METHODOLOGY FOR CREATING BUSINESS KNOWLEDGE

METHODOLOGY FOR CREATING BUSINESS KNOWLEDGE

3RD EDITION

INGEMAN ARBNOR
& BJÖRN BJERKE

Los Angeles • London • New Delhi • Singapore • Washington DC

Second edition previously published with SAGE Publications Inc, in 1997

Originally published by Studentlitteratur. Ingeman Arbnor, Björn
Bjerke och Studentlitteratur, Lund, Sweden, 1994, Second Edition

SAGE Publications Ltd
1 Oliver's Yard
55 City Road
London EC1Y 1SP

SAGE Publications Inc.
2455 Teller Road
Thousand Oaks, California 91320

SAGE Publications India Pvt Ltd
B 1/I 1 Mohan Cooperative Industrial Area
Mathura Road
New Delhi 110 044

SAGE Publications Asia-Pacific Pte Ltd
33 Pekin Street #02-01
Far East Square
Singapore 048763

Library of Congress Control Number: 2008927740

British Library Cataloguing in Publication data

A catalogue record for this book is available from
the British Library

ISBN 978-1-84787-058-2
ISBN 978-1-84787-059-9 (pbk)

Typeset by C&M Digitals Pvt Ltd, Chennai, India
Printed in Great Britain by The Cromwell Press, Trowbridge, Wiltshire
Printed on paper from sustainable resources

TABLE OF CONTENTS

PART I   INTRODUCTION TO RESEARCH METHODOLOGY   1

  1 The Language of Methodology   3
  2 The Act of Creating Knowledge   22
  3 To Become a Knowledge Creator   47

PART II   THREE METHODOLOGICAL VIEWS   79

  4 The Analytical View   81
  5 The Systems View   102
  6 The Actors View   131

PART III   METHODOLOGY   171

  7 Methodical Procedures   173
  8 Methods in Language and Action   208
  9 Methodics   227

PART IV   APPROACHING METHODOLOGY   251

10 The Analytical Approach   253
11 The Systems Approach   273
12 The Actors Approach   298

PART V   METHODOLOGY OF COMPLEMENTARITY   323

13 The Views as Transformative Operators   325
14 Three Cases – Knowledge of Complementarity   349
15 Methodology as Business Creating Intelligence   378

CONTENTS

List of Figures   xviii
List of Tables   xxi
List of Boxes   xxii
Preface   xxiii

PART I   INTRODUCTION TO RESEARCH METHODOLOGY   1

1   The Language of Methodology   3

Methodology   3
Methodological views   3
Methodology and reality   7
Methods   7
Choosing and developing methods   11
Theory of science, methodological views and paradigms   12
Methodology and operative paradigm   17
Awareness and self-reflection   18
The outline of the book   19
Points of reflection   21
Recommended further reading   21

2   The Act of Creating Knowledge   22

A methodological start   22
To think and to reflect critically   23
   Seeing and thinking   24
   The importance of the perspective   29
   Understanding and explaining factors   31
Three methodological views   32
   The study area of entrepreneurship   32
   Some "unconditional" reflections over the area of entrepreneurship   34
   The analytical view   36
     Ultimate presumptions   36
     Interesting issues and perspectives   37
     Conceptualization   37

Methods and methodics	38
Results	38
The systems view	39
Ultimate presumptions	39
Interesting issues and perspectives	39
Conceptualization	40
Methods and methodics	40
Results	40
The actors view	41
Ultimate presumptions	41
Interesting issues and perspectives	41
Conceptualization	43
Methods and methodics	43
Results	44
Points of reflection	45
Recommended further reading	46
3 To Become a Knowledge Creator	**47**
What is science?	47
Being a scientist and creating knowledge	49
"Practised" and "reconstructed" logic	49
A few basic dichotomies to keep in mind	50
Reality assumptions	52
Prerequisites, explanations, understanding and results	55
The analytical view	56
The systems view	57
The actors view	58
A recapitulation	60
More about reality, explaining, understanding and results	60
The analytical view	60
The systems view	63
The actors view	67
Points of reflection	76
Recommended further reading	77
PART II THREE METHODOLOGICAL VIEWS	**79**
4 The Analytical View	**81**
Some basic concepts	81
Reality and models	81
Causal relations, explanations and hypotheses	83

The creation of knowledge problem   88
Deduction, induction, verification – and abduction   90
Operational definitions   92
The concept of analysis   93
Ceteris paribus   94
The philosophical foundation of the analytical view   95
The relation of the analytical view to its paradigm   95
Discovery and explanation   97
General theses   98
Difficulties in relation to explanations   99
Examples of theoretical results   99
Points of reflection   101
Recommended further reading   101

5 **The Systems View**   **102**

The roots of the systems view   102
Systems explanation and systems understanding   104
Examples of classic systems models   105
    Some important concepts of classic systems models   107
Examples of classic systems interpretation   109
Systems view in the twenty-first century   111
A "common" systems language   113
    Systems, subsystems and components   113
    Open and closed systems   114
    Systems environment   115
    Real systems vs. models and interpretations of systems   115
    Magnifying level   117
    Systems relations   117
    Structural and processual perspectives   119
    Systems analysis, systems construction and systems theory   122
        The knowledge orientations of the view   122
Three illustrative studies   122
    The success of Silicon Valley   123
    The Balinese culture   124
    Female entrepreneurship   126
The relation of the systems view to its paradigm   127
Examples of formulation of theoretical results   128
Points of reflection   129
Recommended further reading   130

6 **The Actors View**   **131**

An uncertainty principle in social sciences   131
Some denotations of conceptual meaning   133

Concepts as meaning   133
Intentionality   133
Social science knowledge   134
Dialogue   135
Dialectics   136
Actor   138
Observer   138
Observer–Actor   139
Diagnosis   139
    Development of understanding   139
Language development   141
Action   142
Reality: A social construction   144
Transformation   144
Subjectification   145
Externalization   146
Objectification   147
Internalization   148
Social dialectics   149
    A continuous synthesizing process   149
    Everyday reality   149
The relation of the actors view to its paradigm   151
In general   151
Prerequisites of the actors view: Metatheories   151
Understanding and results   154
    Language   154
    The different levels of language   156
    Scientific language   157
Diagnosis   159
    Engagement   159
    Dissociation   160
    The continuation   160
    A comment   160
The objective of creating knowledge   161
    Actors-based denotation of conceptual meaning   161
    Structurally based denotation of conceptual meaning   161
    Dialectically based denotation of conceptual meaning   162
    Denotation of conceptual meaning and scientific language 163
Some theoretical and action-oriented starting points   166
Social phenomenology and the actors view   166
Developing human procreative power   168
Points of reflection   170
Recommended further reading   170

PART III   METHODOLOGY   171

7 Methodical Procedures   173

Procedures as lessons in harmony   173
Operative paradigms   175
Some "common" groups of techniques   178
  Techniques for selecting units of study   178
  Traditional techniques for collecting data   180
    Secondary information   180
    Primary information: Direct observation   180
    Primary information: Interviews   181
    Primary information: Experiments   182
  The approaches' relation to the traditional techniques   183
    The analytical approach and traditional techniques   183
    The systems approach and traditional techniques   183
    The actors approach and traditional techniques   184
  Measurement techniques and techniques for controlling reliability   185
  Validation techniques   186
Some "specific" groups of techniques   189
  The analytical approach and sampling   189
  The analytical approach and validation of measurements   191
  The systems approach and historical studies   192
  The systems approach and case studies   194
  The actors approach and dialogue   195
  The actors approach and language development   197
    Knowledge creating interface of language development   198
    The procreative report   200
The problem of objectivity   201
  An overview   201
  The analytical approach and the objectivity problem   203
  The systems approach and the objectivity problem   204
  The actors approach and the objectivity problem   204
Points of reflection   206
Recommended further reading   207

8 Methods in Language and Action   208

The three worlds of knowledge   208
Analytical procedures   208
  ANA 1: Professor Peterson on good research   208
  ANA 2: The Service Bank questions   209
  ANA 3: A causal experiment   210
  ANA 4: How to improve response rates   211

ANA 5: Know and "Don't know"   212
ANA 6: Dr Stone's test   213
Systems procedures   213
SYS 1: Professor Anholts's introductory lecture   213
SYS 2: The bank as a system   214
SYS 3: Calmex Co. as an amusement park   215
SYS 4: Rose's final term paper   216
SYS 5: Technical cooperation   217
SYS 6: The answer is written in history   217
Actors procedures   219
ACT 1: Professor Wild on research as an innovative idea   219
ACT 2: Jones and Jones on uniforming methods   220
ACT 3: The number of rejects must decrease   221
ACT 4: An experiment in organization and leadership   223
ACT 5: Graduate paper on the concept of quality   223
ACT 6: Knowledge creating and examination   224
Points of reflection   225
Recommended further reading   226

9 Methodics   227

The analytical approach   227
In general   227
Methodical procedures   227
Methodics   228
The goals of the approach   228
A study plan for determining problems   228
A study plan for analytical studies   229
D: A study plan for descriptive studies   229
E: A study plan for explanatory studies   232
F. A study plan for forecasting studies   233
G: A study plan for guiding studies   233
The systems approach   236
In general   236
Methodical procedures   236
Methodics   236
The goals of the approach   236
A study plan for determining finality relations   237
A study plan for forecasting studies   240
A study plan for guiding studies   240
The actors approach   241
In general   241
Methodical procedures   242

Methodics   243
   The goals of the approach   243
   A study plan for actors studies   243
Excellence in knowledge-creating work   247
Applying the three methodological views   247
Points of reflection   249
Recommended further reading   250

PART IV   APPROACHING METHODOLOGY   **251**

10   The Analytical Approach   **253**

Introduction   253
Case I: Business bankruptcies   253
  Broad outline   254
   Methodics   254
  The case and the analytical approach   254
  Orienting initial study (descriptive purpose)   256
   Methodical procedures   256
   Methodics   256
  Resources and resource transformation in the bankrupt company
   (explanatory purpose)   258
   Formulating the problem   258
   Planning the study   260
   Designing methods for collecting data   260
   Collecting data   260
   Coding and arranging data   261
   Controlling causality   261
   Reporting the results   262
  Assessment and suggested steps (guiding purpose)   262
Case II: Entrepreneurial activities in different countries   263
  Introduction   263
  Overview   264
  GEM Adult Population Survey   266
   In general   266
   Formulating the problem   266
   Planning the study   266
   Designing methods for collecting data   266
   Collecting data   267
   Coding and arranging data   269
   Controlling causality   270
   Reporting the results   270
Points of reflection   271
Recommended further reading   272

11 The Systems Approach   273

Introduction   273
Case I: Electronics Ltd   274
  The start   274
  Planning of the operative paradigm   276
    Methodics   276
  Stewart's ambitions   277
  Systems analysis   278
    Methodical procedure   278
    Methodics   279
    Discussions with senior management   279
    Discussions with the TCM department   280
    Discussions with the CCM department   282
    Stewart's formulation of the problem and his new systems proposal 282
  Reporting the results   283
  And then?   286
Case II: Chinese business culture   286
  How it started   286
  Initial methodical procedures   286
  The operative paradigm   289
    Potential finality relations   289
    Designing methods and collecting data   291
    Do you want to bring in understanding?   294
    Coding and arranging data   294
    Controlling validity   295
    Reporting the results   295
Points of reflection   297
Recommended further reading   297

12 The Actors Approach   298

Introduction   298
Case I: Development of business and activities   299
  Starting point   299
  Operative paradigm as experimental flow   299
  Production philosophical meeting 1   300
    The questions   300
    The deeper undercurrents of business development   301
    Qualification in cultural meeting   302
    Finish   302
  In-between dialogues   303
    The questions and shape of the dialogues   303
  Production philosophical meeting 2   304
    An explorative methodics   304
    Business artistic creation   307

The procreative report   308
  The embryo to businesses   308
  With the disposition of the master   308
  Enriching the encounter with the audience/customer/market   309
  Business embryos as works of art   309
Case II: A line of business with adaptation problems   310
  Introduction   310
  History   310
  The starting point for the study   311
  Problem and purpose   311
  The development of the operative paradigm   312
    Operative paradigms as a continuity   312
    Historical development and description   312
    Actors intentional method   313
    Actors constitutional method   314
    Organizational documentary method   315
    Selection   315
    Classification work   317
    The total methodics of the study   318
  Feedback and the continuing dialogue   318
    Descriptive dialogue as feedback   319
Points of reflection   319
Recommended further reading   321

PART V   METHODOLOGY OF COMPLEMENTARITY   323

13 The Views as Transformative Operators   325

An introductory summary   325
  The continuation   329
    Quality and complementarity   330
Complementary criticism   331
  Back to the future   331
  A warning for the road   332
  Criticism of the analytical view   332
    In general   332
    Criticism from the systems view   332
    Criticism from the actors view   333
    The response of the analytical view to this criticism   334
  Criticism of the systems view   335
    In general   335
    Criticism from the analytical view   336
    Criticism from the actors view   336
    The response of the systems view to this criticism   337

Criticism of the actors view   338
   In general   338
   Criticism from the analytical view   338
   Criticism from the systems view   338
   The response of the actors view to this criticism 339
The idea of reconciliation   340
  Some principles of complementarity   343
   Adapting of existing concepts and theories   343
   Collecting data   344
   Modeling and interpreting data   345
  Exceedance as a methodological result   346
Crealiability of complementarity   346
The thematic language of methodology   347
Points of reflection   348
Recommended further reading   348

14 Three Cases – Knowledge of Complementarity   **349**

Introduction   349
Case I: The analytical approach as transformative operator   350
  Background   350
  First meeting with the study area   350
  The researcher's thoughts in the beginning   351
  Determining the problem   351
  Transformative operations   352
   The study area in theory – primary procedures   352
   The study area in theory – complementary procedures 354
   The study area in practice – primary procedures   356
   The study area in practice – complementary procedures 356
   Methodics   358
  Results   359
Case II: The systems approach as transformative operator   359
  Introduction   359
  Transformative operations   360
   Primary procedures   360
   Complementary procedures   362
  Some results   363
  A comment on complementarity   365
Case III: The actors approach as transformative operator   366
  Starting point   366
  The complementary ambitions of the researcher   368
  Transformative operations   369
   Primary procedures   369
   Complementary procedures   369
   Methodics   370

Results   371
Points of reflection   375
Recommended further reading   377

15 Methodology as Business Creating Intelligence   378

Crealiability of complementarity in focus   378
Knowledge-creating as production factor   378
Knowledge audit   380
   A ground plan for knowledge audit   382
Knowledge intelligence   383
   Business and competitive intelligence   384
   Business creating intelligence   386
Points of reflection   388
Recommended further reading   389

Appendix   390
Glossary   417
References   428
Index   431

LIST OF FIGURES

1.1   Close Connections   5
1.2   How to Avoid Cookbook Knowledge   8
1.3   What Determines What?   9
1.4   Methods and Application of Methods – The Green Light   10
1.5   Theory of Science   13
1.6   Paradigm   13
1.7   Operative Paradigm   14
1.8   Theory of Science and Methodology   15
1.9   Paradigm and Operative Paradigm   17
1.10   Methodics and Methodical Procedures   18
1.11   Plan of the Book   20

2.1   Study Area   25
2.2   With the Naked Eye   26
2.3   "Entrepreneur" in the Seventh Heaven   27
2.4   Seeing is Believing?   28
2.5   On the Whole   28
2.6   The Outlook   29
2.7   What is the Problem/the Opportunity?   30
2.8   Cast a Shadow over the Results!   31

3.1   The Boundary Between Explanatory and Understanding Knowledge   51
3.2   The Analytical View: The Whole is the Sum of its Parts   52
3.3   The Systems View: Synergy   53
3.4   The Actors View: Meaning Structures   54
3.5   The Black Sheep of the Cause-family   61
3.6   Cause and Effect   62
3.7   More Causes Make a Better Explanation in the Analytical View   62
3.8   All Factors are Necessary in the Systems View   64
3.9   Producer–Product Connections   65
3.10   Multifinality and Equifinality   65
3.11   Objectified Reality in the Actors View   68
3.12   Different Meaning Strucures   69
3.13   Finite Provinces of Meaning in Dialectic Relations   71

3.14   A Summary of Actors View Models   73
3.15   The Dialectic Methodology of the Actors View   74

4.1   The Normal Hypothesis   86
4.2   Importance of Background and Intervening Factors   88
4.3   Cyclical Nature of Creating Knowledge in the Analytical View   91

5.1   Is Q a Star?   104
5.2   McKinsey's 7S-model   106
5.3   The Cluster Diamond   110
5.4   The Italian Village Business Circle   111
5.5   Three Principles for Creating Systems Knowledge   112
5.6   A System   114
5.7   Open and Closed Systems   115
5.8   Magnifying Levels of Models and Interpretations   117
5.9   Concrete Systems Relations   118
5.10   Systems Relations in How a Group's Unity Functions   118

6.1   The Arbnor Uncertainty Principle   132
6.2   Knowledge Ambitions   135
6.3   Simultaneous Processes   145
6.4   The Subjectification of a Person or Actor   146
6.5   Social Construction of Reality   150
6.6   Social Dialectics and Everyday Reality   150
6.7   Metatheories   153
6.8   The Actor and the Meaning of Language   155
6.9   Specialized Realities   156
6.10   Dialectically Based Denotation   162
6.11   Actors View Models and Denotation of Conceptual Meaning   163
6.12   Language Development   165

7.1   Operative Paradigms Create Fit   175
7.2   Types of Direct Observation   181
7.3   Experimental and Control Groups in an Experiment   182
7.4   Validity and Reliability   187
7.5   Actors Approach Requirements for Objectivity   206

8.1   A Systems Diagram   218
8.2   O'Brien's Model for Senior Management   222

9.1   A Plan for Determining Problems   228
9.2.   Plans for Analytical Approach Studies   230
9.3   A Plan for Studies Determining Finality Relations   238

9.4   The Dialectics of an Actors Approach Study   244
9.5   The Cores of Crealiability   248

10.1 Potential Causes of Business Bankruptcies   255
10.2 GEM Conceptual Model   265
10.3 GEM Adult Population Survey: Schematic of the
      Interview Structure   268
10.4 Prevalence Rates of Entrepreneurial Activity Across
      Countries in 2006   270

11.1 Organization Chart   275
11.2 Grant's Three-Stage Study   277
11.3 Work Sequence in a CCM Department   284
11.4 Systems Proposal for the TCM Department   284
11.5 Stewart Grant's Formulation of the Problem   285
11.6 Various Ways to Look at Culture   288
11.7 The Methodic Plan of the Cultural Study   290
11.8 The Business Culture from a Structural Perspective   296

12.1 The Flow of Experimental Acts   300
12.2 Groups of Talks and Informal Deliberations   314
12.3 Categories and Sources of Organizational Documentary Material 316
12.4 Recommendation Procedures   316

13.1 An Overview   330
13.2 Methodology of Complementarity   342
13.3 Principal Case A   344
13.4 Principal Case B   345
13.5 Principal Case C   345
13.6 The Cores of Crealiability of Complementarity   347

14.1 External Pressures   352
14.2 The Decision System   357
14.3 Systems Relations in the Experiment   361
14.4 Systems Relations for Energizing the Processes   362
14.5 The Codetermination Act as a Crash   364
14.6 The Innovation System   370
14.7 The Dialectic Methodics of the Actors Approach as
      Transformative Operator   372
14.8 MultiProfessional Dynamics   374

15.1 Business Opportunity.   380
15.2 The Arbnor Business Creating • Intelligence Cycle   387

LIST OF TABLES

3.1	A Recapitulation	61
3.2	Analytical View	63
3.3	Systems View	67
3.4	Actors View	75
5.1	Structural and Processual Perspectives (Examples)	120
7.1	Expectations	194
7.2	Dialogues contra Interviews	196
10.1	Finished Bankruptcies 1996–2000 Distributed in Different Ways to Liquidate the Business	257
10.2	GEM Adult Population Survey: Items Related to Individual Involvement in Entrepreneurial Activity (Reynolds et al., 2005: 213)	267
10.3	GEM Adult Population Survey: Items Related to Individual Attitudes and Perceptions Regarding Entrepreneurial Activity (Reynolds et al., 2005: 213)	269

LIST OF BOXES

1.1	When Methodological Views "Talk and Act"	4
1.2	Why Can't We "Just" Collect Data and Make Statements?	6
1.3	To be a Creator of Knowledge	6
1.4	Which Methodological View is the Best One?	7
1.5	Methods and Methodological Views	11
1.6	Paradigm	14
3.1	Empiricism and Reality	48
3.2	To Become a Creator of Knowledge	50
3.3	Models and Facts	51
3.4	Picture of Reality and Finite Province of Meaning	55
3.5	Causality and Finality	57
3.6	Constitute	58
3.7	Dialectics	58
3.8	Explain, Understand and Emancipate	59
3.9	Average, Typical and Typified	60
3.10	Analysis and Actor	66
4.1	Theory	82
5.1	Be or As a System?	116
5.2	Pragmatism	121
13.1	Methodology in Theory and Practice	326
13.2	The Arbnor/Bjerke Methodological Principle of Complementarity	330

PREFACE

The second edition of this book was published over ten years ago and we, as the authors, have since learnt so much from using that edition that we feel it is now time to come out with a new edition which incorporates that knowledge. We are, therefore, happy to present its third edition.

Over the years the book has been used by us as teachers and as supervisors in various academic contexts in different parts of the world. A very great number of educators in similar roles worldwide have also used it and some of them have sent us useful pedagogical comments from time to time.

Also, as the question of methodology concerns everybody in a position of creating and disseminating knowledge, opinions on what the subject is all about are many. We have participated in many debates and dialogues, in seminar rooms, lecture theatres, conferences of various sorts, cafeterias and bars, as well as in cyberspace, on this subject – discussions which commonly involve our book. We have learnt much from these diverse conversations.

However, outside teaching and supervising purposes in tertiary educational positions, we have also used those ideas on which the book is based in our roles as consultants in industry and elsewhere, and as participants in, more or less public, investigations, commissioned by, for instance, industrial organizations, educators' associations or governmental institutions. This has also provided us with valuable experience about what it means to use the book.

Furthermore, in order get more input about the revision of the book into its third edition, it has been sent out by our publisher to several reviewers. Many useful and progressive comments have come to us by this way as well. Even if the reviewers are, and will remain, anonymous, we thank them for their contributions.

All the above have been with us when writing the third edition of the book, which has taken us about one year. Several changes, modifications and additions have been worked into the book, of which the most important ones are the following:

- The new edition has a *refined pedagogical, linguistic and stringent structure.* With the addition of a couple of new chapters we are also reinforcing its *unique profile* by, in the same book, combining and illustrating both *theory of science/methodological* issues with *business practical/empirical* ones.

- The *unique profile* of the book has been further developed. *The theory of science/ methodological theme* of the book has been *deepened.* At the same time it been made additionally accessible by more *practical* examples, while the discussion of its position among various philosophical "schools" has now been extended and placed in an Appendix. In this way, the book becomes still more useful at several academic levels.

For students at a lower level, the text is free from long and complicated abstract deliberations which could easily hide simpler relations of relevance to the reader, at the same time as there is, for readers who want to go further into the subject, a more philosophically oriented Appendix directly related to what is said in the text itself. This Appendix also includes suggestions for further reading. *All of this will deepen the theory of science connections of the new edition compared to the previous one.*

- *The practical/empirical theme of the book has also been deepened and developed.* The text has, from Chapter 2, *practical examples* where different methodological points of departure are illustrated in concrete terms relevant to the topic of the book. In the new edition, furthermore, most of previous cases have been replaced by new and more pedagogic, as well as more varied, ones, in order to cover a greater number of areas within the subject of business. *The cases* have been chosen and written such that they, in general terms, should be experienced as *more exciting and easier to read.*

- *The terminology has been developed.* An extended set of terminology has been brought into the third edition including, for example, *methodology of complementarity.* This involves extensive discussion of how various methodological views can be approached in reconciliation with each other and assessed as such "combinations". *Crealiability* is another example of this terminology, which refers to the quality assessment of knowledge-creating works.

- *The illustrations in the book are completely new.* All illustrations in the book have been remade and a *unique graphical language of design* has been developed in order to illustratively describe all the methodological and empirical themes of the book. Also, in many cases, the illustrations build on each other in order to extend the *pedagogic ability* of this graphical language of design to communicate aspects in both theoretical and practical areas of methodology, which could be difficult to comprehend.

- *The pedagogical design has been improved.* Every chapter finishes with a "Points of reflection" section, where *the reader* is posed a number of questions. The idea is to intensify the *instructive* capability of the book. In all, there are 162 such questions for the student to answer. *To the instructor* there is an offer of a compendium with suggested answers to these questions as the authors see them.

- *The book has also become part of an interactive effort.* We have *created a website* (knowledge-creator.com) in order to improve communication among our readers, interested in the topic of creating business knowledge and business intelligence. This site will include, among other things, ideas for further reading, a question and answer section, a wiki of methodology for creating business knowledge and a forum for discussions.

However, there are some aspects which have not changed and which have been with us all the way from the first edition of the book:

- It presents a "complete" overview of what methodology is all about, all the way from theory of science and ultimate presumptions, to the practical applications of specific techniques for creating knowledge in business. In fact, if such links are *not considered*, we would not like to call it *methodology*!

- As before, it is based on the belief that *methodology* as such requires its own *meta-language*. The kind of language used in the third edition is, in principle, the same as in previous editions, but several refinements, developments and additions have been made, as mentioned above. We have been very careful to make sure that the new developments and additions *not contradictory* with what is in there from before.

- We keep to our point of departure that the foundation of creating knowledge in business can be comprehended by *three different methodological views*. We call these the analytical view, the systems view and the actors view.

- We still believe that these methodological views are built on paradigms, which cannot be compared or assessed from any logical or empirical grounds. Our methodological views can therefore not, *in principle,* be compared with each other from any neutral points of departure and it is not possible from any general ground to say which of the three views is scientifically best, most profitable, or the like.

The professional relationship between the two of us started more than thirty years ago. However, we have not been working together for many years now. It is therefore not surprising that we have developed differently and to some extent gone our own ways. The past year has therefore involved many and intensive discussions about what the design and content of the third edition of our *Methodology for Creating Business Knowledge* should be and how it should be improved based on our, partly individual, experiences and feedbacks. These discussions have been very fruitful and we are convinced that, without them, the book would not have been so good.

We believe that the book provides an opportunity for the user of its message and terminology to discuss his/her *methodology of knowledge creating* in a kind of language commonality with, in principle, anybody else. Furthermore, we believe that it provides the reader with a unique in-depth understanding of what methodology is all about and his/her role in it. Also, the reader is offered, by our *methodology of complementarity,* the ability to use his/her creativity to go beyond what normally restricts the creation of knowledge. This improves, as we see it, the chance that the reader feels less lost and less strictly bound by whichever *methodological view* he/she intends to be an essential part of.

Ingeman Arbnor
Björn Bjerke

Additional online material for teachers can be found at www.sagepub.co.uk/arbnor

PART 1
INTRODUCTION TO RESEARCH METHODOLOGY

1 THE LANGUAGE OF METHODOLOGY

> In Chapter 1 you will meet a text which aims at clarifying the connections between various main concepts of methodology and their relationships. Those concepts are central to any understanding of different scientific ways of approaching problems and possibilities to create business knowledge in a number of areas.

METHODOLOGY

Methodology is no easy subject, but the more exciting as it concerns one's own personal development as a researcher, consultant or investigator in one direction or another. It is also a relatively young subject, at least in the subject of business. There are contributions to its development, for instance, from philosophy, sociology, logics and mathematics. This, our book about methodology, was, when it appeared in its first edition, one of the first attempts ever to clarify the meaning of methodology in business. Now you hold the third edition in your hand.

Methodology is a mode of thinking, but it is also a mode of acting. It contains a number of concepts, which try to describe the steps and relations needed in the process of creating and searching for new knowledge.

METHODOLOGICAL VIEWS

In business, there are a number of views on when and how to use methods for studying and researching reality. There are also a number of *opinions* on what is really the meaning of "methods". Let us refer to these opinions as *methodological views* and later we will become more precise about what this might mean in various contexts. Our precision does not seek to define any kind of "best practice", but to disclose the complexity of this field, hoping to simplify as well as to clarify the choice of methods available to anyone trying to research the area of business.

Box 1.1

When Methodological Views "Talk and Act"

It is a common use of language to depersonify different social phenomena. We say, for instance, that "research has shown" ..., etc. Of course there are people (researchers) behind these statements. When we in the future talk in terms of "the view assumes", "the view looks at", etc., we use the same way to express ourselves for practical reasons. However, it is not the views in themselves, but their proponents who act and therefore carry full responsibility for what the view stipulates.

The different *methodological views* make certain *ultimate presumptions* beforehand about what we study as business researchers, consultants or investigators. These presumptions differ between views, and the different views, therefore, present different ways to understand, explain and improve. Even if the differences are not as drastic as to compare the starting points of the different views to historical opinions about the configuration of the Earth – flat, round, oval or square – this might nevertheless illustrate what we mean.

If we believe that the Earth is flat, our observations and statements will be based on this belief (as we know, there are historical proofs of this). Our models of, say, navigation, will be concerned with avoiding sailing over the edge, etc. Those who, at that time, started with the assumption that the Earth was round then gained a competitive advantage, of course, by being able to navigate to areas, which were assumed to be placed outside the so-called "edge".

Another interesting parallel is found in what the *New York Times* once wrote about the rocket pioneer professor Goddard set against a recent quotation from the Kennedy Space Centre in the USA. In the *New York Times* they wrote in 1921: "Professor Goddard does not know the relation between action and reaction and the need to have something better than a vacuum against which to react. He seems to lack the basic knowledge ladled out daily in high schools." And in 2006, it was possible at the Kennedy Space Center to read the following quotation from Goddard: "It is difficult to say what is possible, for the dream of yesterday is the hope of today and the reality of tomorrow."

The reason why we have chosen the historic perspective is explained by the fact that it is not until afterward, when we are no longer tied to those assumptions which led to the statements, that we can verify whether they (and thereby the views behind them) have been fruitful or not. We must therefore not be tempted to brush aside the illustrations above by saying, "Oh well, now we know better", because what we know *today* will probably be known better, or rather, differently, *tomorrow*.

One more example of how different *assumptions* may block understanding is found in Watson's (1969) book *The Double Helix*. This describes his and Crick's discovery of the DNA-molecule. When competing to solve the riddle they were convinced that they would get there before other researchers. Their main competitor was, in Watson's words, "so stuck on his classical way of thinking that I would accomplish the unbelievable feat of beating him to the correct interpretation of his own experiments". So, the assumption of the old way of thinking prevented their main rival from interpreting his own actions correctly!

It is relatively easy, afterwards, to see how some assumptions are blocking a successful interpretation in the case of the shape of the Earth, conditions for launching a rocket and the discovery of DNA in the natural science area. It is more difficult in the social area. Such clear cases are more or less non-existing there. Instead, all ingredients are mixed as in a big soup: a soup which is floating around in our brains while at the same time as we must judge its content, consistency and taste in order to create new business-oriented and evolutionary recipes.

By this we want to say that it is only speculatively and reflectively (not logically or empirically) possible to overcome historical verification. From this it follows that there will be problems comprehending the data we collect or try to explain/understand unless we have already reflected upon how the particular view will shape our observations, our understanding and our explanations. As methodological views have different characteristics, it stands to reason that in business, as in other social sciences, there are disagreements between proponents of different *views*. This situation indicates the necessity of a *critical attitude* from the readers' side in relation to different views to avoid being deceived into believing that applying a methodological view in different situations is without conflicts.

It is necessary in these situations to clarify to yourself whether it is of interest to develop business knowledge in order to discover *what is possible in our world of possibilities*. This is even more important if you want to develop models and theories to bring into business as tools/processes adapted to your own situation in order to, for instance, reconfigure a market or create new business-oriented advantages in an existing market, or create completely new markets.

business, with its *models and theories*, is characterized not only by its close relationships to these kind of "philosophical assumptions", but also by its near relationships to "practical reality" where businesses are developed and conducted. This situation is illustrated in Figure 1.1.

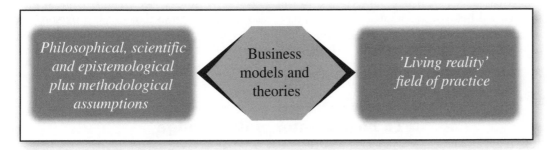

Figure 1.1   Close Connections

In this book we have chosen to talk about this search for knowledge in terms of *knowledge-creating*. The reason why we have chosen *"create"* instead of other concepts like construct or develop is not directly related to how we think that knowledge arises. Knowledge may arise from pure guessing or speculations, through shifts of perspectives, from critical thinking and via anomalies. Knowledge may also be the result of careful planning and field studies, through decoding of information and from simple arithmetic, through experiments, and more. The

---

Box 1.2

Why Can't We "Just" Collect Data and Make Statements?

In order to develop business theories and models, methodological views make *different* assumptions about the reality they try to explain and/or understand. This, in turn, means that observations, collections of data and results are determined to a large extent by the view chosen. Conscious development of knowledge in business – as in other subjects – is therefore far from "just" collecting data and making statements. (Even an "unconditioned" mushroom picker has ideas of where the most sought after mushrooms may grow.) What might be essential data to one view can be completely irrelevant to another. For instance, what value would a calculation of the probability of falling over the edge have for proponents of the Earth being a globe? To take another example: what *statistical use* does a researcher, who is statistically *searching* for only what is *general* as knowledge about, say, entrepreneurship, have for the results of another researcher, who is *searching* for what is *unique* in the entrepreneurially single cases? Can the very search for what is *general* and what is *unique* reflect/reveal other *ultimate presumptions* as well – presumptions about *life*, *reality* and *business venturing*, which are influencing when, where and how we are searching for knowledge and what, we are searching for? And, not to mention, why we are searching at all? We are convinced it does!

---

common denominator in all this is that *somebody* consciously takes on something in order to disqualify existing knowledge, or confirms existing knowledge or enlarges it, that is, that somebody in a critical, conscious and insightful fashion *creates* the *prerequisites* for generating knowledge. This person we have chosen to call a *creator* of knowledge or knowledge creator (see Box 1.3 below). Included in this meaning is also the assumption that this is a person who can consciously and stringently stick to the rules, but also, if necessary, *creatively* transgress them.

Box 1.3

To be a Creator of Knowledge

When are we creators of knowledge, say, within the subject of business? We want to restrict the concept to cover only when such work of developing knowledge and being creative is based on conscious assumptions of reality, and when we understand what knowledge is and how it comes about. Unconscious and naive consultative and investigative activities rarely lead to more than simply confirming what we know already. We have seen this kind of cookbook knowledge develop too often to neglect its existence. In this book we reserve, therefore, the concept of *creator of knowledge* to mean what we refer to a conscious researcher, consultant or investigator.

METHODOLOGY AND REALITY

Methodological views make *ultimate presumptions* about reality! But what does that actually mean? Even to attempt to investigate, explain and understand reality we make certain assumptions about its quality, what it is like. These assumptions become a guide for *the creator of knowledge* in his or her effort to research reality.

The assumptions about reality guiding the creator of knowledge (see Box 1.3) can be conceived as kinds of background "philosophical" hypotheses, but not in the sense that they can be tested empirically or logically, as each view has already postulated its own constitution of reality. In consequence, data collected in that view will be based on these assumptions. If we try to use these collected data to test the assumptions mentioned, they will only confirm their own assumptions in a kind of circular logic. These background hypotheses, or, as we might

Box 1.4

Which Methodological View is the Best One?

You can never empirically or logically determine the best view. This can only be done reflectively by considering a situation to be studied and your own opinion of life. This also means that even if you believe that one view is more interesting or rewarding than another, we, as authors of this book, do not want to rank one view above another. In fact, we cannot do this on any general ground. The only thing we can do is to try to make explicit as best we can the special characteristics on which the various views are based.

better name them, *normative theses*, can only be "tested" reflectively. In such a reflective situation, one might come to the conclusion that the *methodological view* no longer seems able to explain what is personally seen as important. In that case it is possible to shift to another view, or, if this is not enough, to supplement or synthesize. We will be back to this later in the book.

METHODS

The subject of methodology should not be taken lightly. It happens too often, unfortunately, that researchers, consultants and investigators claim that it has nothing to do with philosophy; that there is nothing controversial about conducting an interview, for instance, *as long as you stick to the rules*. According to this opinion, there should generally be one best way to, say, define and quantify something, formulate an interviewer's guide, take a sample, decide when computers should be used or determine the degree of reliability of the end results. If, for instance, you were interested in how a sample is to be taken, you need only walk to the scientific library, pick out *The Encyclopedia of Methods* and look for the answer under the letter "S" (see Figure 1.2).

Figure 1.2   How to Avoid Cookbook Knowledge

Unfortunately, too many so-called "books on methodology" are written as cookbooks. Some author, interested in methodology, modify this slightly, however. They claim, that what is meant by suitable *methods* is determined by the problem at hand. This, in turn, would mean that there would be one best way to develop knowledge, if *only you know which problem is at hand*, that is, a certain *problem* in itself determines the best *techniques* to solve it (see Figure 1.3).

These so-called methodologically oriented authors neglect one important fact: the way a problem appears to a creator of knowledge is intimately related to *the view* he/she is using

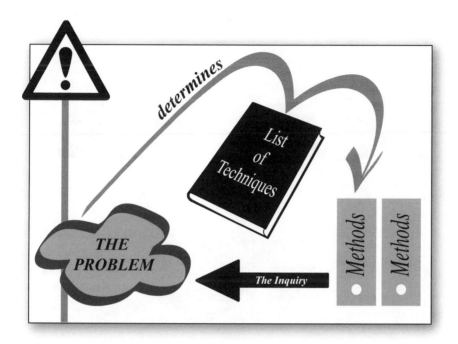

Figure 1.3　What Determines What?

for his/her *reflection*. Methodology is reduced by these authors to relatively simple, instrumental and trivial questions about whether an interview should be conducted in person, over the telephone or by mail, whether it is possible to quantify certain data, etc. Such discussions regard *methodological questions* as mainly choices of suitable *techniques*, against the background of a given problem, considering the researcher's/consultant's/investigator's ambitions and interests. Methodological issues then become operative activities, which in itself is harmless. We all need to be operative and practical as part of our development of knowledge. But, and this is the annoying part, too many business scholars, mostly because of ignorance and fear, never leave this operative level.

Most business scholars who have reflected on methods and methodological applications realize that *every* human being, as a human being, and then as a creator of knowledge as well, carries around certain *ultimate presumptions* (what we previously called background "philosophical" hypotheses or normative theses) about what his/her environment looks like, in principle, and about his/her role in this environment. These presumptions are mostly unconscious on a daily basis and very difficult to change, at least in the short run.

Our ultimate presumptions will have a bearing both on how we look at problems and on how we look at existing and available sets of techniques and at knowledge in general.

The differences between Figure 1.4 below and the previous one are several. In the second case a methodological outfit is *created* out of possible techniques (where single techniques very well may be modified or re-created and where every technique is to be seen in relation to all the others) against the background of a problem *and* the ultimate presumptions. Furthermore, the picture of the problem will be influenced not only by

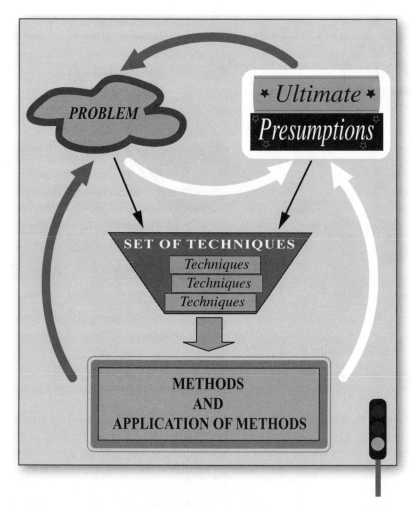

Figure 1.4   Methods and Application of Methods – The Green Light

ultimate presumptions, but also by the methods used. These presumptions will, however, normally reach a certain stability for individual creators of knowledge as they practise their trade – and will thereafter not change in any decisive direction (indicated by the white frame around the Ultimate Presumptions and the white arrows in Figure 1.4).

So, what do these ultimate presumptions (background presumptions, normative theses) consist of? A common *collective term* for such presumptions is *paradigm*. We will return to this concept shortly. However, let us mention here that opinions are divided in the world of creators of knowledge concerning what a paradigm consists of. Some researchers, consultants and investigators claim, furthermore, that this issue is of no interest – or at least unproblematic – when it comes to questions of methods, which in fact in itself is an ultimate presumption as well! Before we take up *the concept of paradigm* we will look at how it is possible to choose and develop *methods* using our point of departure.

CHOOSING AND DEVELOPING METHODS

We see methods as *guiding principles for the creation of knowledge*. But such principles, in order to be useful and effective, must "fit" both with those *problems* which are under consideration and those *ultimate presumptions* held by the creator of knowledge. Otherwise the methods lead, if anywhere, only to platitudes; they may even counteract their own purposes. Another way to express this is that methods must be both *consistent* (fit the problem and the ultimate presumptions held by the creator of knowledge) and *constructive* (fit each other).

Box 1.5

Methods and Methodological Views

Our opinion about the *meaning of the concept of methods* is, of course, also based on certain ultimate presumptions. The two most important presumptions, in our case, are:

1. There are different types of ultimate presumptions.
2. These presumptions are important to how methods are constructed.

One consequence of the above is that there are things we may call *methodological views*.

But how is it possible to choose suitable *methods* when everything seems to depend on everything else? It seems like circular thinking to say that methods depend on problems, which depend on ultimate presumptions, which in turn depend on methods (or vice versa)! The answer to this "paradox" is that the contents of ultimate presumptions, problems, available and developed techniques, and methods, change at different rates and to different degrees over time.

Ultimate presumptions seldom change, as mentioned earlier, and if they do, this normally takes place as gradual modifications of a *paradigm* over a longer time (*evolutionary*). Many people (maybe most) will, in principle, keep their ultimate presumptions all their lives once they have "taken root". But there are those who, once during their lifetime (rarely more than once), change their minds completely about what they earlier believed in and become critical of their own former thinking. Such total shifts of paradigm often take place quickly and radically (*revolutionary*) after a long time of accumulating paradigmatic contradictions and deviations. So, this may be associated with deep personal crises, but also – at least afterwards – with great happiness.

The *available set of techniques* is constantly being added to in the general course of research, consulting and investigation. This set is both broad and deep in Business today. Drastic changes or revolutionary additions rarely take place. *In an individual case and in the short run the creator of knowledge may consider his/her ultimate presumptions and his/her technical possibilities as given, by and large.* They change (if they change) only gradually over a long time, from experience, from problems addressed, from methodological activities, and through curiosity and inventiveness.

Problems are never given. They must at least be perceived by others and/or by the creator of knowledge in order to be of interest as methodological objects. One may even say that they must be "created" or at least be formed, what is sometimes called *being problematized,* in order to be relevant and of interest. Such a creation or constructed result is in itself a creation of knowledge and takes place by the use of methods.

So, *in practice,* choice and development of methods take place in an interaction with a problematization in one form or another, given ultimate presumptions and (on the whole) existing technological possibilities.

THEORY OF SCIENCE, METHODOLOGICAL VIEWS AND PARADIGMS

This book is about *methodology.* As the reader has realized, *methodological views* and *methods* cannot be discussed directly, without showing how they are related to ultimate presumptions. To do otherwise, would be like teaching a navigational approach without explaining that: (a) it is based on the presumption that the Earth is flat; and (b) it is ... etc. (try for the moment to disregard the fact that today we believe that the Earth is a globe). The basic construction of today's social world is an extremely controversial issue – and this book is about views and methods to "navigate" in our social world.

Ultimate presumptions, in the context of this book, are of a *philosophical* character (by all means, study the bookshelves in the scientific library in Figure 1.2). The *relation* between these presumptions and methodological views is studied by theorists of science, whose discipline is consequently called *theory of science* (see Figure 1.5).

Theorists of science have developed a "conceptual language" to describe the relation between ultimate (philosophical) presumptions and the practical use of various methodological views. This "language" contains, as an important ingredient, the concept of *paradigm* (model/pattern). This concept can be seen as the bridge between the two starting points here, which are ultimate presumptions and methodological views (see Figure 1.6).

In the same way as theorists of science have developed a "conceptual language" for *the relation* between ultimate presumption and the practical use of various methodological views, using paradigm as a *bridge,* we will in this book about *methodology* develop a "language of thinking and acting" for the relation between methodology and study area. "The language" is contained in what in Figure 1.7 is called "Methodology". We will use the concept of *operative paradigm* as a *bridge* between methodological views and the study area. The concept is chosen considering its necessary relation to ultimate presumptions, i.e. to some *paradigm.*

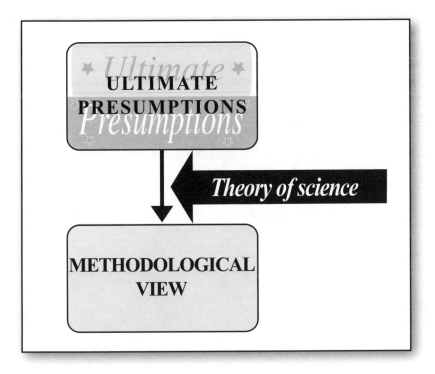

Figure 1.5   Theory of Science

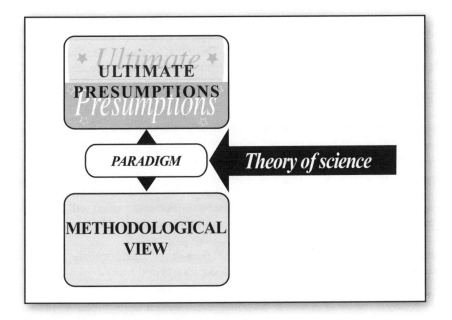

Figure 1.6   Paradigm

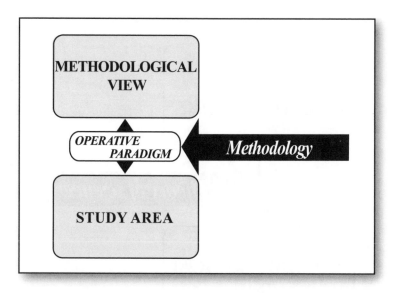

Figure 1.7   Operative Paradigm

Box 1.6

Paradigm

The scientist mostly associated with the concept of "paradigm" today is Kuhn (1922–1996), who first presented his theories in *The Structure of Scientific Revolutions* in 1962. Kuhn was originally rather unclear about what a paradigm consists of, something that he admitted. In later editions of his book, however, he becomes more precise about its components:

1. *Symbolic generalizations*, that is, typical expressions used within the scientific group – what might be called jargon – which are not questioned.
2. *Metaphysical aspects*, that is, typical models (they may vary along the whole spectrum from being heuristic to being ontological). These models function somewhat like symbolic generalizations. Among other things, they offer suitable and acceptable analogies and metaphors. They also assist in determining what will be accepted as an explanation or a solution, which also means that they determine what will be regarded as unsolved problems.
3. *Values* for judging research results (e.g. that they should be formulated quantitatively), or theories (e.g. that they should be simple, consistent and probable) or scientific topics (e.g. that they should be related to specific social use).
4. *Ideal examples* – such as specific solutions to a problem – that scientists confront early in their careers and that can be found in "recognized" scientific journals.

If we choose Kuhn's interpretation of the scientific process of knowledge, there is every reason to doubt the common opinion that knowledge develops linearly and cumulatively.

There are different opinions within the social sciences about paradigms. We (and many others) have found Kuhn's type of analysis rewarding, at the same time that we note an important difference between the natural (Kuhn's field) and the social sciences. In the natural sciences, old paradigms are replaced by new ones; in the social sciences, old paradigms usually survive alongside new ones. This leads us to prefer the scientific theorist Törnebohm's (1974) evolutionary position instead of Kuhn's revolutionary one. There are in social sciences also a lot of proposals for classifying paradigms, of course. Two quite recognized such classifications are by Burrell & Morgan (1985) and by Guba (1990). There are similarities with both these classifications and our own in this book. They use the concepts of ontology, epistemology and methodology to classify different paradigms. We do the same but not in the same way (for further clarification, see our Appendix).

According to Törnebohm, a paradigm consists of:

1. a conception of reality (view of the world)
2. a conception of science
3. a scientific ideal
4. ethical/aesthetical aspects

We have now, in different ways, tried to illustrate, in principle, how ultimate presumptions are influencing the process of creating knowledge. Formulating a problem, collecting data, etc., are to a large extent controlled by the methodological view chosen, which in turn is subordinated to a number of philosophical assumptions and notions. A *methodological view* has, therefore, a double function by *encompassing* some ultimate presumptions at the same time as providing the prerequisites for the *design* of practical instruments, i.e. the development of an *operative paradigm* (see Figure 1.8).

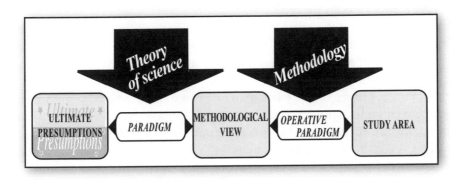

Figure 1.8   Theory of Science and Methodology

Theorists of science use the paradigm concept to describe basic philosophical assumptions that are of importance to practical research. Our use of the paradigm concept consists of a *conception of reality* (vision of the world), a *conception of science*, a *scientific ideal* and *ethical/aesthetical* aspects. Disagreement about the content of any of these components – such as differing conceptions of the constitution of reality – will result in a different paradigm, the same way that different methodological views exist. There is, however, nothing to prevent the existence of more than one methodological view within a given paradigm. And in a similar fashion, a single methodological view can be inspired by more than one paradigm.

Conception of reality has to do with philosophical ideas about how reality is constructed, whether reality exists in and of itself or through our mediation, for example: that reality is ordered and logical in causes and effects, or it has an inherent tendency to dissension with non-linear relations, or it is based on chaotic relations, or it is ordered as well as disordered with a bit of each at the same time.

Conception of science has to do with knowledge we have gained through education, which gives us our concepts or beliefs about the objects and subjects we study, and our knowledge interests, for example: all kinds of pre-scientific concepts and models contained in business, for instance budget, strategic planning, cost accounting, efficiency, calculated risk, market segment and business concept.

A *scientific ideal* is related to the researcher as a person – an expression of something related to his/her desires, for example: if somebody perceives him/herself as being guided by the idea that science is something objective and not influenced by partial interests, or if he/she claims that it is impossible to be impartial and aims therefore at changing some aspects of society.

Ethical and aesthetical aspects have to do with what the researcher claims is morally suitable or unsuitable and claims to be beautiful or ugly, for example: observing people should not be done without their knowledge; well-constructed diagrams and graphs are ideals of beauty; scientific results justify the means used to achieve them.

We understand from this that a paradigm is not usually influenced by any major force of change. It is not possible, for instance, constantly to question the constitution of reality, or our scientific opinion – that would make all practical research and other knowledge creation virtually impossible. The changes that do take place in paradigmatic matters are ultimately derived from the development of different philosophical schools, and may well be of interest for several decades or even for centuries.

An *operative paradigm*, on the other hand, may change fairly often, depending on the *shifting character of the study area* and the type of operative paradigm in question. Differences in rate of change are due in part to the different conceptions of reality that support the various *views*, and in part because of their age. For example, a study area that is based on the concept of an ordered existence should change less than one based on the assumption of a reality with a tendency to contain inherent conflicts.

The aspects we use to describe an operative paradigm are *methodical procedures* and *methodics*. This means that the relation between a methodological view and some actual study area will be determined by the methodical procedures being used and the methodics being implemented.

METHODOLOGY AND OPERATIVE PARADIGM

Methodology is the understanding of how methods are constructed, that is, how an *operative paradigm* is developed. An operative paradigm relates a methodological view to a specific study area. An operative paradigm, as already mentioned, consists of two important parts: *methodical procedures* and *methodics*. The most important mission for methodology, then, is to clarify how different methodologies, problem formulations, study plans, methods, techniques and study areas make up the parts of an integrated whole. In our opinion, one *cannot* talk about a methodology if the components mentioned above are merely described separately and in isolation, instead of referring to their relations to each other and to the whole (see Figure 1.9).

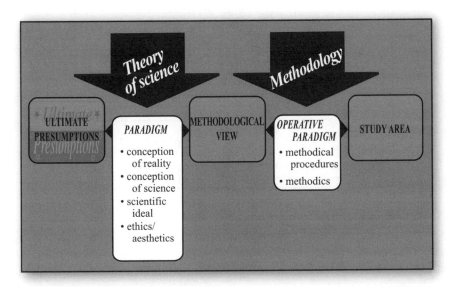

Figure 1.9   Paradigm and Operative Paradigm

A *methodical procedure* refers to the way the creator of knowledge *incorporates, develops, and/or modifies some previously given technique* (e.g. a technique for selecting the units of study, for collecting data, or for analysing results) *in a methodological view. Adopting and possibly modifying a previous result and/or theory is also called a methodical procedure.* So, a technique becomes a method only when, through the application of a *conscious and explicit methodical procedure*, it is incorporated, developed, and/or modified in relation to the methodological view in question, *as well as* in relation to the character of the study area. We point this out because too many studies and investigations take place without any direct or conscious methodical procedures. Such studies or investigations become technique-oriented and mechanical with little or no connection to either the study area or to any preconditions (some methodological view).

The way in which the creator of knowledge *relates* to and *incorporates* these techniques made-into-methods into to his/her study process, and the way the study *is planned and conducted* is called *methodics*. So, adapting a technique to a methodological view is a *methodical procedure*,

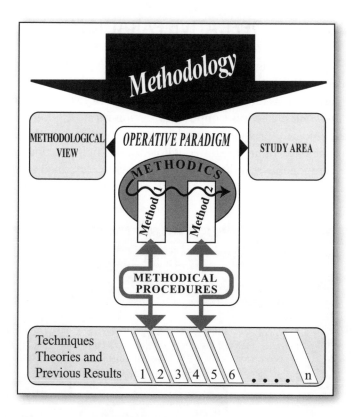

Figure 1.10   Methodics and Methodical Procedures

whereas applying this adaptation (in a plan and/or an implementation of a study) is *methodics*. The study may concern scientific research, consulting and investigation or any business development (see Figure 1.10).

The *methodics* is to be in harmony with the chosen view, the methods and the study area. Lack of harmony either in methodical procedures or in methodics leads to scientifically weak results. All use of theories, previous results and techniques in a study should therefore be taken into consideration within the framework of what we call "development of an operative paradigm", that is, in terms of *methodical procedures* and *methodics*.

From Figure 1.10, and from what has been said before, we realize that *methodology* has more to do with the development of personal insight and understanding in the creator of knowledge than with learning specific techniques and skills.

AWARENESS AND SELF-REFLECTION

To be aware of, and reflect upon, theory of science and the content of methodology is an important task for anyone who wants to understand his/her own studies, and understand what the knowledge that he/she produces is knowledge about. Development of your own *consciousness* about, for instance, the history of the theory of science gives valuable insights into why some views are used the way they are (rightly or wrongly) and why some problems are solved the way they are, etc.

Self-reflection helps the creator of knowledge (see Box 1.3) to orient him/herself within his/her own area, to see its possibilities and limitations and understand his/her own role in the context in question.

As we have found the concepts of awareness and self-reflection central to reading *Methodology for Creating Business Knowledge*, we have chosen to point this out by giving them a section of their own. It is our wish that the reader takes a break here and tries to make clear to him/herself what awareness and self-reflection means to methodology in the area of business.

THE OUTLINE OF THE BOOK

The book is divided into five parts (plus an Appendix and Glossary), and each part, in a pedagogical fashion, deals with the theme of the book within the framework of a specific context.

- **Part I: Introduction to Research Methodology**, contains an introduction to the specific world and language of *methodology*, and consists of three chapters. You have just read Chapter 1. Chapter 2 introduces necessary and reflexive thinking which a creator of knowledge should adopt when facing practical problems and possibilities in business realities in general and, as an example, in entrepreneurship, in particular. Chapter 3 provides an overview of the conditions for creating knowledge and gives a brief summary of the foundation of the three methodological views.
- **Part II: Three Methodological Views**, presents a *principal* description of these three *methodological views* in more detail and consists of three chapters, one for each of the analytical view (Chapter 4), the systems view (Chapter 5) and the actors view (Chapter 6).
- **Part III: Methodology**, constitutes the more *applied* and *practical* part of the book and consists of three chapters: Chapter 7 illustrates different methodical procedures and their design in our three methodological views, considering different available groups of techniques. Chapter 8 provides practical examples of language and action within the framework of such methodical procedures in the three methodological views. Chapter 9 treats methodics in relation to our three methodological views.
- **Part IV: Approaching Methodology**, presents in detail some projects of illustrating the creation of knowledge in more depth than was the case in those short practical examples provided in Part III and consists of three chapters. In Chapters 10, 11 and 12 six (3 x 2) longer examples of methodical procedures and methodics are given for the three methodological views in application (methodological views in application are called *methodological approaches*).
- **Part V: Methodology of Complementarity**, contains our development of some of the complementary possibilities that exist in a reconciliation and transformation of

starting points and techniques in the different methodological views and consists of three chapters: Chapter 13 illustrates our principle of complementarity and presents some of the complementary criticism which the different views direct at each other. Chapter 14 presents three illustrative cases of the methodology of complementarity in business research, where our three approaches act as transformative operators. Chapter 15, finally, brings up some notions about what we refer to as "methodology as business creating intelligence" and the "business knowledge society".

- **Appendix** (Our conceptions of methodology and others) brings up different established thoughts on how to do research in social sciences and relates those thoughts to the methodology presented in this book and to our methodological views.

- The **Glossary** presents the essence of what every conscientious researcher, consultant and investigator should know in his/her relation to methodology for creating business knowledge. It is a condensed result of knowledge creating work for great many years of us two authors together.

As can be seen in Figure 1.11, the design of the book follows the model provided in this chapter of the content of the theory of science and methodology.

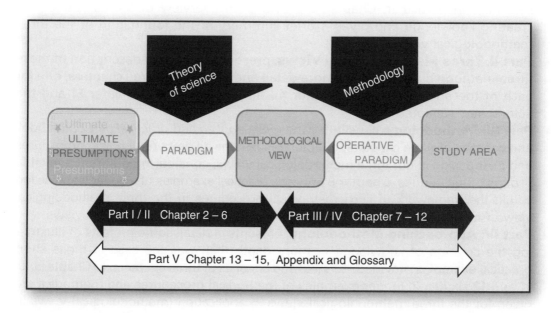

Figure 1.11   Plan of the Book

Methodology means to be aware of, and be able to handle, different relations which exist between participating moments and processes when conducting studies aiming at generating new knowledge. In this chapter we have presented a vocabulary for methodology by introducing concepts like ultimate presumptions, theory of science, paradigm, methodological views, operating paradigm, methods, techniques, methodical procedures and methodics. We have also restricted the term "creator of knowledge" to mean those researchers, investigators, consultants and other business developers, who in a conscious way go about using the language of concepts and action of methodology.

POINTS OF REFLECTION

1. What thoughts come to your mind when you reflect over the *historical* development of science?
2. Name one *important thing* to keep in mind for a creator of knowledge *in spe* (latin meaning "coming, future, to become")!
3. In one of the boxes in the chapter the words *general knowledge* (about entrepreneurship) and *unique knowledge* come up. Can you give some examples of each of those two knowledge formats and what they can be used for?
4. If you enter the *scientific library* (Figure 1.2) you will meet a stop sign. What is it that the scientific library wants to stop?
5. *Ultimate presumptions* are something we all carry with us. As a creator of knowledge we should be aware of these and how they .... What?
6. What do we start from when we talk about different *methodological views*?
7. Which are the most important concepts in the *language of methodology* presented in this chapter?
8. There are two *concepts of relations* that summarize the connections between these important concepts. They are .... and ....!
9. Which different *consisting parts* describe these two concepts of relations?

RECOMMENDED FURTHER READING

See the end of the Appendix and visit the website below.

Become a worldwide partner as a *knowledge creator* in the development of *Methodology for Creating Business Knowledge* by visiting the website: **www.knowledge-creator.com**. Here you can contribute by asking your own questions and you will also find answers to the most frequently asked questions. The website has been developed alongside this third edition of the book and the questions posted there will be used to provide input for future editions.

2 THE ACT OF CREATING KNOWLEDGE

In Chapter 2 you will take part in a number of issues, questions and actions, which you may face, when you are involved in knowledge-creating work. In such real situations, it is necessary that your positions are based on deepened thinking as well as a creative attitude, this in order to build a serious foundation to the "adventure" that is offered by investigative work in general and by research in particular. It is about testing that awareness and self-reflection which we brought up at the end of Chapter 1. In order to illustrate this, we have chosen a practical theme for this chapter, entrepreneurship, which is *indeed* a relevant area for methodology in the subject of business.

A METHODOLOGICAL START

In order to provide a basis for the methodological *modes of thinking* which were developed in Chapter 1, we will here relate these modes to knowledge-creating reflections and actions in relation to a specific study area. It is our hope that this will provide even more substance to the reader's thinking and understanding of what this book on methodology will be all about at this early stage. We have chosen entrepreneurship, which is about the ability to think in new directions and realize them in action. If we, as creators of knowledge, intend to study this phenomenon we have to prepare ourselves for a number of issues to decide on, issues which have a direct connection to those brought up in Chapter 1.

Our purpose is to highlight a number of *aspects of deliberations* which a creator of knowledge should reflect upon during the very process of designing an *operative paradigm*, a process which, according to what has been said before, takes place starting from the *methodological view* chosen by the creator of knowledge, based on his/her convictions, and the study area which is at hand, in this case entrepreneurship. We will, with a number of deliberations, illustrate this complexity following as far as possible the process from beginning to end, but we also intend to make it as easy as possible for the reader, keeping in mind that this is an introduction and thereby renouncing details and excesses. The chapter then becomes a kind of methodological start to that intensification which will gradually take place through the whole book.

TO THINK AND TO REFLECT CRITICALLY

To think and to reflect critically means philosophically to develop alternative ways to think about and to look at things. And this, in turn, requires imagination. Critical thinking is consequently intimately related to a person's creative ability and his/her ability to think unconditionally. And to think unconditionally is not easy. It often calls for more than most people think. We often hear others, or ourselves, saying: "Let's start from scratch", designing a new effort to create knowledge. We then may remind ourselves that it takes longer to be scratch-thinkers than it takes to be scratch-players in golf, that is, to reach a handicap of zero.

Let us, with a very simple example, illustrate this idea about *imagination* as a requirement for critical thinking. In an interview you ask an entrepreneur to present the *unique* characteristics and content of entrepreneurship. As an answer to your question the entrepreneur blinks seven times and says that this is the root of entrepreneurship. You do not get any other answer. Your first thought may be to dismiss the whole thing as a strange quirk. It does not fit with the answers you expected. Seven blinks is also no part of any theory for describing entrepreneurship. So what to do? Well, you may start to generate a number of imaginative deliberations in order to try to get a perspective on the answer. Let us "play" some such answers to illustrate what we mean:

1. The entrepreneur may want with his answer of *seven* blinks to indicate the importance of *uniqueness* and the *childlike mind* of entrepreneurship. In the world of *fairy tales*, it is possible, for instance, to find Snow White and the *seven* dwarfs. It was the first full-length film by the super entrepreneur Walt Disney, and it was his stroke of genius to give individual and *unique* traits to the dwarfs. That entrepreneurship is about daring to be unique, to believe in oneself and always be first, just like Walt Disney was with most of what he did.
2. Maybe he wanted symbolically to point at the wonders of the world, which are *seven* in numbers – to show that entrepreneurship is about creating small or big *wonders*.
3. Maybe he wanted to compare entrepreneurship with what is referred to as the free arts during the Middle Ages – *artes liberalis* – which were *seven* in numbers – demonstrating that entrepreneurship can be seen as *venturesome art*!
4. Maybe he wanted to illustrate the story in the Bible about how the walls of Jericho tumbled down when the trumpets were heard for the *seventh* time – indicating that entrepreneurship is like going through walls of resistance. Sir Richard Branson (Virgin) has likened entrepreneurship to going through a wall.
5. Or maybe he just wanted to say that the soul of entrepreneurship is located in the *seventh* heaven. It is to be in a state of intense, delight or ecstasy.

The pedagogical point is now *not* what the truth is about what the entrepreneur meant with his *seven blinks*. Those far-fetched explanations selected here have been deliberately chosen to inspire the imagination. It is about exercising your own mind in order to come up with new perspectives on what you intend to study. And with new and more perspectives you reach farther, deeper and are able to generate more insightful results. In imagination you may also become emancipated from, and get a new perspective on, your own clichés. Not least, it is then possible to expose clichés that consist of pre-scientific concepts or jargon within the different methodological views, within the subject and in the study area. *So, creativity is a prerequisite for critical thinking and reflection.*

Seeing and thinking

Words can force our thinking and our acting in tracks that we do not consciously choose ourselves. If somebody comes up with a good entrepreneurial idea and some narrow-minded person glues *clichés* on it, like unrealistic, fuzzy, idealistic or naive, then a direct hindrance for getting the idea assessed on its true merits exists. It may be the same in a research process. *Scientific concepts* like reliability, objectivity, dialogue, interview, sample, system, component, structure of meaning, methodics and analysis can directly focus the interest in a way that makes the creator of knowledge think along some predetermined tracks. In the same way *pre-scientific concepts* in our own subject, such as cluster, risk, network, business concept, brand, market, best practice and benchmarking, may make the creator of knowledge follow a certain pattern. Language may consequently be an encyclopedia of what we do not see *as well* as what we do. And the different *methodological views* are in many aspects different linguistic encyclopedias of how research should be done (we know that Kuhn originally picked up his *paradigm* concept from linguistics).

In MIT an experiment was done with a group of students who were about to get a new teacher. They were divided into two groups and they were given the same detailed description of the competence and characteristics of the new teacher, except for *one word*. In the papers one of the groups could read that the teacher was a "rather *warm* person", while the other group could read that he was a "rather *aloof* person". The teacher met the two groups at the same time and gave his lecture. When the students afterwards were asked about their opinion of the teacher, it appears they differed widely. The group we can call "warm" experienced him as very sympathetic, while the group we can call "aloof" experienced him as much more unsympathetic. And what conclusions can we draw from this?

What the students believed to be their own independent thinking was in fact generated by a cliché. The same phenomenon – same teacher and same lecture – was experienced very differently. This type of thinking in clichés triggered by small words also has a tendency to reinforce itself.

There are probably many who ask themselves whether we should throw away our clichés. Of course not! They are in fact a prerequisite for us to be able to handle our environment and ourselves, and to conduct studies creating knowledge. *Our different methodological views could, after all, be seen to represent different forms of thinking in clichés.* On the other hand, it is possible for a person with a critical and imaginative mind to be able, in short intervals, to emancipate him/herself from this kind of mind control. And by doing so, be able, as a creator of knowledge, to experience investigated areas in new ways. This is one of the ambitions of our book on methodology.

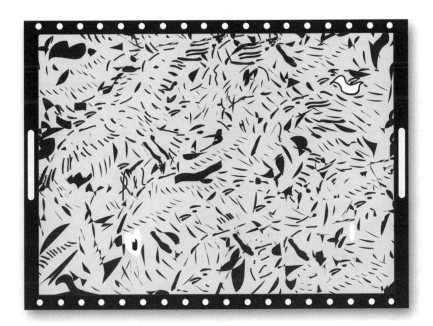

Figure 2.1   Study Area

Among other things, entrepreneurship is about being able to discover that business quality which clichés prevent us from seeing: to see beyond seeing, so to speak, and to develop oneself, new ideas and new ventures. Let us look at Figure 2.1. When facing something as chaotic as this picture seems to be it is easy not to perceive *immediately* what actually exists as the *inner quality* of it. Let us play with the thought that this is the picture of entrepreneurship you meet as a creator of knowledge, when for the second time you experience your study area, keeping your first step, the seven blinks mentioned earlier, in mind.

The feeling of cognitive chaos, meeting what is different, is often related to the fact that our inner map cannot immediately make a clear pattern of what we see. We may perhaps lack relevant *ultimate presumptions* or *clichés* in order to be able to quickly structure what we see. We described this in Chapter 1 as "the way a problem appears to a creator of knowledge is intimately related to *the* view he/she is using for his/her reflection". In real life many people leave this type of situation and call it fuzzy. And they lose the golden nuggets, which are associated with discovering. Research as well as entrepreneurship is basically about *self-reflection* and *awareness* – trying to discover how clichés, or the lack of them, make us blind.

Small things may sometimes lead to quite large changes of awareness. Consider what happened to the students at MIT when the word "warm" was changed for "aloof" in the description of the teacher. Here it is easy to see what the choice of different words can do. This is not an irrelevant experience for all those who want to design an *operative paradigm* and create knowledge by using questionnaires or interviews, for instance. Look at the next picture (Figure 2.2), which is closely related to this phenomenon of words.

Figure 2.2   With the Naked Eye

The picture in Figure 2.2 is a typical *Gestalt phenomenon*, which means that the whole is something more than the parts in it (systems thinking). Here we have only changed the mouth, but suddenly the eyes appear happy or sad. This can give some indication what body language can mean when interviews are conducted. Or what *single details* can mean for the designer of the impression of the whole. Or how a system, something whole (a company), in fact can change through a minor change in some of the internal components.

Let us now see what the "chaotic" picture in Figure 2.1 was hiding for all who did not see what inner quality was in it – see Figure 2.3. That is, entrepreneurship with a unique ability to have an overview and to move fast, combined with the ability to be able to glide in the seventh heaven.

As soon as you see the gull in the figure, something strange is happening. It establishes itself in the brain and occupies seeing. After this, looking at the study area ("the chaotic picture" in Figure 2.1), the gull appears at once – that gull which was originally so difficult to make out. This is experienced by everybody in daily life after having bought a product of a new brand. What before has been seen very little of now seems to exist everywhere. This selective perception is a strength as well as a weakness. Think about when it can be one or the other. Also think about how this thing with selective perception can also influence the choice of different methods and techniques when an *operative paradigm* is about to be developed. And do not forget to keep in mind that a *methodological view,* to a large extent, is controlling how this development process is conducted; that is, what will be seen and what will not be seen.

What *cannot* be seen using *one* methodological view *can consequently*, after having changed to another, be as clear and evident as the gull becomes in Figure 2.1, once it is set out as in Figure 2.3. Then it also becomes difficult to re-create the original, somewhat chaotic picture, where the gull did not appear immediately. You have converted to another seeing, so to speak, which also happens when you change methodological view. We want to stress, however, that our

Figure 2.3   "Entrepreneur" in the Seventh Heaven

simile is very simplified and that change of methodological view is associated with personal ran-sacking and controversies, which are related to *ultimate presumptions* and therefore your whole set of personal convictions.

So, now we have seen a picture which was about *not immediately seeing what was there*, and also about what happens with seeing once you have seen it. But there are also pictures where we *immediately see what is not there*. We add something, so to say, and create an opti-cal illusion. Something to think of as well, when facing a study area. Can my methodological view, my methods, my pre-scientific concepts, create optical illusions? And if so, which ones?

In Figure 2.4 most people see the NATO-type star in the picture, which is *not* there. It exists only as a mental cliché in our heads, not in the picture! And by this we have come to an interesting point in this exposition. Try at this stage to emancipate yourself from the visual impression of the star in this picture, or of the gull in the previous chaotic picture (Figure 2.1). This gives a small taste of how difficult it is to think from scratch, to think unconditionally.

We can go on like this and illustrate things and make small changes, which will completely modify our experiences of them. *This can also give an indication that nothing needs to be too small in a study in order to be able to grow and point at something bigger.*

In the next picture (Figure 2.5), we can see how pairs of *similar* figures assume a *totally* new form with *minor* changes in the broadness of the lines in the figures. Here we can play with the thought that this has been preceded by the ink flow to the different symbols in the figures suddenly having taken new directions, that is, by something insignificant that has been operating for a longer time. Or that the flow of involvement and joy in a company has

Figure 2.4   Seeing is Believing?

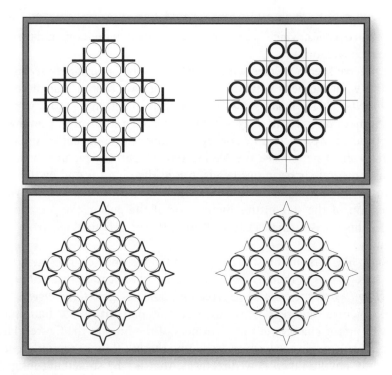

Figure 2.5   On the Whole

declined for a longer time, so that suddenly, the day the company is facing a technological shift in the market, there are no new ideas to be had.

Many small, apparently *insignificant*, changes have consequently "in secret" led to *significant* and bigger changes. In this way we can also look and try to describe what is happening in a research project, in order to better understand *the importance of insignificancies* to the whole. The world as a knowledge-creating *possibility,* therefore, also consists of *the exceptions*, *the paradoxes* and *the deviations*. The ability to discover possible changes in the small, which can lead to something bigger, requires imaginative mental skills in both the creator of knowledge and the entrepreneur.

The importance of the perspective

What does the perspective mean for our seeing? Take, for instance, a map of some well-known area and turn it upside down and it is clearly seen how our ingrained *perspective* has created a *mental cliché.* Maps are a kind of investigative pictures which will give us more detailed information than words can do, just like economic models. *Forms, lines, symbols and colours* are working here as clichés which are supposed to simplify. A well-known map turned upside down will change the prerequisites for these clichés and the map then becomes more difficult to use as an orientation.

Our ingrained perspective in the case of the map, with its clichés of forms, lines, symbols and colours, makes it possible for us to rather unconsciously orient ourselves on the map or in the real world. This is the strength of mental clichés. Their weaknesses include the task for the creator of knowledge to reveal through *problematization*. The *knowledge-creating point* with problematization – to make what is common uncommon – is that we then will think out new points of departure to use for an orientation, and in this way discover new aspects of life.

One perspective brings order and delimits what we look at and reflect upon. It also directs our attention to some specific aspects of reality while others are made invisible. Look at Figure 2.6 and ask yourself what it is and what shape the object has.

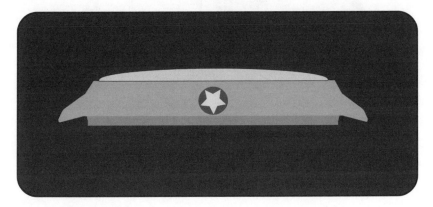

Figure 2.6   The Outlook

The perspective here becomes completely decisive for how one will perceive the shape of the object. The clock is round someone says. The clock is slightly elliptic, almost rectangular, says someone else. Who is right? The perspective becomes the decisive factor, at the same time as we can realize that an object can always be looked at from several different angles.

The French author Jarry (a predecessor to the theatre of the absurd) has commented on this phenomenon:

> Why does everyone claim that the shape of a watch is round – a manifestly false proposition – since it appears in profile as narrow rectangular construction, elliptic on three sides; and why the devil should one only have noticed its shape at the moment of looking at the time? (Shattuck & Watson Taylor, 1965: 23)

This way the perspective also points out a direction from which the onlooker is handling his/her reality. This can also imply what is acceptable knowledge and *normality* in a paradigm. The perspective can therefore be seen as a creator of safety by reducing ambivalence and uncertainty. But precisely because of this the perspective can be the major obstacle to discovering new ways to create knowledge and to develop new business ventures.

To be *able* to look at something from several different perspectives, or to *dare*, which often go together, always gives the creative mind suggestions for new ideas. You should never, therefore, be afraid to put yourself in different perspectivistic positions when looking at something – both mentally and purely physically. To sit down on one's heels, for instance, makes it possible to look at something from a child's perspective. Look at the next picture (Figure 2.7) and speculate over what it can be.

Is it the egg of an ostrich in a jaw? Four hedgehogs eating from the egg of an ostrich? Or is it no ostrich egg? No jaw? No hedgehogs? Then what is it? A four-leaf clover that has been

Figure 2.7   What is the Problem/the Opportunity?

stuck to a black egg? Or is it possibly four elephants, which are drinking from an oval pool? Maybe it is a beginning of what is entrepreneurially possible?

To play with thoughts and perspectives in this way can allow completely new conditions and mind tracks to emerge with the creator of knowledge.

Understanding and explaining factors

In science we often use different *understanding or explaining factors* (variables) when we develop knowledge of situations, problems or phenomena. Transferred to a study of *successful entrepreneurship*, the concepts of *risk taking* and *proactivity* could, for instance, be used as such common *factors* (variables). If we say, then, that successful entrepreneurship is characterized by risk taking and proactivity, then these two concepts for creating understanding or explanation may be defined in many different ways by various entrepreneurs. It is also far from certain that the definitions used by the creator of knowledge will coincide with those in the field being studied. This is the problem of creating knowledge which has to be considered in every study which tries to reflect reality: *that what we study really is what we intend to study*. Sometimes this relation between what we do and what we intend to do, is simple to check. Sometimes it is extremely subtle. And sometimes it becomes totally incorrect and we may not even discover it. One creates fictive explanations or misleading understanding, so to say. In other words, no creation of knowledge!

So, here it is about being very stringent, but also imaginative, with problematizing, defining and determining meaning in order to gain knowledge-creating results of value using *methodical procedures* and one's *methodics*. Let us illustrate this in a simple way by using Figure 2.8.

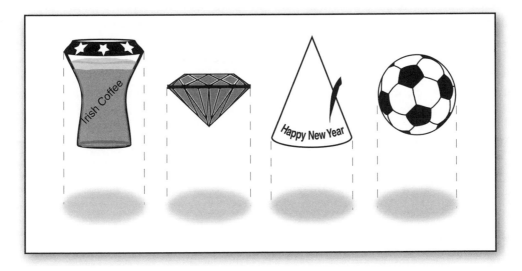

Figure 2.8   Cast a Shadow over the Results!

We see here how four completely different objects, lit from above, give the same *shadow picture*. Have we then found a connection which may possibly constitute an understanding or explaining factor to why all subjects can lead to *successful amusement* (compare successful entrepreneurship)? The question becomes whether that similarity we can now find in *all* objects could explain why these objects in *different* contexts can lead to something linguistically so *similar* as successful amusement.

We can consequently find that successful amusement in the different cases here is related to *one* explaining variable which exists in *all* the objects in question. We may also find that *all* have other variables *in common* such as: (1) that they contain dark sections; (2) that they can roll; (3) that it is impossible to see through them; and (4) that they can be carried one way or another at amusement. All these explaining variables can consequently be seen as valid for successful amusement, together with the shadow picture. But the question still remains whether the variables explain what they are meant to explain: successful amusement (compare successful entrepreneurship, explained by risk taking and proactivity as variables).

So always ask yourself if it is shadow or surface variables you are studying, or if it is real objects in their right context.

THREE METHODOLOGICAL VIEWS

We have previously, on a number of occasions, said that we can see different *methodological views* in our subject and we have done so without providing their names. Not giving their names too early has been a deliberate choice on our side, because we first wanted to build up an understanding that there are different ways of looking at the world in which we act as business economists. And these separate ways also give separate conditions for what we are creating knowledge of. We have also developed a mode of thinking (Chapter 1) in order to be able to describe the look of relations in *methodology* between stages and processes which are in there. Furthermore, in this chapter we have gone deeper into methodology by bringing up a number of aspects and considerations, which a creator of knowledge must keep in mind when designing an *operative paradigm*. We have come to the point, however, when it is convenient to introduce the three methodological views in brief. We do it in the same simplified way as in the rest of this chapter and do not ask for either totality or details at this stage.

We will present the three methodological views – *Analytical view, Systems view* and *Actors view* – in relation to the study area of entrepreneurship. First a few general points about this study area, however.

The study area of entrepreneurship

An entrepreneur's *business concept* is both in small and large part about the *art* of *merging* the passion – the personal inner feeling and the dream of wanting to create something – with an idea rich in points for a market that may not even exist yet. And then in concrete *action* the entrepreneur goes on to develop an exciting and imaginative strategy, where the personal passion/dream and the point in the business concept constantly trigger and inspire each other towards new exciting combinations, in a development complex that will create businesses in a market.

This is normally understood *not* as a linear process from a starting point going straight toward a goal, but rather as a *wandering and searching* development, where one thing gives way to another, and inessentials turn into essentials and vice versa, which may very quickly totally change the prerequisites. Entrepreneurship is also more about creating anew and changing markets than about entering already known and established ground. This opinion we also often find with those we may call business venturers with a capital V, that is, with business managers who are creating the radical innovations or the really big reconfigurations of the market. Thomas Watson, the "true" optimist who created IBM, explained over and over again for his colleagues that every company in the world needs their machines, but the companies just do not know it yet. Watson is often referred to as having said, "We know better than the customer what the customer needs!"

This is an entrepreneurial way to think which can also be illustrated by the following quotation by Apple's founder, Steve Jobs, who supposedly stated: "You can't just ask customers what they want and then try to give that to them. By the time you get it built, they'll want something new."

Another aspect, which also exists within the study area, is the importance of *feeling* for entrepreneurship. We may here quote another super entrepreneur, Sir Richard Branson, the creator of Virgin who claimed: "I never get the accountants in before I start up a business. It's done on gut feeling."

With this so-called gut feeling, the entrepreneurs are "seeing through" our taken-for-granted mental clichés and establishing new perspectives, which give new meaning to realism. The entrepreneurially legend Larry Ellison, who started Oracle, puts it this way: "The secret with entrepreneurship is to identify what is wrong with conventional and traditional knowledge, and in ways of thinking."

The fact that new thinking and innovation also can be more difficult for the environment also belongs to the study area of entrepreneurship. That is, to study those social and business-oriented contexts in which the entrepreneurs are placing their efforts and how they are received. Let us by using a few historical examples describe what in this respect may constitute the context of resistance and inertia of entrepreneurship in that socio-economic world in which they are acting.

In 1878, the chairman of Western Union turns down the exclusive rights to the telephone with the words: "What use could the company make of an electric toy?" He was possibly influenced by the American president at the time, Rutherford B. Hayes, who said in 1877: "An astonishing invention – but who would ever want to use one?"

In 1959, shortly after Ingvar Kamprad had started IKEA, most Swedish furniture dealers said something similar to this: "I would not even like to call this Kamprad with IKEA a furniture dealer. A real furniture shop should have readymade furniture and home delivery. And it should be placed in the centre of the city."

In 1962 the Decca Recording Co. brushes aside the Beatles with the words: "We do not like their sound and their guitar music is on its way out."

In 1997 the administrative manager T. Ruud in the Norwegian K-Bank claims: "Internet is something for young people 14–22 years old. This will not become any important area for K-Bank in the future!" In 2000 the same manager says: "Internet will become the most important distribution channel for K-Bank in the future!"

If people who are deeply involved in business activities have problems in understanding the transforming power of entrepreneurship, we may be able to predict that it is also a delicate task from a research point of departure to create knowledge in this subject and area. We will present some "unconditional" questions in the next section in relation to reflections that may start such a creation of knowledge. Still in the same simplified spirit as before.

Some "unconditional" reflections over the area of entrepreneurship

What we refer to here as "unconditional" reflections are unconditional in the sense that they are not connected to any explicit methodological view or paradigm. This does not deny the fact that different methodological views, through their different *ultimate presumptions* will look different as well as act differently, and also use different language for problematization and come up with different results in the design of the *operative paradigms*. However, as mentioned, we want the reader to consider his/her own answers to the questions below, before we provide our answers later in this chapter.

- *When we start our research process in the area of entrepreneurship should we then first:*
  - o orient ourselves about the *ultimate presumptions* which different views of creating knowledge are based on, or just believe that we could go on unconditionally in the study area?
  - o decide which *methods and techniques* we will use, or first make clear to ourselves how they are related to ultimate presumptions?

- *When we then attack the study area, which questions should we put? Which perspective should we choose? Should we:*
  - o look for similarities in what is different? The regular in the irregular? Or vice versa?
  - o look for what the entrepreneurs have *in common* as explanations and understanding? Or vice versa?

- o   try to understand the individual entrepreneurs and their context? Or look for more general aspects independent of the different contexts?
- o   look for the different contexts which the entrepreneurs are part of and describe those relationships which exist and what they mean for the entrepreneurship in question?
- o   put up hypotheses and test them? Generally en masse or through a few cases where the different opinions of the entrepreneurs are related to their own contexts?
- o   look for answers by studying overall social structures of rewards, laws and taxes?
- o   look for answers by acting together with the entrepreneurs concerned to implement a project?
- o   look in the literature and research reports and then through empirical studies to confirm and/or reject previous theories in the area? Or vice versa, first empirics and then theory?

Your intentions *when looking* will give an answer to your questions In the best of cases. But it is not necessary so that *those questions* you come up with and look for an answer to are the best to explain and/or understand a study area.

- *After these questions should we then:*

  - o   try to clarify the different scientific and pre-scientific *concepts* in the study area to be able to see the mental clichés, or are they embedded beforehand in the questions above? So in this way before we ask our questions we try to clarify them?
  - o   create a set of concepts and definitions by which we can accomplish our knowledge-creating work? Or should we let them develop as we go on with investigating the study area?

- *Are we now clear to design our operative paradigm and:*

  - o   set about which *methods* and *techniques* we should choose beforehand and/or develop? Or is this to be done as we go on in a wandering and searching process similar to entrepreneurship, that is, the study area?
  - o   concretely design a *methodics* for our process of creating knowledge? Or is the methodics also developed by what we meet, so that one thing gives way to another, in a process close to wandering and searching?

- *How are we then to present our results? What type of answers should we provide? Are we to:*

  - o   look for *general explanations* which are seen as valid in most cases? Or are we looking for *understanding-oriented* descriptions, which are connected to the specific cases?
  - o   develop descriptive languages which mean that action is placed in focus, that is, the very act of achieving change and understanding in specific cases? Or are the descriptions to be connected with reports, which are spreading our knowledge further? Or both?
  - o   write and/or act mainly for the scientific community or for the society at large, or only for those involved? Or both?

Starting with this type of question we imagine that the creator of knowledge *in spe* (coming, future, to become) is preparing his/her next investigative and research-oriented study. Once a creator of knowledge has then clarified to him/herself such matters as *ultimate presumptions* and choice of *methodological view*, based on his/her own personal conviction, the process will not be so extensive in the future. A person has then adopted a way of creating knowledge, which is based on *methodological awareness and self-reflection*. That is what this book is trying to teach.

Let us now talk about our *three methodological views* briefly with respect to the questions just presented. Our ambition is to illustrate how the methodological views most likely will present different perspectives when creating knowledge in the study area of entrepreneurship (as well as in other study areas, of course). The intentions of the questions above were to focus the following *five* points of departure:

- Ultimate presumptions (see "Paradigm" Box 1.6 and Figure 1.9)
- Interesting issues and perspectives
- Conceptualization
- Methods and methodics
- Results

The analytical view

Ultimate presumptions

The analytical creator of knowledge is in general not very interested in philosophical matters. Nevertheless, he/she, perhaps unconsciously, makes certain assumptions about the reality in which he/she is operating, or functions as if these assumptions have been made.

The analytical view presupposes that *reality* is *filled with facts* and independent of individual perceivers. Being fact-filled means that it both contains objective elements, that is, external conditions for entrepreneurship, and that it also contains a number of opinions and ideas which people have about entrepreneurship, even though the creator of knowledge, for instance, the entrepreneurship one, may possibly think that several of these opinions and ideas are wrong. *Reality* has also a *summative* character so that new scientific findings about entrepreneurship make the picture of this phenomenon more and more complete.

In the *conception of science* of the analytical view is included a number of entrepreneurship concepts. However, it is a common opinion that, due to the fact that the subject, in the modern sense of it, is so young, there is a great degree of confusion and many unclear points in entrepreneurship as an academic subject and that there are many, often diverging, opinions of the meaning of its central concepts.

One *scientific ideal* is that entrepreneurship scholars will be able to come up with a common agreement about what the subject stands for, what its most central questions are, and how these questions are to be tackled scientifically. Many voices have been aired that this would give the best basis for attacking and conquering the entrepreneurship study area. The majority of (above all transatlantic) entrepreneurship scholars assert that what is needed is *clearer theories, more distinctly formulated hypotheses and, most importantly, statistically secured results.*

One *ethical* aspect of analytical entrepreneurship research is that its creators of knowledge can give advice to different decision makers (which they often do), but they should make a distinction between the role of decision-making and creating-knowledge.

One *aesthetical* aspect of the same is that its creators of knowledge are very fond of "beautiful" graphs and "nicely" presented statistical arrangements.

Interesting issues and perspectives

The scientific ambition of the analytical view is to come up with *explanations* from a general point of departure. This means to come up with patterns, with regularities, with representative models. In other words, the analytical view looks at *regularities* and *similarities*, for what is *common* among entrepreneurs and entrepreneurship. Analytical entrepreneurship creators of knowledge are confident, by doing so, of being able to contribute to the development of the modern society, which in their opinion *stands or falls by its ability to be entrepreneurial*. They are also convinced that that the number of entrepreneurs and entrepreneurial ventures in the world never has been higher than today. For such a creator of knowledge the issue is to discover those *"laws"* that govern society from an entrepreneurial point of departure. They are also interested in finding the conformity to a law of entrepreneurship at the level of a firm and at the level of the individual entrepreneur. *Typical questions* for the entrepreneurship creator of knowledge include:

- What are the relations between entrepreneurship and economic growth?
- Which political measures will encourage entrepreneurship in a country?
- What does the entrepreneurial personality look like?
- Which are the most important success factors in an entrepreneurial environment?
- Which are the most important steps to take at different stages of the growth of an entrepreneurial business venture?
- How critical are different obstacles in an entrepreneurial process?

Conceptualization

The function of concepts, according to the analytical creator of knowledge, is to *catch the truth*. The truth is in the reality. The creator of knowledge is to depict this reality in the closest possible way, as objectively as he/she can. In the entrepreneurship case the mission for the analytical creator of knowledge is to find *the equivalence in reality* of concepts like "entrepreneur", "opportunity recognition", "business idea", "risk taking", "profit orientation" and others. There is also a general belief here that some concepts are more important than others to *explain* entrepreneurship. The analytical entrepreneurship creator of knowledge is looking for them all the time.

Methods and methodics

Methods in the analytical view rest, of course, on the premise that they, as closely as possible, shall "hit" those forces which are governing the fact-filled reality, reality then seen as built up by laws of causes and effects. It is under such circumstances quite natural to look for two sources of data: (1) public statistics, above all such information, which has been collected by impartial agencies and institutions; and (2) answers to those who know and who have been there. It is important in the second case for an interviewer to influence the answers as little as possible. Another important source of information for the analytical creator of knowledge in entrepreneurship is to acquaint him/herself with results from research done already.

Based as much as possible on what the creator of knowledge judges as of interest in this previous research, when trying to *explain* and not only to describe the study area in question, he/she feels that he/she is best guided by formulating *hypotheses*, that is, preliminary explanations which are formulated in the beginning of the study and which are to be tested (be confirmed or rejected) as the study goes on. One problem sometimes expressed by analytical creators of knowledge in entrepreneurship is that there are so many *contradictory results*, which are caused by, they say, the fact that the subject is so young. However, they are convinced that as knowledge of entrepreneurship will gradually improve, existing conflicts and paradoxes will be eliminated or at least explained.

The methodics in the analytical view consists of well-defined steps to take. Following these steps is seen as a guarantee that valid results will be coming up as a result.

Results

The analytical creator of knowledge in entrepreneurship looks at his/her results as one more contribution to the truth of the subject in question, at best as *generalizable* explanations. As he/she feels as one part of a larger collective of researchers aiming in the same direction and guided by common *methodical procedures* and *methodics* (the analytical view is seen as very homogeneous), he/she asserts that it is of minor importance whether the results are conforming to what has been found out elsewhere, brings some clarity to some scientific entrepreneurship issue, or comes up with some new findings. In the last case it is not appreciated, however, if the results are based on definitions and conceptualizations, which differ radically from what is seen as the *dominant opinions* of the meaning of key terms.

Those concepts and definitions, which the analytical creator of knowledge in entrepreneurship is using when presenting his/her results are important in order for them to be accepted by other creators of knowledge in the same field and with the same orientation. This is clearly in line with the importance which the analytical view points out for language as a depicting and clarifying tool.

The result of a study based on the analytical view, it may be a consulting report, a general investigation or a research effort, is often based on clearly designed rules as far as general design and sections to be included are concerned.

The systems view

Ultimate presumptions

Philosophical assumptions made by a systems creator of knowledge are, consciously or unconsciously, as well as in the two other views, a kind of their own. The systems view looks at *reality* as consisting of fact-filled systems structures in the objective reality and of subjective opinions of such structures, which are treated as facts as well. Unlike the analytical view, however, a creator of knowledge in, say, entrepreneurship cannot see how different parts of reality can be simply added to each other and combined without those parts influencing each other. In other words, reality is *not summative* here.

The *conception of science* of the systems view implies studying the entrepreneurship reality as different wholes and patterns, where the entrepreneur is not looked at as an isolated individual.

The *scientific ideal* is to find these wholes and patterns as objective structures and to try to make every new systems picture better than the last, partly as more valid systems structures, partly as pragmatically more favourable concepts. There are a number of such systems pictures within entrepreneurship at present.

The *ethical* dimension has become more powerful in the systems view. This means in entrepreneurship, for instance, that because different *components* in a business system, like employees, the founder of the business, financiers, environmentalists, feminists, etc., depend on each other and because none of them favours negative results of entrepreneurship, different kinds of systems consequences of the phenomenon have more and more come out into the open.

Aesthetical aspects of the use of results from a systems-based study play a minor role according to the systems view. However, aesthetical aspects on the content of the report, its language, its graphs and its figures are often of great importance.

Interesting issues and perspectives

The systems creator of knowledge is convinced, of course, that entrepreneurship can only be explained or understood in its *context*. This context is therefore the place for the creator of knowledge to start from and interesting issues, according to him/her, are raised there.

The creator of knowledge sees the context as a system, where he/she is looking for *regular patterns, interactions and relations*. However, he/she also allows him/herself to bring *irregular aspects* of the context into the picture as well. All of this is to be part of a *systems model* or a *metaphor*, which is to *describe* and *explain* or provide an *understanding* of the entrepreneurial reality.

To be inspired and to relate to other research done, the creator of knowledge usually (but not always) starts in existing *literature* to look for research/consulting/investigations being done in the same field. These other efforts may also provide inspirations for interesting *analogies* to use, guiding the creator of knowledge in his/her design of the operative paradigm.

The perspective of the creator of knowledge has, as a consequence, that his/her interest is directed more towards different *situations* of structures and relations than towards general factors en masse, taken out of context.

The systems oriented creator of knowledge more often works as a discussion partner to, and as an interviewer of, entrepreneurs in the study area than as an actor taking part in co-creating the future.

The basic perspective is that the right combination of circumstances at national, regional, industry and individual company levels will provide the solutions – and the systems creator of knowledge has a rather pragmatic attitude to which they should be.

Conceptualization

The systems oriented entrepreneurship creator of knowledge claims that a systems oriented view is the most successful way to go to bring the subject forward. The systems view has also entered the entrepreneurship area *with gusto*. There are few texts on entrepreneurship, which do not contain terms like clusters, industrial parks and regional development, to give a few examples of terms normally studied with a systems view. Concepts like network, interaction, organizational learning, innovation and design are also very common in system view studies with all the specific questions these concepts will raise.

Methods and methodics

Researching systems has several consequences. One is that a system can be extensive as well as complicated with many people involved. It might therefore be *a huge job* for a systems creator of knowledge to study, say, an entrepreneurial issue with a systems view, to participate in discussions and conduct interviews in a number large enough for a comprehensive and clear systems picture to develop in his/her mind. This requires also, normally, that the creator of knowledge should try to lay his/her hands on as much relevant secondary information as possible in order to supplement the picture.

Another methodological consequence of the systems view is based on the fact that a system does not appear overnight and that it has often existed for a long time. It is therefore often important for a systems creator of knowledge of, say, an innovation system, to clarify *the system's history*, including critical events that have taken place and important decisions that have been made along the way.

What has been said above naturally leads to a situation where an individual systems research effort rarely covers more than a few cases in the study area at the same time.

An interesting (or rather natural) aspect of methodics in the systems view is that its design is done to generate *pictures* of those systems which are believed to be there out in the fact-filled reality, that is, to *gradually* move forward to get better and better pictures of those real systems.

Results

It is quite natural that a more comprehensive report from a systems study contains empirical results that to some extent are *unique* to the study. What it might have in common with other systems studies are two things.

It may be based on the same *systems theory* as some other study or studies. This could, in entrepreneurship studies, be theories like necessary components in an entrepreneurial system, common mistakes made in an entrepreneurial start-up, or roles played by different participants in an entrepreneurial network.

Another aspect that a systems study report quite often has in common with other reports is that he/she often will come up with some (what he/she considers to be) *representative metaphor* (which the systems creator of knowledge can see as providing a kind of understanding, that is, it clarifies to him/her the system being researched in a deeper sense than just explaining it). In the old days, it could be a metaphor like a machine or an organism. In modern times, metaphors like power structures or value hierarchies are more common.

The actors view

Ultimate presumptions

When the creator of knowledge confronts his/her study area and starts to reflect on the ultimate presumptions of the actors view, it may in a simplified description look like this.

The actors view assumes that *reality*, as it exists for us, is a social construction, filled by chaos and uniqueness in the case of entrepreneurship, but also relatively stable structures, mentally anchored with those actors, who maintain the structures. It is a world, which to the largest extent is dependent on us human beings, where the creator of knowledge also participates as one of its constructors.

In the *conception of science* of the actors view, it is included that all pre-scientific concepts must be objects of reflection in all kinds of work of creating knowledge. The view claims that taken-for-granted concepts may become obstacles to real understanding and renewal.

As the actors view starts from the idea that research – the work of creating knowledge – always has self-reference to the society at large, that is, participates as one of the constructors of the social reality, it becomes natural that the *scientific ideal* of the actors view advocates a knowledge creating and consciously active interaction. This may mean everything from the language style of reports to an active changing and developing work in the study area at the same time as the area is researched.

Ethically this is about taking responsibility for his/her part of the construction of reality, which the creator of knowledge cannot disclaim responsibility for, whether he/she wants it or not.

Aesthetically it may be so that the actors view, perhaps more than any other view, wants to come up with descriptions and interpretations which are close to being artistic. The actors view also has an expressed concern in an innovative knowledge interest, that is, not only to describe but also to drive change.

Interesting issues and perspectives

When the creator of knowledge has reflected on the paradigm and view he/she has chosen, he/she may, but not necessarily, continue by taking account of what other creators of knowledge have done in the study area (*the actors oriented creator of knowledge may choose to first go to the study area and then study what others have done*). To study what has already been done in the area is about getting an understanding of where the research front is and what questions might be of interest. Included here, of course, are studies which are not done by the actors view alone. When these results are problematized, in relation to the presumptions of the different views, the creator of knowledge may have sorted out the following as a *starting actors orientation* for his/her own *perspective* in relation to his/her own *issues*.

Economic growth in a country depends on the *individual* entrepreneurial act. An entrepreneur is a person who thinks what is impossible and approaches reality without taking cover against it with the use of established and "correct" thinking. He/she does not drive any linear process or start from what exists, but creates his/her own story and lives his/her dream. It is a person who with ideas is happy to surprise his/her own rationalistic sides. He/she is also happy to place him/herself in situations, which are difficult to master in order to consciously loosen their grip, thereby being forced to look for new and untested roads out of the difficulties. The entrepreneur is the person, who with a glint in his/her eyes walks right through the wall of resistance which everybody claims that he/she will face. The entrepreneur is like a court jester of the present who dares to do what others do not. It is easy to laugh at him/her, but the risk is always that the laughter will stick in the throat. And the only medicine being offered is total devotion to what is not possible to understand immediately.

Then one is offered a possibility to reflect on one's own taking-for-granted explanation models.

The possibility of being heckled for one's ideas can only function as a trigger for the true entrepreneur. The entrepreneur has an ability to marvel at *everyday matters* as others do when faced with incomprehensible tricks by a magician. Entrepreneurs often talk about their ideas as magical, almost like spiritual experiences. And these intuitive visions and breakthroughs in their personal development must be caught, understood and constituted in works of creating knowledge.

It is generally possible to say that entrepreneurship is a *non-linear process*. It is *unique*, *chaotic* and *specific*, and it is related to *single individuals*. Then the overall perspective and issue is raised with the actors oriented creator of knowledge: *is it possible to study entrepreneurship with linear and general methods which are searching for what is similar in what is dissimilar – which are searching for general explanation factors?* Is it possible to *explain* entrepreneurship? Is this not a phenomenon, which must be made intelligible by deepened *understanding*? That is what the actors creator of knowledge is thinking.

An actors oriented creation of knowledge also tries to entice the master talent, which is in every individual! In consequence, this creator of knowledge asks him/herself whether it is possible, as in statistical studies, to "bring together" what is *qualitatively different* with individuals into something *quantitatively similar* (measurable), and by doing so exclude what is *unique*. The actors view does not, however, try to isolate what is rationally sensible and exclude what is emotionally creative. What is unique and what is emotional for the individual are both what is essential, because it is the *personality*. And feelings and imagination are the very detonating composition which actives reason. The actors creator of knowledge therefore asks him/herself whether it is possible in a study to separate the entrepreneur from his/her situation of feelings and practical reality. Does not every entrepreneurial answer have to be interpreted relative to the uniqueness and context (lifeworld) of the individual entrepreneur?

Conceptualization

The actors view, just like the other views, has an established set of concepts, which we will come back to in later chapters. One of the most prominent characteristics of this set is, however, the concept of *language development*, which means, among other things, that the creator of knowledge attempts to develop a language that will bring *understanding* and *action* when facing the study area. It is a *conceptual development*, which in the study is linking the actors' *own* mental language with the developing descriptive language of the creator of knowledge. This is to be seen as a mirror of feedback as well as of providing understanding for the actors involved, and a description for bringing insight and action for those who also may take part in the results.

The actors view is encouraging its creator of knowledge, when facing the study area, to be open, devoted and start by throwing away all previously given categorizations and clichés. Entrepreneurship is to be understood on its *own conditions. Improvisation* and *creativity* in the process of creating knowledge then become important concepts in the actors view. *The feeling* for the aspects of entrepreneurship, which are more difficult to catch and which are truly different, like lust, force, dream, imagination, chaos, perseverance, artistry and free thinking, must be given their place in the developing conceptualization. The individual/entrepreneurial "language of adventure" is not to be transformed into some kind of phraseology of scarcity.

Concepts of shaping, connected with the established conceptualization of the view in question, are to be specifically developed for the study area with a capacity to catch the entrepreneur's creation of him/herself as well as the essence and socioeconomic context of entrepreneurship. These concepts become decisive in the process of making the innovative power of language come alive to describe and clarify the "discoveries" and ideas of the creator of knowledge, and to create action.

Methods and methodics

That *choice of methods* that are to come forward, using the articulated issues, perspectives and conceptualization above, is first of all the *dialogue*. According to the actors view the important thing here to be able to approach a reality – the reality of entrepreneurship – on its own terms. And then it is also important to understand what the dialogue can do in this context.

The actors oriented creator of knowledge searches in every possible way for the *inner quality* of those entrepreneurial masterpieces he/she is facing. And at the same time, he/she takes pains to re-create this *quality* within him/herself in order to able to *understand* the *masterpieces* and bring the experience forward. He/she is listening to the "harmony" of the entrepreneurs, follows their rhythms and tries to distil the essence of the quality of the whole thing.

For the creator of knowledge it is necessary here to enter a dialogue with a reality that he/she *identifies* with at the same time, in order to emotionally, imaginatively and *qualitatively* look for what is *different*, and to make this reality intelligible using the *first hand expressions* of the entrepreneur and the concepts of shaping by the creator of knowledge, where participating actors are made into *subjects* for an *innovative* knowledge interest. *Methodics* becomes *processual*, that is, it is worked out gradually by what is happening in the dialogues and the choice of leading actors. Historical, economic and other sociostructural studies may be added in order to supplement the contextual aspects of the statements of the entrepreneurs themselves. This becomes a constant work of interpretation which in several aspects is similar to the entrepreneurs' own processes of trial and error and creativity, where one thing gives way to another. If in the process questions and answers arise which can be seen as more or less depending on the context, the actors oriented creator of knowledge may also use questionnaires, but in a fashion which usually differs from the way they are used in other methodological views (exemplified in Chapter 14).

Results

The actors oriented creator of knowledge does not try to *explain* that entrepreneurship which he/she is facing in the study area, as *general* explanations of what is *unique*, according to its conception of reality, only become shallow clichés, and also become outdated the moment they are stated. Every free human being (so also an entrepreneur) may, of course, at the same time as he/she hears the explanation do exactly the opposite of what the explanation says. This is, according to the actors view, part of the peculiarities of social reality, a reality in constant interactive change, if, for no other reason, because of the *self-reference*, which is built into the work of creation of knowledge.

The creator of knowledge talks instead of creating *understanding* and *insightful action*. This is about *making* the rich possibilities of entrepreneurial reality *come alive* (the irregular in the regular). The answers are to reinforce what is unique for the subject. Be deep and penetrating. Clarify the vital interaction, which exists in the study area. Point out what is different in what is similar. No quantitative, statistical study can liberate this thematics according to the actors view. *Ponderanda sunt testimonia, non numeranda* (The testimonies are counted through their weight, not through their numbers). This is how the creator of knowledge is thinking here.

Metaphors (language pictures) as *concepts of shaping* become for the creator of knowledge one of the most important elements in that *descriptive language*, which he/she develops to present his/her "discoveries" in the study area. It also becomes one of the most important forms of shaping for linguistic/semantic innovation in the social science area according to the actors view. The *second forms of shaping* for the creator of knowledge are the *symbols*. They can be seen as taking over where metaphors are no longer enough. Symbols (e.g. road signs, pyramids, pentagrams) are instrument of knowledge which can be used to disclose sides of reality, which get away from all other languages. Like the metaphors, the symbolic language may awaken our imagination and offer us a trip into the "magic" kingdom of the "wordless" entrepreneurial thought.

The actors oriented creator of knowledge will in his/her report present *results* as *reflections on shaping* related to the theories of the area. This way he/she attempts to summarize the experiences in a metaphoric and critical language into order to go deeper down into human life in the entrepreneurial portraits. For the reader it then becomes possible, in the borderland between the descriptive language of the creator of knowledge and the actors' own linguistic descriptions, of either experience that "Yes, it is probably so", or to argue against and reject. The creator of knowledge wants with this to create an intellectual as well as exciting reading, in which the reader can participate actively. *The essence of the acting of the actors oriented creator of knowledge is more of a wish to excite the dialogue about entrepreneurship at all levels, no matter how it develops* – a dialogue that the creator of knowledge wishes to see as a kind of *meta-production* of new entrepreneurial thoughts in the social construction of reality.

What can be more important than immediately reflecting when approaching a study area with ambitions to create knowledge? In this chapter, a number of such aspects have been raised. The fact that critical thinking is associated with imagination is perhaps not the first thing on the mind of a knowledge creator *in spe*. Here we have given it a prominent place as part of the mental activities that are presented as part of the development of an operative paradigm. We have also raised some small examples of warning: clichés and thinking in clichés have been illustrated, and the importance of perspective has been focused. The chapter also points at the importance of being observant so that those explanations and that understanding used in the study really illustrate what they are supposed to illustrate. As a theme throughout the chapter, we have used the study area of entrepreneurship. At the end of the chapter, the three methodological views, the analytical view, the systems view and the actors view are briefly presented in relation to entrepreneurship as a study area. Here we illustrated for the first time in our book how the various methodological views may reflect and act facing the tangible task of creating knowledge.

POINTS OF REFLECTION

1. To *think critically* is not as simple as is sometimes presented. What a person may not think at first as an important characteristic of critical thinking is ....!
2. Give some examples of what could be called *clichéd thinking* and *optical illusions*. Why is it important to be observant of these in one's methodical procedures?
3. A thing, a phenomenon, a set of events can be seen from different *perspectives* and through them specific aspects will also appear more often than others. Take one example where you describe one thing, a phenomenon or a set of events out of different perspectives and illustrate how these may influence the general opinion of the matter in question.

(Continued)

(Continued)

4. At one place in the chapter we can read: *that what we study is what we intend to study*. What does this mean?
5. In the chapter three *methodological views* are introduced. Which ones? Why are they called methodological views?
6. When you read the description of how the three methodological views look on the specific study area of entrepreneurship, what did you think then? Which important *differences* do you see between the three methodological views?
7. Those *differences* that exist between the methodological views can also describe/explain their different names. Something where you think this is clearly seen.

RECOMMENDED FURTHER READING

See the end of the Appendix and visit the website below.

Become a worldwide partner as a *knowledge creator* in the development of *Methodology for Creating Business Knowledge* by visiting the website: **www.knowledge-creator.com**. Here you can contribute by asking your own questions and you will also find answers to the most frequently asked questions. The website has been developed alongside this third edition of the book and the questions posted there will be used to provide input for future editions.

3 TO BECOME A KNOWLEDGE CREATOR

In Chapter 3 our comparison between the various methodological views, the analytical view, the systems view and the actors view, is deepened. This is done primarily by, under specific headings, stressing their similarities and differences. What it means, "to become a knowledge creator" will be explored further in this chapter, especially in the sense of personal development.

WHAT IS SCIENCE?

Every serious attempt to explain the world or to understand it includes the following five questions as *points of departure* (compare with our three examples in Chapter 2):

1. Which are the *ultimate presumptions* held by the creator of knowledge?
2. Which *kinds of questions* are asked and from *which perspective*?
3. Which *kind of conceptual set* is used to formulate these questions and point out the perspective?

The answers to these first three questions are of decisive importance to the last two:

4. Which *kinds of methods* and *methodics* are used to explain or understand the world?
5. Which *kinds of answers or solutions* are given to the questions and how are the results *presented*?

Answers to each of these five questions should have a solid philosophical foundation.

From the answers to these five questions, it is possible to distinguish *various ways of creating knowledge*, that is, the various approaches to gaining knowledge about the world.

One of the ways of creating knowledge about the world can be called *scientific*. Sometimes it seems like there are as many "expert opinions" about what science is as there are "experts". Still, we maintain that there is a relative unity in terms of explaining or understanding the world the scientific way – compared with other ways of doing so. The scientific way is specific in three aspects, all of which are both necessary and interrelated.

First, each attempt that claims to be scientific is based *on an explicit relation between ideas and empirical observation* and on an attempt to be relevant to a reality. What is "empirical" and what is "reality", however, is debated in the scientific community (see Box 3.1). Therefore, one problem that every scientist has is that of convincing colleagues that his/her results, descriptions, explanations or understanding are supported or can be confirmed by empirical reality.

Box 3.1

Empiricism and Reality

What "reality" is and what the experience of this "reality" is – in other words "empiricism" – is a question that has been debated by philosophers for millennia. In order to illustrate the issue, we provide a few examples of ideas of "reality" and "empiricism" among "ideologists" in the history of science and philosophy:

- There are those (e.g. Durkheim) who claim that creators of knowledge researching reality should look for "objective facts", as "unspoiled" by "biased" subjective impressions as possible.
- There are those (e.g. Russell) who ask that every statement of reality should follow a certain logical form; otherwise the statement cannot be called "scientific" or "true".
- There are others (e.g. Schutz) who claim that social science cannot progress if it is not based on an understanding of how subjective (and thereby social) reality emerges.
- There are people (e.g. Weber) who throughout their scientific life aim at making subjective reality objectively understandable.
- There are people (e.g. Kant) who assert that we cannot reach objective reality per se. Because we, through human necessity, always "cultivate" this reality when it is experienced, it can only appear to us in this cultivated form.
- There are those (e.g. Husserl) who believe that there is also a reality that does not depend on our sensory experiences, that is, a so-called transcendental reality. This reality is more a basic result of human conditions in reality than accumulated experiences as life progresses. There has been a lively discussion in philosophy whether or not this experience of reality can be called "empirical". Husserl chose to talk about this reality as eidetical, to separate it from empirical reality.

So, there are truly different opinions about what "reality" and "empiricism" are. The reader should keep this in mind in order to understand the breadth we want to impart to what we mean by "scientific". What is contained in the concepts of "reality" and "empiricism" is a decisive issue between different scientific schools in general and between different methodological views in particular. (For references and further reading on the subjects, see the Appendix.)

Second, using a scientific methodology necessarily means *a conscious application of reasonably clearly formulated rules*. Opinions vary about how strict these rules or methods should be – which will be evident in this book. In other words, all scientists worthy of the name attempt to find an explicit way of showing others – particularly other members of the scientific community – how they arrived at their results.

Third, using a scientific methodology means that the scientist acknowledges that *every member of society has a legitimate right to protection from public scrutiny or of his/her private life*. In other words, there are limits to the research that can be done on the public.

These characteristics of scientific activities are general enough to allow for a variety of opinions. They are valid whether you are dedicated to explaining, interpreting and/or understanding or whether you base your research on a specific philosophical school or research tradition. The concepts of *explaining* and *understanding* will be brought up later.

BEING A SCIENTIST AND CREATING KNOWLEDGE

It is not necessary to be a scientist to be a creator of knowledge. There are many studies that are based on "an explicit relation between ideas and empirical observations" and on "a conscious application of reasonably clearly formulated rules", and that acknowledge that "every member of society has a legitimate right to protection from public scrutiny of his/her private life". Such works, without claiming to be scientific, change our state of knowledge just as surely as advanced works of science.

A principal difference between knowledge created the scientific way compared with other ways (say as a consultant or as any other kind of investigator) is that some kinds of studies do not present their methods and results for public and critical scrutiny by other creators of knowledge (e.g. for reasons of confidentiality). This *"principle of publicity"* is central to scientific works.

From a methodological point of departure, however, there needs to be no major differences between various ways of creating knowledge. From this particular point of *departure*, we treat them as equal in *Methodology for Creating Business Knowledge*.

"PRACTISED" AND "RECONSTRUCTED" LOGIC

The American theorist of science Kaplan (1918–1974) makes an important distinction between "practised logic" and "reconstructed logic". *Practised logic* is the path that researchers/consultants/investigators follow de facto (this path can be rather meandering); *reconstructed logic* is their *presentation of this path* (often somewhat straightened out). Some communities may simply demand a certain type of presentation of how a study was conducted and its results. Even if there were no such requirements, the presenter might still want to make the text more "pedagogic", that is, to reconstruct his/her logic (compare with the aesthetical aspect of the paradigm concept).

Box 3.2

To Become a Creator of Knowledge

As mentioned in the text, it is not necessary to become a scientist (junior or senior) to become a creator of knowledge (see also Boxes 1.2 and 1.3). To become a creator of knowledge the way we look at it means as a *first step* to acquire that *basic methodological thinking* which is presented in this book. It means also, as a *second step,* that this consciousness includes being *creative, open, aware* and *self-reflecting.* So these are the qualities that you are training yourself for if you want to become a creator of knowledge, for instance, as a student. This is, of course, easier said than done, but we can assure you that it is worth the effort of trying! And the value includes not just a possible professional career, but, in the highest degree, also personal development. To be able to "decode" different research results of their ultimate presumptions is, in fact, very much about personal freedom. The freedom to be able to have one's own ideas about research and science. The freedom to be able to handle adaptation and usage of business theories and models in completely new contexts.

Even if it may seem difficult to become a creator of knowledge in the meaning of this book, there are a few simple rules of thumbs, which might be of value in the process. You will never become a creator of knowledge if you are not willing to:

1. embrace curiosity and imagination
2. ackowledge the insight that knowledge involves manifestations of ultimate presumptions as well
3. seek training in the concrete handicraft to develop knowledge
4. present new knowledge to others and be accountable for it

When reading presentations of how other creators of knowledge have proceeded, remember that in reality there is always a difference between practised and reconstructed logic.

We also want to mention that some of the allure of creating knowledge is being able to participate in "Aha!-experiences". This is the creative side of these activities. And *real* creativity can hardly be presented at all!

A FEW BASIC DICHOTOMIES TO KEEP IN MIND

Most of this chapter will contain a more detailed comparison of our three methodological views. Before we proceed, however, we need to clarify some fundamental dichotomies that can be seen in Figure 3.1.

The *analytical* view has a sole ambition to *explain* reality, a reality that it looks at as fact-filled with objective and subjective facts which are summative, that is, its parts can be considered in isolation from other parts.

The *systems* view may have as an ambition either to *explain* or to *understand*. In both cases it looks at reality as full of facts as well, but unlike the analytical view it looks at reality as

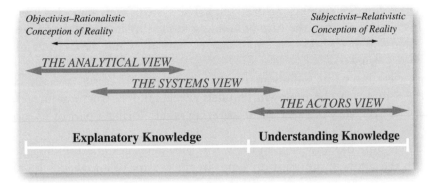

Figure 3.1   The Boundary Between Explanatory and Understanding Knowledge

systemic, that is, its parts cannot be seen in isolation from each other but as more or less structured as relative wholes, called systems.

When the analytical view and the systems view are looking for explanations, they build *models*, mental constructions made by the creator of knowledge where he/she is *subtracting* (neglecting) irrelevant facts and circumstances from the fact-filled (see Box 3.3) reality

---

Box 3.3

Models and Facts

In everyday language it is common to associate the concept of "model" with "prototype", "paragon", or "example", that is, with some kind of ideal situation. This may also be the case in the context of creating knowledge. It is more common here, however, that a model stands for a reproduction of a piece of *existing* reality rather than a *desirable* reality (i.e. a picture or a representation vs. a prototype of a paragon).

A photo is not, according to the analytical view, a "model", however, nor are novels, poems, or works of art considered to be "models". What is required in order for a picture to be called a model according to this view is that the picture in question is *deliberately simplified* in order to highlight some important relations or circumstances.

So, a model – in the context of creating knowledge in the analytical view and in the systems view – is a *deliberately simplified picture or prototype (representation) of a piece of the fact-filled reality*. In the continuation of the book we denote this so-called "fact-filled reality", as *factive reality*. The statement that the two views in question have different opinions of how this reality is based and arranged makes no difference to their perspective on what a model is – in principle.

The concept of model is given another meaning in the actors view, as models are part of constituting reality, not representing it only. An additional concept in this view that is given another meaning is *fact/factual*. The meaning of these two should be read as "factified". Something socially constructed.

(seen as either additive or systemic respectively). The systems view may also look for understanding. This is pursued as in the case of building models by its creators of knowledge, but here he/she is *adding* metaphors, structural images, narratives and the like but all along they are seen as *representing* it.

The *actors* view has as its ambition to *understand* reality, seen as socially constructed. Whenever the actors view comes up with models as metaphors, structural images, narratives and the like, however, they are seen as *constituting* reality (being a part of it), not only representing it (as stand-alone pictures).

Also, when creators of knowledge in the actors view aims at understanding, they do it in dialogues with the actors in the study area, not by the creator of knowledge on his/her own, which can happen in the case of the systems view.

Understanding through the systems view could be called *representative understanding*. Understanding through the actors view could be called *constitutive understanding*.

REALITY ASSUMPTIONS

The first methodological view we consider is the analytical, which is also the oldest of the three. The analytical view is common in business research and consulting today, and it is also well represented in various public investigations. A large number of books on methodology for creating business knowledge take only into consideration the analytical view, even if in the preface and in the use of terminology they sometimes attempt to give a more "comprehensive" impression.

The analytical view has its origins in classic analytical philosophy and has therefore a deeply rooted tradition in Western thinking. Its assumption about the quality of *reality* is that reality is factive and has *a summative character*, that is, *the whole is the sum of its parts*.

This means that once a knowledge creator gets to know the different parts of the whole, the parts can be added together to get the total picture (see Figure 3.2).

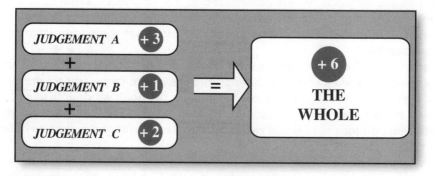

Figure 3.2   The Analytical View: The Whole is the Sum of its Parts

Knowledge created based on the analytical view is characterized as being *independent of the observer*. This means that knowledge advances by means of formal logic that is represented by specific *judgements,* which are supposed to be independent of the creator of knowledge's individual subjective experience. These judgements consist of assumptions that can be verified or falsified (hypotheses).

Historically, the systems view is next. It came into business in the 1950s, partly as a reaction to the summative picture of reality in the analytical view. It is no exaggeration to say that systems *thinking* is the dominant point of departure in business (in theory as well as in practise) today. It is very common in business to attempt a rather holistic perspective on problems.

Early writers on the systems view in business include von Bertalanffy, Buckley, Churchman and Emery.

The assumption behind the systems view is as in the case of the analytical view that reality is factive, but the systems view holds, unlike the analytical view, that *reality* is arranged in such a way that *the whole differs from the sum of its parts*. This means that not only the parts but also their relations are essential, as the latter will lead to plus or minus effects (*synergy*) (see Figure 3.3).

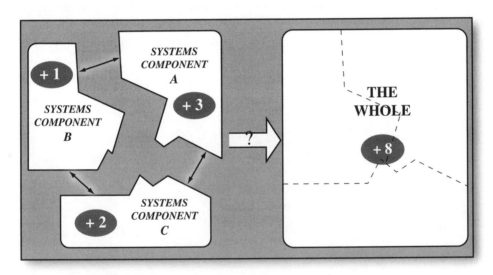

Figure 3.3   The Systems View: Synergy

Knowledge developed through the systems view *depends on systems*. The behaviour of individuals, as parts of a system, follows systems principles, that is, individuals are explained in terms of systems characteristics. Consequently, the systems view explains *parts through the characteristics of the whole* (of which they are parts).

If we say instead that *the whole is understood by the characteristics of its parts*, we describe the third view, the actors view, the most recent of the three. It appeared, shaped clearly enough for us to be able to talk about and develop it as a specific view, at the end of the 1960s. The person probably most associated with an actors perspective in business at its beginning was the English organizational sociologist Silverman, who had adapted the more important contributions to his "action frame of reference" from men like Husserl, Schutz and Weber.

The actors view is not interested in explanations; rather, it is interested in understanding *social* wholes. This is accomplished through the pictures of reality – *the finite provinces of meaning* – held by individual actors. The actors view is directed at reproducing the *meaning(s)* that various actors associate with their *acts* and the *surrounding context*. *Reality* is therefore taken as a *social construction* that is *intentionally* created by processes at different levels of *meaning structures*. From this it follows that our common language is given a different meaning relative to these levels. Wholes and parts are ambiguous and are continuously reinterpreted.

In the actors view, systemic characteristics are not relevant to understanding businesses and organizations. Interest is instead directed toward the finite provinces of meaning held by leading actors in a particular social context. Organizations as such cannot act, only their individual members can. According to this concept, systems – as these are seen in the systems view – are not real. The actors view asserts that such systems exist only in the head of the systems view knowledge creator and are therefore not based on the way actors interpret themselves in relation to their own experienced and constructed totality of meaning structures (see Figure 3.4).

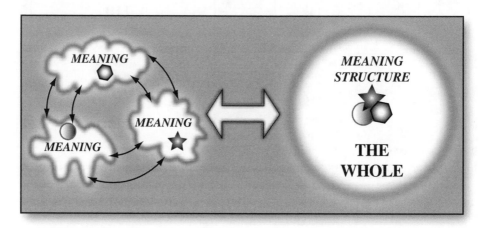

Figure 3.4 The Actors View: Meaning Structures

Knowledge developed with the actors view is therefore dependent on actors, even though it follows certain phenomenological principles (see Chapter 6 and the Appendix) as to how social reality is constructed.

A review of the reality assumptions made by the three methodological views is presented below:

Analytical view	The whole, which is factive, is equal to the sum of its parts. As long as it contains facts, knowledge can be objective as well as subjective. Parts are explained by verified judgements.
Systems view	The whole, which is factive as well, does not equal the sum of its parts. Knowledge depends on systems. Parts are explained or understood by the characteristics of the whole.
Actors view	The whole is socially constructed and exists as meaning structures, which are socially constructed. Knowledge depends on individuals. The whole is understood via the actors' finite provinces of meaning.

Please *be aware* that the systems view is critical of the analytical view, and the actors view is critical of both the analytical view and the systems view and that this criticism is by no means a one-way affair (even if it may appear that way in the text above). The three views currently direct various kinds of criticism at each other, which has led not only to fruitful development within the views themselves but also to various attempts at combining the three different methodologies. We will return to this criticism and these attempts in Chapter 13.

We present each of the three views on its own terms, and we need additional bases for this comparison so the reader will be able to compare them better. Remember that these bases can never be completely consistent across the views: each view shapes its own base according to its own individual logic. This gives the views partly separate content and meaning (see Box 3.4).

Box 3.4

Picture of Reality and Finite Province of Meaning

The reader has probably noted that we use the concept of "picture of reality" in the analytical and the systems view and that we use the concept of "finite province of meaning" in the actors view. These concepts are, in a way, related. They both refer to means by which individuals orient themselves in this world. The difference between the two, a difference that the reader will learn to appreciate more in the course of this book, is that the "picture of reality" stands for *an image of an external world*; "finite provinces of meaning" *is* reality.

PREREQUISITES, EXPLANATIONS, UNDERSTANDING AND RESULTS

Based on the different assumptions about reality made by our three views, a number of subsequent theses have been developed that specify the prerequisites in order for each of the three views to function. These prerequisites in turn determine the form of explanations and understanding involved, and the results to aim for.

Consider the following: You want to expand your company. You have a well-established position in the part of the country where you started, and now you want to go further by opening a new branch office in region C, where you have never operated before. You want to be just as successful there as you are now at your original site. You set up certain objectives for market share, turnover, customer value, and profit – these are your desired *results*.

In order to accomplish this, you decide to develop a *model* (a crib) or an *interpretation* on your terms of the relations that you believe to exist among the various factors – pricing, product choice, employee motivation, customer preferences, competition and organization. You are looking for *explanations* in the first case and *representative understanding* in the second.

If, however, you believe that results are inevitably connected with the individuals involved in your expansion project, the language and symbols they use or the interpretations they make, and the relation of it all to customers as individuals as well, you are seeking a *constitutive understanding*.

Your explanations or your understandings are based on certain assumptions, such as, the size of the new market you are looking at, the experience and background of your employees and customers, the financial power of your company, your desire to build up an organization at the new site that will be similar to the successful one you already have, and your belief in the will power and creative ability of those involved. These are your *prerequisites*.

The initial conditions just referred to determine to a large extent the forms of explanations, understandings and results. This example should be regarded *only* as an illustration of the relations among prerequisites, explanations, understandings and results: It is not intended to illustrate a specific methodological view, because each of our three views would present both objections and additions to the example.

The analytical view

Prerequisite: existing theory and a number of *techniques* given in advance that make rendering the *verification or falsification* of stated *hypotheses* possible when the techniques are used properly. Verified or falsified hypotheses clarify facts that are subsets of the factive reality. When these facts are added together, a more complete picture is obtained. This follows from the assumption of the summative character of its factive reality.

Explanation: in the ideal case reproducing causal relations, which means seeking to explain some *effect* by finding the prior or current *cause*. The view's assumption about reality gives the following situation: *the greater the number of proven causes (or proven effects), the stronger the explanation*. The analytical view assumes that it is possible at all levels to argue "ceteris paribus", that is, "other things being equal" or, "all other things remaining unchanged".

Result: _cause–effect relations, logical models and representative cases._ The result should have a generalizable character in order to be a prerequisite of continuing research/consulting/ investigation. The character of the result follows naturally from the factive and summative assumption of reality. The fact that reality is seen as factive and summative and independent of its observers leads knowledge creators who use the analytical view to express themselves in relation to their results with the words: "These explanations are good, but they can always be improved!" The conception of reality held within the analytical view also makes it important to keep in constant contact with what is called the research front. It is from this front that judgements are made whether progress in the process of a summative creation of knowledge has taken place.

The systems view

Prerequisite: _existing systems theory_, which, however, is not used in the same general way, as are theories in the analytical view. This follows from the assumption that wholes in reality are always seen to differ from the sum of their parts. For this reason the systems view operates with _analogies_ normally based on _similarities in structure and form_ with other findings as a prerequisite of research/consulting/investigation.

Explanation or understanding: _reproducing finality relations_, which leads to seeking to explain or understand a particular result by finding a _force with a structural pattern_.

Result: Starting from the assumption of synergistic effects in reality (e.g. $2 + 1 + 3 \neq + 8$), the results yielded by the systems view will be structural models or representative interpretations delivered by the creator of knowledge. This in turn will lead to _typical cases_ and certain _general classification mechanisms_ for _different kinds of cases_ (see Box 3.5).

Box 3.5

Causality and Finality

Relations between various phenomena and events can be seen in different ways. If a relation is seen as _causal_, it means that an event either must lead to another event by necessity (_deterministically_) or with a certain probability (_stochastically_). If the result is explained by the purpose behind the driving force, the relation is called a _finality_ relation (sometimes called _teleological_). If we ask, for example, why a company has a budget, a causal explanation could be: "The budget was established by the founder of the firm and the bank requires a continuation." A finality explanation could be: "Senior management feel the budget makes them better able to plan the company's future."

Note that teleological explanations only are meaningful in the human world, that is, where conscious actions can take place in order to achieve some purpose. For example, explaining, "Why do birds have wings?" by saying "They must to be able to fly" sounds frivolous.

In order to separate finality relations in the systems view from causal relations in the analytical view, we will talk in the systems view about _producer–product_ relations instead of _cause–effect_ relations.

The actors view

Prerequisite: various *metatheories* (more fundamental "theories of theories" that inevitably include the people using them) that give general starting points for *the function of human consciousness* and *the social construction of reality*, along with *guidelines* for different *constitutive interpretive procedures* and *interactive actions* in the study area. Furthermore, previous actors view research/consultations/investigations will result in certain *"general" contributions* as far as *constitutional factors* are concerned; constitutional factors are part of what is denoted as an *ideal-typified* language (see "Result" section below). These theories and contributions are associated with the knowledge creator's development of understanding in interaction with the other actors.

The assumption in the actors view that reality is socially constructed means that the *situational contributions* (descriptive languages) from previous actors' research/consulting/investigation can only be included as *experiential* material (for developing and maintaining skills in the area of knowledge creation), and can therefore never constitute starting points given in advance (see Box 3.6).

Box 3.6

Constitute

Constitute as a concept, stands for constructing social reality and/or making it visible. In this process it is possible to find "general" factors that make the construction of reality understandable. The quotation marks here indicate that this is not the same type of generality as is the case for the conception of a factive reality in the other two views. The generality as a social science phenomenon is also regarded by the actors view as socially constructed (a social invention, as it were); for which reason it can be questioned, changed, and transformed.

<u>Understanding</u>: *describing dialectical relations*, which means trying to understand relations among (constitutive) *interpretations* made by various actors in relation to different levels of *meaning structures*. The relations being sought are not relations in the sense used earlier, but rather how various constitutive interpretations and factors mutually and in constant *transformation* influence each other in a continuous *developmental process* in which reality is socially constructed (see Box 3.7).

Box 3.7

Dialectics

The word *dialectics* comes from the Greek word *dialektos* (through "discourse"). The dialectic procedure brings to light contradictions and other types of opposition. The origin of dialectics may be attributed to Socrates and Plato, with the Sophists in a supporting role.

The role of the dialectic process, the interpretation of its nature and the understanding of its importance vary widely in the history of philosophy, depending on the position of the philosopher in question.

For Plato, dialectics embodied the highest knowledge and formed the capstone of the sciences. For Kant, dialectics became the term for man's misguided effort to apply the principles governing phenomena to what we can never completely reach, that is, "things-in-themselves". The German Kantian Fichte (1762–1814) was the first to present the process of dialectics as involving the triad *of thesis, antithesis* and *synthesis*. He also regarded the process as one of posit, counterposit and synthesis. Hegel and Marx frequently used the dialectic process as a model for development.

For us, dialectics stands for *the logic of ambiguity*. "Dialectic relations" mean that the relations are ambiguous and change qualitatively in a continuous transformation. To describe dialectic relations means, for the actors view, to make this socially transforming and transcendental interaction visible and comprehensible.

The actors view also aims at pointing out "general" *constitutional factors*. The relations that are sought in this methodological view can be seen as having both an *internal* and an *external* character. The internal character is related to getting the actors to understand their own situation better – a kind of (internally) *emancipative* understanding. The external character can be seen as consisting of *procreative* understanding. To create, to transform, to vivify and to change hold unique and desirable positions in this view. Because reality is perceived as a human construction, why shouldn't creators of knowledge actively participate, expressing responsibility for their actions? This is both the question and the answer that the actors view gives because of its own prerequisites (see above).

Result: Depending on the type of understanding sought – the description of dialectic relations with or without aiming for internal and/or external emancipation – the result of the actors view commonly consists of *descriptive languages* such as situational interpretive models; *ideal-typified* languages that concern typified cases and constitutional ideals; and *emancipatory interactive action* out in the study area (see Boxes 3.8 and Box 3.9; see Table 3.1 for a review of the foregoing discussion).

Box 3.8

Explain, Understand and Emancipate

Earlier, we made a distinction between "explaining" and "understanding". In the latter case many creators of knowledge go further, looking for possibilities for "emancipation". This can be internal, that is, it can "end" with the creator of knowledge making the actors aware of their locked-in frames of reference. It can also be external, with the creator of knowledge actively creating conditions for a genuinely new kind of thinking, transformation and change.

Box 3.9

Average, Typical and Typified

To create knowledge means almost by definition to make descriptions of more than one perhaps unique case. Such "more general descriptions" can be based on different assumptions and therefore acquire different characteristics.

If we believe in a factive (but generally describable) reality that is independent of us as observers, we may calculate statistically average descriptions – for example, that "an average small exporting company in Country S has 4.3 employees per country being exported to, and that its general manager has an average education of 12.5 years" (*the analytical view*).

With the same objective basis we might instead say, as an example, that "a *typical* (most frequent, modal) small company in Country S can be described as a system with four employees per country being exported to, and its general manager is an educated economist of some sort" (*the systems view*).

If we don't believe in a factive reality we talk about another type (or *ideal type*). We say, perhaps, that "a *typified* (*ideal-typified*) Country S small export company consists of a smaller group per country being exported to, which constitutes just the critical mass of actors necessary to develop the company in this country, where the leader as far as relevant areas are concerned is somewhat more educated than the others". The purpose in this case is not to *reproduce* (statistically or in any other way) an external independent reality (which we in this case consider to be constantly moving), but deliberately to *isolate certain* relations to improve the understanding of what *may* happen in "Country S's small export companies" (the potential as an intrinsic part of what is, or seems, factual) (*the actors view*).

A recapitulation

Table 3.1 provides a recapitulation of what has been said so far. As it is based on partly incompatible presumptions (it would be interpreted differently from the actors view point of departure compared with starting from the other views, for instance), it is better seen as a typified description (compare Box 3.9).

MORE ABOUT REALITY, EXPLAINING, UNDERSTANDING AND RESULTS

The analytical view

The goal in the analytical view is to explain the factive reality as exactly as possible. Explanations of this reality take, ideally, the form of causal relations. The terms *cause* and *effect* are then used. In all versions of the analytical view, reality is assumed to be built up by *summative* components.

Table 3.1   A Recapitulation

	Analytical View	Systems View	Actors View
Prerequisites	• Existing analytical theory • Verified/falsified hypotheses	• Existing systems theory • Analogies (Homologies)	• Metatheories • Constitutional factors • General pre-understanding • Interactive development of understanding
Explaining/ Understanding	Causality Cause–effect (explanation)	Finality Producer–product (explanation or understanding)	Dialectics Thesis–antithesis–synthesis (understanding)
Result	Cause–effect relations (as an ideal)	Classifications • Structural representative models • Representative interpretations	Descriptive languages • Situational interpretive models • Institutional models • Process models
	Logical models	Classification mechanisms	Ideal-typified language • Ideal-typified cases • Constitutional ideals
	Representative cases	Typical cases Partly unique cases	Emancipatory interactive action • Creative action • Direct action

According to the *analytical* view, a causal relation exists between two groups of factors, X (the causes, sometimes called *independent* variables) and Y (the effects, sometimes called *dependent* variables), if the following three requirements are met:

Requirement 1   There must be a relation between X and Y.
Requirement 2   Y must not precede X in time (but X and Y can be contemporary).
Requirement 3   Relations other than X→Y are excluded, or at least do not give a better explanation (see Figure 3.5).

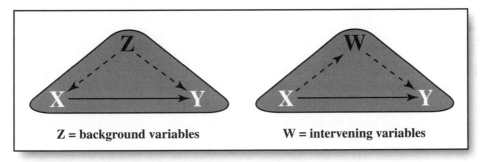

Figure 3.5   The Black Sheep of the Cause-family

In order to achieve an acceptable explanation of a certain effect, a sufficient number of causes is required. The view leads to the ambition to find causes that are independent of each other (see Figure 3.6).

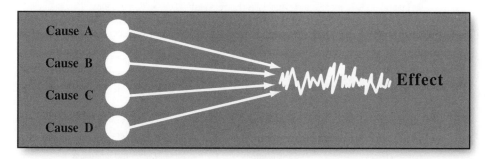

Figure 3.6   Cause and Effect

Causal relations can be of two kinds: *deterministic* or *stochastic*. In deterministic causal relations, the causes give both necessary and sufficient conditions for an effect. In stochastic causal relations, on the other hand, the causes may be necessary, but they are not sufficient. In other words, there is a "chance" that the effect in question will not take place in the given situation even if the causes are present. This may be because the model constructed is not inclusive enough (there are other causes that are not included) or because it is not detailed enough.

These conceptions mean, among other things, that if a cause is not included in a model, the result will be a less good (but possibly still acceptable) picture of the phenomenon (see Figure 3.7).

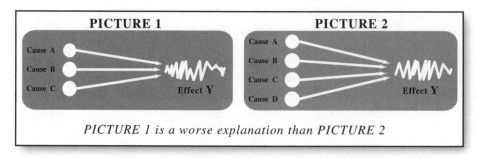

Figure 3.7   More Causes Make a Better Explanation in the Analytical View

Another basis for the analytical methodological view is that, when moving from one research/consulting/investigation *situation* to another that is similar, the former situation could be very useful. Similarity between the two *situations β and Ω* below may be such that it is possible to use the *same model*, even though the causes themselves might be different.

Situation β	*Situation* Ω
$Y = 4 + A + 6B + 2C - 4D$	$Y = 4 + A + 5B - C - 4D$

Consider the mathematical expressions in the above two situations as pedagogic examples only. Although it is common to do so, it is in no way necessary to work with mathematical symbols in the analytical view. Also, the expressions above do not have to be linear for the logic to be valid.

A constant goal of the analytical view is to collect data about factive reality. This data collection is controlled by *hypotheses*, that is, by possible descriptions and explanations that are formulated at the beginning of the study.

Such research/consulting/investigation results in a theory constructed of verified hypotheses – descriptions and explanations of factive reality – that have not been proven false. As more and more of the hypotheses in a theory are verified, the theory is considered to be a better and better representation of factive reality. It gains a *general* character. Its use does not depend on any individual; it is at the disposal of anyone with the interest and competence to use it. The theory also becomes *absolute* in the sense that users do not have to go back to the situation in which the theory was developed in order to use it. The theory is therefore assumed to be true and not dependent on anyone's idiocracy. We may call this *knowledge independent of individual observers* (see Table 3.2 for a recap of the analytical view).

Table 3.2   Analytical View

• *Conception of reality:*	A factive (objective and/or subjective) reality that can be described as consisting of summative components.
• *Knowledge independent of individual observers:*	Descriptions and explanations of reality are general and absolute.
• *Explanations:*	The analytical researcher/consultant/investigator seeks causal relations, that is, necessary and sufficient relations between cause and effect (deterministic relations) or necessary but not sufficient relations between cause and effect (stochastic relations).
• *Result:*	The theory of reality becomes ever better, consisting of more and more verified hypotheses.
• *Prerequisites for continuing:*	When studying new problems the researcher/consultant/investigator can build on existing theory for the problem area in question. However, new results may falsify earlier results.

The systems view

The systems view also assumes the existence of a factive reality that researchers/consultants/investigators consider their primary field of interest. Creators of knowledge presume that this "systems" reality is constructed somewhat differently than the reality of the analytical view. Systems reality is assumed to consist of components that are often mutually dependent on each other – which means that they cannot be "summed up". The structure of these components brings about *synergistic effects*. This means that not only the content of the individual components, but also the way they are put together, provides information. The whole is more (or is less) than the sum of its parts. What is required for reaching an acceptable explanation or understanding of a specific situation is to consider the more total picture. The systems researcher/consultant/investigator asserts that it is possible to discern such "wholes" or "more total pictures" in factive reality.

In the systems view, it is not possible to remove any of the factors from a systems picture without risking that the more total picture will be seriously affected. Note the difference in the two structures in Figure 3.8.

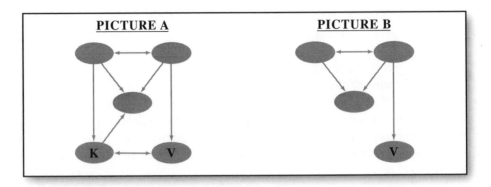

Figure 3.8   All Factors are Necessary in the Systems View

In Picture B, component K has been removed, which also removes all connections with K. Picture B differs so much from Picture A that it may no longer give a satisfactory image of the whole. This is easy to see if Component V is the one we want to explain or understand. It is not possible to add the separate components together (they are not independent of each other). We may well have to consider all five components in Picture A in order to reach an acceptable explanation or understanding of what we are looking for – hence the name "system", or whole.

Another important difference between the systems and the analytical views is that the systems view denies the usefulness of looking for single-dimensional causal relations. In the systems view, the creator of knowledge looks instead for *forces* that influence the system as *a whole* (or results which the system as a whole will contain). Such a force might be that one *constellation* of components proves to be more or less functional in a specific situation than another constellation. Another possibility is that the force is a *goal* perceived by the system (or its members). A third possible force is the *active behaviour* (or ambitions) of individuals who are part of the system. There are further possibilities. These forces may (or may not) be part of what is normally called the *systems structure*.

We will call these *finality* connections between forces and their results in the systems view *producer–product connections* (see Figure 3.9) to differentiate them from the *cause–effect* relations in the analytical view.

Working with *producer–product* (vs. cause–effect) connections means – among other things – not having to satisfy Requirements 2 and 3 of the requirements for causal relations listed above (p. 61). Furthermore, the background and intervening variables may be exactly the kind of relations we are looking for to improve our picture of the real system and of the possible synergistic effects embedded in its relations.

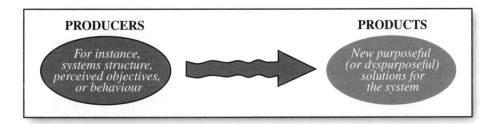

Figure 3.9   Producer–Product Connections

It is also possible for a producer to lead to alternative products (*multifinality*) and for alternative producers to lead to the same product (*equifinality*; see Figure 3.10). This is because there is always a time lag between producer and product, and an interaction between the system and its environment in the meantime. During this interim period, interaction with the environment or active interference by the members of the system may change the course of the system.

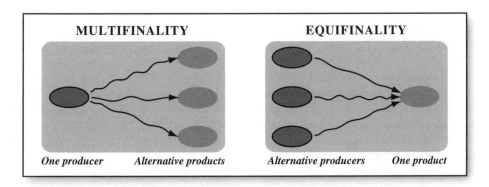

Figure 3.10   Multifinality and Equifinality

Note the difference between Figure 3.10 and Figure 3.6, which depicts the analytical view. In Figure 3.6 we referred to several *simultaneously operating* causes, whereas the systems view has *alternative* (mutually exclusive) producers or products.

The systems view also leads to a different attitude toward using the experiences from *one* study in *another* (similar) study. The results of a systems study (and therefore the prerequisites for another) do not result in an absolute theory (as understood in the analytical view), neither for the components of a model, nor for the way such components must be structured or behave. Systems creators of knowledge use the experience and the results from earlier studies only as mental inspiration for analogies or metaphors when they conduct studies of systems with similar orientation and content (see also Box 3.10).

Box 3.10

Analysis and Actor

There are many conceptual confusions in our subject area of business. Two of them should be brought up here. An *analysis* can be made within all three of our methodological views. Also, it is possible to be an *actor* within the systems view.

An analysis, according to the analytical view, consists of dissecting an object into its parts, studying the separate parts, and then putting them back together again in the same relationship to each other. This dissection and recombination can take place either in imagination or in reality.

An analysis in the systems view consists of explaining or understanding the relations of an object's parts to each other, to the totality, and to the environment (including the relations of this whole object as such to the environment) while keeping the object as a whole entity. Alternatively, we can say that a systems analysis always leads to a *systems synthesis*. An analysis as understood by the analytical view does *not* lead to some kind of total combination.

The analysis concept is also sometimes used in the actors view in order to emphasize an interest in looking at different parts and their ambiguous (dialectic) relations to each other. More common within the actors view, however, is the concept of *diagnosis*, to stress an interest in understanding (we will come back to the concept of diagnosis in Chapter 6).

The concept of *actor* is sometimes used in the systems view. Then it is not a question of causal relations (as in the analytical view) because individuals (especially if they are powerful) can "destroy" or change any such relation if they want to. Nor is it a question of any dialectic relations (as in the actors view) even if this term is sometimes used carelessly here. It is rather a question of finality relations (as in the systems view), that is, a behaviour (among separate individuals or in the system as a whole) aimed at achieving certain results.

The fundamental difference between actors in the systems view and in the actors view is that the former act within a *factive* framework. (Creators of knowledge mean here that subjective conceptions are facts as well.) Within the actors view, actors are regarded as free creators who nevertheless *objectify* various phenomena (i.e. treat them as *if* they were objective; we will return shortly to this concept). An emancipatory knowledge interest, however, aims at making visible to the actors that these phenomena are merely treated as objective without them having to be so.

These definitional and conceptual displacements between the different views are extensive. They are fully visible only when used against a background of the separate ultimate presumptions made by these same views.

An early version of systems theory, the so-called *general systems theory* (which will be treated in Chapter 5), claimed that the goal of the systems view should be to find different systems and to derive typical behavioural patterns for these types. In its early days, the systems view was also seen as a way to bridge the gaps among various disciplines in the technical, biological and social (including business) fields. In fact, some of the terminology of these "bridging" goals are still with us in Business today: for instance, *survival, adaptation, domi-nance, niches, dynamics* and *feedback* (terms that are taken from biology and technology).

It is fair to say that the systems view still has some of its interdisciplinary ambitions, even if they are much more limited. Many commentators claim, for instance, that Business is essentially a conglomerate of selected parts of, say, Sociology, Psychology, Ethics, Economics, and Economic History that, lacking a core of its own, is placed in a systems-oriented framework.

Modern systems view is also more ambitious to gaining than was traditionally the case (more of this in Chapter 5).

Knowledge developed by the systems view does not become general in the same absolute way as knowledge developed by the analytical view. Theoretical knowledge becomes related to one or several types of system or to specific systems phenomena, and we therefore speak of systems-dependent knowledge. Table 3.3 presents a recap of the systems view.

Table 3.3   Systems View

• *Conception of reality:*	A factive (objective or subjective) reality, consisting of wholes, the outstanding characteristic of which is synergy.
• *Knowledge dependent on system:*	The description of reality consists of pictures of systems or parts of such systems. These pictures, however, are normally not regarded as general but as valid only for specific systems classes.
• *Explanation or understanding:*	The researcher/consultant/investigator seeks finality relations (producer–product relations), i.e. relations among (systems) forces and their (positive or negative) results as explanations, or comes up with representative interpretations as understanding.
• *Result:*	The theory of reality becomes an ever better explanation or understanding of the behaviour of different classes of systems. Even the classification itself is changing and improving.
• *Prerequisites for continuing:*	When studying new problems, the researcher/consultant/investigator is relatively free to draw analogies or come up with metaphors being inspired by the results of earlier (similar) studies. These analogies, however, must be adapted to the specific case, which could mean a rather unique (or at least contingent) picture of the new system.

The actors view

The actors view differs markedly from both the analytical and the systems views and their assumption of a factive reality, independent of its observers. The reality assumed by the actors view (or at least the reality of interest to the social sciences) exists only as a *social con-struction*, which means that it is not independent of us, its observers. Reality is thus regarded as consisting of a number of *finite provinces of meaning* that are shared by a larger or smaller number of people. These different provinces have separate sociocultural significances. The finite provinces of meaning can overlap to varying degrees. The overlapping parts constitute common parts of reality for an inclusive group of people, which may be an organization or an entire society. The parts that are held in common by the group, organization and/or soci-ety (see Figure 3.11) can be called an *objectified* reality, but this reality is not objective in the sense of the other two views.

Figure 3.11   Objectified Reality in the Actors View

This objectivity is created by people and can therefore be questioned and changed. Furthermore, these objectified parts of reality or their meaning influence, in turn, the people who created them. The *relations* between that which people create and how these creations in turn influence the creators are *dialectical*. We continuously reinterpret the sets of meaning that are in play in these *relations*, resulting in meaning that becomes ambiguous and relations that therefore becomes *dialectic*.

One very fixed objectified meaning structure, shared by practically everyone, is that we should not kill any fellow human being – but this objectified reality is reinterpreted if we enter a state of war. The concept "to kill" is then given a quite different meaning, one that even the clergy can justify. In war, we substitute the concept *enemy* for *fellow human being*, because this concept legitimizes killing, legally as well as ethically and morally.

If we move down the hierarchy of meaning structures, we come eventually to the level of subjective finite provinces of meaning. As an example, consider the two different meanings the concept "poor" will probably have for one and the same actor, first when applying for a bank loan (to be able to borrow money you must, as we know, have assets that enable you to pay it back with interest) and then when applying for social welfare (which will not be granted if you do have any direct assets). Similarly, we can think of other conflicting meanings a person might have, depending on the situation in which he or she is placed.

An actor's various meanings and interpretations acquire their structure from the *finite provinces of meaning* by which actors *orient* themselves, and also from those that actors orient themselves *toward*, that is, other actors' provinces. These finite provinces of meaning are further developed through these interpretations and significances. Reality (the provinces of meaning – the *thesis*) and the actors' interpretations (the *antithesis*) stand in a mutual dialectic relation to each other – they are reformulated in a continuous process of change (*synthesis*).

Over time, change becomes more evident at the subjective than at the objective level (compare the interpretation of "to kill", which in many countries has not been changed for hundreds of years). In this sense we can regard subjectivity and objectivity as endpoints on a scale. That is, the more *objectively* something is socially constructed, the fewer reinterpretations; and the more *subjectively* something is socially constructed, the more reinterpretations. So reality consists, as mentioned before, of different levels of meaning structures, and language will be given different meaning in relation to these levels.

This means that in the actors view, social science, unlike natural science, studies phenomena that consist of concepts – the actors' conceptions of their experiences. Because phenomena are constituted by the actors' experiences, which are constructed through their *egological sphere*, this finite province of meaning and egological sphere must be comprehended before any kind of understanding can be reached. Criminals do not perceive the law code as a guide (see Figure 3.12); in their finite province of meaning it is seen as a threat to their existence.

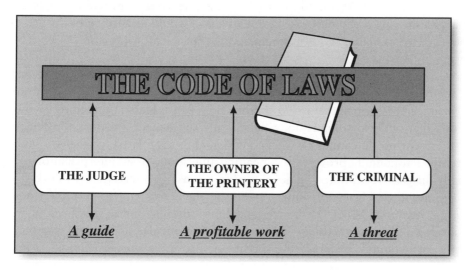

Figure 3.12   Different Meaning Structures

How criminals establish meaning and interpret this threat, along with their total life situation, makes it possible for us to understand why they repeatedly commit crimes in spite of knowing the legal consequences. Similarly, a purchasing manager who always buys too much of a particular product is none the less rational if this is seen in the light of the finite province of meaning (and egological sphere) that controls the interpretation. The behaviour of this manager will hardly be changed by pointing out that, once again, too much has been purchased. The purchasing manager might well be aware of this, but gives it a different interpretation than the environment does – in a way that relates to his or her finite province of meaning and egological sphere, which are, after all, what control the purchase.

The same idea, but to a greater degree, is valid for people who have developed a pathological pattern of action. No matter how hard a psychotherapist might try to explain to a patient that a particular problem might be due to a dysfunctional relationship between the patient and the patient's mother, it doesn't help. The patient, like the purchasing manager, may know this, but it does not help because the action is interpreted through the finite province of meaning (which is consistent with the person's egological sphere) that led to the pathology in the first place. In the actors view, the therapist must try to make the patient aware of the finite province of meaning that led to the disturbance. This means that there are people who are unable to see certain things in spite of the fact that nothing is wrong with their eyes or their neurological functions. The problem is that their finite province of meaning neither allows nor makes it possible for them to see these things.

When talking about information in everyday life (e.g. business, organizations, society), the expression "in one ear and out the other" is all too often confirmed. According to the actors view, the problem is usually that the people who receive information do not have the finite provinces of meaning from which the information was developed and that would allow them to interpret the information in a way that is meaningful for them. Compare this *ideal-typified* description of an information problem with how politicians and people in senior positions often believe that this kind of problem can be solved by providing more information. Having a more insightful outlook on this situation would, according to the actors view, make it possible to save large sums of money in the transfer of information in both business and society.

The above can be called the *first* basis for *understanding* in the actors view. According to this view, the creator of knowledge must *first understand* the finite provinces of meaning by which different actors orient themselves before they can understand actions in the social world. If this first understanding is not reached, any subsequent understanding of why the actors act the way they do cannot be reached either. If this is related to what we said earlier about different actors' finite provinces of meaning and these actors' interpretations standing in a mutually dialectic relation (being developed in a constant interaction with other actors), we will have the *second* basis for understanding in the actors view – an understanding of these *dialectic relations*. When we understand how different finite provinces of meaning interact, develop and change through these relations, we can also understand why something changes in a sociocultural *life-world* the way it does, to use a phenomenological term (see Figure 3.13).

As mentioned earlier in this chapter, the understanding that is sought in the actors view may have both an *external* and an *internal* character. The internal character has to do with getting actors to come to a better understanding of their situation – that is, how their finite provinces of meaning both control and are related to their interpretations and acts, and to the organizational and taken-for-granted social structures in which they exist. This *emancipatory* interest can, in turn, create circumstances for a genuinely *new way of thinking, acting and of creating*, which is the *external* character of understanding.

So far, understanding is done by the actors themselves. The creator of knowledge (who is an actor as well, of course) also reaches an understanding that is expressed. This *explicit understanding* (which is based on the understanding reached by the knowledge creator) in turn aims at bringing the actors to an understanding and/or creating circumstances for a new way of thinking and acting. This brings us to the form of the results in the actors view.

The knowledge creator's understanding is presented as results in the form of a *general language* for the actual problems or phenomena. The different parts of understanding are

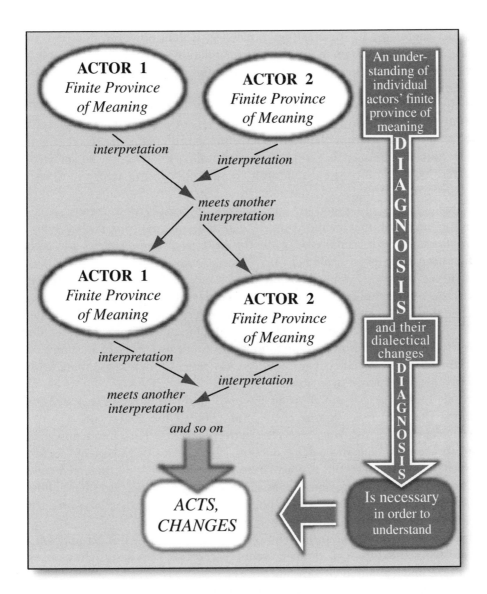

Figure 3.13   Finite Provinces of Meaning in Dialectic Relations

related to each other and are connected to previous experiences and results, as well as to what we earlier referred to as metatheoretical starting points, whereby such general languages can be developed. We will henceforth talk about *descriptive languages* and *ideal-typified languages* – or simply language/language development – to represent the various interrelated models that depict the results of the actors view.

Language/language development, then, means that the everyday language used by actors is transformed or *abstracted* to a *scientific language* (lacking a better word, we call this language "scientific" although it is not restricted to scientists; any researcher/consultant/investigator can construct and/or use it) for creating knowledge, which, however, does not mean that the language as such becomes more abstract (in relation to concrete), but only that the *descriptive elements* of the language are separated and developed (more about this below and in Chapter 6).

Knowledge developed by means of the actors view is *dependent on individuals* in the sense that it refers to the ways in which different actors or groups of actors perceive, interpret and act in the reality they themselves have helped to create. Yet the results from the actors view must not be seen as giving an understanding relative only to specific individuals. The results, because of the assumption about reality in the actors view, also have a broader significance in that they contribute to a *general understanding* of different contexts of structural meaning and of the dialectic processes that create social reality. Furthermore, the results may include certain "general" contributions, such as *typified cases* and *constitutional factors*. Figure 3.14 on the next page demonstrates the actors view models mentioned earlier in Table 3.1.

As descriptive languages, *situational interpretive models* focus on how different actors' finite provinces of meaning lead to the same or to different interpretations and acts.

Institutional models focus on how objectified provinces of meaning develop a life of their own as taken-for-granted structures in relation to an individual actor's interpretations.

Process models focus on how interpretations and finite provinces of meaning are developed in actor relations. Social change is understood based on how these finite provinces of meaning develop and change over time.

Ideal-typified language is a more "general" contribution from actors' research/consulting/investigation. The ideal types consist of an abstraction of the above said. The abstracting involves development of the language's descriptive elements. This abstraction takes place, though it may sound strange, through a reduction, which means that the creator of knowledge gradually separates interpretations and acts from what is factual and actual, and concentrates on the functions of human consciousness as such. Ideal-typified languages have an important *dialectic function* because they also tend to point out that which is potential as an intrinsic part of what is factual (the antithesis of everyday language).

Models of typified cases contain descriptions of different groups of actors from the perspective of "typified actors with typified actors' perceptions (finite provinces of meaning) acting as a type under typified circumstances".

Models of constitutional ideals describe the constitutional ideals of social reality.

For creators of knowledge who choose the actors view as their starting point, it follows as a natural consequence of the reality assumptions about a socially constructed reality that they, during their knowledge-creating work, are also active parts of this dialectic. Among the prerequisites of the actors view (see below) is an interactive development of understanding by the creators of knowledge as an indispensable part of the everyday dialectics in the research/consulting/investigation field.

When we then look at the actors view results, we can see how this everyday dialectic process of *thesis–antithesis–synthesis* accumulates different interpretations and is transformed into a higher, qualitative form through the language developed by the creator of knowledge. The *descriptive* and *ideal-typified* languages emerge as the *antithesis* of everyday

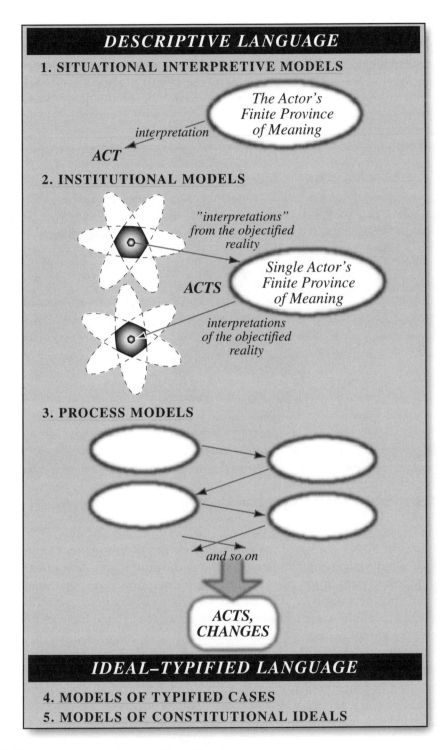

Figure 3.14   A Summary of Actors View Models

language. The creator of knowledge's *emancipatory interactive* action in the research/ consulting/investigation field constitutes the *synthesis* – that is, the active *process that creates* new social reality together with the actors in the field. From a methodological point of departure, in other words, it is the active part, the creative process itself, not its result, that *constitutes* the synthesis. This dialectic methodology of the actors view might be illustrated as in Figure 3.15.

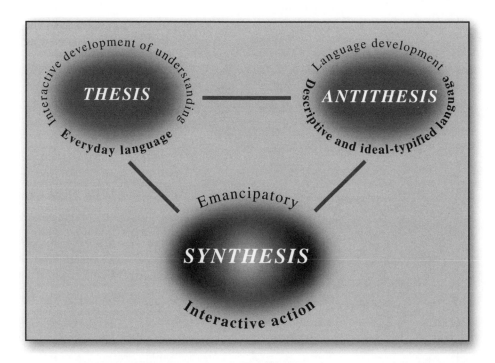

Figure 3.15   The Dialectic Methodology of the Actors View

Models 1 to 5 in Figure 3.14 and the *emancipatory interactive action* can, to a certain extent, be seen as a developmental hierarchy in which the most highly developed form is the fifth model together with interactive action. This does not mean that the results of the actors view must necessarily contain all five models and the interactive action element. How far the creator of knowledge goes is decided on a case-by-case basis and depends on the purpose of the study.

How the language of the actors view is developed and what it might look like will be presented in Chapters 6, 7 and 12. Circumstances for continued research/consulting/ investigation, as mentioned earlier, consequently become a "general understanding of different situations of meaning structure and those *dialectic* processes creating social reality" (Models 1, 2 and 3 in Figure 3.14), and "general" contributions (Models 4 and 5 in Figure 3.14) and the experiences of the researcher's/consultant's/investigator's emancipatory interactive action out in the study area. It is important to realize that this is related to the *interactive development of understanding* in future studies. Furthermore, creators of knowledge have different metatheories at their disposal (we will come back to those theories in Chapter 6). Table 3.4 offers a recap of the actors view.

Table 3.4   Actors View

• *Conception of reality:*	A socially constructed reality that consists of different levels of meaning structures. Human beings (the generating actors) and reality (what is generated) stand in a mutual dialectic relation to each other (we create reality at the same time as reality creates us).
• *Knowledge dependent on individuals, including the knowledge creator:*	Reality is described by denoting conceptual meaning at various structural levels, which is based on how different actors (individuals) perceive, interpret, and act in reality (their egological sphere).
• *Understanding*	The researcher/consultant/investigator attempts to understand and describe dialectic relations, i.e. ambiguous relations that are continuously reinterpreted and given different meaning.
• *Result:*	Through the understanding sought for, our knowledge of those processes that socially construct reality will grow. The result is presented in various forms of descriptive language and ideal-typified language and by emancipatory interactive action out in the field.
• *Prerequisites for continuing:*	Use of the actors view is very much based on a personal and conscious development within the creator of knowledge himself/herself. The actors creators of knowledge will over time develop something we might call craftsmanship in creating knowledge (*craft* as creative activity and not as a repetition of routines). This will be of help in attacking new problems. Researchers/consultants/investigators also have metatheories at their disposal that provide essential starting points for a "general" understanding of the function of human consciousness and for the construction of social reality. Furthermore, these metatheories give guidelines for constitutive interpretive procedures to be applied by the creator of knowledge to him/herself and to others. The "general" contribution provided by previous research/consulting/investigation as constitutional factors also gives starting points a priori. Other "general" contributions, that is, typified cases, are only a guide for thinking in analogies. Experiences from emancipatory interactive actions out in the field raise the quality of "craftsmanship" resources as well, of course, in order to continue to create knowledge within the framework of the actors view.

This chapter has presented the basic conditions for the three methodological views, their similarities and differences, describing how the views are focusing relations in reality and how they differ. As the analytical view chooses to look at these relations as causal, the systems view talks about the relations in terms of finality and the actors view them as dialectical. Furthermore, the chapter has illustrated how the views lead to different results and conditions for further development of research. We have gone deeper into each of the three views under their own headings and illustrated them through a number of figures and sketches, which, also in the way they have been designed, try to convey some of the differences between the views. There are also several summarizing tables to simplify comparisons between them.

POINTS OF REFLECTION

1. At the end of Chapter 2 you could follow how a number of *questions* evolved in front of an imaginative knowledge creation task in the study area of entrepreneurship. These questions can also be seen in this chapter. When looking at various answers given to these questions it is possible to separate ... What?

2. In the chapter we can find words like *explain* and *understand*. Give a short description of these concepts as you see them "in everyday life". Relate your opinion to how they are looked at from a scientific point of departure. Which differences and similarities can you see between everyday life opinion and the scientific one?

3. The methodological views represent different *conceptions of reality*. Give your version of them and clarify to yourself what the different views mean for working with creating knowledge.

4. In the chapter concepts like *finality*, *dialectic* and *causal* relations are mentioned. Describe the relations between a company and its customers in a finality way, dialectical and causal. Discover the differences!

5. What does it mean that something is *general*?

6. From what *view* did you start when you answered the question above about the meaning of general? Can you summarize how the different views look at what this "general" issue is?

7. What are "*Cause–effect relations, classifications* and *descriptive languages*" examples of?

8. Sometimes there is a mention about *background* and/or *intervening* variables. Can you give an example to illustrate what these two concepts stand for?

9. Sometimes there is a mention of *multifinality* and/or *equifinality*. How would you argue with these concepts as a background if you were a research manager and were in a situation where you want to initiate a project to develop a new mobile phone? Justify your arguments.

10. What does your *finite provinces of meaning* look like?

11. In the chapter you can read about *models* in several different ways. Detail some of the different definitions/conceptualizations that exist in the chapter.

12. *Thesis–antithesis–synthesis* are three important concepts, but in what methodological view? And what do they stand for?

RECOMMENDED FURTHER READING

See the end of the Appendix and visit the website below.

Become a worldwide partner as a *knowledge creator* in the development of *Methodology for Creating Business Knowledge* by visiting the website: **www.knowledge-creator.com**. Here you can contribute by asking your own questions and you will also find answers to the most frequently asked questions. The website has been developed alongside this third edition of the book and the questions posted there will be used to provide input for future editions.

PART II
THREE METHODOLOGICAL VIEWS

4 THE ANALYTICAL VIEW

This chapter will present the analytical view in detail. Concepts on which the view is based will be provided, such as models, causal relations, hypotheses, problem formulations, deduction, induction, verification and abduction, operational definitions and *ceteris paribus*. The relation of the analytical view to its paradigm and some typical results from this view will also be provided.

SOME BASIC CONCEPTS

There is good reason to say that a methodological view is its concepts. Major parts of this chapter are therefore devoted to presenting concepts that are often used by proponents of the analytical view: *reality and models, causal relations, hypotheses, deduction, induction, abduction and verification, operational definitions, analysis and ceteris paribus* ("other things being equal"). We will finish by discussing how the analytical view relates to its paradigm and look at various ambitions associated with being an analytical creator of knowledge.

REALITY AND MODELS

The analytical view is based on the assumption that reality is factive. There are *objective* facts and *subjective* facts. Both are looked at as *true*. Objective facts are circumstances, which, in principle, are indisputable, not questionable and not influenced by somebody's opinion. This could be the age of a company, which product is selling best or the telephone number to the present general manager of the firm. There are also subjective facts. These are true opinions that people may hold. To the extent that they are facts, they are, from a methodological point of departure, treated in the same way as objective facts. When looking for facts, especially in the subjective case, the question of whether a finding is true or not often arises.

In the case of the analytical view we are faced with the task of discovering elements (things, events, opinions) that are *invariant* in spite of changes in the environment and variations in perceptions among different individuals. These have always been the requirements of the analytical view. That which is invariant is seen as more "true". Two questions are consistently asked:

- Which are the facts?
- How can we explain these facts?

Being so concerned with invariance, it is natural that logic and mathematics have a dominant position in the analytical view. The following arguments are considered valid.

a. Logical and mathematical knowledge is not subject to sensory illusions.
b. Results from logical and mathematical analyses are universal and valid; they are not subject to change.
c. The only results that are precise and not subjective are those that can be formulated in mathematical terms resulting from calculations and measurements.

The ambitions in the analytical view are to work up pictures of factive reality (ambitions that the analytical view shares with the systems view). Some of these pictures can be called *models*. An analytical approach (we remind the reader that analytical "approach" means analytical view "in application") is to look for representative models (many systems creators of knowledge have the same ambition).

Models in the analytical view tend to contain *quantitative* elements. Models that are quantitative, but do not adhere to laws of mathematics, must meet strict requirements as to their origin and form to qualify as models. In the analytical view, the researcher/consultant/investigator therefore has some guarantee that a model – if it is quantitatively based – actually reflects the *invariant* phenomena in question.

Models with at least a certain minimum of generality can be part of the *theoretical concepts* of the analytical view (see Box 4.1).

Box 4.1

Theory

Theory (from the Greek word *theoria*, reflection) is a term with various meanings, among others the following:

1. a hypothesis
2. a strictly verified assumption (vs. a hypothesis)
3. a purely intellectual explanation or understanding (vs. application or practice) ("theory and practice")
4. a set of systematically constructed theses.

In the analytical view we can say that theory contains models of factive reality, models that are valid for more than one case in real life. (The concept of theory is used in the systems and actors views as well. We will return to this.)

CAUSAL RELATIONS, EXPLANATIONS AND HYPOTHESES

A very important concept in the analytical view is *hypothesis*. In this view, a hypothesis is a suggestion of an explanation of certain facts and a guide in surveying others.

Not all analytical studies *start* with the formulation of hypotheses. Studies for creating knowledge might be *explorative*; in other words, their objective can be to *formulate hypotheses*. Furthermore, there are a large number of studies that are of a purely *descriptive* character. The goal of these studies is to present facts without trying to establish the "logical consequences" of these facts; that is, without attempting to explain any described invariance.

Hypotheses may include possible factive patterns – guides or templates that give structure to purely descriptive studies. But because the highest ambition of the analytical view is to find explanations, we will reserve the concept of hypotheses to apply to what might be called "*statements* (confirmed or not) *about causal relations*", or the assumption that one factor (or group of factors) determines the emergence of another. Traditional psychoanalytical theory provides an example of a hypothesis of this type: the hypothesis that asserts that a person's early childhood experiences are an important factor in *determining* the person's adult personality.

"Hypothesis" is a concept that can also appear in the systems and actors views, but in those instances it is usually given a less precise meaning – namely, a general assumption or an idea about how something is constructed or that a phenomenon will occur. What's more, it is not related to *causal* thinking and *determinism*, and the close connection to theory is missing.

Hypotheses can originate from various sources. A hypothesis may simply be based on a *guess*. It can be the outcome of *results* from various studies and an *expectation* that a similar relation among two or more variables will be valid in the current study as well. A hypothesis can also come from existing *theory* that allows a creator of knowledge to predict that if specific circumstances are present, certain results should follow.

No matter where a hypothesis comes from, it has the following important purposes right from the start for those analytical studies whose aim it is to find explanations. It is the lodestar for:

a. the type of data to be collected in order to confirm or reject the question formulated in the study
b. the extra data to be collected to test the veracity of the question formulated in the study
c. the best way to organize these data for the analysis.

The background of a specific hypothesis is of great importance to the contribution the study can bring to the state of general knowledge (to existing theory). A hypothesis that originates in *intuition* or a mere *guess* can eventually offer an important contribution to the state in an effort to create knowledge. Yet if it has been tested in only *one* study, it has two limitations to its usefulness. *First*, there is no guarantee that the relations that were discovered between two variables in the study will appear in other studies. *Second*, a hypothesis based on a mere guess is probably not directly related to other knowledge or to existing theory. In consequence, results based on it have no clear connection to the great amount of social science knowledge that is now available. The results may well pose interesting questions or stimulate further studies and eventually be incorporated into existing theory. But until that happens, the results provide only some isolated information.

A hypothesis that emerges from the *results* of other studies escapes the first of these two limitations, at least to some extent. If the hypothesis is based on what other studies have stated and the subsequent study supports the hypothesis, the results verify that some kind of *regularity* in factive reality has been discovered. The possibility that the relations that have emerged depend on specific circumstances in a given situation is reduced, if not completely eliminated.

A hypothesis that originates not only from the results of previous studies, but also from a *theory* that is formulated in more general terms, is free of the second limitation as well – that is, of isolation from general knowledge. If connections are satisfactorily established between general theory and specific data from a study, and if the results from the study confirm the idea on which the hypothesis is based, the creator of knowledge has provided a two-way contribution. First, the results of the study assist in confirming that the theory holds in this new case as well as in previous ones. Second, by applying general theory to the specific case, the creator of knowledge is assisted in interpreting the results, that is, gets an answer to why he/she has come up with the results in question.

Whether the character of an expected relation can be expressed explicitly from the start (i.e. be formulated as hypotheses at the beginning of the study) depends primarily on the state of knowledge of the study area being focused on. Studies for creating knowledge can either be based on well-formulated hypotheses or they can produce them. From this it follows that *formulating* and *verifying* (or falsifying) *hypotheses* is *one* goal of studies that proponents of the analytical view want to call *creation of knowledge*. This goal cannot be reached without effort. In several business areas significant hypotheses are missing, which means that many *explorative* studies must be undertaken before hypotheses can be formulated. Such explorative work is an inevitable part of any effort intended to develop better knowledge about companies and related social phenomena.

It does not make sense to say that studies that start by formulating hypotheses are more knowledge-creative than others. Just when it is appropriate to formulate such hypotheses varies with the nature of the problem and the extent to which knowledge of an area already exists. Formulating and reformulating questions to create knowledge is a *continuous* process. A hypothesis implies that a special characteristic or event (X) is one of the factors that determine another characteristic (Y). Studies designed to test such hypotheses must result in data that allow creators of knowledge to conclude that X does or does not help *determine* Y. This leads us to *causality*.

The concept of causality was discussed to some extent in Chapter 3. A deeper discussion than that is beyond the scope of this book. Causality is, incidentally, a very complicated philosophical concept and has long been an issue on the agenda in many philosophical discourses. "Common sense", in the context of causality, usually follows the idea that one circumstance (characteristic or event = cause) always leads to another circumstance (characteristic or event = effect). In analytical research, however, it is more usual to search for a *number* of *determining* factors (not just one) that, taken *together*, make possible the appearance of a characteristic or the occurrence of an event. Furthermore, basic and more advanced theoretical thinking may be focused on finding *necessary* and *sufficient* conditions for a characteristic or an event. However, the methodological issues are the same whether limited to one characteristic or event or considering several simultaneously, which means that our discussion can be based on the premise of *one* cause → *one* effect.

A *necessary* condition (circumstance or event) is, by definition, a condition that *must* exist if the phenomenon of which it is a cause is to appear or happen. If X is a necessary condition for Y, Y cannot appear or happen unless X exists or happens. A *sufficient* circumstance is one that *always* will be followed (contemporarily or later) by the phenomenon of which it is a cause. If X is a sufficient condition for Y, Y always appears or happens when X appears or happens.

According to the analytical view *in general*, a condition can be both necessary and sufficient for a phenomenon to appear or happen. If that is the case, Y will never appear or happen if X does not appear or happen. Furthermore, Y will always appear or happen if X appears or happens. Taken together, this means that Y appears or happens *if, and only if,* X exists or happens. However, in *social sciences* it is in practice impossible to find necessary and/or sufficient *causal* (*extrinsic*) relations. Social sciences usually go no further than presenting *intrinsic* or *logical* relations (compare the discussion in Chapter 3). The reason why the social science creator of knowledge cannot find causal necessary or sufficient relations in his/her reality is, according to the analytical view, understood to be that the social science creator of knowledge is not able, like the natural science creator of knowledge, to control his/her environment enough during various studies to be able to isolate what such causal relations might possibly be.

> *Example of an intrinsic necessary relation:* More than one company must exist in a market in order for that market to be competitive.
>
> *Example of a logical sufficient relation:* If a machine breaks down, manufacturing done on that machine must stop.

A strict creator of knowledge would probably say that neither of the above examples is an explanation! However, to clarify, nothing in the analytical view in social sciences prevents them from generating causal relations. It happens all the time. However, they are never of a necessary or sufficient kind!

As the reader has noticed, cause as well as effect can indicate a state (a characteristic) or a course (an event). It is often arbitrary, or more the matter of how to interpret the meaning of a word, how we express it.

As mentioned before, in the normal case a single cause and a single effect are not enough to explain social events or phenomena. Creators of knowledge, therefore, try to find a group of causes that, combined, makes it more probable that an effect will take place or emerge. Conversely, most creators of knowledge search for several effects from a given cause.

A usual additional complicating factor in business is that causes in a given situation *interact* with each other. The cause–effect relation is rarely (if ever) one-dimensional, even though that is the ideal situation in the analytical view. Many analytical operative paradigms are nevertheless set up as if this ideal were possible. Creators of knowledge then consciously get a bundle of causes (or effects) as the outcome of the study (see Figure 4.1).

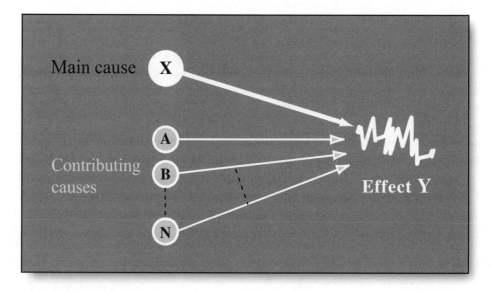

Figure 4.1   The Normal Hypothesis

Most hypotheses in business (and in the social sciences in general) are associated with *contributing* or *alternative* conditions and prerequisites under which the hypothesis is valid. It is therefore usually not possible to demonstrate *directly* that a given characteristic or event (*X*), either by itself or in combination with other characteristics or events (*A*, *B*, *C*, etc.) will automatically lead to an Effect Y. Instead, creators of knowledge find themselves, from the data observed, having to draw the conclusion that the condition *X* is a condition of *Y* is (or is not) defensible with a specified degree of certainty (if the study is done in quantitative terms, this degree may be possible to state in statistical numbers). Three stipulations are, as mentioned in Chapter 3, necessary to draw a certain and safe conclusion that the causal connection proposed between factor *X* and *Y* in a hypothesis is valid.

1. *Relation between the Factors*. The first stipulation is that factor *X* and factor *Y* co-vary in the way stated in the hypothesis. Let us assume that we want to test the hypothesis that *X* is a contributing cause of *Y*. If we find that the number of cases that contain both *X* and *Y* are fewer than the number of cases that do not contain *X* but do contain *Y*, we draw the conclusion that the hypothesis is not defensible. Furthermore, if our hypothesis also specifies the

amount of Y that is determined by X, we should also find that cases showing a higher amount of X also show a higher amount of Y. (Instead of a positive co-variation between X and Y it is possible, of course, to consider hypotheses that suggest that the existence of X prevents the existence of Y or, if the creator of knowledge wants to express it more quantitatively, that Y increases as X decreases – or vice versa. In this case, our discussion would be analogous.)

Suppose we want to test the following hypothesis: large market share for a product results in high profit from the same market. We reject the hypothesis if our data do not show that in more cases where a product has had a large market share, the profit is higher than among those cases where a product has had a small market share. Two alternative relational forms of X causing Y may, however, be valid under these conditions:

a. What we thought was a cause might actually be an effect (X could be an effect instead of a cause), and vice versa (Y could be a cause instead of an effect).
b. External or specific circumstances other than X could be the "real" causes of X being related to Y.

To return to our example, it might well be that high profit brings large market share instead of the other way around (see (a) above). It could also be the case that the cause of high profit as well as a large market share can be found in good senior management or that the study has looked only at industries that are particularly conducive to high profit no matter what. Other industries might have shown other results (see (b) above).

2.   *Chronological Order of the Factors*. The possible alternative hypothesis – that high profit will cause large market share – leads us to the second stipulation necessary for saying that a hypothesis has been verified. A characteristic or an event cannot be considered a cause of another if it exists or happens later in time than the other one. A cause must always exist or happen before – or possibly at the same time as – an effect. Moreover, two factors can be each other's causes and effects. The relation is then said to be *symmetrical*. In our example, it might be possible that large market share normally brings high profit. Yet this profit may be necessary for maintaining the large market share, by enabling the use of new resources.

Even so, the chronological order itself, even if combined with an existing relation between two variables (factors), is not enough for us to say that a causal relation has been found. A third prerequisite is necessary.

3.   *Elimination of Other Possible Causal Factors*. In order to be able to say that X is a cause of Y, it is necessary:

•   that there is no *background factor Z* that can explain X as well as Y
•   that there is no *intervening variable W* that gives a better picture of the causal relation.

The most serious of these is, of course, the background factor. If an intervening factor is present, it might simply improve our explanation. Examples of what having to deal with background and intervening factors could mean are illustrated in Figure 4.2 (compare Figure 3.5).

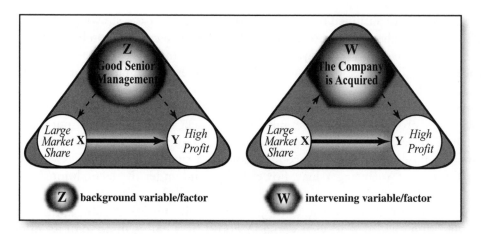

Figure 4.2   Importance of Background and Intervening Factors

Let us summarize the three requirements for drawing the conclusion that a hypothesis is an expression of a particular established causal relation:

1. An existing covariation. *X (the causing or independent variable)* and *Y (the affected or dependent variable)* shall vary in a way that is predicted in the hypothesis; *X* and *Y* shall tend either to assist or counteract each other.
2. *Y* shall not have existed or taken place prior to *X*.
3. It shall be possible to eliminate other factors determining *Y*.

It must be pointed out that even if these three requirements are met, they are not *proof* (in practice) that X actually causes Y. It is possible to have overlooked a decisive cause other than X; alternatively, X might cause Y only under certain circumstances that are not determined in the study. In other words, we draw the conclusion that it is probable that X causes Y, but we can never be absolutely certain. Further studies will have to disprove or support our conclusion; in practice, it will never be absolutely proven.

THE CREATION OF KNOWLEDGE PROBLEM

As the reader has probably understood, the analytical view is rather formalistic and full of rules. There are rules for what should be seen as reality, there are rules for what is science and what is not, there are rules for what should be counted as an explanation, etc. The reader will later discover that there are rules in the analytical view for how to incorporate, develop, and/or modify previous techniques, results and/or theories, that is, methodical procedures and rules for how an analytical study is designed, that is, methodics.

One aspect of the relatively tight discipline which is associated with the analytical view, is its attitude to what is a *creation of knowledge problem*. Generally, when possible, the analytical view recommends that already at the beginning of the process of creating knowledge – even before the project starts – the creator of knowledge should state the research problem, and, if applicable, also the practical problem, which is to be studied.

One may ask, of course, whether the creation of knowledge problem can always be described at the start of a study and, furthermore, whether it is always connected to a practical problem? Of course not! There are projects, which could be called *explorative*, which are designed to clarify a problem more than anything else. However, according to the analytical view, such studies should also be governed by a problem formulated in the beginning, even if a very preliminary one. As far the second part of the question is concerned, the creator of knowledge has the right, of course, to formulate problems, which have not yet been recognized in practice and/or concentrate on theoretical issues, which eventually will have a practical application in the future.

Whatever type of analytical study is at hand, a problem should be guiding it, so the view in question says. Also, there are several types of analytical studies in terms of what they aim for (this will be discussed further at the end of this chapter). Each of those should be introduced by a clear definition of the problem according to the analytical view. In this respect and with this view, there are basically three types of studies, that is, *explorative*, *descriptive* and *explanatory*.

- The problem for the *explorative* study is to come up with a more precise statement of the problem, which can be brought forward in further efforts of creating knowledge.
- The problem of a *descriptive* study is to come up with as detailed a map as possible of some factive reality.
- The problem of the *explanatory* or *hypothesis-testing* study is to explain the connections between causes and effects of some characteristics or events.

The details of what is to be contained in these different formulations of a problem differ, but one thing is certainly common to all. *Definitions* of key terms and concepts should be given as early as possible in the study, according to the analytical view.

The three studies above are of a more scientific type. The consultant and/or an investigator outside the academic arena have, on top of these, almost always an ambition to suggest solutions to specific problems. If this is the case, in the ideal case, a formulation of a problem should answer the following questions:

- What?
- Whom?
- How?
- When?
- Why?
- With what effect(s)?

For consulting and similar studies, it is possible to see a problem hierarchy in the analytical view. At the most general level, there is a *management problem*. The management problem represents a decision that a manager must make and is the problem prompting the research. At a more specific level, there is a *research problem*. A research problem is the single question or hypothesis that best states the objective of the research study. A study, which answers these questions or attacks these hypotheses is supposed to provide the manager with the desired information. On occasion, it may be more than one question, but often, it is just one. At the most specific level, there is an *investigative problem*. The investigative problem contains those more specific questions that the creator of knowledge must answer in order to satisfactorily answer the general research questions.

There is, of course, nothing preventing an original problem formulation in an analytical approach to be modified as the study goes on, depending, perhaps, on the fact that new information is received or new experiences are gained. New directions in the original design of the study or even restarts may be necessary.

DEDUCTION, INDUCTION, VERIFICATION – AND ABDUCTION

The analytical view is always focused on *facts*. From this it follows that creators of knowledge in this view are first of all *collectors* of *facts*. Second, they attempt to *describe*, in general terms, both what *facts* they see and what *facts* they hear people talk about in terms of what they have seen and what they think. Third, they make a *prediction* based on their theories and explanations, which – again – can be verified against *facts*.

The most characteristic aspect of the analytical view and its operative paradigms is that they are cyclical. They start with *facts* and ends with *facts*, and the *facts* of one cycle are the *facts* that begin the next. Creators of knowledge regard their theories, however, as only *probable* and are therefore always prepared to give them up if the data that emerge are not consistent with the predictions based on the theories. If a series of observations developed to verify certain predictions forces them to abandon a theory, they look for new and better theories. Because in the analytical view they expect the progress of knowledge (gained through scientific or other means) to go on in a chain of successes, they expect that this cyclical process will continue. See Figure 4.3 opposite for an illustration.

The horizontal dashed line in Figure 4.3 separates the empirical world (the factive world) from the theoretical world, which, in accordance with the analytical view, is more or less quantitatively constructed. In the world below the line we see creators of knowledge who, for instance, look into microscopes or observe behaviour or interview people. In the world above the line, we see a chain of mathematical formulae, logical sequences and systematically arranged data. We also notice three steps in the figure. The first step involves moving from original observations towards theories. This is known as *induction* – a way of creating knowledge whereby creators of knowledge conclude general laws from individual cases, that is, construct theories using factive knowledge. This can mean, for instance, that a mathematical formula is found that is perceived to suit the facts that a creator of knowledge is trying to incorporate in the theory. Then the creator of knowledge asks, "Is this really what I want?" The creator of knowledge is then forced to go back to the world of facts (factive reality) to verify his/her construction.

A creator of knowledge cannot, however, check on a general law without first asking what it says about specific cases. The course of the stock market, for instance, cannot be observed

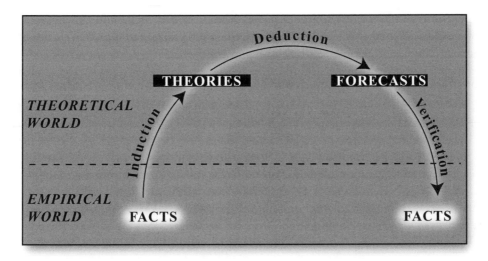

Figure 4.3   Cyclical Nature of Creating Knowledge in the Analytical View

indefinitely. The creator of knowledge may perhaps observe that average prices rise one day, that they rise the following day as well, and then, after one more day, fall, and so on. Any limited number of cases can be observed. Creators of knowledge using the analytical view must therefore decide what their general theory says about tomorrow's development, for example. This step is reached through *deduction* – a way of creating knowledge whereby the creator of knowledge infers single cases from general laws; that is, a logical analysis of what general theory says about a specific event tomorrow. Not until then will creators of knowledge be ready to return to facts and find out whether or not their predictions were correct. This third and last step is the *verification* of the theory.

So, in principle, the deductive mode means that the creator of knowledge goes from theory to facts and the inductive mode means that the process goes the other way around. The most common criticism directed at the pure deductive approach is precisely its dependence on theory, and the influence on sampling and operationalization of variables in the models being constructed that follow. There is a risk that those observations which are made will not fit that reality which they are meant to describe. This is a criticism of the deductive approach which is directed by Glaser and Strauss (1967), who with their so-called *constant comparative method*, based on an analytical view, recommend induction. However, in their version of methodology, they claim that the objective is not verification but to generate *a grounded theory* (more about grounded theory can be read in the Appendix): "Generating a theory from data means that most hypotheses and concepts not only come from data, but are systematically worked out in relation to the data during the course of research" (Glaser and Strauss, 1967: 6).

Apart from induction and deduction, sometimes a third method is mentioned in this context, that is, *abduction* (Peirce et al., 1998). Abduction means that a single (often surprising) case is placed in a general hypothetical pattern, which, if it is true, will explain the case, in question. The explanation should then be confirmed by new observations (new cases). The method then becomes a kind of combination of induction and deduction, but it also brings on new steps. Another way to put it is to say that induction and deduction can be seen as two alternative research strategies, while abduction is more of a research tactic. Induction starts from facts and deduction from theory. Abduction starts from facts like induction, but it does not turn away theoretical knowledge and is, to that extent, closer to deduction. The analysis of facts may very well be combined with, or preceded by, studies of existing theory in the literature, not as a mechanical application to single cases, but as a source of inspiration to discover patterns for further explanations. This means that the research process consists of alternations between (existing) theory and facts, where both are seen in the light of each other. The single models of explanations, that is, deduction and induction, are then seen as too one-dimensional and unrealistic, compared with how research is done in practice.

OPERATIONAL DEFINITIONS

All creators of knowledge must use a set of concepts when they organize their data so as to discover relations. A *concept* is an abstraction of observed events or characteristics, a short verbal representation of them. Some concepts may be relatively easy to relate to the phenomena they attempt to represent – such concepts are price tag, factory or machine. It then becomes possible to point out the corresponding phenomenon in factive reality. Phenomena represented by other concepts, however, can be more problematic to point out, observe or measure. These concepts are more abstract, more distant from the empirical world. Examples of such concepts might include creativity, image and organization. These more abstract concepts are sometimes called *constructs*.

The closer a concept is to factive reality, the more *operational* the concept is said to be. Because the analytical view is, to a large extent, occupied with creating knowledge of events, characteristics and behaviour in this reality, the creator of knowledge tries as much as possible here to formulate *operational definitions*, that is, concepts that in themselves contain a description of how a specific phenomenon is to be discovered in factive reality. Using the rules the definition provides, anyone should be able to discover the specific phenomenon in the reality represented by the definition. An operational definition should contain the following parts:

1. A statement of which object(s) or subject(s) are to be observed or questioned.
2. A description of the situation in which the observation or questioning is to take place.
3. A determination of the type of measuring scale to be applied to the observations made or answers obtained.
4. Rules for how to handle the data obtained through the observation or questioning.

Here are two examples of operational definitions:

Level of stock: Average book value of a company's stock during a year, calculated as the arithmetical mean of the public figures that can be read in the company's accounts in the beginning and at the end of a given financial year.

Improved product quality: More yes-answers than no-answers to the question: "Do you think the quality of Product X has improved since the last time you used it?" The answers should come from a random sample of at least 100 customers among those who have actually bought the product in question at least twice. The latest purchase must have taken place within the past 2 months. Each customer is to answer individually and independently from other customers. The survey can be conducted by phone or by mail, and the questions are to be posed by an impartial third party with no connection to the company that manufactures and markets the product in question, such as an employee of an independent marketing research firm.

THE CONCEPT OF ANALYSIS

We have given the name "analytical view" to the methodological view described in this chapter. It is therefore reasonable to justify the label of the view and to clarify the meaning of the concept of analysis.

In our everyday language we make a distinction between *analysis* and *construction*. Without going into a detailed and sophisticated discussion of the demarcation of different schools of philosophy, we can say that this distinction exists there as well. Analysis, then, means *a thorough investigation* of an *existing* situation. Construction has to do with *putting together a new* (and, perhaps, better) situation. (There is, in fact, a philosophical school, which is called *the analytical school*, a school, which the analytical view leans heavily on and which is, therefore, another reason for our name "the analytical view". We will return to this shortly.)

The analytical view, like the systems view, contains the concept of "analysis". The concept is, in fact, central to both. However, the analytical view, in its analytical concept, is oriented primarily toward the *techniques* used by *the creator of knowledge*, whereas the systems view is oriented mainly toward the *results* that can be employed by *the user* (the one who may use the results provided by the creator of knowledge). Analysis is therefore of *primary* (general) interest to the creator of knowledge representing *the analytical view*, whereas it is of only *secondary* (or rather of *starting* and *finishing*) interest to the creator of knowledge representing *the systems view*.

The concept of analysis also has different meanings in the two views. In both cases, however, *analysis* means a specific treatment of factive reality (or a model thereof), the existence of which is acknowledged both by those who represent the analytical view and those who represent the systems view. Factive reality, according to the analytical view, is best clarified by what can be characterized as *disintegration* or *decomposition*, that is, by studying its smallest components *by themselves*. The sum of these partial results becomes knowledge of the whole.

Analysis as seen by the systems view (systems analysis), however, means that any part of the factive reality is best clarified by studying components *in relation to the whole*. Yet the sum of the study of these individual components in relation to the whole does not constitute knowledge of the whole. In addition, it is possible to talk about the totality *as such* (the system) – for example, in relation to its environment (*placing the system in its larger context*). We return to the systems view in the next chapter.

The analytical view is therefore based on a very important *theoretical* assumption:

a. That the elements of an object or subject under study can be regarded as relatively independent of each other.

And a *practical* assumption:

b. That the intrinsic properties of the object or subject under study does not change rapidly or in such a way that it is not possible to explain this object or subject by explaining its separate elements.

The systems view denies assumption (a) and sometimes assumption (b) as well. But both the analytical view and the systems view make the following assumption:

c. That the analysis of an object or a subject can be done without influencing it in a manner that cannot be controlled.

Because analysis plays such a central role in the analytical view (plus the fact that "its" philosophy is the analytical philosophy), but only constitutes one part of the systems view, we see the name of the former view as totally adequate. Besides, the term *analytical view* is not our own. It was used more than fifty years ago by those who "launched" the systems view, and it is still used today in the sense of "the analytical view" versus "the systems view".

CETERIS PARIBUS

The assumption in the analytical view that elements of the objects and subjects being studied are relatively independent of each other makes it possible for results that are developed from various operative paradigms of the analytical view to be formulated "*ceteris paribus*" (as if "all other things remain equal", i.e. unchanged). Among other activities, sampling, hypothesis testing and theory construction in the analytical view are based on this assumption. In consequence, causal relations that have developed are considered to be valid provided "nothing else has changed". Study the following three statements:

1. If the price of a product is falling, the demand for that product will tend to increase.
2. If the price of a product is falling and nothing else changes, the demand for that product will increase.
3. If the price of a product is falling and the product is sold in a situation of perfect competition, the demand for that product will increase.

Case 2 is what we mean by *ceteris paribus*. This is the usual case for business theories in the analytical view (although Case 3 could also exist). The systems view might accept Case 1.

THE PHILOSOPHICAL FOUNDATION OF THE ANALYTICAL VIEW

The philosophical foundation of the analytical view is definitely analytical philosophy. Just like any part of philosophy, explaining what analytical philosophy is isn't straightforward. However, providing such as explanation is not the intention here. Rather, we want to bring up some points that have been raised by analytical philosophers over the years, points, which by no means have been left unopposed and some which are even not valid today, but they provide a kind of panorama which still flavours the analytical view today:

- About philosophy:
    - Can philosophy be done the way that science is?
    - Can more rigor be introduced into philosophy by proceeding in a logical fashion?
    - Can philosophy be *reduced* to logic?
- The structure of reality is essentially the same as that of mathematical logic, that is, *atomistic*. Studying mathematics can tell us more about reality.
- Science is to be advocated as the *only* way to truly learn about the world (this is sometimes referred to as *positivism*, a stream which gave a start to analytical philosophy, but is no longer seen as of stand-alone interest within this philosophy)
- *The principle of verification*: only those propositions that can be verified are meaningful.
- An *interesting* statement can always be reduced to *observation* statements.

Analytical philosophy is largely a twentieth-century story. Famous analytical philosophers during the last century include Russell (1872–1970), Moore (1873–1958), Carnap (1891–1970), Wittgenstein (1889–1951), Ryle (1900–1976) and Austin (1911–1960).

Analytical philosophy is active today in many areas, particularly the philosophy of mind. What we can call meaningful, how we find out about the factive world and what kind of facts it is composed of are central questions for analytical philosophers today.

More about analytical philosophy (and positivism) can be found in the Appendix.

THE RELATION OF THE ANALYTICAL VIEW TO ITS PARADIGM

What the analytical view stands for today can be summarized in terms of the description of *paradigm* provided earlier in the book:

1. Conception of reality
2. Conception of science
3. Scientific ideals
4. Ethical/aesthetical aspects

Let us look at business through "the lens of the analytical view".

Conception of reality, or What Does Business Reality Actually Look Like? Business reality exists objectively in itself, independent of us as theorists and/or creators of knowledge and it exists subjectively as relatively stable opinions of, and beliefs in, this objective world. Such objective and subjective parts of reality can together be classified as *factive*. Even if we, through interference or through change of mind can make this reality appear in various forms, it is *basically* a stable construction. This basic construction has a *summative* character consisting of explanatory links that can be studied relatively independently of each other.

Conception of science, or How Do We Look at Business as a Science? Business as a science (and as it is applied by researchers, consultants and other kinds of investigators) is a picture of business reality. This picture consists of more or less definite facts that can be discussed in terms of "all other things remaining equal". This picture will improve as time goes on and as more knowledge is created.

Theories (as language) can be discussed with regard to how they are constructed (*syntax*), in relation to what they stand for (*semantics*) and in relation to their users (*pragmatics*). Because theories should be based on facts, their terms (e.g. *cost accounting, budget, matrix organization, long-term planning* and *advertising*) should be as syntactically and semantically correct as possible, yet – as far as possible – be made independent of pragmatic controversies. It is therefore natural that the terms are, to a large extent, defined operationally, based on logics and mathematics.

Business knowledge is logically separated from moral matters and ethics. This means, for instance, that business can argue about which consequences different alternative actions will have in terms of formulated objectives, but deciding which objectives should actually be chosen is beyond its domain. According to analytical creators of knowledge, science (this pertains to business (practice) as well) should not take a definite position on which business objectives to choose, and related matters.

There is also a sharp boundary between philosophy and creation of knowledge. Philosophy can be used as a basis for discussion, but it can never provide the truth. That is the task of the creator of knowledge as researchers, consultants or other kinds of investigators.

Scientific ideals, or What Do We Want From Business as a Science? Gradually, the study of Business will fill in as many "empty squares" in our knowledge of business reality as possible. This knowledge will consist of verified assumptions (hypotheses) in factive reality, assumptions which follow certain formal rules. Knowledge emerges most surely with the use of well-tested techniques, many of which have been picked up from the natural sciences. The results will be an increasing number of, and ever more refined, logical models and representative, generalizable cases.

Even if we aim for explanations that are as simple as possible (but nevertheless true), we know that generally the more causes we find, the more complete the explanation of a given effect will be. We will continue to get increasingly more deterministic relations, but in the meantime we will have to be satisfied with results that are sometimes stochastic.

Business knowledge is to be used to make better and better predictions of the consequences of various alternative actions that could be taken, and consequently to steer BUSINESS reality in a desirable direction.

Ethical and aesthetical aspects, or *What Can and Should Business Creators of Knowledge Do, and What Attitude Should They Take Toward What is Done?* These are relatively uninteresting questions to proponents of the analytical view. It is instead seen as important to regard creation of knowledge as progress; as business creators of knowledge we do not have to take responsibility for how people in business reality use the knowledge that will be presented as we go on.

We present further thinking associated with the analytical view under the headings "Discovery and explanation", "General theses" and "Difficulties in relation to explanation". Before we do so, however, we remind the reader of the outline of the book. Our intent, as far as possible, is to present each of the methodological views on its own terms. If you believe in the analytical view, you accept Chapter 4, and so on. This also means that the descriptions in Chapters 4, 5 and 6 are in several basic respects often not comparable. It is important to remember that the different views are based on their own paradigms.

DISCOVERY AND EXPLANATION

From a *methodological* point *of* departure, the analytical view treats all social sciences as one. The reason is that all of them relate to humans and that they all use the same explanatory principles (if a creator of knowledge in that science has an analytical orientation).

The view also often sees classical natural sciences as an ideal to emulate, because the natural and social sciences are seen as having similar *purposes*, if not the same *results*. If an objective of creation of knowledge is to establish various general relations among phenomena in factive reality, *if* the test of veracity of relations relies ultimately on data, and *if* these data are collected in factive reality, then, according to the analytical view, you are doing science. All social sciences, basically, meet these expectations, according to this view.

The differences between the classical natural sciences and the social sciences (to which business belongs) are then more a matter of degree than of kind. Being engaged in the work of creating knowledge means, according to the analytical view, that you always face the same basic problem: *to discover and to explain.*

In certain respects, the social sciences have not reached as far as the more exact sciences. Furthermore, if some of the social sciences have established less reliable answers than others, this is not because the creators of knowledge were less ambitious or less intelligent. Nor is the reason, essentially – according to the analytical view – that less successful subjects are younger. Nor could the situation be explained by different methods being used in different areas, because the methods in analytical operative paradigms are the same. So, the differences are not caused by level of ambition, intellect, the age of the subject or the methods employed; they are caused by the built-up (complexity) of the problem being approached.

According to the analytical view, every science has *two basic levels of ambition*: to discover and to explain. To discover can mean either to explore or to describe. Descriptions and explanations, in turn, may be used to forecast and to guide. The *first* (discover) determines whether the study area is to be called an area of interest to science, the *second* (explain) the extent to which we are entitled to call the science successful. To discover is either the same as developing problems of creation of knowledge or, if they already exist, to show the characteristics and the behaviour of objects and subjects in reality. This can be called discovery because the problems or the characteristics or behaviour might be unknown (at least in this format) until the creator of knowledge reveals them. To explain is to present more or less general relations among characteristics, behaviours, or both. Explanations in this sense are far more common in natural sciences than in social sciences, which some claim is a striking difference between the two.

Descriptions and explanations are invaluable results of all creation of knowledge efforts conducted according to the analytical view. Such results, that is, empirical theses, are more or less *generalizable*. So that they are not misunderstood, they should contain operational definitions as far as possible. Otherwise there is a risk that, for instance, explanations might be based on concepts that are not related to factive reality.

Over the years, the social sciences have, through their use of the analytical view, put together a huge number of empirical theses, some examples of which are given at the end of this chapter. If the first task of a science is to establish generalizations, the social sciences have established quite a few. Yet these generalizations are neither so general nor so exact as those in the biological or technical sciences, for instance. Among other things, the results are valid primarily for the industrialized part of the world, and they are stated with a number of provisos.

It is difficult to find strict explanations in business. This is partly because we cannot easily manipulate the objects and subjects being studied or the circumstances around them. For instance, it is difficult (even unethical) to experiment with people, compared with experimenting with things. Furthermore, people cannot be exposed to the same treatments or conditions as when testing new situations among animals and physical objects. This is also the reason why the creator of knowledge using the analytical view in a business context applies a number of statistical techniques as a control mechanism, even though they are considered to be less reliable than physical control.

The *most important* task for business when creating knowledge with the analytical view is to find explanations. Explanations are based on discoveries (formulations of problems and descriptions). *To explain* means to answer the question "Why?" Explanations should not only be directly supported empirically, but also indirectly follow as a natural consequence of existing theory (be deduced). This is so whether interest is directed towards a single phenomenon or a more generalizable thesis. It is in the area of *finding explanations* that the social sciences face extra problems.

GENERAL THESES

The longer a science has been on "the road of explanations", the greater the number of general theses it tends to contain. It is unfortunately true that business contains a relatively small number of such theses under the analytical view.

It is also true that what can be claimed, as belonging to the subject of business is rather vague. What should (or should not) be included (or omitted) from business is primarily determined by *the problem*: to occupy oneself with business. Often, therefore, results from such related subjects as Economics, Sociology and Psychology are used. From this point of view, the situation is considerably brighter. Acknowledging that they contain the same principles would, according to the analytical view, promote the development of knowledge. Business would, in this case, be further stimulated by the larger number of theories, concepts and methods.

DIFFICULTIES IN RELATION TO EXPLANATIONS

So, the difficulties of business are related more to finding explanations than to making discoveries.

Business, in this context, operates (like other social sciences) at two levels at the same time. It contains empirical theses about individuals (often collected from psychology), but also of aggregates of individuals – groups, organizations, classes and societies. The relationships between these two levels are not simple. In both the analytical and the systems view we treat organizations as if they were objective entities. This, of course, is only a simplification of factive reality. If we want to explain in greater detail why an organization behaves the way it does, why it behaves differently from other seemingly similar organizations, we would probably have to consider its individuals (although external circumstances could also explain different behaviour, of course). But this does not mean leaving the analytical view for the actors view. Instead, this can take place through what in the analytical view is called a *reduction*, in this case a reduction of organizational theory theses to psychological ones.

There are difficulties associated with such reductions in business. There are certainly many relatively rested theses in psychology, but they are only statistically true and they usually have a very limited scope. In business, for instance, we often find that a thesis that is valid under *one* set of circumstances is not valid under another set. When this happens, it is more likely that *another thesis, sometimes the opposite*, is valid.

According to the analytical view, business does progress in its search for explanations. Even so, there is still a gap between general business theses and the numerous empirical results that exist. This distance will most likely remain into the foreseeable future. One problem is that new (general) explanations are more difficult to find, because the new hypotheses (suggested explanations) that are formulated do not (yet) have a solid theoretical support on which they can be based.

EXAMPLES OF THEORETICAL RESULTS

Let us point out a few examples of theoretical results from the analytical view. The results presented here are not meant to be in any way verified as absolutely true according to the basic idea behind the analytical view, even less to be inclusive. The results are presented only to give the reader an idea of *what kinds* of theoretical results can be developed by starting from the analytical view, *how they are usually formulated* and at *what level of general applicability* they are normally kept. The examples are from an area that we could call "Organizations".

Example 1.   The larger, the more complex, and the more heterogeneous the society, the greater the number of organizations and associations that exist within it.

     1.1.   Organizations tend to call forth organizations. If people organize on one side of an issue, their opponents will organize on the other side.

     1.2.   There is a tendency for voluntary associations to become more formal.

Example 2.   The larger an organization becomes, the more levels of personnel it will tend to have.

Example 3.   A period of innovation and change affecting an organization is likely to produce a heightened amount of communication among the members, communication oriented both toward the task and toward mutual emotional support.

Example 4.   Other things remaining equal, the more friendly and helpful the boss,

- the lower the absenteeism
- the higher the productivity
- the more likely that subordinates feel that the organization's requirements are reasonable, and the more willing they are to accept changes in organizational practices
- the better liked the leader is
- the more strongly the subordinates associate with the organization
- the less tension there is within the organizational unit and the greater the internal cohesion
- the higher the subordinates' morale

Example 5.   The leader's style of leadership tends to be influenced by the style in which he/she was led.

Example 6.   The more closely a member holds to the organization's professed values, the more likely he/she is to be promoted within the organization.

This chapter has only discussed the analytical view, the oldest of our three methodological views. As with all methodological views, it is greatly concerned with concepts. The concepts of the analytical view have consequently been presented in this chapter, including its fundamental concept of "*ceteris paribus*". Also presented here is some basic thinking in the analytical view, like having definitions as operational as possible and regarding steps in creating knowledge, like deduction, induction, verification and abduction, as distinctly different from each other. At the end, the relation of the analytical view to its paradigm and some typical results of knowledge being created from this view have been provided.

POINTS OF REFLECTION

1. The analytical view talks about *invariance*. Explain this concept for your fellow students!
2. What is *determinism*?
3. Formulate what you consider to be three well-formulated *hypotheses*.
4. Think about and describe a cause/effect relation consisting of a *main cause* and at least two *contributing causes*!
5. What does it mean to conduct an *explorative* study?
6. In the analytical view *deduction*, *induction*, *verification* and *abduction* are some central concepts. Without any problem you may surely explain the first three concepts, but what is *abduction*?
7. To *operationalize* something means .... What?
8. *Ceteris paribus* is Latin, but what does it mean?
9. What would your story look like if somebody asked you to present the relation of the analytical view to its *paradigm*?

RECOMMENDED FURTHER READING

See the end of the Appendix and visit the website below.

Become a worldwide partner as a *knowledge creator* in the development of *Methodology for Creating Business Knowledge* by visiting the website: **www.knowledge-creator.com**. Here you can contribute by asking your own questions and you will also find answers to the most frequently asked questions. The website has been developed alongside this third edition of the book and the questions posted there will be used to provide input for future editions.

5 THE SYSTEMS VIEW

The systems view contains many variations in practice, but, from a methodological point of departure, we believe it can be summarized in terms of philosophical influences, similarities and differences when explaining and understanding using the systems view, basic systems language, the relation of the systems view to its paradigm and typical theoretical results from the systems view. Such a summary will be provided in this chapter.

THE ROOTS OF THE SYSTEMS VIEW

Three overlapping philosophies make up the paradigmatic thinking behind the systems view. They are:

- systems theory
- holism
- structuralism

Systems theory, in its broadest sense, is the interdisciplinary study of organizations with systems language and thinking. More specifically, it is a framework by which a creator of knowledge can analyse and/or describe any group of objects that work in concert to produce some result. These objects can be, for instance, the components of a single organism, any organization or society, or any electro-mechanical or informational artefact. Systems theory as a general academic area of study predominantly refers to the science of systems that resulted from von Bertalanffy (1901–1972), who in relationship with many other scholars, for instance Rapoport (1911–2007), Boulding (1910–1993), Ashby (1903–1972), Mead (1901–1978) and Churchman (1913–2004), launched the General Systems Theory (GST) in the 1950s.

As a transdisciplinary, interdisciplinary and multiperspectival domain, General Systems Theory tried to bring together principles and concepts from Ontology, Philosophy of Science, Physics, Computer Science, Biology and Engineering and, later, Geography, Sociology,

Economics and Business, among others, serving as a bridge for an interdisciplinary dialogue between autonomous areas of study as well as within the area of systems science itself.

Systems theory was based on two fundamental ideas. First, all phenomena can be regarded as a web of relationships among its components, that is, as a system. Second, all systems have common patterns, behaviour and properties which can be explained and/or understood to develop greater insight into the behaviour of complex phenomena and move closer toward the unity of science.

Systems theory became a nomenclature that early creators of knowledge used to describe the interdependence of relationships in organizations by defining a new way of thinking about science and scientific paradigms. A system from this frame of reference is composed of regularly interacting and interrelating groups of activities. This was different to conventional models at that time that centred on individuals, structures, departments and components separate in part from the whole, instead of recognizing the interdependence between components and groups of components that enables an organization to function. The basic idea was that the whole sometimes has properties that cannot be known from an analysis of its components in isolation.

General Systems Theory is seen as part of the history of science, but in business, like in several other disciplines, its influence still lingers on to some extent.

Structuralism refers to various theories across the humanities and social sciences, which share the assumption that structural (patterned) relationships can be usefully exposed and explored. More accurately it could be described as a perspective in academic disciplines in general that explores the relationships between principal elements in their fields, where these elements are built up as tangible structures, cultural structures and/or structural networks.

In the second half of the twentieth century, it grew to become one of the most popular approaches in academic fields concerned with the analysis of language, culture and society. Structuralism can be found in, among other areas, Psychology, Linguistics, Anthropology, Sociology and Literary Theory.

Structural thinking is also often seen in business. However, due to its nature of ultimately looking for better economic and human solutions, it is commonly called *structural functionalism* there.

Holism is the idea that all the properties of a given system (biological, chemical, social, economic, mental, linguistic, etc.) cannot be determined, explained or understood by the sum of its component parts alone. Instead, the system as a whole determines in an important way how the parts behave. *Reductionism* is sometimes seen as the opposite of holism. Reductionism in science holds that a complex system can be explained and understood by reduction to its fundamental parts.

In the second half of the twentieth century, holism led to systems thinking and its derivatives, like the science of chaos and complexity.

Scientific holism holds that the behaviour of a system *cannot be perfectly predicted*, no matter how much data is available. We will be back to this last point a bit later in this chapter.

The systems view could also be called the *structural* or *holistic view*. However, we prefer *systems view* as it seems to be the most established term of the three in business.

SYSTEMS EXPLANATION AND SYSTEMS UNDERSTANDING

We have, on a number of previous occasions, mentioned that the systems view can have an ambition to explain as well as to understand (one of the two ambitions might be in focus; a combination of the two is possible as well). Let us explore what this means by first looking at Figure 5.1.

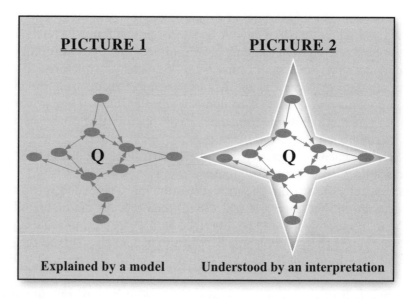

Figure 5.1   Is Q a Star?

Picture 1 in Figure 5.1 is a *model*. The idea is here to depict the reality as it is, in fact, in this case in a *systems model*. A good model is supposed to include aspects of the factive reality which are of importance, say, to *explain* the centre Q of the system, for instance its behaviour, etc.

Picture 2 in Figure 5.1 is an *interpretation*. Apart from depicting reality as it is, something else is added. A common way to do this is to bring a *metaphor* into the picture. A metaphor, in the systems view, is invented by the creator of knowledge and therefore not, strictly speaking, part of the reality of the study area per se. Such a metaphor is placed on the systems model in order to give further insight into what is going on, that is, to *understand*, and to do this by inspiring and generating some new questions, which are intended to guide the creator of knowledge in his/her further endeavor into the study area. So, the metaphor of a star in picture 2 may, for instance, lead to the following questions:

- Is there really a star (recall Chapter 2, and compare with Figure 2.4)?
- Is Q really the centre of the star and what does it mean to be a centre?
- Have all the tips of the star been identified? Have any tips been missed?
- Are the tips of the star equally strong or which is the balance of power between them?

There are other ways to try to *understand* real systems, for instance by concepts or models added by the creator of knowledge, which do not have the *symbolic* aspects of a proper metaphor (the star in the example above is a symbol, that is, something is seen *as if* it were a star, which it is not in reality). Also, metaphors are used in the actors view as well, but then they are a result of a procreative effort by the creator of knowledge (see Chapter 6).

EXAMPLES OF CLASSIC SYSTEMS MODELS

Let us look at some models and interpretations that have been presented in business during the last few decades. The illustrations are from organizations and organizing in business in general without going into functional areas like marketing, finance, manufacturing, service or human resource management, where in all cases a large number of models and interpretations have been suggested with a systems view over the years.

Let us start with some examples of models and, then, in the next section look at some examples of interpretations using metaphors. There are many classic systems models, some of which are based on concepts and ideas that are still in use:

- March & Simon (1958): organizations are *decision-making and problem-solving mechanisms*.
- Burns & Stalker (1961): different kinds of environment require different organizational structures; the faster moving and the more unsettled the environment is, the looser the organization's structure should be to succeed. Burns and Stalker refer to this as being *organic* instead of being *mechanistic* in your organization structure.
- Thorsrud & Emery (1964): organizations should best be seen as *sociotechnical systems*, that is, a mix of social and technical aspects.
- Etzioni (1966): *power structures* are important in organizations.
- Katz & Kahn (1966) derived the following *eight characteristics* that they claimed was a pattern *for all human organizations seen as open systems*:

  o   The system imports energy into itself from the environment. Energy consists of resources, raw material, competence, and so on.
  o   The system processes resources and transforms them into products that are delivered in different forms to its environment.
  o   Activities have a cyclical character and there are dependent relationships between input and output.
  o   Negative entropy in living systems means that they tend to die. This is to be counteracted by the organization through importing resources and energy from the environment.
  o   Information and negative feedback makes it possible to control the activities of the organization within certain critical limits.
  o   Balance (homeostasis) among different components of the system must exist in such a way that the relationship to the environment is maintained.

- o Differentiation, integration and coordination are necessary when handling complex relationships to the environment and trying to incorporate these variations with the system's own structure.
- o The system can reach its objectives in different ways. It can arrive at the same result through different types of structures (finality).

- Thompson (1967): organizations are governed by the *law of requisite variety* and the need for *buffering systems*.
- Buckley (1968): organizations are *complex, but socially adaptive systems*.
- Lawrence & Lorch (1969): the importance of *differentiation and integration* differ between different environments.
- From the 1970s, consultants took on systems models. One such, then, commonly used model is shown in (Figure 5.2).

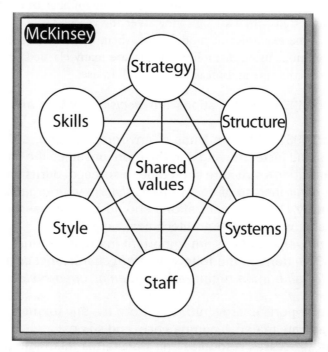

Structure: The basic organization of the company and how the units relate to each other, communication and responsibility.

Strategy: The direction and scope of the company and the plans for the allocation of the company's scarce resources.

Systems: The formal and informal processes, procedures and routines that support everyday business activity.

Skills: The company's excellent capabilities of personnel and/or of the company as a whole.

Style: The leadership of the company and the all over cultural style, and how key managers act in their business achievements.

Staff: The company's human resources and how they act and develop.

Shared values: The interconnecting center of the company's values, attitudes and beliefs. The ultimate guide for the employees.

Figure 5.2   McKinsey's 7S-model
Source: McKinsey. Reproduced with kind permission.

The idea with this model, of course, is to say that seven aspects of an organization, which could be referred to as *components*, should be identified in the company as a system. If you want a well-running firm, the seven components should fit each other, support each other and not counter and block each other. Then you will have the *synergy* effect, which is possible in systems, that is, to have a situation where the whole is more than the sum of the parts.

Some important concepts of classic systems models

We consider it to be possible to see some kind of common vocabulary or concepts in the above classical analyses of business systems as models. The words actually used in specific cases may not be the same as the following ones, but the thinking behind them and the orientations of the concepts are, in principle, along the same lines.

Variety. Variety is the more or less distinguishable components, states, events or behaviours shown from systems either as structures or as processes, components etc., that a system has the potential of showing and using at any given moment. A *law of requisite variety* of systems was formulated in systems theory a long time ago; it states that systems, in order to survive, must have at least the same amount of variety as their environment (for a *business* application of this law, see Thompson 1967).

Depiction. Depiction is the ability of a system to "reproduce" positions of the environment, the ability to allow the structure of the system to be "similar" to that of the environment.

Adaptability. Systems are adaptive. In order to be so, they require: (a) a certain degree of plasticity or irritability toward their environment, so that they have a continuous interaction with the events in the environment, considering them and if necessary reacting to them; (b) some source of mechanism for variety – to manage the problem of depiction and to introduce a new or a more detailed variety in a changing environment, if necessary; (c) a set of selective criteria or mechanism by which "the source of variety" can attract the variations in the system that reproduce the environment well and that deflect those that do not; and (d) an arrangement for keeping and/or developing successful reproductions (compare Buckley, 1968).

Existence of tensions and conflicts. Tensions and conflicts might exist in all systems. Systems that function well have the ability to use these in order: (a) to obtain information about what is happening out in the environment (what has caused the disturbance); (b) to obtain new ideas of suitable arrangements via deviations from existing ambitions; and (c) to create new, more purposeful arrangements.

Systems objectives. One outcome of the systems view is the realization that it is possible to talk about a system without having to talk of its parts. For instance, it is possible to talk about the system of a company and then state that the system has objectives. There are many suggestions for what objectives companies have and should have. The trend is definitely to combine strict financial objectives, like cash flow, profit and turnover, with softer objectives, like being socially and environmentally sustainable and the like, often in more process terms than before.

Management system. Systems, run by people, do not just develop by themselves, of course, even if from outside this may seem to be the case. They are a result of conscious efforts by what could be called "the management subsystem" of the company. By studying this subsystem, the creator of knowledge may get an explanation of how the system works as a whole.

Fit. Two or more interacting systems or subsystems that cooperate and support each other are said to fit each other. Systems that disturb or destroy each other are unfit to each other. To survive, a system should develop such that it fits the environment with all its changes and it should develop subsystems that fit each other.

Reactions to and in the environment. Open systems depend on their environment, which means that it is important for them to interact purposefully with the environment in order to derive a goal-oriented behaviour – and to behave accordingly. Researchers often talk about *three kinds* of environment and the associated purposeful reactions of the system, if the system reacts actively, which is not always the case. (There is a natural tendency among systems made up of people to resist change, even if the environment insists. This can express itself in the system neglecting external changes and continuing as before – which probably will not be a purposeful behaviour for long).

The first of the three kinds of environmental change is *variation* (*reversible* change), that is, a temporary deviation from a "normal" situation. This kind of change is often answered by the system varying its behaviour *within* existing areas of competence, provided the system has a sufficiently varied repertoire. The environment will eventually return to "normal".

The second kind of change in the environment is a *structural* change (even called *displacements*), which is an *irreversible* change, that is, a permanent departure from a previous situation. Systems theory claims that organizations (as systems) *must* adapt with new structures to such a situation, that they must create a new *fit* with the environment in order to survive and grow. This can take place in several ways (that can be combined):

- *Reproducing* the environment (see previous treatment)
- *Matching,* or a mutual adaption to another organization followed by exploiting the environment together
- *Simultaneously optimizing and consulting,* which means partly to cooperate with and support another organization in order to exploit the common environment, and partly to see the other organization as part of the exploitable environment (to cooperate and compete with the environment at the same

time; a situation which is often claimed to be a characteristic of a good functioning business cluster)
- *Domination*, which means that systems may be able to dominate their environment all the way from having a superior variety to subduing the environment
through force.

The third kind of change in the environment is also an irreversible one. It is what we might
call a *paradigmatic shift*. In this case the environment changes so radically that only a *completely* new "model of the environment" can handle the new situation.

Dynamic conservatism. So far, our discussion has been almost exclusively about adequate
behaviour of systems. Schon (1972) provides an interesting example of the opposite. His
example has proved to be very common in general. A system often displays considerable inertia as far as changing its structure is concerned (this is sometimes called "the human factor").
According to Schon, members of the system then use various means in an attempt to maintain
the system as it is:

a. They ignore facts that influence and/or change the way the environment
behaves.
b. They pursue an internal economy in which changes in one area are offset by
higher stability in another.
c. They each have an active interest in maintaining the subsystem of which they are
a part.

Later behaviours in the sequence are not considered until previous ones have failed (first (a),
then, of necessary, (b), and finally, as a last resort, (c)). Schon calls this *the strategy of
dynamic conservatism*.

This strategy may be dysfunctional – not purposeful – for the system as a whole, but is
understandable from the point of view of the individual participants.

Recipe. Every human system has members that have gradually established mental clichés
for how to manage its operations in the light of the environment in which they operate. Like
all mental clichés, they are simplified versions of what is going on, but are generally considered as successful (at least as judged by performance in the past). This is what might be called
the *recipe* for the system (Johnson & Scholes, 1999). This is a set of unquestioned beliefs and
assumptions about what to do and what not to do in order to do well. Such a set is, of course,
very much a result of the history of the system.

EXAMPLES OF CLASSIC SYSTEMS INTERPRETATION

The variety in using metaphors in the systems view as means of an interpretation in order to
get an understanding of a system is not smaller than the variety in using models, which are
used as a means of explanation – rather the opposite. Furthermore, it is fair to say that the

use of metaphors has grown among systems creators of knowledge over the years, partly due to the fact that these creators of knowledge increasingly stress *the importance of symbols* in understanding real systems and their environments. Some examples of metaphors used are, to understand organizations as *living mechanisms*, the survival of which depends on *financial capital* (Miller, 1977), or as *holograms*, or to go beneath the surface of what appears to be happening by studying them in terms of *cultures*, *conceptions* and *psyches* (Kilmann, 1984), or as *jingles* (Pfeffer, 1992), as *music* (DePree, 1992), as *factories* (Hammer & Champy, 1993), as *theatres* (Jeffcutt et al.,1996), as *jamming* (Kao, 1997), as having *souls* (Salzer-Mörling, 1998) or as *cognitive fields* (Morgan, 1998).

Let us finish this list of examples of metaphors by bringing up two examples from regional development – Figures 5.3 and 5.4.

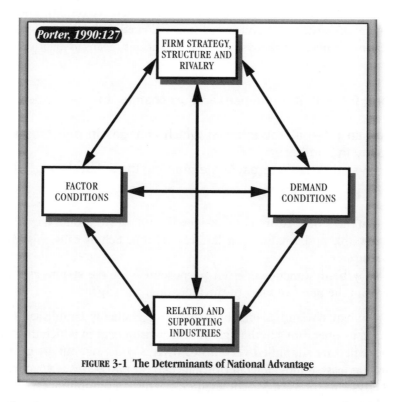

FIGURE 3-1 The Determinants of National Advantage

Figure 5.3   The Cluster Diamond

These two last metaphors tell a story of the systems they portray more effectively than a simple snapshot would. This is what we have referred to as "understanding," which, in a way, goes beyond "explaining". In the first case, you think of a "diamond," where all parts are to shine equally bright and in harmony for the system to work at its best. In the second, if you break the "circle", the system will not work as well any longer!

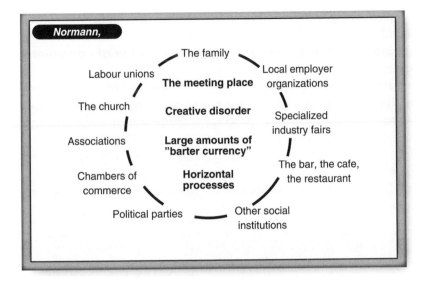

Figure 5.4   The Italian Village Business Circle

Source: Normann, 2001: 302. *Reframing Business. When the Map Changes the Landscape*. Normann, R. (2001), © John Wiley & Sons Limited.
Reproduced with permission.

SYSTEMS VIEW IN THE TWENTY-FIRST CENTURY

During our present century, the number of proposals for suitable systems models and systems interpretations has grown ever bigger. However, it is possible to see aspects of systems being stressed more often than others:

- *Processes more than structure.* In the modern life of constant change, so also in business, this is quite natural.
- *Good relations to customers.* Increasingly, customers are seen as components of the business system, not only as people to whom you try to sell your goods and services.
- *Team-building.* The fact that the company's people are its most important resource is true – and having them work in concert is often necessary and a great asset for business.
- *Temporary organizations/project organizations.* Another aspect of (or rather response to) change is that no organization should be built up to stay that way for too long any more. New temporary project organizations should be designed to face new problems, always slightly different from before.
- *Entrepreneurial organizations/organized chaos.* It is less and less possible to forecast the future. The future is increasingly built by resourceful individuals and they seem to thrive best in a kind of organized chaos.
- *The network perspective.* It is often no longer most important what is happening inside organizations, but outside and between them in a kind of mutual adaptation.

- *The innovation system.* New situations require new solutions – and this at an increasing rate.
- *The virtual system.* This is due to an increasing range of computer information technology applications.
- *Deep structures.* Increasingly, systems are analysed in order to trace so-called deep structures, that is, patterns and processes which are not possible to see directly, but which, if assumed, can provide a good understanding of what is going on.

We believe that, before as well as today, it is possible in the systems view both to explain by models as well as to understand by interpretations (in the latter case to use, for instance, metaphors) and that there are certain *guiding principles* to keep in mind by the creator of knowledge using this view (Figure 5.5).

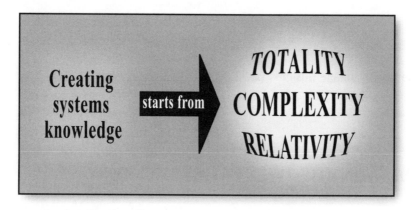

Figure 5.5   Three Principles for Creating Systems Knowledge

The *first principle* is that it is important to stress the *totality* of a complicated world in which the parts are more or less dependent on each other (totality). Nevertheless, no matter how a picture of this complexity is created, every picture becomes relatively limited. Delimitations of two types have to be made:

- *external delimitations:* It is necessary to delimit the picture of a system, if for no other reason besides a practical one, at the same time noting the systems relations to and from this environment.
- *internal delimitations:* There is a limit to how much detail can be considered in the picture of the system. It is always necessary to choose a certain *magnifying level.* (We will be back to this concept shortly.)

The second principle means that:

- Every systems model or interpretation is a limited picture of reality, real or imagined.
- Every delimitation can be questioned. There are no absolute systems delimitations, only more or less *useful* ones in relation to a certain purpose. Being so multidimensional as real systems are, there are many options to choose from (*complexity*).

The *third principle* is that every systems picture becomes partly dependent on the one who constructs it. This is an important dissociation from the analytical view. The systems creator's frame of reference is of great importance; it depends on the creator of knowledge as a person and how his/her angle and focus is delimiting the model or interpretation. To phrase it differently: there are no absolutely true or false systems pictures, only more or less comprehensive ones (to express it in more positive terms), or ones that are more or less dependent on the frame of reference of the creator of knowledge (to express it in slightly more negative terms). Churchman (1968), one of the first who introduced the systems view into social sciences, said that all systems models are "deceptive", even "untruthful", in the sense that it is not possible to present the whole truth in such models. In the system view, one can say that the American courtroom oath, to tell "the truth, the whole truth, and nothing but the truth", is a myth (*relativity*).

A "COMMON" SYSTEMS LANGUAGE

In a sense, every methodological view *is* its language. So also the systems view, in spite of large variation in its structural and holistic attempts to explain and/or understand systems. The following systems language concepts will be illustrated here:

- Systems, subsystems and components
- Open and closed systems
- Systems environments
- Real systems vs. models and interpretations of systems
- Magnifying level
- Systems relations
- Structural and processual perspectives
- Systems analysis, systems construction and systems theory

Systems, subsystems and components

The systems view in business started in the 1970s. At that time it came along as a way of looking at different academic activities as well as at industry outside the universities, in everyday language and in mass media. New titles and professions emerged, some of which are still in use, such as systems analyst, systems engineer and systems designer (which is not limited to associations with computers). And what student has not heard of concepts like control systems, information systems and reward systems? These (and similar concepts) have become a natural part of the vocabulary of business in practice as well as in business as an academic discipline.

The background to this development is quite multi-dimensional. One dimension is the development of energy and of technology, everything from feedback-controlled mechanisms like thermostats and missiles to modern communications and computers. This development, according to the systems view, has contributed to the tendency to talk, for instance, about technical systems instead of single, isolated mechanisms or machines.

Another dimension of this development is the increasing complexity of society, for instance, from an organizational point of departure. Now we talk about, say, the hospital system, the educational system, the political system, and more.

What is the meaning of the concept "system" in these various constellations? Although there are nuances in practice, in the context of creating knowledge from the systems view, there is general agreement on the following, seemingly simple, definition: a *system* is a set of *components,* which can be subsumed into *subsystems* and the *relationships* among them all (compare Figure 5.6).

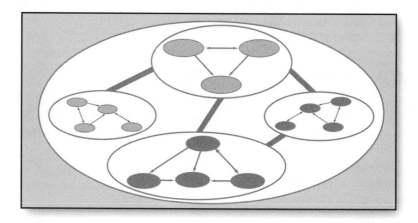

Figure 5.6   A System

Open and closed systems

The definition of *systems* demands a couple of additions:

- A systems view is not an analytical view model that is exceptionally comprehensive or that considers more aspects than simpler one-dimensional models do. It is some-thing much more fundamental than that. It is a *reorientation of thinking* compared to the analytical view. This reorientation means studying components that are in inevitable interaction with each other instead of in potential cause–effect relations.
- In order to explain or to understand an individual component it is not enough to study the component itself in isolation. A creator of knowledge must put the com-ponent in context. This reasoning can be carried to a higher level. In order to explain or to understand a system it is sometimes necessary to place it in its own context or environment; this makes it possible to distinguish between *open* and *closed* systems. Open systems are studied in the context of their environment; closed systems are not (see Figure 5.7). Business is normally not interested in closed systems.

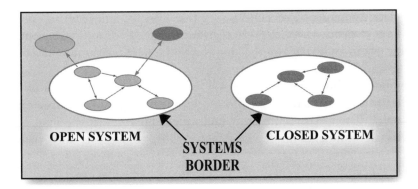

Figure 5.7   Open and Closed Systems

Systems environment

The systems environment is what lies outside the "boundary" of the system. This environment is usually seen as the *factors* that are important to the system to consider but beyond its control.

It is always so that the environment of an open system is important. A large number of theories from the systems view refer to how a system should act in a given environment. To give just one example: the more complications there are from outside, the more flexible the system needs to be from inside (compare the *law of requisite variety* mentioned earlier). Therefore, in business (using the systems view) there are a number of suggestions about how to *classify* the systems environment, for instance, shifting or not, demanding or not, friendly or not, and more.

Real systems vs. models and interpretations of systems

Just as the analytical view did, the systems view makes a distinction between factive reality (reality itself) and representations of this reality. Misunderstandings can arise in discussions if it is not made clear whether manifestations of factive reality (i.e. *real systems*) or representations of this reality (i.e. *systems models* or *systems interpretations*) are the topic.

In the systems view, creators of knowledge are very open to what a systems model or interpretation might contain. In the ideal situation, this is determined by the *use* for which the model or representation is intended and by the *magnifying level* desired. If the model or interpretation is intended only for descriptive purposes, the creator of knowledge may include a huge number of factors from reality. If, on the other hand, the model or interpretation is to be used for controlling the future of the real system, several factors in the real system might have to be omitted in order to make the model or interpretation manageable to use, not including too much detail.

To take an example: a *model* of a university as a system might contain a list of different subjects and departments, a list of available educational programmes, a map pinpointing off-campus localities related to the university, and – this is decisive for the systems model – the mutual relations among these subjects, departments, localities and so on. A model intended to show new students where to go to register for the Business department needs only a map of the city where an arrow is indicating the building in question and another arrow shows where the student is now.

One might possibly criticize the person distributing the map of the university mentioned above if it turns out to be ten years old and if the names of several streets and locations were omitted or outdated. The criticism is unjustified, however, if the map is up-to-date in the aspects that new students need, that is, informative enough to show them how to find the Business department.

Suppose a new student wants a deeper insight into what world he/she is entering by studying business at the university in question. He/she meets another student who has been studying the subject for one year already. This other student says:

> Remember that the Business department is the biggest department at this university in terms of number of students. You will feel like you are spending your student life on a lush and green hill with many dull small villages around on the university campus. You will have the impression that you are spending your life on the top and isolated from the rest of the world at the same time.

This is a systems *interpretation* and it might give an additional feeling to the new student of being prepared for something extra.

Every systems model or interpretation is just *one* among many possible *aspects* of a real system. If a creator of knowledge claims, therefore, that something takes place in a "system", it should be made clear sometimes whether this "system" is a real system, or a model or an interpretation of the same, or possibly all of it (see Box 5.1).

Box 5.1

Be or As a System?

The reader should realize that in *one* respect there are two kinds of creators of knowledge in the systems view. There are those who believe that reality in itself is systems-like and that the task of the creator of knowledge is to reproduce it or interpret it as such. On the other hand, there are those who see no reason to take a definite position for or against the way reality is ultimately constructed, but nevertheless find it useful, interesting, or both, to reproduce it or interpret it as *if* it behaved like systems.

Similarly, there are two kinds of analytical creators of knowledge reproducing reality in the form of cause–effect relations, in one case because it is assumed to be that way, in the other case because it is treated as *if* it were (in the latter case without taking a position on how reality in itself is constructed).

Distinguishing between those two kinds of creators of knowledge is of minor interest here. *From a methodological point of departure* they behave in the same way.

Magnifying level

Sometimes there is a reference to *the relativity principle* in the systems view: every component in a system is a potential system of its own. Every system is a potential component in a larger system. This smaller system is, as mentioned above, called a *subsystem*. The larger system, correspondingly, is a *supersystem*.

This makes it possible to talk about various *magnifying levels* for systems. A low magnifying level means that a model or an interpretation contains a number of details. Conversely, a model or interpretation with a high magnifying level would have few details (compare with a magnifying glass: the higher level, the fewer details, and vice versa; see Figure 5.8).

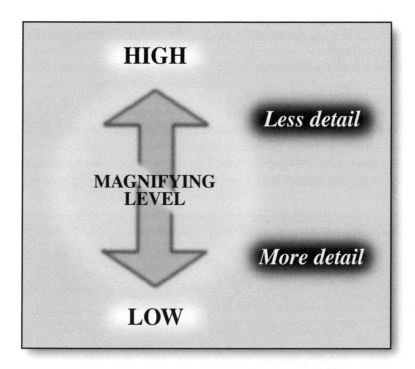

Figure 5.8   Magnifying Levels of Models and Interpretations

Systems relations

What do relationships in a system actually consist of? The concept of "relation" could be seen as having a concrete or an abstract content (or a combination). We might, for instance, describe relations among different stages in a manufacturing process as the flow of material passing between workstations or as a flow of information progressing among different decision makers at these different stages. This gives the concept of relation a *concrete* meaning, which can be studied in Figure 5.9, where every relation in the figure is an expression of something concrete.

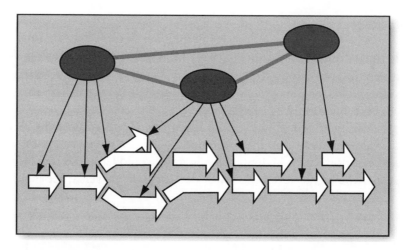

Figure 5.9   Concrete Systems Relations

In another system, for instance, a creator of knowledge might want to *explain* how a group's unity functions. It would be possible to talk about relations among the members of the group, for instance, in terms of their attitudes toward each other, of their family connections, of similar opinions about the value of unity, or of relations between the system and its environment as various threats that forge the workers into a group (see Figure 5.10).

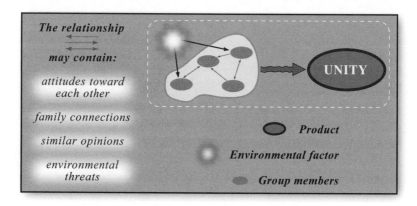

Figure 5.10   Systems Relations in How a Group's Unity Functions

Note the differences in the content of relations in the systems view and the analytical view. In the latter case, relations do not *contain* anything. They purely *point out* which causes are connected with which effects (see Figure 4.1).

It is possible, in principle, to illustrate models (or interpretations) in the systems view as diagrams of the kind we can see in Figure 4.1, that is, where the components contain variables, in this systems case *producers* and *products* (terms which we, as mentioned before, use in the systems view to point out the differences from causes–effects). However, such illustrations become much more complicated than they are in the analytical view and not very illustrative. It is such, for instance, that what is a *producer* in one model or interpretation can easily be a *product* in another – and vice versa. To give one example: in network analysis the following variables can be used to characterize a network (a kind of systems view model) (Shaw & Conway, 2000):

Morphological dimensions

- Anchorage
- Reachability
- Density
- Range

Interactional dimensions

- Content
- Intensity
- Frequency
- Durability
- Direction

However, these variables might as easily be seen as reasons for a specific network behaviour (*producers*) as the results of such behaviour (*products*).

Due to the complexity of producer–product relations, relations which are far from so direct as the cause–effect relations are regarded in the analytical view, we can formulate two more principles for the systems view apart from those three we have already examined (in the section, "Systems view in the twenty-first century"). The *fourth* one is:

The principle of mutuality. (Producers and products can easily change place.)

We can also add a *fifth* principle to our systems view, based on what was said when we talked about holism at the beginning of this chapter:

The principle of unpredictability. (Due to the way a system is constructed and because it is in constant interaction with its environment, there is *a definite limit to* predicting its future.)

Structural and processual perspectives

To describe a real system, creators of knowledge would have to indicate the positions of different components and relations at a given time. By indicating the position of all components and relations in the system and considering all characteristics of the system, the creator of knowledge indicates a *systems state* (remember that we refer here to a *model or interpretation* and not the real thing when we talk about "systems". To indicate the position of all the components and relations in a system *in reality* would be theoretically and practically impossible). The description of the real system should be complete enough for the creator of knowledge to feel that he/she has explained or understood the real system in relevant aspects. Stressing the different *characteristics* of components and relations in a model or the interpretations of real systems, is traditionally called a *structural perspective*.

The description of real systems may alternatively be intended to indicate the *flow* of different components and relations over time. This has been called a *processual perspective*. It is, of course, possible, in one and the same study, to describe real systems in structural as well as in processual terms, as shown in Table 5.1. In traditional terms we can say that a structural description gives a static picture, whereas a processual description gives a dynamic picture.

Table 5.1   Structural and Processual Perspectives (Examples)

Structural perspective of System A

- The system is three years old.

- The system's objective is to represent its members.

- The system is constructed in a relatively simple way.

- One of the rules of the system prescribes that the leadership consists of M., B. and K.

Processual perspective of System A

- The system added a new member during the past year.

- The system has a continuous interchange with System B.

- The system issues a newspaper three times a year.

- The system is stable.

Many creators of knowledge are of the opinion that it is sometimes difficult to differentiate between structures and processes in real systems. For instance, let us look at the three last examples of systems aspects from the list in the beginning of the section "Systems view in the twenty-first century" earlier in this chapter. When we talk about *innovations systems*, it is, almost by definition, something that is constantly changing *in content as well as in form* (otherwise it would not be very innovative). The word "innovation" in English can even be read as a *creative process* or as a *new result* (which might be a new structure). When we refer to a *virtual system*, this might be a large number of computers that are linked up with each other. It might be impossible in practise to provide a model of this build-up (its *structure*). But is this of interest to anybody? Is it not more interesting to get an understanding of what goes on in this system, its *process*? And is the distinction between structure and process useful here, really? Let us consider a third example, that is, *deep structures*. How can we call something a *structure* when it cannot be seen but only be *assumed* that it exists? Is it not rather a behavioural pattern we are talking about here (which *can* be seen)?

Such "indistinct" circumstances as those just mentioned are not uncommon in the systems view. It can be seen as a result of the *pragmatism* so characteristic of the systems view (see Box 5.2).

Box 5.2

Pragmatism

Languages can be characterized as sign processes. Those signs can be analysed in three "dimensions" or aspects of how they function: in relation to other signs (*syntax*); in relation to what they represent (*semantics*); and in relation to their users (*pragmatics*).

Pragmatism also stands for the epistemological orientation that claims that the value of knowledge is equal to its practical use. This is what we normally associate with the systems view. "The truth" of a statement of a systems description becomes equal to its consequences. See also "Validation techniques" in Chapter 7.

The realities that the business theorist is interested in never stand still in their concrete forms of expression. One could, therefore (and maybe rightly so), ask oneself whether the models and interpretations intended to describe this reality should not be dynamic as well. There are authors who claim that the interesting structures of real systems in social contexts are the *stable behaviours* that can be distinguished over time. It is therefore possible to differentiate between *dynamic* and *static* structures. In such a case, the statement "The system issues a newspaper three times a year", for instance, would indicate a dynamic structure and "The system's objective is to represent its members" would indicate a static structure. This would give a classification of:

- *static structures* (fixed, stable characteristics)
- *dynamic structures* (regular processes)
- *non-regular processes* (which may even lead to a change of structure)

Non-regular processes are the aspects (characteristics and behaviours) of the system that are not stable. It is a question of one-time phenomena of various kinds. They do not necessarily have to be without interest; on the contrary, they may have a decisive influence on the course of the system (they could be *critical events*). Such singular phenomena may even lead to the system changing its structure (static and/or dynamic).

We want to introduce the following distinction concerning systems perspectives:

- *Structural* perspectives focus on stable and dynamic structures and on non-regular processes that mean (or can mean) a change of structure.
- *Processual* perspectives focus on dynamic structures and non-regular processes.

There are studies carried out according to the systems view in which these perspectives are combined so that in some stages the creator of knowledge has a structural perspective and in others a processual perspective.

Systems analysis, systems construction and systems theory

A creator of knowledge working according to the systems view may have several *orientations*. These orientations, systems analysis, systems construction and systems theory, do not exclude one another.

The knowledge orientations of the view

Systems analysis means to depict a real system in a systems model or interpretation without changing the real system, and to make clear to oneself the internal and external factors influencing this system. In a way, this is as much a question of *synthesis* as of analysis. In other words, systems analysis has both a descriptive and an explanatory or understanding purpose. We may say that it is partly a question of synthesis because systems analysis also includes the study of the totality of the real system, including its relations to the environment. Recall that in the analytical view totality did not have its *own* meaning as an object of study; there the situation is broken up into its elements and *only* the relations among those elements are studied. If the totality is discussed in the analytical view, it simply means the sum of the individual elements. In systems terminology we could call this a closed system without synergy – that is, no system at all.

Systems construction means to develop a new system, that is, a systems model that the creator of knowledge may hope to be able to construct in reality (a new combination in factive reality). The need for a new real system may emerge when, while analysing a real system, the creator of knowledge finds that it does not function very well. The creator of knowledge then might try to construct a new real system (on paper and possibly in reality as well).

When talking about *systems theory*, either of two things may be referred to (usually the latter):

- General systems theories. These are inspired by the General Systems Theory mentioned earlier in this chapter, that is, they are theories of systems in general – alternatively, theories of different classes of systems – that do not allude to any specific *real* systems. Often the *structure* in such general systems theories is seen as *the essential producer* to bring about certain (hopefully purposeful and functional) products. General systems theories are therefore sometimes said to be *homologically* constructed, that is, based on similarities in structure.
- Specific systems theories. These theories are less general and refer to specific types of real systems or even a single real system. These theories often classify systems into different categories, but structure might not be the decisive producer anymore. These categories may instead be, for instance, types of technology, age, type of environment, size, complexity, strength of culture and many more. The ambition is to find similarities *within* these categories.

THREE ILLUSTRATIVE STUDIES

Let us look at three real studies based on the systems view to illustrate how this language may be expressed in practice. We will see that these three studies have some thinking in common, even if they were done in three very different fields.

The three studies are:

1. The success of Silicon Valley (Saxenian, 1996)
2. The Balinese culture (Geertz, 1973)
3. Female entrepreneurship (Ahl, 2007)

The success of Silicon Valley

Saxenian's study is an attempt to explain why the region of Silicon Valley in the United States has been such an economic success when the region of Route 128 has not.

Silicon Valley has been created by people brought together from different firms and industries, from public and private sectors, and from financial, educational and training institutions. An industrial community has been created where traditional boundaries between employers and employees and between corporate functions within firms have been eliminated. Instead, interdependent project teams linked by intense, informal communications mirroring the region's industrial structure have been growing in large numbers.

Individuals have also moved from firm to firm, both within and between industrial sectors, from established firms to start-ups, and vice versa. At the same time, an expanding network of specialist suppliers and service providers has facilitated start-ups.

This has resulted in a complex, highly social process rooted in an industrial community. Silicon Valley's producers are embedded in, and inseparable from, these social and technical networks. As a result, the region's engineers have developed stronger commitment to one another and to advancing technology than to individual companies or industries. Informal conversations have been, and still are, pervasive and serve as an important source of up-to-date information about every issue that concerns business and technology in the region. They also function as efficient job search networks. This has been essential in Silicon Valley, where engineers move so frequently between firms. Mobility is not only socially acceptable, it has become the norm. The preferred career option in the region has traditionally been to join a small company or a start-up.

The Silicon Valley culture has encouraged risk and accepted failure. Less formal social relationships and collaborative traditions have developed that support experimentation. The geographic proximity of the firms in Silicon Valley has facilitated occupational mobility. Moving from job to job in that region has not been too much of a disruption from a personal, social and professional perspective. However, unlike Silicon Valley, the Route 128 region is so expansive that sometimes helicopters are used to link its widely dispersed facilities.

Furthermore, in Route 128, entrepreneurs inherited and reproduced an industrial order based on independent firms which, by and large, kept to themselves. The region is dominated by a small number of relatively integrated corporations. Secrecy and corporate loyalty govern relations between them and their customers, suppliers and competitors, reinforcing a culture that encourages stability and self-reliance. This has been valued over experimentation and risk-taking in the Route 128 region.

Managers and executives in Route 128 firms are typically in their fifties and sixties while in Silicon Valley, by contrast, they are often in their twenties and thirties.

The blurring of social and professional identities and the practices of open exchange of information that distinguished Silicon Valley never developed on Route 128.

Illustrated in our systems language, we can say about Silicon Valley that *processes are more important than structures*, that *team-building* across the functions of firms and between firms have been decisive, that many of these teams are *temporary*, *entrepreneurial*, of a *network* type and devoted to *innovation*.

The system is very *open*; its *environment* is that part of the rest of the world operating in similar industries. This environment is certainly very shifting, complex and demanding.

The study is made at a *magnifying level* where individual firms are of minor importance and *the relations* between various *components* contain the latest necessary information to take the road to the commercialization of new technological ideas.

The Balinese culture

Geertz believes that human thought is social in its origin, social in its function, social in its forms and social in its applications. He spent quite some time in Bali to prove his point, examining how the cultural apparatus of that place make its people refine, perceive and react to each other.

In Bali, there are six sorts of labels which one person can apply to another person in order to identify him/her as a unique individual. These are: (1) personal names; (2) birth order names; (3) kinship terms; (4) teknonyms; (5) status titles; and (6) public titles. These labels are, in most cases, used simultaneously. Geertz (1973) refers to all this as "symbolic orders of person-definition".

Personal names. The symbolic order defined by personal names is the simplest to describe for a foreigner, because it is in formal terms the least complex and in social terms the least important. All Balinese have personal names, but they rarely use them to refer to themselves or others. In general, personal names are rarely heard and they play very little public role.

Birth order names. The most elementary, standardized label bestowed upon a child, when born, is whether it is the first, second, third, fourth, etc., member of the sibling set. These birth order names are the most frequently used terms of both address and reference for children and young men and women who have not yet produced offsprings in Bali. They can be used on their own or supplemented by the personal name, especially when no other way is convenient to get across which is meant.

Kinship terms. Formally, Balinese kinship terminology is quite simple. An individual classi-fies his/her relatives primarily according to the generation they occupy with respect to their own, like siblings, half-siblings, cousins, uncles and aunts. The interesting fact about Bali, however, is that these terms are used very infrequently. With rare exceptions, one does not actually call one's father (or uncle) "father", one's child (or nephew/niece) "child", one's brother (or cousin) "brother", and so on. Kinship terms in Bali appear in public discourse only in response to some question or event, where the existence of the kin tie is felt to be a relevant piece of information.

In short, the Balinese kinship terminology defines individuals in a cultural map where certain persons can be located and certain others, not features of the landscape, cannot.

Teknonyms. If personal names are treated almost as secrets, birth order names are used only with children and not yet parents and kinship terms are invoked at best sporadically, how, then, do most Balinese address and refer to each other? For the great mass, according to Geertz, it is by teknonyms. This means, in Bali, that as soon as a couple's first child ("X") is named, they start to be referred to as "Father-of-X" and "Mother-of-X". This is what they will be called (and will call themselves) until their first grandchild ("Y") is born, at which time they will begin to be addressed and referred to as "Grandfather-of-Y" and "Grandmother-of-Y". A similar transition may occur if they live to see their first great-grandchild.

This means that what identifies a Balinese is reproductive continuity, his/her ability to perpetuate him/herself. This has very great economic, political and spiritual consequences in the country.

Status titles. Almost everyone in Bali bears one or another title placing that person in an all-Bali status ladder. However, status in Bali, or at least that sort determined by titles, is a personal characteristic and independent of any social structural factors. It has, of course, important practical consequences and influences a wide variety of arrangements, from kinship groups to business organizations and governmental institutions. From a person's title you know, for instance, what demeanour you ought to display toward that person.

The human inequality embodied in status titles is neither moral, nor economic, nor political – it is religious.

Public titles. Balinese have a high sense of responsibility and everybody's duty as part of the public as a corporate body is charged by the special status that public titles express. At the same time, Balinese look at the public sector of society as a number of self-sufficient and self-contained realms, including the hamlet as a corporate political community, the local temple as a religious body, the irrigation society as an agricultural body, and, above these, the structures of regional government and worship, centring on the nobility and the high priesthood.

It is easy to understand that all this has great consequences for business life in Bali. Illustrated in our systems language, we can say that the Balinese culture is a *closed* and rigid system, where *structure is much more important than processes* and which has been built up by generations. One might even say that this system is closed and has no environment of interest to identify in order to understand the system.

The content of its *components* differ with social situation and role, but its *relations* always include religious aspects. The *magnifying level* to understand the Balinese culture should include all its members but their labels differ with social occasions. The details at individual or family level are of less importance for such an understanding.

Female entrepreneurship

Ahl's (2007) study is about women's entrepreneurship. She undertook a discourse analysis of a large number of research articles on women's entrepreneurship published from 1982 to 2000 in order to find out how they regarded the female entrepreneur. The material was analysed using a framework by Foucault.

In general she found that a female entrepreneur was consistently positioned as inferior to her male counterpart, irrespective of which facet of entrepreneurship was studied.

Ahl asserted that feminist theories are examples of how different versions of knowledge imply different sorts of social order. Feminism is defined as the recognition of women's subordination, and the desire to do something about it.

The definition of discourse in the Ahl study is that it:

- is a group of claims, ideas and terminologies that are historically and socially specific
- is a set of metaphors, representations, images, stories and statements that in some way presents a version of reality
- has some kind of effects, including power implications.

Some of Foucault's procedures and principles as seen by Ahl and used in her study were:

1. You do not speak about everything, what is of most interest to a researcher here is the ideas and assumptions that are taken for granted about women, society, entrepreneurship, and so on, that are reflected in the reviewed articles.
2. What is true and what is false is historically contingent and dependent on institutional support.
3. Discourses are repeated and reproduced; founding fathers and the foundational texts on entrepreneurship can therefore not be neglected.
4. Writing and publishing practices are part of shaping and delimiting the discourse.
5. The disciplines, in this case entrepreneurship, carry out a restricting function and provide regulations for research methods.
6. There are rules and rituals pertaining to who is allowed to speak (and write) on the topic of women's entrepreneurship in the research community.
7. The principle of discontinuity says not to forget that there is no grand narrative.

Ahl concluded that the entrepreneur was described in words such as bold, rational, calculative, firm, strong willed, achievement oriented and detached and that these words are male gendered. The words describing masculinity and entrepreneur are very similar. The femininity words are mostly their direct opposites. The most common research question was related to differences between male and female entrepreneurship in areas like personal background and firm characteristics, attitudes to entrepreneurship and intentions to start, psychology, access to capital, and performance but, contrary to expectations, few such differences were found. Within-group variation was typically larger than between-group variation. The arguments for studying female entrepreneurship in the reviewed articles were largely the same as for studying male entrepreneurship – to see how it contributes to employment and economic growth. It turned out, however, that the women's businesses in comparison with that of men were, on average, a little smaller, grew a little slower and were somewhat less profitable. This was seen as a problem and a further reason for investigation.

Illustrated in our systems language, we can say that the above study is an attempt to find a *deep structure* an implicit arrangement between entrepreneurship scholars that contained opinions of female entrepreneurship. This structure seems quite *closed*, and the different *components* of it, like claims, terminology, models and findings, seem to support each other in their version of reality. Discourse *processes* in the system are consequently repeating and reproducing each other in their content as far as the topic of women's entrepreneurship is concerned. They are so repetitive that they even might be seen as a *structure* which is constantly confirming itself. Another *magnifying level* than the usual one has to be taken in order to break the existing order.

THE RELATION OF THE SYSTEMS VIEW TO ITS PARADIGM

Let us, just like we did in the case of the analytical view, summarize what the systems view stands for in terms of:

1. Conception of reality
2. Conception of science
3. Scientific ideals
4. Ethical/aesthetical aspects.

Conception of reality, or, What Does Business Reality Actually Look Like? We can look at reality as either independent from, or dependent on, us as theorists and/or creators of knowledge. In the first case, we assume that it *is* systemically constructed; in the second case, we treat it *as if* that were the case. From a methodological point of departure the two cases are the same. In both situations we accept that reality contains objective as well as subjective facts. The subjective facts, however, can be treated as objective according to the systems view conception of reality and be described as systemic.

Conception of science, or, How Do We Look at Business as a Science? Business-as-a-science is a representation of business reality, either in models or in interpretations. The terminology developed within the framework of the systems view (which is plentiful by now) is related to various systems pictures. These pictures cannot be treated in terms of "other things being equal", and they are mainly assessed in relation to their users and to the consequences they have when explaining, understanding and adding value to the purposefulness of different systems, and/or parts of these, to the members of corresponding real systems (*pragmatics*).

Scientific ideals, or, *What Do We Want From Business as a Science?* Eventually, Business is to provide better and better pictures of systems in business reality. This takes place as formulated producer–product relations. These relationships are strengthened as we,

- reach better explanations and understandings of how various types of systems behave under different internal and external circumstances. The types that a creator of knowledge is studying change as we reach ever better systems knowledge.
- develop new concepts that better cover what happens in the systems world.

Ethical and aesthetical aspects, or, *What Can and Should Business Creators Do, and What Attitude Should They Take Toward What Is Done?* Systems creators of knowledge believe that the ethical and aesthetical consequences of the knowledge we gain through the systems view are increasingly emphasized as we consider the relationships between companies and their surroundings in the form of employees, consumers, environment, technology and energy. This is in keeping with the belief in increasingly interdependent relationships in the world, not only among different parts of the company but also between the company and its surroundings. Aesthetically, the systems view wants to provide holistic descriptions which, as illustratively and knowledge-creatively as possible, provide overviews and facilitate practical action at the same time as these descriptions can inspire other researchers/consultants/investigators as analogies.

EXAMPLES OF FORMULATION OF THEORETICAL RESULTS

Let us show a few examples of how theoretical results are formulated in the systems view. Again (as for the analytical view), we want to point out that these results are presented only to offer a perception of *the type* of theoretical results that emerge from using the systems view, *how they are usually formulated* and *at what level of generality* they can be kept. The examples are therefore not meant to be either important or comprehensive.

General systems theories tend to be both abstract and general, as shown by the examples that follow:

- Different environments give different systems. How well they succeed depends on their structure.
- The systems structure is conditioned by history and can become an obstacle to future development.
- Demand for variety in a system is conditioned by the variety in the environment.
- If open systems are not provided with input from the environment, they will die.

- Mechanistic systems structures tend to prevent entrepreneurship while organic structures seem to facilitate it.
- What is the best system should most often be judged by what it leads to for its environment.

As we have seen quite a few examples of in this chapter, modern systems theories are usually of a more specific type.

The systems view is, in a sense, broad as well as having a focus and an orientation. It has spread into a number of different applications in business, in fact, too many to summarize or classify in any meaningful way. Therefore, in this chapter, we have tried to illustrate some of these applications by using those which we see as more typical than others. In doing so, we have made a distinction between explaining reality in (representative) models and understanding reality in (representative) interpretations. However, we believe that there is a central nucleus in the systems view. All its applications emanate from the same philosophical roots, there is a reasonably common systems language and the relation of the systems view to its paradigm is quite clear. This has also been presented in this chapter.

POINTS OF REFLECTION

1. The systems view talks about being *holistic* and *structural* in it orientation. Explain what this means to your fellow students.
2. Why is there an *unlimited* number of possible *pictures* of a *real* system?
3. In the chapter you could read about both the *understand/interpret* and *explain/ models*. These are two very important concepts in the systems view, concepts which you are not allowed to use among the set of concepts in the next point of reflection, but what do these two conceptual constellations mean?
4. When interviewed for a position you are asked to come up with six important *systems concepts* and describe what they stand for. Which ones would you choose? And what would your descriptions look like?
5. Why is there, in principle, a definite *limit to perfectly predict* the future course of action of a system?
6. Think about and describe a cause/effect relation consisting of a *main cause* and at least two *contributing causes*. Repeat the description in finality terms using *producers* and *products*. Differences?

(Continued)

(Continued)

7. Come up with a *metaphor* for the place where you work or study or for any situation with which you are very familiar. What does this metaphor say over and above a description based only on a model of this situation, where the model is based only on an attempt to depict as truly as possible what is going on?

8. Suppose you characterize one business firm in terms of "summer" and another one in terms of "winter". What do these *metaphors* tell you about the firms in more practical terms?

9. What would your story look like if somebody asked you to present the relation of the systems view to its *paradigm?*

10. In the chapter we talk about *five principles*. What are they? What do the principles say to a person who wants to use the systems view?

11. In Chapter 2 you can find a heading "The importance of the perspective". If you reflect on the essence of that heading and relate this to the perspectives of *Structural* and *Processual* in this chapter, how could you describe that reflection in terms of its *characteristics* (structure) and/or in terms of its *flow* (process)?

RECOMMENDED FURTHER READING

See the end of the Appendix and visit the website below.

Become a worldwide partner as a *knowledge creator* in the development of *Methodology for Creating Business Knowledge* by visiting the website: **www.knowledge-creator.com**. Here you can contribute by asking your own questions and you will also find answers to the most frequently asked questions. The website has been developed alongside this third edition of the book and the questions posted there will be used to provide input for future editions.

6 THE ACTORS VIEW

This chapter will present the actors view in detail. Fundamental concepts such as meaning, intentionality, dialogue and dialectics on which the view is based will be provided. The relation of the actors view to its paradigm and some typical results from this view will also be provided.

AN UNCERTAINTY PRINCIPLE IN SOCIAL SCIENCES

In modern Physics there is, among other things, talk about an *uncertainty*, which means that physical *phenomena* in micro-cosmos are not only *particles* but also *waves*. This aspect means the particles do *not* have any definite *demarcation*. The uncertainty, then, says that it is certainly possible to close the *waves* in between two obstacles in order to better *determine* the position of a *particle*. But *the closing in* is then decreasing the wavelength, at the same time as the frequency is increasing. The outcome is that what was supposed to provide a more precise measurement in reality is changing the *energy* of the particle.

The actors view might, in parity with this, claim that man too should be seen both as a particle (*being*) and a wave (*becoming*) with indefinite demarcation (*freedom*). What will then happen if we as creators of knowledge are closing her in – the authentic human being – between some items in a questionnaire in order to *quantitatively determine* the "position" of isolated *characteristics* of her? What type of *knowledge* will be the result of such a *closing-in*, asks the actors view? Is not the "energy" of this "particle" also changed by the very moment of measuring?

Like the uncertainty principle that Heisenberg brought into modern physics (*the Heisenberg uncertainty principle*), Arbnor asserts (2004) that it is possible to formulate an uncertainty principle even in the social science area by starting from the ultimate presumptions of the actors view (see Figure 6.1 on next page):

From this principle it follows that every kind of statistical measurement as *explanation* of human aspects/behaviour in social contexts (micro-cosmoses) leads to a gradual decreased *understanding* of ourselves as *authentic* totalities. And the opposite: the better we *understand* ourselves as authentic totalities, the more uncertain the quantitative aspects become – they can take any expressions, whenever, wherever. Because, as men we are *free* to act as *unique* subjects! Unlike phenomena in nature we also have the unique ability to think critically of what we are exposed to as well as uncritically be manipulated by it. We are creatures *creating meaning* one way or

> *The more precisely you determine isolated characteristics of a human being and her activities, quantitatively and statistically, the less you understand of her as a whole. And the better you understand her as a whole, the more uncertain the quantitative/ statistic aspects become.*

Figure 6.1   The Arbnor Uncertainty Principle
Source: Arbnor, 2004: 362

another. If we lose the *qualitative* feeling of totality and the *meaningful* context – our ability to create ourselves, as free actors in our own micro-cosmos – then we lose some of what is human, according to the presumptions of the philosophy of life according to the actors view.

As creators of knowledge in the actors view we must therefore never stand outside in order to observe others as *objects*, because in such a case the others and their situation would appear as *strange*. Appearing as strange is a function of not participating ourselves. And if we do not participate as actors creating knowledge, that which appears as strange also looks like something *determined* (= conditioned by external factors and not by human free will). Because, if we participate ourselves, we will notice, as creators of knowledge, that things are moving by our own choice and actions and by others. Then, we will not be *strangers* to the dynamic flows of the present in human micro-cosmoses. (This problem of free will and determinism is one of the most disputed questions in the history of philosophy.)

In the "closing in/locking" perspective of statistics/questionnaires most characteristics may, according to the actors view, appear as *determined* and even *similar on the surface*. And according to the uncertainty principle above we will, by this *explaining* knowledge, *understand* human situations as *free dynamic totalities* increasingly poorly! We develop and measure us, so to say, into "unfreedom" in the sign of *self-reference*. The *explanatory knowledge* here becomes, according to the actors view, a kind of *constructivistic vicious circle of unfreedom*.

Using the presumptions of the actors view as a basis, researchers, investigators, consultants and business leaders are instead building their activities on developing and clarifying others as creative subjects (actors) in order to make themselves free. If we, as creators of knowledge, are aiming for human development and freedom, then the purpose of "making ourselves free" also becomes a prerequisite for this ideal. If we are better at realizing our own freedom, we also have better possibilities to realize this life value first in the study area and then also in society at large through that *self-reference* which always exists between scientific results and the development of society according to the actors view.

The actors oriented creator of knowledge is therefore, in all different ways, searching for the *inner quality* of those human micro-cosmoses he/she is meeting. And also, at the same time, he/she tries to re-create this *quality* in him/herself in order to be able to *understand* and to transfer these experiences through "the *emancipatory interactive action*" (see Table 3.1).

SOME DENOTATIONS OF CONCEPTUAL MEANING

The section title mentions denotation of conceptual meaning (vs. providing definitions) because of the ultimate presumptions the actors view is based on, for example, that concepts within social reality are ambiguous and continuously reinterpreted.

Concepts as meaning

As stated earlier, the actors view postulates that reality's ambiguity and changeability are a result of (among other things) the creator of knowledge's interaction with, and search for, *dialectic* connections (knowledge that is dependent on the observer/actors). The actors view claims that the core of knowledge consists of understanding/meaning for the subjects; ambiguity is therefore as desired as it is essential to the creation of knowledge. The actors view talks for that reason about denotations whereas the other two views talk about definitions. A *denotation of conceptual meaning* refers here to the general understanding, meaning and significance that we, the authors, associate with the concept, while a specific meaning is given by the context in which it appears.

Intentionality

The concept of intentionality is an essential part of the basic assumptions of the actors view. It constitutes the foundation on which actors' egological spheres (the internal logic of actors that constitute their subjective conceptual meaning) and finite provinces of meaning are postulated (see Chapter 3); that is, it describes how egological spheres and finite provinces of meaning can exist.

Intentionality refers to the structure that gives a *purpose* to experience. Intentionality is not the same as intentions; it is the dimension *behind* intentions. It is through intentionality that we bridge the gap between *subjects* and *objects*. The concept of intentionality is not used by traditional *empirical* researchers because it does away with part of their foundation. In strictly empirical thinking, people are seen as "passive" experiencers and interpreters of objects in external reality. That which is contained in intentionality, on the other hand, makes people active creators of the objects in their environment. May (1969) expresses it this way: "What really happens is that objects themselves conform to our ways of understanding. A good example of this is mathematics. These are constructs in our minds; but nature conforms 'answers,' to them" (1969: 226). May continues by quoting Russell, "Physics is mathematical not because we know so much about the physical world, but because we know so little; it is only its mathematical properties that we can discover" (1969: 226).

The concept of intentionality overturns traditional empirical thought, which states: we are attracted by surrounding objects through our senses, and our senses make it possible to perceive them (the objects). On the other hand, intentionality asserts that via our purposeful consciousness, we reach out by using our senses and find or mould objects according to our purposes. This ability to create our environment is called *intentionality*.

Consider how one and the same house can alter its look depending on the intentionality present. Suppose we work with the following alternative starting points for our intentionality: (a) We are to conclude a "quick deal", that is, buy and then sell the house for a good profit; (b) we have been invited to spend a weekend with friends in the house. We will certainly experience the house completely differently in the two cases. This means that the house as an *object* will be molded according to the intentionality we have as a starting point for our sense impressions. The common saying that "seeing is believing" is consequently, according to the actors view, highly relevant to everyone.

Intentionality connects us with the environment and makes us *act* as *creative humans* instead of passive receivers (the result of the strict empirical idea). The degree of vitality and engagement among people is to be found in intentionality. It also directs our attention as creators of knowledge toward trying to understand the roots of intentionality in order to make the actors' egological sphere and finite provinces of meaning intelligible.

Social science knowledge

According to the concept of intentionality, social science knowledge also becomes socially constructed with a self-reference to the society at large. The creator of knowledge should, according to the actors view, therefore consciously use this reference and construction in an *open, ethical* and *emancipating* way. This means, among other things, to work for a form of knowledge that emancipates one's own thought as well as others and one's own power, urge, passion and commitment as well as others. The conception of knowledge of the actors view is therefore *procreative* with a clearly expressed ambition to *be present* and *to act* – not to stand outside as an observer.

The actors view claims that an action-oriented social research is needed which aims at reaching deepened understanding as well as extended freedom in society, at the same time as research is providing a knowledge which is extending understanding of the complexity of the human society. And what is *complex* can *not*, according to the actors view, be divided into simple relations of causes and effects – in the spirit of *determinism* – because what is humanly complex will then be erased – that which we intended to understand! Complexity has the peculiarity that it can only be clarified through descriptions, which are rich in aspects and which show depth and composition and *show* the *unique* human/the actor behind and in this composition. Similarly, as Sartre once formulated his criticism of the *labels* of generality for human activity, "Franz Kafka is an intellectual-bourgeois, but every intellectual-bourgeois is not a Franz Kafka."

The knowledge interest of the actors view is definitely innovative, oriented towards understanding, emancipation and action, unlike an *explaining*, deterministic search for generality of a cause–effect type of knowledge. As creators of knowledge we are always co-actors in a constant flow of the development of reality. And here the issue is, according to the actors view, that we are like "*artists*" who procreate and shape this interactivity and do not believe that it is possible to stand outside like observers and register something which afterwards is reconstructed in general models – statements which might not make one single man feel freer or more alive.

What happens, says the actors view, if we more generally were to say yes to actors oriented premises for what we call social science knowledge? And the actors view answers, according to Arbnor (2006), by providing the ambition criteria for actors oriented social and business knowledge shown in Figure 6.2.

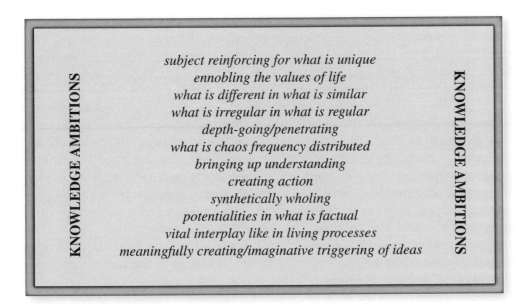

KNOWLEDGE AMBITIONS

subject reinforcing for what is unique
ennobling the values of life
what is different in what is similar
what is irregular in what is regular
depth-going/penetrating
what is chaos frequency distributed
bringing up understanding
creating action
synthetically wholing
potentialities in what is factual
vital interplay like in living processes
meaningfully creating/imaginative triggering of ideas

KNOWLEDGE AMBITIONS

Figure 6.2   Knowledge Ambitions

So, the actors oriented creator of knowledge aims at *delivering what is potential in what is factual* and, at the same time, aims at describing and shaping this process. It also becomes a means for critically reflecting the self-reference of general social science knowledge. In the process of *realizing* the knowledge ambitions (Figure 6.2), the creator of knowledge will also discover the existing social science knowledge *representation* of generality, normality, clichés, uniformity, etc. in individual human beings. The creator of knowledge therefore asks continuously what really should be called social and business *knowledge*, emphasizing science.

To be a *creator of knowledge in the sense of the actors view* consequently means, as an actor, to enter a *dialogue* with that reality which you, in a flow of the present, are at the same time part of creating in order to *emotionally*, *imaginatively* and *qualitatively* look for what is *irregular*, and *clarify* this reality using an *authentic language* (first hand expressions), where participants are made into *subjects* of an *understanding, emancipatory* and *innovative* knowledge interest.

Dialogue

The word *dialogue* is from dia (through) and logos (words), and is characterized by the interplay between "talking" and "listening" that takes place on equal terms for the participants. The *word* is the "instrument" of the dialogue, and it consists of *two mutually dependent* elements: *reflection* and *action*. If a word loses its element of action, reflection is affected. Words drained of action become elements of an empty language game – babbling – from both a scientific and an everyday point of departure. If, on the other hand, a word loses its reflective element, it becomes an empty activity, action for action's sake; scientific as well as everyday activism. Words that have lost their intentionality – one or both of their elements – bring out what is *not genuine* (not dependent on individuals) in existence, in thoughts, or in both.

The methodological purposes of the dialogue are twofold. Firstly, to *clarify* differences (thesis–antithesis) in which the participants can reflect their original opinions. Secondly, to *go beyond* (synthesis) the original opinions with which you enter the dialogue as a participant.

The interplay of questions and answers in the clarifying phase of the dialogue is close to what we might call an "honest question". *To ask an honest question, you have to know that you don't know. And when you know that you don't know, you don't use a direct method, because that implies that you only want to know something more thoroughly in the way you already know it* (compare understanding an actor's actions based on his/her finite province of meaning and not your own). Dialogue leads to a more intensive interaction than, for instance, questionnaires with their prepared questions. In a dialogue the creator of knowledge can *not* stand outside as an observer. The dialogue is based on nearness, authencity and willingness to emancipate and go beyond (create syntheses). In the continuous *first hand expressions* of the dialogue the subjectivity of man is refined.

Dialogue could be called the basis of dialectics (see below).

- A asserts *a1* (thesis)
- B asserts *b1* (antithesis)
- A asserts *a2* (synthesis), which encompasses or is based on both *a1* and *b1*, and which contains something over and above the pure combination of *a1* and *b1*: A adds new information and/or gives *a2* a specific structure. (Out of the clarified differences something new and qualitatively different is developed. In the ideal case the dialogue continues until a common understanding/action develops – a kind of meta-synthesis.)

The dialogue is a necessity in the social world of reflection and action between people. To interview someone in depth or to plant one's own ideas with somebody else has nothing to do with the dialogue. Carrying out a dialogue is the basis of the *act of creating* knowledge and the *participation* of the creator of knowledge in the world. The dialogue as a method in the actors view therefore necessitates humility, undivided attention and a genuine curiosity on the part of the creator of knowledge, as well as a belief in fellow humans as actors who have their own free will and right to create social reality.

Asking *honest questions* and being *genuinely related to the words* makes it natural for actors creators of knowledge to use *an interactive development of understanding* as a *prerequuisite* and to carry on *emancipatory interactive action* as part of *the result*.

Dialectics

The word *dialectics* comes from *dia* (through) and *lektos* (conversation). It was stated in antiquity that the best method for reaching "the truth" was to converse/argue (shed light on) an issue from a number of different angles (perspectives) so that various opinions could *contradict* each other. Dialectics is basically the study of the inherent *contradictions* in phenomena. By *contradiction*, we mean that everything contains its own negation; that is, what is general can only be revealed if what is specific exists: the finite only in relation to the infinite, what is quantitative in relation to what is qualitative (see "the Arbnor Uncertainty Principle", Figure 6.1).

In the previous illustration in which A and B made statements in a dialogue, we can reflect on how contradictions appear in the dialogical situation itself. The concepts that might perhaps be used by A in the first statement *a1* (the thesis) are given as something *immediate*. This immediate (*the first*) is later shown as *the second* in relation to itself; that is, as something *mediated* or referring to something else. This something else is the statement of the dialogical partner B (*b1*). That could therefore be called *the negation of the first* (antithesis). The immediate (*a1* – the thesis) has *been subordinated* to the second (*b1* – the antithesis), but the second is *not* an empty negation. The second is what is mediated and contained in the denotation of the first. The first is therefore preserved in the second even though it has been subordinated to *b1* through the fact that it has been given another shape in relation to the negation (the antithesis).

The second is simultaneously the mediat*ed* and the mediat*or*. The second denotation mediates something that is related to itself, that is, *b1* to *b1*; it therefore contains its own second in itself. In this way the second denotation – as a *contradiction* – leads to its own dialectic. The negation that the second in itself will give rise to *invalidates* the contradiction (two minuses equal a plus, a double negative is a positive) and thereby *restores* the first immediateness. This immediateness is, in fact, part of the process of *the third* in relation to the first immediateness (the thesis) and the second mediated (the antithesis). The third is the *unity* (the synthesis–*a2*) between what is *immediate* and what is *mediated*. This is the *trinity* of dialectics (thesis–antithesis–synthesis).

This is the basic idea of what we call dialectic relations, connections and/or circumstances.

Everything in our social lives originates in these starting points, according to the actors view. This leads to social phenomena becoming *ambiguous*. What *my* actions are and what they become is partly fixed by *others'* significant ambiguous denotations of these actions.

Acknowledging that every social phenomenon in and of itself carries *contradictory* tendencies and has an inherent capacity to accumulate quantitatively to new *qualitative* states will clarify why everything that exists (in the social world) is in the process of continuous development or intrinsic movement. It is because of this, according to the actors view, that we are able to understand the contradictions and breaks in continuity in our social lives. At the same time we can also understand the knowledge ambition of the actors view to emancipate what is potential (the antithesis) in what is factual (the thesis) and develop and create something new (synthesis).

The meaning of dialectics can be summarized in three paragraphs:

X. *The unity and struggle of contradictions.* Contradictions condition each other and bring meaningfulness to the poles. Day conditions night and night, day. The day does not take the night and vice versa. The phenomena are each other's prerequisites and create in their struggle a movement (e.g. learning – unlearning, quantity – quality, reflection – action, and other polarizing concepts).

Y. *The transition of the quantitative accumulation into a new quality.* Quantitative change can quickly change into completely new qualitative configurations. Cold water can quickly turn into ice. A seed in the ground can suddenly start to grow after lying dormant for several years. A work team can quickly change qualitatively if some members leave and/or others are added.

Z. *Everything undergoes development and becomes its own contradiction.* The seed in the ground becomes a plant – the negation (antithesis) of the first – that becomes a seed-case – the negation of the negations (the synthesis). This contradiction, once again, becomes its own negation, which may be the same as at the beginning but at a higher level – plants and more seeds. The synthesis looks like the thesis but at a higher qualitative level. For example, the need for the increase in knowledge within an area leads to specialists who carry their own contradictions around – a need for overview, more complete orientation, and so on.

The meaning of dialectics is also contained in the dialectical methodology of the actors view (refer back to Figure 3.15 at the end of Chapter 3). The simple circumstance of a *theoretical* person entering *practice* starts *a unity and a struggle of contradictions* (X). *The accumulation of everyday language* – the development of language by the creator of knowledge, *leads to a new quality* (Y) – descriptive and ideal-typical languages, *that will negate what is immediately given* – the descriptions in everyday language. The original interactive development of *understanding leads to its own contradiction* (Z) – *the act*, the emancipatory interactive action. Recall under "Dialogue", above, that the genuineness of a word (its intentionality) is related to reflection and action as contradictory partners indispensable to each other.

Actor

To talk about *actors* is important in the actors view, because it indicates an interest in *people* as *intentional*, that is, as *active, reflective* and *creative* individuals. In a dialogue, interest is directed at *understanding* and postulating people as free, active, reflective and creative, not as conditioned by external factors by which they might be explained as components with systemic characteristics. It is therefore natural to talk about actions instead of behaviours. Action gives a person the role of an *active* creator of understanding, whereas behaviour gives a person a *passive* role as a receiver of stimuli and a generator of responses.

To the creator of knowledge, the actor is an "object" to be studied as a free human being who in the ideal case thinks freely and acts responsibly. This actor is often placed in a context that is more or less organized and that is also an object to be studied by the researcher/consultant/investigator. This context consists of other actors – other people with their own finite provinces of meaning.

Observer

Observers in the sense of the actors view start from the fact that they must engage themselves humanly in the situation of the actors being studied in order to understand social action, but must periodically increase their dissociative distance in order to *broaden the perspective* of the data being collected. This method of working should not be confused with what is called participative observation, which can in principle be conducted without any engagement at all. The combination of engagement (interactive development of understanding) and dissociation (reflection), furthermore, minimizes the risk that observers will "drown" in the organizations they study.

The observer's course of action must be flexible and interactively oriented. Stringent and well-regulated study plans will therefore hinder more than they will help. When the observer has reached a suitable combination of *engagement* and *dissociation*, a more coherent total understanding can be developed.

Recall that observers can have *more than one interest and knowledge ambition*, and that these can be incorporated in the descriptions the observers later provide. An individual observer might be interested in creating *understanding, new thinking, emancipation*, or some combination of these. This can be accomplished in many different ways, depending on the organization and the actors that creators of knowledge, as observers, work with. It is also important, because observers do work with creating understanding, new thinking and/or emancipation in the organization, for them to detach themselves more and more from any engagement in the organization.

Observer–Actor

An observer of social action will of necessity, according to the actors view, also retain the role of an actor. This means that at the same time that an observer (the creator of knowledge) observes other actors, these actors will observe the actions of the observer – who becomes an actor to them. In these constant role shifts, where the observer becomes an actor and the actor an observer, the observer's knowledge and theories as well as the actor's understanding of his/her own situation will be improved.

Observers of social action can never stand outside of what they are studying. According to the actors view, it is a dialectic necessity that observers appear as actors at the same time that they influence and are influenced by what they are studying. To believe as a creator of knowledge that it is possible to stand outside and observe others creates a kind of estrangement, which is deceiving the creator of knowledge into seeing what is happening as something *determined* (by different causing factors and not by human free will). A researcher/consultant/investigator as an observer might therefore be called an *observactor*.

Diagnosis

Development of understanding

The word *diagnosis* is from *dia* (through) and *gnosis* (deeper insight). To diagnose is a way to understand and interpret actors and situations through deeper insight, so that "tools/processes" can be developed that can increase self-understanding among actors and help them in their future actions.

In the actors view, the most important aspect of the diagnosis is to see actors as human beings with intentional characteristics, rather than as artificial beings arranged in some a priori descriptive scheme. As creators of knowledge we are human beings as well and therefore constructed basically the same way as our studied actors. This gives a unique *potential* possibility for *understanding* others (and really, understanding would not be possible without it). The possibility is, however, potential because training and reflection are necessary to be able to understand others through oneself: the risk is great that only such experiences of others that suit the finite province of meaning held by the creator of knowledge will be *observed and noted*. In the same way, there is a risk that the experiences of the actors will be *interpreted* from the finite province of meaning held by the creator of knowledge, instead of from those held by the actors themselves. It is therefore important for the actors oriented creator of knowledge to search for the *inner quality* in those human micro-cosmoses he/she meets and at the same time re-create this *quality* within him/herself in order to be able to *understand* and bring the experiences on.

We describe the purpose of diagnosis in social science (i.e. business) as a three-step process for an interactive development of understanding: preunderstanding, understanding and postunderstanding.

Preunderstanding

Diagnostic preunderstanding is supposed *to bridge* the differences that exist between the finite province of meaning held by the creator of knowledge and the finite provinces of meaning held by the (other) actors. Preunderstanding can then function as *a linguistic bridge, a dialogue*, between the intentionality of the creator of knowledge and that of the actors. A *genuine* relation to the words and *honest* questions are the starting points for this interactive development of understanding (see "Dialogue" above where one of the two methodological purposes of the dialogue is described as to clarify differences).

Diagnostic preunderstanding is not to be confused with the general preunderstanding brought up in Chapter 3 (see Table 3.4, summarizing the actors view, at the end of Chapter 3). General preunderstanding is related to the collected experiences that creators of knowledge bring to *every* new study situation, whereas *diagnostic preunderstanding* is always *developed* in a *specific* study situation and becomes associated with that situation.

In order to develop diagnostic preunderstanding, a *historical* study of the actors of interest (and their organization) is necessary. It is only against the background of such a study that it becomes possible to understand the finite provinces of meaning that guide the actors' actions. This preunderstanding or *language commonality* is the eventual basis of the continuing dialogue and development of understanding in the next two stages, understanding and postunderstanding.

Understanding

The development of understanding itself comes about by using the relations and the dialogue that the creator of knowledge established during the preunderstanding stage. It is worth remembering that the ultimate purpose of this situation and the ongoing dialogue is to *improve the ability* of the actors to be free to solve their *own* problems. For this reason it is essential to see the development of the diagnosis as a development of an understanding that is *shared* by the creator of knowledge and the actors. This is supposed to take place through the earlier described "observer–actor" relation in which mutual development and an increase in knowledge takes place.

This second stage (diagnostic understanding) consists of a *reflection process* in which the researcher/consultant/investigator, in both dialogue and action with the actors, tries to find essential patterns in the information that are based on the actors' everyday language. During this dialogical reflection process, the creator of knowledge as well as the actors grow in capacity. At the same time, the creator of knowledge gradually *develops* descriptive and ideal-typified languages (see "Dialectics", above).

Postunderstanding

Diagnostic postunderstanding is the third stage in the development of understanding. Here a process is initiated whereby the languages developed are related to what is factual and actual, as well as to existing theory. In this stage, the languages being developed become an integral part of the knowledge creator's "tools", which means that these languages will provide the bases for the continuing *emancipatory interactive action*, an interactive action that creates a solid understanding among actors of what is old – and what is new.

Language development

To develop *descriptive* and *ideal-typified* languages, in other words to develop "language", might seem somewhat obscure. How do you develop a new language – like the creation of Esperanto or what? Language development in the sense of the actors view has nothing to do with this kind of language. When we talk about language development in the way the actors view does, we have in mind all the instruments that creators of knowledge can use, antithetical to the everyday language, to express their experiences and understanding.

Actors creators of knowledge are intent on communicating through actively forming what they experience as subconsciously and unconsciously significant in their relation to the actors' life-worlds. The word *communicate* is from the Latin *communis* (common), and is the road to common experiences and insights. To *form*, in this context, means to "vivify" something, where the observer becomes an important part in creating meaning around what is vivified. The processes, the means (the instruments) that actors creators of knowledge develop and use understandingly, emancipatorily and creatively in order to express themselves are what we call languages. Recall that we earlier divided these into *descriptive* and *ideal-typified* languages (a further development of this dichotomy is illustrated later in the chapter).

We can, in this respect, compare creators of knowledge who use the actors view to artists, poets, composers and the like, as far as "the passion" for communicating new dimensions of experience is concerned. May (1969) explains what we mean:

> It is the artists who teach us to see, who break ground in the enlargement of our consciousness; they point the way toward the new dimensions of experience which we have, in a given period, been missing. This is why looking at a work of art gives us a sudden experience of self-recognition. Giotto, precursor to that remarkable birth of awareness known as the Renaissance, saw nature in a new perspective and for the first time painted rocks and trees in three-dimensional space. ... The new view of space by Giotto was basic for the new geographical explorations of oceans and continents by Magellan and Columbus which changed man's relation to his world, and for the explorations in astronomy by Galileo and Copernicus, which changed man's relation to the heavens. These new discoveries in space resulted in radical upheaval of man's image of himself. ... The psychological upheaval and spiritual loneliness in this period was expressed by the poet John Donne. (1969: 320–1)

Actors researchers/consultants/investigators normally do not communicate their insights in the form of drawings, films, or paintings. But to indicate the road to *new dimensions of experience*, they must be able to use all possible linguistic features. Actors creators of knowledge must therefore not be ignorant of such methods as slide shows, light and sound shows, or multimedia combinations of these means of expression in order to create an antithesis to everyday language. The actors view agrees entirely with the philosopher von Wright (1986) who, in *Vetenskapen och Förnuftet* [*Science and Reason*], asserts: "The understanding of reality in earlier scientific categories has reached its limits. In order to go beyond the limit, these categories must be transformed or replaced by new ones" (1986: 46; our translation). It is through a conscious and re-creative development of language that we, according to the actors view, give ourselves the chance to emancipate "the potential in what is factual". Then we can go beyond old categories of created knowledge and make more cost-effective and attractive ways of life and work for ourselves. Business revival, according to the actors view, necessitates this language development, too.

When constructing language expressions and phrases, which are condensed through the use of various artistic means of expression, creators of knowledge can use new well-connotated word combinations, analogous concepts, contradictory terms, new concepts and terms, metaphors, analogies, simplifications, newly constructed words, and illustrations and drawings to advantage.

When researchers/consultants/investigators, using the instruments just described within the framework of various models of the actors view (i.e. using scientific language; we remind the reader that it is not necessary to be a scientist to use a "scientific" language), develop a coherent *formative pattern* in relation to some area under study, we talk about *language development* – a discourse.

Action

Intentionality makes us *acting* subjects. The word is the instrument of the dialogue and consists of both reflection and action! *Action* is, in reflection, its own contradiction and vice versa – the contradictions condition each other and give each other a meaning. An actor is an *active*, reflective and creative human being. We have come to understand that these are some of the implications of using action as a concept and a practice in the process of creating knowledge within the framework of the actors view.

The opinion that I as a creator of knowledge have of others must, according to the actors view, be one to which I myself am willing to conform. It therefore becomes natural for actors creators of knowledge to engage in active emancipatory *action* as an important part of the process of creating knowledge. At the same time that this role of action is criticized by the two other views, the actors view asks whether creators of knowledge who are analytical and systems-oriented might not like to have their own knowledge-creating activities explained/understood as they explain and understand the activities and development of others; that is, as an expression of various *external* factors – causes or producers – that *determine* what they do or that arrange them as components of a system.

An actors creator of knowledge who does not take the role of action seriously is as defective, in the actors view, as analytical and systems-oriented creators of knowledge who do not accept that what they posit for others and their environment applies to themselves as well.

It is often language that limits the actions of creators of knowledge when in the field. What at any moment is *the given language* (whether everyday or scientific) limits the potential that creators of knowledge have for structuring their experiences out of the interactive development of understanding. Creators of knowledge who do not progress in *language development* and *action* can *speak* and *write* about only the characteristics and relations for which there are words in the given language. If a transformation of what is given does not take place, the work of these creators of knowledge leads only to a confirmation of what is already known, because every existing life-world also constitutes a knowledge-world in which language is an important part of the structure of reflection, action and legitimacy.

Co-reflecting and co-creating with the actors in the field become important prerequisites for a transformation of what exists in the everyday world as well as in the scientific (research/consulting/investigation) world. Through action, meaning can be wrung from reflection, and through reflection, action can be scrutinized. As much as action designates reflection, reflection designates action – the unity and struggle of contradictions. *This distinguishing mark of actors is a guarantee that the creator of knowledge has a genuine relationship to words* (see "Dialogue", above).

Business as research/consulting/investigation and research/consulting/investigation as business could be the motto for the business researcher/consultant/ investigator who wants to be involved with *creating knowledge through emancipatory interactive action* within the framework of the actors view. This includes the *creative* act and the *direct* act as important elements. The *creative act* encompasses the "artistic" development of language (see above). The concrete participation of creators of knowledge in practice – such as creating businesses, starting ventures, transforming organizations – constitutes the *direct act*. The reason the actors view talks about these acts as "emancipatory interactive action" is related to what we have described as the solid connections between language and existence – in both directions. If the knowledge ambitions of the actors view (see Figure 6.2) and the potential in what is factual are to be made visible, intelligible and believable, emancipatory interactive action in the form of *creative* and *direct acts* out in the field is necessary.

In the actors view, it is important to convey the message actively to the actors out in the field that the alternative to the laws of causality does not have to be vagueness and make-believe. The alternative is meaningfulness and freedom in reflection and action.

REALITY: A SOCIAL CONSTRUCTION

Transformation

The central assumption of the actors view is the existence of a social reality. This means that reality is *not independent* of us, but consists of an interaction between our own experiences and the collected structure of experiences that we have over time created together with others. The process by which we create our own experiences is called *subjectification*. This process is prescribed by the concept of intentionality and by *the Arbnor Uncertainty Principle* (see Figure 6.1) and constitutes the basic idea that *humans are a subjective reality*.

When through our common language we make these subjective experiences externally available, we talk about *externalization*. With externalization we create the surrounding reality and can therefore say that *society is a human result*.

The process by which an externalized human act might attain the characteristic of objectivity is called *objectification*. Through objectification, externalization loses its subjectively significant structure and becomes a *typification*, that is, it is given a virtually objective significance structure. Typification is related to our way of attaching various labels and typical designations to – having different understandings of – the people and things around us. Examples of such typifications could be, commuter, entrepreneur, chief, Englishman, snob or scorcher. We expect, and then take for granted, that what is typified behaves according to the understanding mediated by the typification. The typification is not completely objectified until it has gone through a process of *institutionalization* and *legitimization*. The process of objectification, in turn, constitutes the basis for the assumption that *society is an objective reality*.

The fourth and last of these processes in social reality is called *internalization*. This stands for taking over the world in which others already live, and so it constitutes *the* dialectic process through which we *become* members of society. We are not born as members but become such via internalization with its primary and secondary socialization phases. This is the basis of the fourth assumption, that *humans are a societal result*.

SUBJECTIFICATION	→	*Humans are a subjective reality*
EXTERNALIZATION	→	*Society is a human result*
OBJECTIFICATION	→	*Society is an objective reality*
INTERNALIZATION	→	*Humans are a societal result*

We have now described four different *transforming* elements in the total dialectic process that molds our reality. It is important to remember that they work simultaneously at all levels of the social order. In order to understand organizations/companies, it is essential that these transforming elements – processes – are considered with a perspective of totality in their simultaneity (see Figure 6.3).

It is not possible to understand any of these processes in isolation. They must be understood in relation to each other, to their constant movement – dialectics. They constitute transforming elements in the unity and *struggle of contradictions* at the same time as they are each other's prerequisites for the transition of the *quantitative accumulations to a new quality*, in which they again develop and *become each other's contradictions* (see "Dialectics" above).

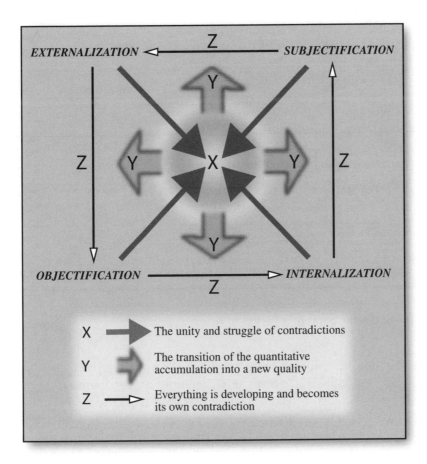

Figure 6.3   Simultaneous Processes

For ease of description, we will describe each of the elements – the processes – separately. The reader is therefore asked to keep the *dialectic idea* in mind and to relate the following presentation to Figure 6.3.

Subjectification

We experience our fellow human beings in a direct way when we share a community in time and space. When we share this community with another, we reach a contemporaneousness in our consciousness. We perceive each other's bodies as an unspecified field of sensations by which this consciousness manifests itself in us. In these dialogical, everyday meetings with others we continuously externalize ourselves and consequently lay the foundation for social dialectics. This dialectic relationship also lays the foundation for various finite provinces of meaning that are developed by society's actors. How externalization and development of these finite provinces of meaning take place is to a large extent related to what we call the *subjectification* of a person or an actor (see Figure 6.4).

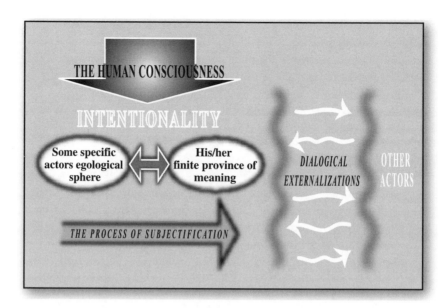

Figure 6.4   The Subjectification of a Person or Actor

This subjectification is attributed to how individual actors develop themselves as *subjects* on the social stage. An individual actor's interpretations are attributed to his/her *subjectification process*. How each actor makes this interpretation is related to the finite province of meaning by which he/she is oriented and the egological sphere and interpretation he/she uses. That this finite province of meaning and egological sphere are possible at all is based on the assumption of intentionality, which describes the principles of human consciousness as such. If these principles are *related* to an actor's *total situation* and *factual way of interpretation*, we can infer the actor's *egological sphere* and *finite province of meaning*, that is, we can develop an understanding of the *subjectification process*.

The *knowledge ambition* of the actors view (see Figure 6.2) to act *reinforcing the subject for what is unique* relates directly to this process of subjectification. It is the belief of the view that unique individuals in a dialogue support a creative development of the society, which in turn relates to the *innovative knowledge interest* of the view.

Externalization

Externalization stands for the assumption that we take part in creating our surrounding reality (society is a human result). When we communicate our subjectification to others through our common language, that is, make something *externally* available, we enable them to react to our previous subjective experiences and thoughts. We *externalize* ourselves continuously in various actions that we communicate to fellow humans in everyday relations. These other human beings then function as reflections of our externalizations. By means of this communication we may possibly transform the original content of a thought and formulate a new or refined thought. This mutual relation with others is *dialectic* and leads to the continuous reinterpretation and change of meanings.

A creator of knowledge should therefore, according to the actors view, interest him/ herself in a *language development* (see above, p. 141–2) which is extending our externalization possibilities to express, vivify and clarify what is pregnant, sublime, subtle, creative, difficult to express etc. This is also about the special knowledge ambitions of the view (see Figure 6.2).

Objectification

Our externalized subjective thoughts and intentions constitute *moments* (stages) or *parts* of complicated dialectic processes. After several reflections (reinterpretations), and changes in the original subjective thoughts, these thoughts may finally approximate the character of being objective. The environment, then, has generally started to accept the externalization as meaningful. This process of acceptance is what we call *objectification*. What was earlier externalized has now become part of our objective reality.

We can divide objectification into two phases: *institutionalization* and *legitimization*. When, between different actors, there is a common *typification* of some habitual act, we can say that an *institution* has emerged. (By "institution" here can be meant everything that we go on, from the established descriptive language of the society and its applied social science research, to different public authorities.) All human actions are in one way or another subject to *routinization*. These habitual acts are incorporated into our experience as knowledge routines, and because they are characteristically taken for granted we call this type of knowledge *cookbook knowledge*.

The origin of all *institutionalization*, in other words, is in the typification of one's own and others' conduct. We typify not only the actors but also their actions. This makes it possible for us to handle others' (as well as our own) performances safely as generally accepted and objective acts. In this way we assign to ourselves and to others certain *typified roles* that are attributed to typified action patterns. If these partially objectified, finite provinces of meaning become too much a part of our interpretation of ourselves, there may be negative consequences for our self-experience. An objectified finite province of meaning can completely paralyse our subjectification, leading us to develop normal pathological acts – that is, acts that are so normal in our society that they are active obstacles to a renewal that might be necessary and desirable. It is in situations like this that creators of knowledge work with an emancipatory knowledge interest; that is, they work to emancipate the actor from this paralysing basis of interpretation and action. Because this situation is more or less valid for all of us, we have a tendency to express our purposes and action patterns from a basis of objective meaning structures. We unconsciously hide our subjective meaning, a fact that in the actors view is worthy of thought for all researchers/consultants/investigators engaged in interviews of any kind.

For the next generation of individuals, those who will take over the institutions, some kind of *social control* is necessary because at different ages these individuals "are forced" to become members of a number of different institutions and cannot return to conditions as they were before. The *second* important phase in the process of objectification, therefore, is *legitimization*. This works as a kind of *second degree of objectification* in which we weave legitimization into the institutions themselves in order to explain and to justify them.

We can divide the legitimization process into three stages: *linguistic legitimization, proverbial legitimization* and *theoretical legitimization.*

Linguistic legitimization is already built into our everyday language, because it comes from and is developed in the objectified reality (see "Action", above). Most words in our language already contain "objective" information. For example, a child learns that another child can be called a cousin. This word (*cousin*) conveys certain information about how the child might act in relation to the other child and, therefore, legitimizes this specific "cousin" action. Or a new employee finds out that the boss is the founder of the company as well, or he meets other so-called pre-scientific or subject-specific concepts which exist with inbuilt "directions of use" for thinking beforehand.

Proverbial legitimization can be attributed to our use of proverbs to legitimize some of our actions. If a child or anyone else asks why you act as you do, you might answer: "Many a little makes a mickle." Any other explanation becomes unnecessary. In fact, such a question asked at the workplace may well be justified, but because the typification on which the institution is based has the characteristic of taking things for granted, nobody reflects on why they act as they do and instead uses the proverbial legitimization built into the typification as an answer to the question. By taking too much for granted, according to the actors view, we become "slaves" to institutions we ourselves have created.

Theoretical legitimization is more sophisticated and is used at a higher level than those mentioned above. This can be related to all kinds of quasi-scientific explanations given to legitimize an institution.

According to the actors view these processes are operating together and in parallel with that form of knowledge creating activities that are going on within a large number of social *institutions* with different *legitimizing* dignity. Knowledge creating activity does not then stand outside this social dialectics and the view speaks therefore about the *self-reference* of knowledge creation. We can therefore, according to the actors view, develop knowledge about ourselves which is reducing us – making us unfree in the sign of this self-reference (see Figure 6.1 and for a reminder of the meaning of "self-reference", see the Glossary). We can alternatively work with emancipating acts within the knowledge ambitions of the view (see Figure 6.2). This is a choice that the knowledge creator makes in what we call the *scientific ideal* in a paradigm.

Internalization

Internalization stands for the element with which we accept a world in which others already live. In other words, we *become* members of the society. The internalization process can be seen in the phases of *primary* and *secondary socialization* (Berger & Luckmann, 1966).

Primary socialization, which takes place in childhood, is the most important phase for a person's development. Most of the "objective" world that is accepted by a child is imparted by others. Therefore, knowledge being transferred becomes emotionally conditioned and identification becomes a necessary prerequisite. Children, for instance, identify themselves with a role or an attitude. This identification is a continuous dialectical process between the experience of others and the identification of oneself. It is in primary socialization that the first understanding of reality is founded. *Language* becomes the most important internalizing factor of primary socialization. Yet socialization is a continuous process that does not end with the primary phase but continues throughout a person's entire life as secondary socialization.

Secondary socialization mainly encompasses the internalization of specific institutional sub-areas. The content of this internalization depends on the complexity and the work specialization in the area in question. In this phase, the learning of *role-specific knowledge* and the *professional language* associated with the area are often necessary. The learning situations of the two socializing phases are different to the extent that the degree of anonymity is considerably higher in the secondary phase. For this reason there is not the same demand for *identification* as in the primary socialization.

Social dialectics

A continuous synthesizing process

Just as we have described how reality is socially constructed in a society, we can describe various organizations in the society. This means that we can talk about the *social reality* of a company and can follow its construction using the *four elements*. It is only a question of levels in the social order – while keeping in mind that a company is only a small piece of the total social dialectics.

In order to understand what this social dialectics means, we have to realize that each individual actor simultaneously represents both subjectified reality and objectified reality. We have to understand how we can see the *general* in what is *personal* and the *personal* in what is *general*. These contradictions are inseparable and, in fact, produce the transformation in the thesis–antithesis relationship, which becomes a continuous *synthesizing process*, namely, the *development* and *self-movement* of social reality (see Figure 6.3 above and Figure 6.5 overleaf).

In the development process just described, society's actors construct their finite provinces of meaning, which then reflect simultaneously both what is *subjective* (personal) and what is *objective* (common). The *common set* that emerges when all the finite provinces of meaning are *aggregated* in a society, a company or any organization constitutes the *objectified reality* for that organization. This is the reality in which we live our daily lives as members of society. It is always there before us; its total existence is very rarely or never in doubt, only minor aspects of it are questioned. This objectified reality is what we call *everyday reality* (see Figure 6.6).

Everyday reality

Husserl (1931) described everyday reality as the reality in which we find ourselves at every moment of our lives (the *Lebenswelt*), where we accept it exactly the way it presents itself to us in our *everyday experiences*. This reality is extended in an indefinite way in both time and

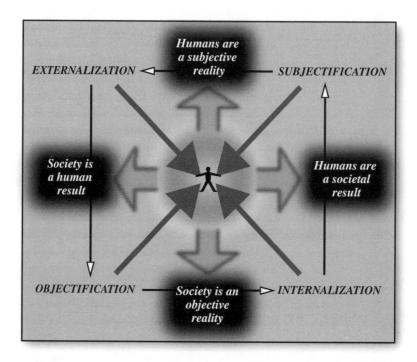

Figure 6.5   Social Construction of Reality

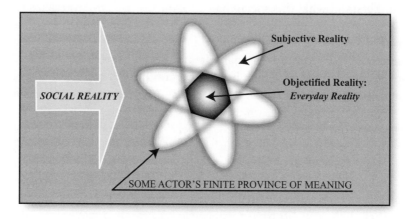

Figure 6.6   Social Dialectics and Everyday Reality

space. Its existence is never in doubt; this applies to both its physical and its sociocultural aspects. Doubts, of course, do arise and things often prove to be different from our previous experiences. Yet these doubts, questions and corrections concern mainly details within this reality and never reality as such and in its entirety. So when we face problems that are not routinized we try to relate them to our "cookbook" knowledge: we try to find some kind of everyday life explanation rather than worry "unnecessarily". Sometimes we don't find such an explanation and so have to turn to our own, very subjective, reality. The subjectivity we experience as a result can hardly be communicated to others in a meaningful way because our common language is based on everyday reality; trying to externalize this very subjective experience will necessarily distort it.

It is therefore important for a researcher/consultant/investigator to consider language barriers when subjectification processes are to be made intelligible.

In the section titled "Language Development" (above), we stated that the creator of knowledge should not be unfamiliar with various instruments for communicating and for manifesting the *antithesis* of everyday language. We want to stress the importance of this once more.

THE RELATION OF THE ACTORS VIEW TO ITS PARADIGM

In general

In Chapter 1, "The Language of Methodology" we described a paradigm as a model or a general mechanism for controlling the creation of knowledge and as consisting of the following parts: a conception of reality; a conception of science; a scientific ideal; and an ethical aesthetical part.

In the previous section we presented the most central standpoint in the actors view, that is, the *conception of reality* on which the view is based. This description is a thorough presentation of the first part of the paradigm to which the actors view is related. The second part encompasses the *conception of science* on which the view is based. We have already described this conception as the *prerequisites*, the *development of understanding* and the *results* with which the view works. In the rest of this chapter we will concentrate on this second area, the conception of science held by the actors view. This means that its *scientific ideal* and *ethical aesthetical* parts will not be specifically described because they, as mentioned earlier, are more associated with the goals of individual creators of knowledge than with any specific theory. The content of the two latter parts of the paradigm of the actors view, however, is implicitly intimated throughout the whole chapter and more specifically under "Action" (above) and "Some theoretical and action-oriented starting points" (below).

Prerequisites of the actors view: Metatheories

Of the conditions we brought up in Chapter 3 concerning the methodological views and their prerequisites, explanations/understanding and results, all, except what were referred to as metatheories, are attributed to contributions from previously conducted actors research/consulting/investigations. These contributions from such previous actions cannot be regarded as parts of the paradigm, so they will not be treated here (see Chapter 12). What we earlier described as *constitutional factors* under the results of the actors view in Chapter 3 can, however, in some situations contribute to a development of the metatheories mentioned and, as such, be incorporated into the paradigm.

When we talk about metatheories we refer to the background theories in the *conception of science* that are held by creators of knowledge and that, in general terms, guide their practical research/consulting/investigation and are therefore related to the paradigm. These are the guiding theories in the actors view, which means that creators of knowledge use them to *develop* not only an understanding of their object of study – understanding others – but also for understanding themselves. Because creating knowledge in the actors view is to a large extent aimed at understanding others by understanding oneself, we realize that creators of knowledge who within themselves are not trying to re-create that *inner quality* they meet in the actors, are not creators of actors knowledge.

We can say that a person (an actor) is simultaneously *psychological, social, historical* and *political*. Political in the sense of power-political; that is, various actors (including creators of knowledge) both exert power and are subject to power. In association with each of these basic aspects of human life, we talk about *metapsychology, metasociology, metahistory*, and *metapolitics* – different meta-areas that become part of the conception of science in the actors view.

Metapsychology points out that human beings are *subjective* interpreters of their reality in accordance with *being, becoming* and *freedom* (see the beginning of this chapter and Figure 6.1). People cannot be described and explained in terms of their environment alone. The researcher/consultant/investigator must therefore, according to the actors view, try to understand the *subjective constitution* of knowledge, interpretation and action. This understanding can be developed by trying to get the actors to express problems and opportunities in their own words – *first hand expressions*. The *meaning* of formulated problems and opportunities, and the corresponding language, can be seen as the knowledge that opens the creator of knowledge's understanding of the actions among the actors. It is of great importance in the actors view that an interpretation of an actor corresponds to certain action patterns.

The actor, however, does not live in a social vacuum. Interpretations and actions take place in a social reality with *several other actors*. We can also talk about the actor's structural environment, which – as mentioned earlier – is, according to the actors view, *dialectic* as far as its intrinsic character is concerned. The actor shares a number of things with other actors such as interpretations, actions and language. Many of our actions, however, are controlled or influenced by the *objectification* that historically emerges around various patterns of interpretation, action and language.

In these historical processes we also discover how various *power-political* games have taken place in the interface between externalization and internalization, and have been powerful forces behind many objectifications. In consequence, the historical and political aspects are included as essential metatheories in the conception of science in order to understand the psychological and sociological aspects (see Figure 6.7 and study it in relation to the previous Figures 6.3 and 6.5).

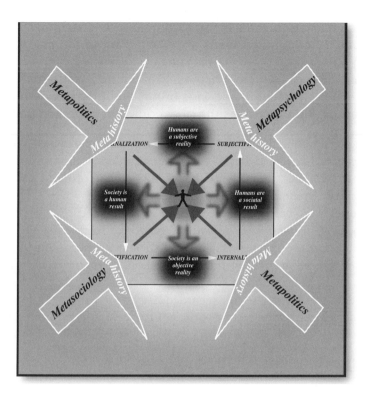

Figure 6.7 Metatheories

Looking at Figure 6.7 we can say that:

A. *Metapsychological* theory, with such advocates as Husserl, Merleau-Ponty, Fromm, Kelly and Heidegger, offers guiding principles to creators of knowledge for interpreting the subjectification process of individual actors. Yet this is not enough to make intelligible what happens in the illustrated interaction among several actors.

B. *Metasociological* theory, with such advocates as Schutz, Fromm, Berger & Luckmann, and Mills, offers an understanding of how externalized meanings become objectified and how reality is socially constructed. This makes visible the "game" that is played among actors. Even so, what may seem like inexplicable "game patterns" can appear. These cannot be understood without a full understanding of the power-political elements to which the illustrated group is either subordinated or else dominates.

C. *Metapolitical* theory, with advocates like Weber, Schutz, Marcuse and Foucault, can bring an understanding of why an actor acts in a way that might contradict his/her personal convictions. Why are, for instance, these specific individuals where they are, and why do they act as they do? What brought them there? How and where have they acted before? Or questions such as why certain actions, thoughts and ideas are given a better externalization space than others, and why certain actions, thoughts and ideas are given a more tangible legitimizing and internalizing power than other, similar ones.

D. *Metahistorical* theory, with advocates like Schutz, Habermas and Foucault, bridges the historical vacuum and thus brings an understanding in terms of historical processes, which clarifies the questions that have just been raised.

These metatheories are among the prerequisites of the actors view as well as part of the interplay when the creator of knowledge tries to reach an understanding and give a meaning to that understanding. They are therefore not arranged in a fixed order of 1 through 4, but are all used simultaneously in the development of understanding.

These metatheories were partly explicated in the section titled "Reality: a social construction" (above, p. 144) when we described how the elements of subjectification, externalization, objectification and internalization socially construct our reality. The rest of the description that can be devoted to them in this book is intertwined in the presentation of the other parts of the conception of science in the actors view, that is, the *development of understanding* and *results*. They are not regarded as part of what we refer to as methodology. We believe that our coverage will be sufficient to begin applying the actors view.

Understanding and results

Language

In this book, language is regarded primarily as a social science phenomenon, as a way of externalizing social reality. We experience the world in language. We act in, and reflect on, the world through language. We hold conversations, exchange thoughts, express feelings, create technology and cooperate. Using language we build our companies and organizations. The generally oriented social scientist (as a researcher, as a consultant, or as a general investigator) in the actors view is guided by what language *means* to people's way of life as a means of expressing and intermediating knowledge and information in the form of language. It is through language that the knowledge creator attempts to catch what Max Weber called "the subjective logic of actors". We call this "a person's egological sphere".

What goes on between people in, say, an organization can therefore be seen as a *language game*. The actors view thus postulates that the *use* of language is controlled by more or less visible rules that give meaning to the symbols and the actions. We can talk of language games as containing ideological, referential and technological rules in which different language games also reflect different life practices (see also, for instance, Arbnor, 1976; Winch, 1958; Wittgenstein, 1953).

The various *relationships* that an organization has with its environment can also be seen as language games in which the actors of the organization interpret the environment by using the rules of their language games, and in which the environment in turn, using its own rules, interprets the organization. In this language game and the interpretive processes that are shaped by it, we can find connections and relations to various patterns of activities, actions and interactions. These connections are based on the assumption that behind every human act there is a more or less conscious *process of interpretation*. The assumption is related to the conception of social reality, of man, and so on.

Language is a means and a medium for describing our interpretations, activities and actions. People use *language* to *describe* and to *intermediate* reality to themselves and to others. In the same way, creators of knowledge use language in their interactive development of understanding, externalizing descriptions in order to describe and form the reality being studied so they themselves and others can visualize "the egological sphere of actors" and "the finite provinces of meaning" (see Figure 6.8).

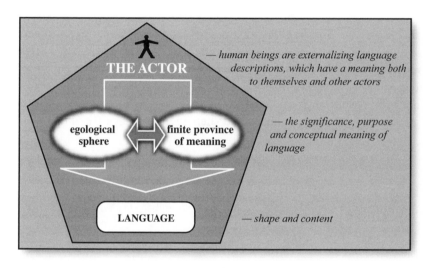

Figure 6.8   The Actor and the Meaning of Language

While we are making it clear to ourselves that language is of essential importance to the construction of social reality, we must not forget that language can be inadequate for capturing the egological sphere. People have a *number of systems* and *means* of expression apart from language – gestures, physical movements, and "internal brain work", to name a few. Furthermore, linguistic descriptions of reality are *ambiguous*. People show an amazing flexibility when it comes to attributing varying meanings to words and actions, in spite of the fact that social language games throughout history have attached many stable and objectified meanings to words. In consequence, as an actors creator of knowledge one faces an almost impenetrable surface that can *hide* the *original* and most important meaning. At the same time that language is the most important tool for the actor creator of knowledge, it has serious shortcomings that he/she often can do nothing about. Human beings are at the same time, according to the actors view, conscious and unconscious, complex and simple, subjective and objective, ambiguous and unambiguous, *dialectic*.

From the conception of science represented by the actors view, as far as the vision of human beings and social reality is concerned, it follows that there is no *single* answer that provides the truth about a problem. Creators of knowledge must admit that reality has such a *simultaneousness* of uniqueness and generality (dialectics) that it cannot be subjected to experiments in a laboratory. Subjective reality concerns *subjective meaning and logic*, the pattern of which creators of knowledge should try to verify in as many ways as possible, but the procedures of control and validity must not be based on "faulty" conceptions of the nature of reality. Reality, according to the actors view, is a *relativity* that can only be "disclosed" by *awareness, action* and *self-reflection*. Language – the object of study according to the actors view – is a *social invention* that is used by and for human beings in this relativity. As such, language is a *social* and *historical* construction and should therefore be understood and studied accordingly.

The different levels of language

Hand in hand with the building of societies over time, people have invented various specialized realities to solve various types of problems. This has resulted in a division of work into a number of dissimilar specialist roles. In each of these specialized realities, more or less unique languages are developed. Handling and developing these specialized realities would not be possible within the framework of everyday language. Scientists (researchers/consultants/investigators) have therefore also constructed their own language (see Figure 6.9).

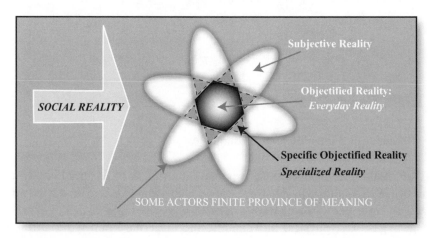

Figure 6.9   Specialized Realities

Within social science research/consulting/investigation, such a development of specialized languages has also taken place. The actors view claims that this language development has to a large extent forgotten the connection to what is most fundamental, that is, to everyday language. Language development so far has been based too heavily on analogies from the worlds of mathematics physics, mechanics and biology. According to the actors view, it is as if one were describing summer by the language usage of winter. For lack of a more suitable term, we use the word "bureaucratic" for the type of scientific language that, according to the actors view, has *lost* its *dialogical* connection to the language base of the described phenomena themselves.

The starting point for the creator of knowledge should therefore be actors' everyday descriptions, which are then interpreted in a creation-of-knowledge way. This actors-based interpretation is thereby different from a bureaucratic knowledge-based interpretation. This is because other *knowledge interests* and demands govern the actors researcher/consultant/investigator.

From different realities (subjective, specialized and everyday) follow also different forms of language use in which the meaning of knowledge differs in relation to the various realities. According to the actors view, we must learn to understand how language and the quality of reality stand in a mutual dialectic relationship to each other (reality constitutes language – language constitutes reality). With this in mind, we also realize that we can only understand a reality in and through the language that is related to it. Creators of knowledge must therefore use *interpretation, action* and *reflection* to be able to "translate" the language of *one* reality into the language of *another* reality (in particular, everyday language into a scientific language).

According to the actors view, social phenomena must be *understood* on their own terms, and what they mean in the language game and in the reality in which they appear. The knowledge will otherwise become rootless in relation to practical and emotional actions in everyday life. The expression "Theory is one thing and practice is another" is possibly an expression for such a kind of rootlessness.

Scientific language

It is through the processes of *interpretation, action* and *reflection* talked about thus far that scientific language is developed in the actors view. It is important to keep in mind that this development takes place starting with what phenomena *mean* in the *reality* in which they appear and in the *language* with which they are described. This meaning becomes externalized, however, after the process of interpretation, action and reflection into a language other than everyday language. This is because everyday language cannot go beyond its own phenomena. *Phenomena* in any reality appear when the given language in this reality does *not* allow a description of them. When we talk about phenomena in everyday reality, we must understand that we are actually referring to experiences that cannot be totally externalized through everyday language. Actors research/consulting/investigation aims at depicting this immanent, not externalizable, understanding. *Language development*, therefore, means expressing experiences in a language in which they can be externalized (compare to a poet's language for expressing what is difficult to express). Yet this translation cannot be made unless phenomena have been *interpreted* in the light of *the finite provinces of meaning* and that *egological sphere* that has produced them (see Figure 6.8). To help in their interpretations, creators of knowledge have the four metatheories (see Figure 6.7); the *historical* one takes on a decisive meaning. The actors view therefore stresses the historical perspective when studying social phenomena.

To be able to express an experienced phenomenon (consciously or unconsciously) in our everyday reality scientifically, the phenomenon must, through *action*, be "extorted" for significances and *interpreted*, because the phenomenon has a subjective, social, historical and political connection to its language as well as to its reality. Only after such a process of interpretation, action and reflection can the researcher/consultant/investigator externalize the phenomenon by means of language – a scientific language. Remember that the criticism that the actors view directs against the other methodological views has to do with their *neglecting* this process of *interpretation, action* and *reflection*, and instead describing the phenomena of everyday life in terms of what they mean in their scientific language. If phenomena are experienced starting from the scientific pictures of reality, it is not certain in the actors view that they constitute real phenomena in everyday reality.

If we were to describe the construction of the scientific language in the actors view in dialectic terms (see above and compare "Dialectics") we might say that this language is the *second* in relation to the *first immediate* (the first hand expressions by the actors). The first immediate (the thesis – the positive) is the phenomenon as expressed in everyday language, which in a scientific language appears as the *second* in relation to itself, that is, as the *mediated* (the antithesis – the negative). The *immediate* now appears as something *mediated* in relation to itself. This mediated (the phenomenon in the scientific language) is at the same time the *mediating* (it is fed back to the actors in everyday reality) and the *second* (the scientific language) therefore negates itself (– –) and thereby becomes the origin of its own dialectics. The self-negation of the *second* nullifies the contradiction (– – = +) and restores the immediate, which is then the *third* in relation to the first immediate, that is, the *synthesis* is at hand.

As actors creators of knowledge, we understand from this: if the *first* immediate does not *refer* to the experienced phenomenon by the *actors* in everyday reality but to the creator of knowledge's experience of the phenomenon starting from the reality of the community of knowledge creation, the scientific language will *not* appear as something *second* to the actors (they simply feel like strangers in the presence of the scientific language – knowledge has become *rootless*). This is because the creators of knowledge *did not* enter into a dialogically honest relation with the actors; nor did they try to *interpret* the phenomenon starting from *its* egological sphere. That is, they did not lay a foundation for any *mutual* dialectics (creator of knowledge ⇔ actor — scientific language ⇔ everyday language). The dialectics that now emerges is related only to the reality of the scientific community; that is, the *second* (the antithesis) appears in dialogue with colleagues in the *scientific reality*. In other words, there will never be a *mutual dialectic* relation *between the different realities*. Because no mutual dialectic relation is developed, there is a great risk that the relation becomes *unilaterally dialectic*. Creators of knowledge will then, according to the actors view, use their language in a way that implicitly denies other people's freedom (see Figure 6.1) and thereby they will stretch and mold everyday reality and people in the same way a potter controls a lump of clay (*human beings are made into things*), because our relation to things are then unilaterally dialectic.

We use this to direct the reader's attention to the most important starting point for the actors view: namely, that *phenomena* must be *interpreted* according to the *meaning, significance* and *purpose* they have for the *actors*. After such a process, phenomena also become phenomena to the creators of knowledge, who then attempt to externalize these interpreted phenomena to the actors by means of a scientific language. This means that the descriptive and ideal-typified languages developed by researchers/consultants/investigators must reflect the richness of variety in social reality, its dialectic nature, its relative and its unique characteristics – in other words, be based on the reality they try to describe. The languages can then be developed with various degrees of specificity and detail. In this way we can find various levels of abstraction, not only in everyday language but also within the framework for handling the scientific language. It then follows, according to the actors view, that actors creators of knowledge use their language also to clarify their special responsibility for the *self-reference* of creating knowledge and such actions in social development.

Diagnosis

In denoting the conceptional meaning of diagnosis, we began with three stages of understanding: *preunderstanding, understanding* and *postunderstanding*. We also brought up the objectives of the stages and what they contained in general. We did not, however, illustrate the way of thinking that guides the diagnostic work of the actors creators of knowledge during these stages.

During the entire diagnostic process – all three stages of understanding – creators of knowledge work by placing themselves *alternately* in *two* different situations: by personally *engaging* themselves in, and *dissociating* themselves from, the actors being studied. While personally engaged, the creators of knowledge have an opportunity to co-act with and interpret the actors in a *dialogical* relationship (see "Dialogue" above) and thereby attain an *immediate understanding*. In order to get *perspectives* on the immediate understanding, the creators of knowledge dissociate themselves from the actors for a while and attempt to disregard *factual* circumstances. They then use metatheories – referred to earlier – for interpretation. During this dissociation an *intermediate understanding* is developed. Through this *interplay*, both actors creators of knowledge and other actors grow in capacity and insight. This means, of course, that the first engagement situation and the *immediate* understanding associated with it will not be the same as the second one, and the second not the same as the third, and so on. This is also true for the dissociating situations and the *intermediate* understanding (a dialectical process of development).

Below, we describe some of the thinking in a *first* situation of engagement and dissociation.

Engagement

The actors bring data and information to the creators of knowledge through externalized language descriptions. In principle, the steering that the researchers/consultants/investigators have means only that they want to achieve a *dialogical* situation, by means of which they hope to capture an actor's egological sphere. They know that this result is not obtained at once. The process is considerably longer, with learning/unlearning and development of understanding. Creators of knowledge have something in their background that initiates an interest in an organization even before arriving on the grounds. Certain problems, questions, motives and actions work as incentives to this interest. An actors creator of knowledge wants to understand the *significances* behind problems, opportunities, questions, motives, actions, and more. Based on these conceptions, the creator of knowledge attempts to guide the dialogue. The actors, on the other hand, are expected to share their versions and interpretations within these restrictions. In this case, the actors have the leading role, at least quantitatively.

The working results of this *first phase* depend on the spirit and actions that can be created between a creator of knowledge and the (other) actors. The possibility of sustaining an inter-subjective communication depends on whether the parties see each other as genuine parties to the conversation. This of course requires that both parties are open and honest during the dialogue. In this first phase, an *immediate understanding* is developed that is, however, created in a dialectic relation that is still weak.

Before entering a *dissociative* situation, creators of knowledge must be reasonably sure of the actors' denotation of the conceptual meaning of various questions. Creators of knowledge therefore implement *a kind of validity control* that has possibilities for a *corrected immediate understanding*. This takes place in such a way that the actors are allowed to check their own interpretations from the *first phase*. The feedback may result in new dimensions of the problems, new self-interpretations, new awareness, new repressions, new defence mechanisms and new tendencies to cover up. This can lead to a *change* of, or *supplementation* to, the original externalized descriptions. The finite provinces of meaning held by the actors may therefore seem to change in this *second phase*. The creator of knowledge, however, should not take these new versions for granted. The interpretive creation of knowledge in the *dissociative* situation, therefore, should encompass versions from both the first and the second phases.

Dissociation

In a dissociative situation, creators of knowledge free themselves from the actors for a short time in order to make a further "validity check" based on other sources. They try during this time to place the whole problem or opportunity complex within brackets in order to separate it from the actual situation. They do this in order to obtain *further perspectives* on the finite provinces of meaning, to discover *the potential in what is factual* and thereby obtain an intermediate understanding. The actors' own interpretations of the egological sphere are related to other sources of interpretation and to *metatheories* described earlier. The development of understanding and the "validation" thus continue by means of the creator of knowledge's attempts to interpret the reasonableness of the externalized descriptions. The creator of knowledge therefore supplements the actors' original descriptions with other sources and his/her own interpretation of reasonableness. The actors' original descriptions and self-interpretations nevertheless remain important sources of knowledge in the diagnostic process.

The continuation

This alternation eventually continues with a new situation of engagement in which the knowledge from the dissociative stage is fed back to the actors. The objective is to allow the actors to obtain *deeper insights* into their own interpretations. In return, the researcher/ consultant/ investigator is given the opportunity to obtain a *deeper interpretation of the reasonableness* of the consistency among manifested actions, alternative actions not taken, and the actors' denotations of the conceptual meaning of various actions and non-actions. As a result, the creator of knowledge obtains a new *immediate understanding* and continues his or her work with a new dissociation, and so on. During this continuing dialectic process, a larger and larger co-created awareness of what is *factual* and what is *potential* is developed.

A comment

These alternating procedures continue throughout all three of the diagnostic stages described above: *preunderstanding, understanding* and *postunderstanding*. The number of alternations necessary within each stage in order to fulfil its purposes and knowledge ambitions (see Figure 6.2) must be decided from case to case.

The objective of creating knowledge

The knowledge-creating objective of *understanding* conceptual meaning and egological spheres is related, among other things, to the actors view opinion of the social sciences as a science of *conceptually denoted meaning* and the idea of how *social reality is constructed*. In this context, the egological sphere (the logic in constructing subjective conceptual meaning) is sovereign. Human beings do not act without *interpreting* reality. The actors view postulates that there is a *connection* between *interpretation* (the actual denotion of conceptual meaning of action) and *action*. In the terms of an egological sphere, the actors view creators of knowledge attempt to understand this *dialectic* relation typical of human beings as sensible social creatures.

Individual actors *ascribe* a *significance, a purpose, an understanding*, to themselves and their actions that is noted by the creator of knowledge. Added to this are a number of different interpretations that other actors make of these actions, as well as the designation of meaning, which is viewed as controlling their actions. Researchers/consultants/investigators must therefore give *variety-rich* descriptions of the content of the egological sphere of the specific actor in order to reflect the *potential in what is factual* through the *ambiguity* that is an inherent part of social reality.

Creators of knowledge now act at two levels of language. At the "lower" level, they give extensive and manifold descriptions of the content of various conceptual meanings that are denoted as action by the actor in question. At the scientific level, on the other hand, the point is for researchers/consultants/investigators to *denote* the *egological sphere* from an *actors* and *structural,* as well as from a *dialectic*, point of departure.

Actors-based denotation of conceptual meaning

An actors-based denotation of conceptual meaning can encompass both concrete and ideal-typified actors. Creators of knowledge may then, if they wish, verify the actors-based denotation of conceptual meaning against the structurally and dialectically based denotations of conceptual meaning. In this way the creators of knowledge may, through their overview, bring understanding to a large number of actors-based denotations of conceptual meaning. The strategic question for such a study of conceptually denoted meaning is: *"What does it mean?"* If this question is prescribed in the "right" way, it can result in an experience of "damn it!" or of "aha!" or of "what is going on?" – that is, the potential in what is factual is manifested.

Structurally based denotation of conceptual meaning

When creators of knowledge form structurally based denotations of conceptual meaning, they try to clarify how *typifications* and *institutions* (see above) emerge (e.g. "business concepts") as taken-for-granted structures in the dialectic play among the denotations of conceptual meaning by various actors in and through a life practice. Over time, these institutions will acquire a more and more objectified and unambiguous character in a social reality that is otherwise highly multifaceted; they therefore tend, for good or ill, to create a strong prescribing power on patterns of interaction and action, and on the way of thinking within a particular life practice (e.g. a company, a family, a political party). Structurally based denotations of conceptual meaning reflect entire organizations, and they exist as "the organization's finite province of meaning to itself", constructed by – yet at the same time independent of – the denotations of conceptual meaning of individual actors. It is these institutionalized, somewhat rigid, provinces the creator of knowledge attempts to form for the purpose of making them understood.

Dialectically based denotation of conceptual meaning

The dialectically based denotation of conceptual meaning refers mainly to a diagnosis of the denotation of conceptual meaning as a *process* among various groups of actors, institutions, and single actors. With its starting point in the construction of social reality, a dialectic play takes place (see Figure 6.10).

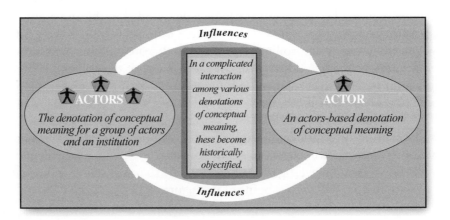

Figure 6.10   Dialectically Based Denotation

A denotation of conceptual meaning for groups of actors consists of a *historical* diagnosis. Through such a diagnosis, the researcher/consultant/investigator may find various epochs with different types of patterns that give structural characteristics to the period. The creator of knowledge should ask for the *meanings* of different periods of history, the implications of different patterns, what was significant in different epochs and how different epochs were understood by *different types* of actors. A historic diagnosis also involves a study of *changes* and *change potentials*. What does the change imply? What are the characteristics of different change potentials? In this dialectic play, many denotations of conceptual meaning will be *objectified* – acquire stable structural characteristics – but many others will change with time.

Forming a dialectically based denotation of conceptual meaning obviously becomes more extensive than working with the denotations of conceptual meaning for a few specific actors. We are here dealing with larger social groups or with a more complicated actor level than the one involving individual and specific actors. The dialectic, the language and the actors all bring an ambiguous character to social reality. The possibilities for *change* and *stability* exist simultaneously as expressions of human unfreedom and/or freedom.

Denotation of conceptual meaning and scientific language

The denotation of conceptual meaning is consequently the basis on which the scientific language of the actors view rests. This language is there to communicate (to form) these denotations of conceptual meaning, which will then appear as the second in relation to the first immediate denotations (so-called *first hand expressions*) of conceptual meaning given by the actors. The language will then give rise to its own dialectics in the formation dialogue with the actors. Through this dialectic play, a development of understanding is made possible for the creator of knowledge as well as for the (other) actors. This could be called the third stage of diagnosis – *the postunderstanding*.

We have divided the scientific language of the actors view into two levels: *descriptive language* and *ideal-typified language*. We have also explained some of the basic differences between the two levels. We now continue this presentation by describing the connection between the denotations of conceptual meaning described above (actors-, structurally and dialectically based) and the two language levels.

Under *descriptive language* we can find *three* kinds of models: *situational interpretive models*, *institutional models* and *process models* (we recommend the reader look at Figure 3.14 again, where the different language levels and models are illustrated). We relate the situational interpretive models to the *actors-based* denotation of conceptual meaning; the institutional models to the *structurally based*; and the process models to the *dialectically based* denotation of conceptual meaning (see Figure 6.11).

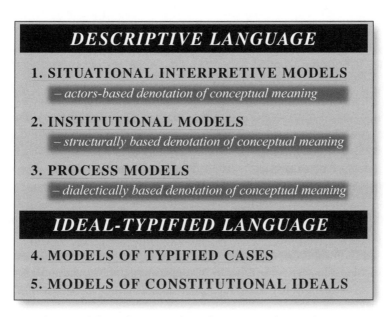

Figure 6.11   Actors View Models and Denotation of Conceptual Meaning

A *descriptive language* is based on a *direct connection* with the part of the social reality that it describes. The main purpose of the descriptive language is to communicate understanding and initiate action *in relation to* this *specific* part of reality. By giving the actors an opportunity – in the form of a descriptive language – to experience the various denotations of conceptual meaning formed as something *mediated*, a dialectic process will emerge in which the potential in what is factual can be developed.

In order for the interpretations and clarifications presented in the three models of the descriptive language to convey more universal knowledge, the creator of knowledge must refine the results; "take away" what situationally influences the shape of the descriptive language. This condensation/qualification leads to the *second* language type in the actors view: *ideal-typified language*, in which we again find the two kinds of models, *typified cases and constitutional ideals*. By condensation the different models in the *descriptive language*, a case description of typified actors who carry typified actors' conceptions and pursue typified actions under typified circumstances can be developed – namely, models for *typified cases*. These models have an *ideal* character because in their condensed form they describe various *ideal states* that "imaginatively" can reflect human freedom and potential, and thereby engage various actors in *procreating* dialogues in which the potential will be transformed into the factual, that is, into a *new social reality*. Typified cases, in spite of being ideal, have a *connection* to the "living" social reality, although no longer characterized situationally, but *essentially*.

In order not to bring the description too far into the concept of essence, we can, as a simplification, use the examination of a musical piece as an analogy. In the three models of *descriptive language* (see Figure 6.11) the "denotation of melody" of the social reality is presented by (starting from) the *situational* "denotation of tones". In a model of *typified cases*, on the other hand, the situational "denotation of tones" is deepened, and the "denotation of melody" *as such* is studied and described. This "denotation of melody" (essence) we can produce only through a *process of interpretation, action* and *reflection*.

If we go further in the process of condensation/qualification, we can ask ourselves what *constitutes* the "denotation of melody" and find that the answer is "the theme". The second form of *ideal-typified language* is therefore about *constituting ideals*: in our musical analogy, the "denotation of theme" (*theme* in the meaning of motive for creating a melody).

In models of typified cases the "denotation of theme" is *described* by the "denotation of melody". In a similar fashion, the "denotation of melody" is *described* by the "denotation of tones" in the models of the descriptive language. We can thus see how various forms of models (except models of constitutional ideals) describe something by the use of something at different levels (see Figure 6.12 opposite).

So, models of *constitutional ideals* belong to the final "core" in which something cannot be described by anything else, only by itself. By going beyond the "denotation of melody", "denotation of beat", "denotation of tempo", "denotation of harmony", and so on, we achieve the "denotation of theme" that *constitutes* higher levels; that is, we get the constitutional factors of social reality. Similar to models of typified cases, models of constitutional ideals have an ideal character, but by means of the condensing process retain a connection to social reality.

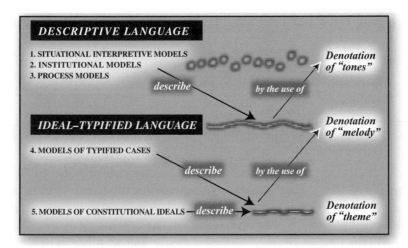

Figure 6.12   Language Development

The condensing referred to can be seen as an *understanding* of the radical shifts that creators of knowledge make in their *interpretive, active* and *reflective* orientation in order to reach the "hidden" subjectivity of the knowledge of social reality; that is, in order to clarify both the *historical* and *future meaningfulness* in the *potential* and (at the same time) in the *factual* present.

Using this kind of *language for creating* knowledge the actors oriented researcher/consultant/investigator is developing something *unique*, but something which also goes beyond what is singular to something as *universal* as music.

Like a composer, to continue the music analogy, he/she wants with his/her *language development* to create excitement and a mood by varying "rhythm, tonality and timbre" in the descriptions. The *"rhythm"* we could call the "pulse" of the activity/text, which is increasing and decreasing in a conscious way, in order to create a tight and varying experience. *"Tonality"* is an implicit *keynote*, which is there all the time, even if it is not heard – to compare with denotation of theme. To break the keynote – the theme – and do this without "playing out of tune", is called the composer's modulation. The actors creator of knowledge is happy to modulate his/her descriptions and actions in order to create moments of surprise or situations that require imagination, interpretation and insight – a way to mark or reflect on the denotation of theme. The *"timbre"* – the instrument or voice that performs the tone – is created in commonality in the actors view by personalities from different life-worlds – everything from participants in the researched activities in the study area to the readers of the different descriptive languages. The *dialectics* in social reality then becomes visible in an understanding and action-oriented way. When all the actors involved are given the possibility to feel their own participation in the resulting knowledge creation, they will understand that things are moving through their own choices and actions and by those of others. One does not, then, become *alienated* facing the inner flow of the dynamism of our socially constructed reality. When you are participating as a knowledge creating actor, everyday life does not appear as something *determined* (= conditioned by different external factors and not by the free will of man).

SOME THEORETICAL AND ACTION-ORIENTED STARTING POINTS

Social phenomenology and the actors view

The actors view developed in this book is inspired by a social phenomenology tradition with Alfred Schutz as the major representative scholar. Social phenomenology attempts to make clear the variety and the relativity of social reality and how it is maintained by the language used to describe it (see Appendix). In this way, the actors view stipulates that all collected data are "impregnated with theory" from the social sciences, alternatively from less systematic theories like the basic conceptions of everyday life, or from both (we have previously in the book called this phenomenon "the self-reference" of social science).

It is therefore in the interest of the actors view to use, among other things, linguistic innovations, pictures, sound, and more, as working tools/processes in order to puncture taken-for-granted structures in the conception of reality that often stifle development and that are maintained by scientific as well as everyday theories from the language fields. In order to make creators of knowledge aware that data are never theoretically neutral, the actors view prefers to refer to the *construction of data* instead of the collection of data. If we accept this premise, that data are "impregnated with theory", it leads us, according to the actors view, to acknowledge that a "fact" is a *variable* thing, in time as well as in place. This is the background for why the actors view does not accept the idea of an objective, observer-independent reality against which we can test our statements.

A creator of knowledge, according to the actors view, cannot be objective in the sense stipulated by the analytical view (see Chapter 7). Instead of, as the actors view puts it, conducting an artificial struggle by trying to isolate the creator of knowledge in a kind of external relation to what he/she is studying, the actors view makes the creator of knowledge a central figure *responsible* for how data are constructed and how knowledge is created. In this tradition, the opinion is that it is not possible, and therefore not desirable, to establish a clear boundary between the subjects aiming for knowledge and the "objects" providing it. But don't misunderstand this, it does not mean that knowledge is subjective in the sense of not being accessible or of not being capable of testing for reasonableness by others.

Subjects and objects as understood in the actors view exist in a *meaning situation*, a meaning context. We always meet subjects and objects in connection with import and meaning. According to the actors view, objects cannot exist in a social vacuum. *Ob-ject* means *for-somebody* in this view. The consequence is that what we call the object of a study will always be woven into a fabric (a net) of relationships of understanding that consists of everything from the creator of knowledge's own pre-scientific and scientific theories to the actors' "theories" of meaning. For instance, using a questionnaire to ask people about matters whose personal *significance* (engagement or, interest in, significance for, in their everyday actions) we cannot possibly know, will, according to the actors view, produce meaningless knowledge for the actors in question and most likely also for the creator of knowledge. Knowledge becomes knowledge of object-like things (an objective, independent, artificial world) that, according to the actors view, triggers a biased and unethical knowledge of other human beings (see Figure 6.1). The only meaning relation the questionnaire has as a technique for asking questions, according to the actors view, is to the creator of knowledge's own engagement and understanding, not to the individual respondents' worlds. This is what keeps expressions like "theory is one thing, practice is another" alive, according to the actors view.

Social reality consists of people – human beings – and their freedom to interact. The phrases *human being* and *freedom* are important in this context. In fact, this orientation is embedded in the denotation of "the actors view" (see Figure 6.2). By stressing the term *actor*, an important characteristic of social reality is described. A person is also dependent on other people in social reality. The position of dependence among human beings must consequently require interaction in *various forms of externalization*, such as when we talk with each other and when we work together. Social interaction is based on people being generously equipped with the ability to interpret their reality. *Dialectics* is characterized by this interplay of interpretations being based on interactions and interactions based on interpretations. The dialectic is marked by *multiplicity, ambiguity* and *change,* among other reasons because people are subjects who come from different environments, have different historical backgrounds, and, furthermore, play different roles in social reality. Social multiplicity can be externalized and described via different human vocabularies. The *denotation of conceptual meaning* that is expressed by the human *use of languages* is an important *constitutional factor* for the way social reality looks. The actors creators of knowledge take great pains to study this social *language game*. This is because the opinion of the actors view is that the language game in dialectic terms simultaneously shows subjective ambiguity and structural non-ambiguity.

We reproduce in a number of theses a basic perspective of social reality based in social phenomenology and the actors view:

1. A theoretically articulated agreement between reality and view/ approach is needed.
2. Social reality can be seen as a language game in which it is important to understand the three kinds of denotations of conceptual meaning of various phenomena.
3. The pre-scientific idea stipulating that the more accurately a phenomenon can be measured the better it can be understood, is of no relevance to the actors view (see *the Arbnor Uncertainty Principle,* Figure 6.1).
4. Various dialectic processes characterize the construction of social reality.
5. Everyday reality is fundamental to the understanding of social reality.
6. That which is expressed in everyday life as factual has an important significance in terms of diminishing what is potential.
7. Free human beings are seen as carriers of interpretations, having the ability to create knowledge and actions in a net of meaning relations.
8. In order for new knowledge to breed insight, development of personality, and direct action, it must be related to meaning and purpose – i.e. the actors' own emotional relations (including those of the creator of knowledge).
9. Business is a human science. Human beings construct social business reality.
10. Business is about transforming resources, where the most important 'capital' is made up of the human ability to interpret, create knowledge and act (an engagement in the world) within the framework of structural denotations of conceptual meaning (see Figure 6.2).

From the above it is apparent that the actors view consciously encompasses the philosophical aspects of life as well.

Out of the ultimate presumptions on which the actors view is based, what is known as the *network* idea as a model for social organizing and change has also emerged. The idea of being able to describe social phenomena simultaneously as structure and process by seeing phenomena in terms of network relations is based on the central idea that it is common value structures that connect people to each other and give them the power to create unexpected changes. In terms of the actors view, this can be described as a meaning context in which the quantitative accumulation is transformed into a new and unexpected quality (see Figure 6.3). The original network idea, according to the actors view, was nevertheless distorted when it entered the world of researchers/consultants/ investigators because the analytical and systems views chose to start to "construct" networks for others, thereby losing the very essence of the genuine construction of networks: the *spontaneous* and *free* driving force in meaning relations among people. Despite this, the actors view regards the network idea as an interesting descriptive language for making social change understood.

Developing human procreative power

The intent of the actors view is to achieve understanding, insight, emancipation and action for various actors in society (e.g. business leaders, researchers, consultants, investigators). In order to create this, creators of knowledge (being business leaders, researchers, consultants, or investigators) can, within the framework of the models described above under the heading "Denotation of conceptual meaning and scientific language", use various instruments to develop language. These instruments are not only of a purely descriptive nature referring to actors concerned in the study area, but should also be seen as serious instruments of communication that, at the end of a project, can produce understanding in the meaning relations for other actors and other creators of knowledge as well.

The *written word*, emanating from the *creative act*, is one aspect of the way the actors view communicates via *procreative reports* (see Chapter 7 "The procreative report"). Another is the *direct act*. In both cases the *dialogical structure* is central.

In the same way as we in a dialogue can use the language subconsciously, we may here be able to use it consciously to create new thoughts, open new perspectives, create involvement, etc. This is all related to those *knowledge interests* (understanding, emancipating and innovative) and those *knowledge ambitions* (see Figure 6.2) which engage the actors oriented creator of knowledge to use language in a way where life is enriched.

Working with reports that create knowledge, in the actors view, is a means of communication that should attempt to go beyond the traditional research/consulting/investigative report. Compared with a rational ideal picture in which descriptions are assumed to be expressed objectively and perceived unambiguously, the descriptions here are intended to give possibilities to interpretations and actions as objects for the development of knowledge – that is to release *the potential in what is factual*.

This is a kind of knowledge development where metatheory, empirical reality and ultimate presumptions are up against each other in a parallel fashion, where creation of knowledge and action are inside and outside of the same helix. The totality is polyphonic if we use our earlier musical analogy, but we don't find the music by *explaining* the instruments. We have to *understand,* according to the actors view, the complex interrelation between actors and their construction of meaning in the social reality as denotation of "tones, melody and theme" (see Figure 6.12).

In this area, with reports that create knowledge according to the actors view, we find ourselves at the beginning of an exciting development. The actors view encourages legitimate experiments. Furthermore, there is a striking similarity between the almost bewildering confusion that is revealed by the actors approach's view of the knowledge-creating process of description and Bohr's principle of *complementarity* in modern physics. Bohr's principle claims that it is impossible to reduce the nonreducable variation in reality to one single language. And this, according to Bohr, is not a resignation but a development in thinking that Bohr himself, apparently, said made him dizzy.

The actors view often borrows *complementary* ideas from other areas, including artistically oriented activities, that can lead to a situation in which knowledge recognizes previously unseen connections, or in which out-dated knowledge can be overcome, and so on. By means of a theoretically well-founded actors view, theory will, through its proponents, become *the best practice. Theory* will *not* be something that is done before or after *practice* but will become an integrated part of practical development.

In pedagogic contexts, therefore, the actors view recommends *the objective* (the ob-ject) of creating knowledge that alternates between theory and practice, rather than the *time periods* of creating knowledge that are to be sequentially partitioned into practical and theoretical stages, a view that is common in many educative contexts. As the actors view sees it, a partitioning of time may lead instead to the possibility that an old-fashioned theory based on meaningless generalizations might survive. And this could, in turn, eventually give nourishment to what is otherwise such a mistaken opinion about the strict difference between theory and practice. Theory and practice, according to the actors view, are two sides of the same progressive coin – our social life.

Reality is, according to the actors view, a human construction in which actors are involved. "Actor" here becomes a central concept when studying the individuals of society. It is a person with the potential freedom to act and to create his/her own life-space. Other concepts like intentionality, dialogue, understanding, denotation of conceptual meaning, action and others, are in this chapter given a dialectic significance. The chapter describes how these and other ultimate presumptions of the actors view together create the frames for a view with an understanding, emancipating and innovating knowledge interest and with knowledge ambitions to reinforce what is unique, look for what is different in what is similar, be meaning- and action-oriented, emancipate the potential in the factual, etc. The chapter also provides the necessary "philosophical" and theoretical background in order to be able to practically apply the actors view in different research/consulting/investigation situations.

POINTS OF REFLECTION

1.   *The Micro-cosmos* of man and *the Arbnor Uncertainty Principle* are two analogies to natural sciences used in the chapter. Talk to your friends about what in the chapter has been described as *being, becoming* and *freedom*. What do these three concepts mean in relation to what is called *determinism*?
2.   Please illustrate what the actors view talks about as *intentionality*?
3.   The actors view has several explicit *knowledge ambitions*. Which ones? And *knowledge interests* as .... Which? What would these ambitions and interests mean to you personally as a creator of knowledge?
4.   Why should a *dialogue* not be mixed up with discussion or debate? Which are the two *elements* of the dialogue and its two *methodological purposes*?
5.   Construct an example that can vivify the concept of *dialectics*?
6.   *Actor* is the very central concept of the view. Which important qualities of the view are indicated with this concept?
7.   If you were to *develop language* in order to describe the actors view to your fellow students, what *metaphors* and concepts would you then use in order to come up with a *procreative* description?
8.   Why is the knowledge creating *act* so important in the actors view?
9.   What does *reality as a social construction* mean? And which are the *processes* by which this construction is described?
10. The construction processes are *dialectically related* to each other. Can you present what is meant by "a dialectic relationship" in this context?
11. *Meta-theories* are mentioned in the text and they are four in number, but how are they denoted and what do they stand for?
12. What is meant by *denotation of conceptual meaning*?
13. Which *models* do you come up with when you describe what is contained in *descriptive language*? And how do you make the models comprehensible for those who do not know what descriptive language is all about?
14. Which *models* are described under *ideal-typified language*? And what is an *ideal type*?

RECOMMENDED FURTHER READING

See the end of the Appendix and visit the website below.

Become a worldwide partner as a *knowledge creator* in the development of *Methodology for Creating Business Knowledge* by visiting the website: **www.knowledge-creator.com**. Here you can contribute by asking your own questions and you will also find answers to the most frequently asked questions. The website has been developed alongside this third edition of the book and the questions posted there will be used to provide input for future editions.

PART III
METHODOLOGY

METHODICAL PROCEDURES

In this chapter we present a number of different techniques, which by the method-ical procedures (see Figure 1.10) for the different views can be designed as effective methods for creating knowledge. The chapter also takes up issues around validity, reliability and objectivity. Presented here are some techniques that are specific for different methodological views as well, techniques that in several respects charac-terize these different views and their actions in the study area.

PROCEDURES AS LESSONS IN HARMONY

The description of the different methodological views has, for defensible reasons, not fol-lowed a completely uniform line. One methodological view is not like another, which means that we need somewhat different ways of describing them. We would like to add to this treat-ment a bit before we proceed.

The descriptions of the first two views – the analytical view (Chapter 4) and the systems view (Chapter 5) – were illustrated, among other things, with examples of different *theories and results* to which they have led. This was less appropriate for the actors view (Chapter 6); there we referred to *metatheories*, which are *not* comparable to the theories of the other two views. This is explained by the presumptions or lack of presumptions about reality made by the vari-ous views. From this it also follows that the analytical view and the systems view, to a greater extent than the actors view, stress the importance of charting earlier studies and their results within a given field of research/consulting/ investigation before the next study is undertaken.

This will be fairly obvious if we consider the following. If reality is presumed to be *filled with facts*, interest will of necessity be directed toward how this objective and/or subjective factive reality appears, that is, the researcher/consultant/ investigator aims at using or devel-oping *reproduction theories*. If we instead presume, as in the actors view, that reality is basically a *social construction dependent* upon us as observers/actors, interest will be directed toward the way this reality is *constructed*, that is, the researcher/consultant/investigator aims at developing *construction theories*. But the actors view, as we know, also "reproduces" a social reality by using its *descriptive* and *ideal-typified languages*. These constructions are called metatheories because they not only include these languages (their *own* construction), but are also the prerequisites of their development.

This could be perceived as the actors view going one step further than the other two views (it brings an understanding of, or depicts, *both* the construction of reality *and* its appearance). But this opinion is wrong insofar as the other two views' conceptions of reality and science do not presume a construction process – reality as such is a given. In this sense we *cannot* say that one view goes further than another.

At the same time we should point out that the proponents of the actors view claim that they *can* go further (or rather deeper) by presuming reality to be a social construction. What they are saying is that it is not until one realizes that reality is and will remain a social construction that many of the unsolved problems of business (and of society in general) can be studied. It is pointless for us to argue for or against this opinion here. What we can say, however, is that the different conceptions of reality that are associated with our views lead to different ways of doing research/consulting/investigation and to differently created worlds of knowledge, in both practice and theory; whether any view can go further or deeper than another view can only be decided by reflecting on the different conceptions of reality. The question thus becomes: can you go further – can you explain and understand more – by changing (changing yourself) to another view's *conception of reality*, instead of staying with the one being used? This leads to something we have already pointed out: "You can never establish empirically which view is the best one."

Because we are attempting, as far as possible, to present each of the views on its own terms, it becomes necessary to let the descriptions of the different views vary. The reason we have devoted so much time to ultimate presumptions is because we hope through this book on methodology to create conditions for independent and critical thinking in the reader. The reality that creators of knowledge face when conducting a study is not exactly the reality described in textbooks. Modifications must therefore always be made to textbook presentations. These modifications cannot be made without first having gained an insight into the ultimate presumptions on which a view is based. Otherwise it would be like opening and changing a car's gearbox without understanding the "presumptions" on which it is based, namely, its relations to the engine, the road, and the use of the car generally.

We mentioned earlier that methodology's task is to clarify how different methodological views and study areas harmonize in terms of problem formulations, research/consulting/investigation plans, methods and techniques. Because it is not possible to define this "harmonology" in advance in an "instrumental" way, methodology will to a great extent be about developing the *insight* and understanding that make it possible for creators of knowledge to develop some degree of "harmonology" on their own.

The presentation so far has aimed at producing independent and critical thinking about what the three methodological views try to achieve and under what circumstances they should be used. These are necessary prerequisites for developing an *operative paradigm*. An operative paradigm cannot be developed just from technique centered knowledge and associated skills; also necessary are a deep insight into, and feeling for, that which is being studied and for how the "tools/processes" the creator of knowledge uses for orientation are related to ultimate presumptions (the foundation of any methodological view). This is because the purpose of an operative paradigm is to create a *fit* between ultimate presumptions about a *methodological view* and the nature of the *study area* (see Figure 7.1).

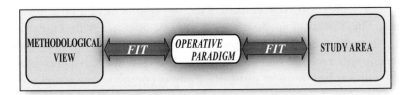

Figure 7.1   Operative Paradigms Create Fit

OPERATIVE PARADIGMS

In the introductory chapter of this book, we described how scientific theory uses the *paradigm concept* to describe the relation between *ultimate presumptions* and *concrete methodological views*. In the same way, we proposed our idea of being able to describe the relation between a *methodological view* and *an area under study* by using the *operative paradigm concept*. Through this concept, which is determined in terms of *methodical procedure* and *methodics*, we have acquired a means of communication that will allow us to compare various studies, reports, essays, and the like. If this can function as a bridge of *language commonality* among the proponents of various methodological views, we have come very far on the way to both a better understanding and a better communication within the area of methodology, which continues to be characterized by a high degree of conceptual confusion. This becomes especially important with the intensification of knowledge in production, service, marketing, and other areas in business.

To invest resources strategically in developing knowledge without making it clear in advance what the knowledge is knowledge about – that is, what ultimate presumptions it is based on – would not be cost effective (more about this kind of "knowledge audit" in the final chapter). Therefore, we can expect an increasing interest in the questions that methodology addresses.

In our earlier descriptions of the operative paradigm concept we stressed its character of aspiring to fitness, in other words, that it might function as a general instrument for testing relations between a chosen methodological view and the actual study area. From this it follows naturally that the development, as well as the form, of the operative paradigm will be *different* for each of the three methodological approaches (in the text from now on we use both the concepts of view and approach, alternating depending on whether we are referring to the view as such or to its use in practical application – the use of either one concept or the other is, however, not something which the reader needs to attach any greater importance to than has already been stated).

If we were to describe the development of an *operative paradigm* in each of the approaches in terms of their degree of formalism and instrumentalism, we would find that the *analytical* approach ranks *highest*, the *actors* approach ranks *lowest* and the *systems* approach is somewhere *in between*. This, of course, would also characterize when in a study the operative paradigm is ready as well as its *final form*. Because of its greater degree of formalism and instrumentalism, the analytical view considers the development of an operative paradigm as less problematic. The analytical approach, as we know, operates with a greater number of a priori starting points than the other approaches, which leads to its operative paradigm being ready relatively *early* in a study. This also indicates that the operative paradigm in an actors approach study will not be complete until the study is complete: an actors approach operative paradigm is developed *gradually* over the course of a study. The time for developing the operative paradigm in the systems approach varies between these two points, depending on the circumstances of a given study.

What happens in the development of an operative paradigm can, as mentioned before, be divided up and described in terms of *methodical procedures* and *methodics*. We remind the reader of our definitions:

Methodical Procedure: the way in which researchers (or any other creators of knowledge) arrange, develop, and/or modify any technique, theory, or previous result in a methodological approach, or, alternatively, develop a new technique.

Methodics: the way in which researchers (or any other creators of knowledge) relate and arrange the techniques-become-methods in their study plans, and the way in which a study is actually approached.

Researchers/consultants/investigators, just like other people, have access to a number of means in their work. These means vary. There are physical means like paper and pen, microscope, computer, and the like; what we might call instruments or *tools*. Among the tools used by creators of knowledge we can also count the special terminology available for the purpose of creating knowledge. In business we have a set of such terms, such as costs and revenues, budget, manager, brand, segmentation.

By a *technique* we mean the way in which a subactivity of creating knowledge is carried out. The tools just mentioned (and others) will be useful in this context. When a sample is taken (a technique), a random numbers table (a tool) can be used. When a personal interview is carried out (a technique), a digital recorder (a tool) can be used. Furthermore, the interview must be conducted in a terminology (a further tool) that the respondent can understand.

One could also say that *available* techniques are the alternative actions open to the creators of knowledge. Part of their work may also be to *develop* new techniques, increasing the number of alternative actions available.

The interesting question is, of course: *When* should the researcher/consultant/ investigator carry out, for instance, a face-to-face interview, *where* should it take place and *how* should it be arranged? If we also keep in mind *why* a technique is used, we have four questions with which we can assess techniques. In other words, if for each technique we ask:

- When?
- Where?
- How?
- Why?

a specific technique should be used, we arrive at the *level of methods*. We maintain that a technique in itself is worthless. A technique has no value until it becomes a method. To turn a technique into a method or to develop a new technique into a method is what we call a *methodical procedure* (please note: adapting and possibly modifying previous results and theories is also referred to as methodical procedures). This implies a serious answer to the four questions above.

Whether a new technique is to be *developed*, or which technique is to be *chosen* and how it might be *modified*, are determined by:

- the methodological view chosen
- the character of the study area.

It is to some extent possible to examine in principle what a technique should look like in relation to a particular methodological view. But it is not until it is related to the study area that a technique takes on its definite shape, that is, becomes a *method*.

In other words, the *methodological view* and the *character of the study area* (e.g. which problem and/or opportunity seems to be at hand) will determine the rules for choosing, arranging and developing techniques into methods, that is, the alternative actions to create knowledge.

The connections between techniques and methodological approaches – in other words, the development of *methodical procedures* – are the subject of this chapter.

From methodical procedures we take a further step when we come to *methodics*. We then come to the study plan as a whole, and to the actual conduct of the study. This will be illustrated in Chapter 9.

There are major differences among methodological approaches as far as methodical procedures are concerned, but the differences are even greater for methodics. Methodical procedures and methodics go hand in hand. *In practice they cannot be fully separated.*

Every methodical procedure pays attention to its background, the methodics of which it is, or will be, a part. Any methodics would be empty if it did not contain seriously prepared methodical procedures. Nevertheless, in this chapter we will treat only methodical procedures and how they can be related to various methodological approaches. We do this in order to initiate the reader gradually into understanding the relations among the methodological view, the operative paradigm, methodical procedures and methodics – in other words, the development of an *operative paradigm*.

We believe that an exchange between "theory" (this chapter) and "practice" (Chapter 8, "Methods in Language and Action") is useful for continued learning. After reading Chapters 9 to 12, where we deal with methodics vis-à-vis our methodological approaches (in Chapter 9 in theory, in Chapters 10, 11 and 12 in practice), we are confident that the reader will have a practical and consistent methodological orientation.

We begin by reviewing what are considered to be "common" groups of techniques:

1. selection techniques (for units of study)
2. traditional data collection techniques
3. measurement and reliability techniques
4. validation techniques.

Even if our three methodological approaches often regard/make use of these groups of techniques differently (sometimes even define them differently), we believe they constitute something of a common ground for every effort to create knowledge. We are aware that several groups of techniques are thus excluded, for instance:

a. techniques for making definitions
b. techniques for relating to previous knowledge
c. mathematical and logical techniques
d. application techniques.

We covered *techniques for making definitions* in the illustrations of the basic concepts of the three methodological views presented in Chapters 4, 5 and 6. *Techniques for relating to previous knowledge* were brought up at the ends of these same chapters. *Mathematical and logical techniques* belong primarily to the analytical view (see brief discussion in Chapter 4), and will be considered later in this chapter when we treat techniques specific to the various methodological approaches (e.g. sampling). The differences in *application techniques* for each of the views should be clear after reading the examples.

After treating some "common" techniques, we will further clarify the differences among our methodological views. This will be done within the framework of one approach at a time, by specifically describing:

For the analytical approach:

- *sampling*
- *validation techniques*

For the systems approach:

- *historical studies*
- *case studies*

For the actors approach:

- *dialogue*
- *language development*

We treat these techniques separately even though they could be used in more than one methodological approach (but with modification, and often after redefinition). For instance, validation techniques are presented in the group of "common" techniques as well as under "specific" techniques.

This chapter ends with a reflection of how our three methodological views position themselves in relation to the problem of objectivity.

SOME "COMMON" GROUPS OF TECHNIQUES

Techniques for selecting units of study

In this section we provide certain general principles for using techniques to select units to be studied when creating knowledge. We will not go into deep mathematical or statistical aspects (they belong mainly to the analytical approach, which we will come back to). Our goal here is only to present a sufficient basis for understanding the different methodological views' relation to such techniques.

Every study (no matter which view it uses) wants to reach certain results, even if they are only preliminary. Reality (no matter how it is defined) can never be encompassed in its entirety. In every effort to create knowledge we can attempt to study, explain, and/or understand only a part of it. This part we can define as "a piece of history" (i.e. a temporal limitation) or "a piece of the existing state" (i.e. a spatial limitation). No matter how we do it, our area of interest becomes limited, that is, we must select only what seems relevant for the study.

In the analytical view reality is seen as a great number of independent units, which means that statistical sampling theory can be a decisive means for achieving the ambitions of the view (we will return to this theory in further detail). *Representativity* (i.e. how selected units represent the larger totality that is to be described or explained) becomes crucial for whether or not the research ambition will be generalizable. Finding the *average* and the *pattern around this average* is what every analytically based person trying to create knowledge aims for. If this is the case, it means that when the description or the explanation of the selected units is present, the description and the explanation of the area of interest as a whole is also present.

The principle of independent units of study is not accepted by the *systems view*. A systems-based person trying to create knowledge perceives his or her reality as consisting of systems, which by definition means *dependent relations* on the one hand, and sometimes *partly unique cases* on the other. The concept of representativity, in a strictly statistical sense, is therefore not valid for the systems view in general. It is therefore common to work with *case studies* here (more on these later). Another reason for working with case studies in the systems approach is simply that from a practical point of departure, analyses of complex objects require extensive effort. The cases studied by the systems creator of knowledge cannot be selected on the principle that they will represent all other systems (in the sense of being constructed the same, or of behaving the same way). Nevertheless, in the meaning given them by the systems view, they can represent *a certain type of system* (if the intention is to study a system *type*). So, the real systems selected for study within the systems approach usually follow other principles:

- They are *versatile* and can therefore bring comprehensive light to phenomena being studied.
- They are *interesting* in the sense of leading the development in some direction. This could mean that we will look for unique, or at least divergent, cases.

The concept of *representativity* is rarely used in the systems approach.

Because the *actors view* is primarily interested in *specifying the meaning* and *the construction* of social phenomena, starting from its inherent *egological sphere*, the talk about representativity is of less interest here too, and can even be seen as invalid. According to the actors view, representativity makes no sense in a socially constructed reality because it represents only shallow clichés of statistically generalized situational "tones of meaning" (see the subheading "Denotation of conceptual meaning and scientific language" in Chapter 6). The concept of representativity is therefore extremely rare in the actors approach. It is customary, however, to *apply* principles similar to those used for selecting cases in the systems approach when selecting individual companies in the actors approach. When selecting individual actors within those companies or elsewhere, some of the following principles, alone or in combination, are usually applied:

- recommended selection
- understanding selection
- problem/opportunity-oriented selection.

A *recommended selection* means letting different actors recommend other interesting actors. By an *understanding selection* we mean a selection of actors who, in the diagnostic development of understanding, turn out to be important in some way. A *problem/opportunity-oriented selection* means choosing individuals who are in some way connected to the problem/opportunity being studied. These people may not have been seen as important in the diagnostic development of understanding, but in order to get a versatile description of the significance of the problem/opportunity and possibly raise the level of understanding, certain actors are nevertheless chosen. This might in turn raise the level of understanding with which new selections will be made, but now as *understanding selections*. In other words, there is often an extensive *interchange* between these three types of selection.

Traditional techniques for collecting data

There are two main categories of traditional techniques for collecting data.

- using material previously collected, so-called *secondary information*
- collecting new data, so-called *primary information*.

Primary information can be collected in three ways:

- direct observations
- interviews
- experiments.

Secondary information

When using *secondary information*, the creator of knowledge often faces two problems:

1. *Compatibility*. Previously collected or secondary information might have been collected for another purpose, from another perspective, and so on. Existing data may therefore be classified differently or start from a different measurement scale and/or from other definitions. Consequently, these data might not be compatible with those the researcher/consultant/investigator wants.
2. *Trustworthiness*. Researchers/consultants/investigators can be unsure about the extent to which previously collected data are correct.

Primary information: Direct observation

You are observing when you conduct a face-to-face interview. Studies of secondary information, including viewing all types of recording or listening to recordings, are also a kind of observation. Both of these cases are what we might call *indirect observation* (and/or *listening*).

Direct observation, on the other hand, consists of a situation of creating knowledge that, *as a whole*, is arranged around observing what happens in the present. Four types of direct observation can be differentiated, as shown in Figure 7.2.

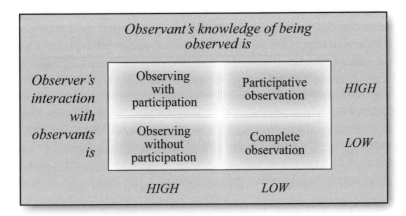

Figure 7.2 Types of Direct Observation

A situation with "complete observation" is difficult to achieve. It is *technically* complicated to arrange a situation in which you can observe without those being observed knowing it. It is also *morally* questionable whether a researcher/consultant/investigator should observe people without their knowledge and consent. Another technical problem, of course, is that you can directly observe only what is happening *here and now* (including directly observing something taking place *"there"*, if you have a camera pointed at the place). So a researcher/consultant/investigator must know *when and where to observe*.

Primary information: Interviews

A very common traditional technique for collecting primary information in business is through *interviews*. The following types can be differentiated:

- personal interview (face-to-face)
- telephone interview
- mail questionnaire
- group questionnaire (a questionnaire constructed by the interviewer and administered to an entire group at the same time and place).

Some important concepts for this traditional technique for collecting data are:

- *standardization:* the same questions for everyone
- *nonstructured interview:* interview with a low degree of standardization
- *open questions:* questions without fixed alternative answers
- *closed questions:* questions with fixed alternative answers
- *interviewer effect:* the respondent is influenced by the interviewer
- *panel effect:* the panel (a group of individuals who are repeatedly interviewed) usually develops to a point where it consists of "specialists" who are no longer representative of the social group, consumer type, and so on, from which they were originally selected.

Primary information: Experiments

The traditional technique for collecting data referred to as *experiments* is aimed directly at reproducing *causal relations* and therefore regarded as a technique for collecting data only in the analytical approach. However, this does not prevent the other methodological approaches from using the term "experiment", but as the other two views consider causal relations as irrelevant descriptions of social relations, the term will have a very different meaning in these other two views, and even a different meaning in between the two.

Successful experiments in the analytical approach starts with creators of knowledge finding (or arranging) two identical situations. Then they *deliberately* interfere with one of the situations so they can study the effects of this interference. After the interference has established itself, they measure the difference(s) between the two situations. The *effect* of the deliberate interference is the difference in the measured results between the experimental group (interfered with) and the control group (not interfered with). The interference is the *cause* of these effects (see Figure 7.3). We call this an *experiment with a control group* and *with post-test measurement only*.

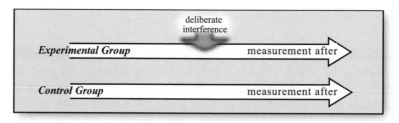

Figure 7.3   Experimental and Control Groups in an Experiment

There are a number of variations in how experiments are arranged. Researchers/consultants/ investigators can measure both the experimental and the control group before the experiment takes place in order to check for differences that may exist between the groups even before the experiment. These differences will have to be considered later when the effects of the interference are evaluated. Another variation when working with the experimental group only (i.e., omitting the control group) is to measure the experimental group's characteristics both before and after interference. There are yet other experimental variations.

A complete traditional experiment in the analytical approach should make two kinds of operations possible:

1. *Manipulation:* manipulation of the independent variable
2. *Control:* elimination of any influence from background or intervening variables, either by eliminating the variables or by isolating their influence. This means, among other things, that the researcher/consultant/ investigator is clear about the experimental context and that it is possible to repeat the experiment, preferably in an identical context.

Conducting experiments in a "natural context" is called *field experimentation*. The possibilities for manipulation and (above all) control are less in field experiments.

The approaches' relation to the traditional techniques

The analytical approach and traditional techniques

The *analytical view* is based on the assumption that all creation of knowledge should be *cumulative* (larger and larger slices of factive reality will be mapped as one proceeds). This approach therefore uses *secondary information* extensively. When presenting the results of a study, the analytical approach consequently attaches great importance to disclosing the way data were collected, how samples were taken, what definitions were made, what measurement scales were used, and so on.

The analytical approach also tries to collect all sorts of *primary information* and then uses all three of the above-mentioned methods of collecting data. One can therefore say, without exaggeration, that the traditional techniques for collecting data to a large extent are related to this approach.

Within this approach it is also usual to standardize the *interview questions* in order to be better able to compare the different answers. The analytical researcher/consultant/investigator aims (if possible) at closed questions. This will simplify the compilation of the results (the so-called coding). The analytical view points out, however, that it is difficult to conduct strict experiments in practice in business, no matter how desirable they may be.

The systems approach and traditional techniques

The *systems approach* does not conduct experiments as they are defined above, because experiments as they are done the analytical way are based on conditions that are not valid for systems. The systems approach uses *secondary information* and *primary information* from *direct observations* and *interviews,* however. Even so, experiments in a "looser", trial-and-error sense are, in fact, often undertaken in the systems approach. As we have seen, a correctly conducted experiment in the analytical approach requires that two essentially identical situations can be found or created. Furthermore, analytical approach experiments attempt to establish a causal relation whereby the independent variable (which is deliberately interfered with) explains the dependent variable, *all other things remaining equal* ("the experimental philosophy"). The systems view questions both the possibility of finding two such similar situations and being able to discuss matters in terms of causal relations and of "all other things remaining equal".

Secondary Information. Because the systems view's conception of reality claims that it has to deal with a more complicated reality than the analytical view, and that real systems are often relatively different from each other, secondary information concerning the environment of the real system being studied, and, above all, concerning other real systems, is used with great care. However, secondary information within the real system being studied (minutes, statistics, documents, etc.), material that may very well reflect both the environment and other real systems, is used extensively (this source of information is also common in the two other approaches).

Direct Observation. This is used almost to the same extent as in the analytical approach. The conditions permitting direct observations and the interest in doing so, however, are not as common. (Among other things, the systems view is very interested in explaining and understanding the history of real systems – which by definition is not directly observable. We will come back to studying the history of systems.) On the other hand, direct observation is frequently combined with interviews.

Interviews. Interviews are used extensively in the systems approach, usually in the form of *personal interviews*. Rarely, if ever, are broadly elaborated questionnaires administered.

The actors approach and traditional techniques

Virtually all methods of collecting data used in *the actors approach*, where the egological spheres are to be apprehended, start with the *dialogical situation*. For the creator of knowledge collecting data for use in the actors approach, a dialogue is an *engagement* in a situation on equal terms with other participants. You talk, listen, notice, question, observe and, on the whole, act as you do in everyday life – but with a disciplined reflective attitude (we will return to the actors approach and the dialogue in further detail). In this context, what separates creators of knowledge from other actors is the way in which the creators of knowledge *interpret, notice* and *arrange* data. The engagement varies, of course, with the degree of information the researchers/consultants/investigators are trying to obtain, what *understanding* they are aiming at, and what *actions* they intend to conduct. Actors must never feel that researchers/consultants/investigators seem belittling, self-righteous, supercilious, critical or triumphant when feeding back an interpretation. This would strongly bias their ability to receive any potential insight. Because this insight is *not* the researchers'/consultants'/investigators' private "invention"; it is also the actors'. It was developed through their cooperation in constructing a fresh social reality.

It follows from this that only personal "interviews" as dialogues, and what we have referred to as indirect observation (and participative observation – see experiments below), should be used when reproducing the egological sphere.

Historical material is collected through various kinds of documentary analyses and the time frame that selected actors cover. We will not take up how to do a documentary analysis now; the reader can find some information in the discussions of applications using the actors view (see Chapters 8 and 12). We want to stress again what we said at the end of Chapter 6 about using historical descriptions in the actors approach. It is through such descriptions that the approach aims, among other things, at creating meaningful "mythical images" – the "truth" of which can be proven by the actions they trigger.

Depending on the study area, there may be certain "hard" factors that can be of interest for *reflecting* denoted conceptual meaning in another perspective. These include any that answer questions in terms of:

- how many?
- how often?
- is it associated with something special?
- what colours?
- what age, sex, and so on?
- what income?
- and more.

When charting these, researchers/consultants/investigators can, in principle, use all of the techniques for collecting data described above under "Traditional techniques for collecting data". But keep this in mind: a *denotation of conceptual meaning* as used in the actors view can *never* be structured in a questionnaire or be studied in terms of, for instance, "how often?" Denotation of conceptual meaning can *only* be interpreted and understood, not explained or quantified (see Figure 6.1). Sometimes in the actors approach we refer to data obtained from "hard" factors as "actual/factual data" to stress that "factual" data, according to this approach, are *given* their actuality by the actors involved, and it is not permanent.

Experiments in the sense used in the analytical approach do not exist in the actors approach. The actors approach does, however, use *"experiments"* (emancipatory interactive action) in the sense of creative experimental activities (as creative and direct action – see Chapter 6 under "Action") together with actors out in the field, in an attempt to receive information, discover the potential in what is factual, and develop descriptive languages. These experiments of a creative character can contain anything from pedagogic dramas presented on film to direct business activities.

Measurement techniques and techniques for controlling reliability

In principle, there are four measurement scales:

1. *Nominal scale.* Nominal scales only allow the creator of knowledge to place measurements in *groups* – such as man/woman, foreman/worker, or inside/outside the factory – but not to indicate any order among those groups. Two measurements can therefore only be equal or not equal to each other on this scale.
2. *Ordinal scale.* Ordinal scales include the possibilities of nominal scales and also allow *ranking* among the measurements, such as larger or smaller (or possibly equal). Many attitudinal scales are of this type.
3. *Interval scale.* Measurements are further specified on interval scales. They make it possible to tell the *distance* between the measurements. Because an interval scale does *not* have a natural *zero point*, the whole scale can be moved (allowing scale transformations) without making it less useful. One example is the Celsius scale. Its zero point is arbitrary, and the scale can be easily transformed into a Fahrenheit scale. Many exam-grading scales are of the interval type.
4. *Quota scale.* Quota scales are the most "precise" of the four types. Their *zero point is fixed*, and all possible mathematical operations can be applied. Examples include height, weight and length, as well as profit, market share and salary. Interval scales and quota scales are both called *cardinal scales*.

In the *analytical approach*, the terms *sensitivity, precision* and *reliability* are used for characterizing scales. *Sensitivity* is increased when a scale is refined, such as when it measures dollars singly instead of by the thousands. *Precision* can be increased only by shifting to a new scale (downwards in the categorization above), going from an ordinal to an interval scale, for instance. The scale with the highest precision is the quota scale. A *scale* is reliable if it gives the same results under repeated use. Similarly, a *measurement* is reliable if the same result is obtained with repeated measuring. The *reliability* of, for instance, a test of a person's suitability for a certain position or task can be controlled in several ways. One way is to conduct the same test more than once; this is called *test-retest*. Another way is to conduct *two similar, parallel tests* at about the same time. A third method is called *split half*, which means that a test is divided into two halves, each containing similar questions, and so on. If a whole group is tested, two similar tests can be allocated *randomly* in the group to check the tests' reliabilities against each other.

The analytical approach (which is often very quantitatively oriented) aims at increasing sensitivity as well as precision. It also recommends controlling reliability as often as possible.

The systems approach is less quantitatively oriented than the analytical approach. Its measurements are therefore not as precise (as defined above). Such precision is also not considered worth aiming for. As in so many other contexts, the systems approach takes a *pragmatic* position (see Appendix). The important thing is what a measurement can be used for, not the way a measurement was made or its precision. The concept of reliability is rarely used.

Considering what has already been said in this chapter about *the actors approach* in the contexts of techniques for selecting study units and collecting data, we remind the reader that denotation of conceptual meaning as an expression of the logic of ambiguity and social movement cannot be quantified, which means that scales, as they are defined above, and control of reliability are not used. This is a natural consequence of the ultimate presumptions on which the actors view is based. What is commonly referred to as a "lack of reliability" in social science results is, according to the actors view, not a deficiency but rather proof that the ultimate presumptions of the actors view are relevant. A social life that is presumed to be in a state of constant dialectic flux with a subjective status cannot be studied in a traditional reliable way. In order for that to be possible, according to the actors view, an ultimate conception of reality as an objective possibility, with a summative and causal character – that is, in accordance with the analytical view – would be required.

When it comes to other "hard" factual factors, factors that can be treated quantitatively, the actors approach uses scales just like the analytical approach does. It is very rare, however, for these to be used in actors-oriented studies.

Validation techniques

Because validation techniques are rather different for the different approaches, we discuss them under each individual approach.

The most important factor for assessing the quality of different measurements in *the analytical approach* is their *validity*. This concept can be seen in two ways: (a) concerning a *test or a measuring instrument* one can ask: "What is measured by this test (or measuring instrument)?"; and (b) concerning the *measurement* itself one can ask: "Does this result reproduce factive reality: that is, is it true?" Unless a relatively adequate answer to each of these questions can be given, all measurements will be useless, according to the analytical approach.

They may not only be useless but even become harmful. This is easy to see when considering the following:

A company is about to enter a new market with an existing product and is using a sales forecast based on a number of different measurements as a guide. If these measurements do not *measure what they are supposed to measure* but instead measure something like the demand for a supplementary product, or if they are wrong (even if measurements are about future demand for the product in question), the results will not only be useless, they may be frankly "disastrous".

Validity in *the analytical approach* can therefore *first* be said to be the extent to which the indicators of a measuring instrument *correspond to a definition*. This means that validity affects the core of the relation between theory and data. Validity can therefore be improved by a continuous adjustment between our methods for constructing theories and for conducting research/consulting/investigation. This again emphasizes the importance of using *methodical procedures* to choose and develop the right techniques for the particular methodological view and study area. It is pointless to develop or to choose techniques, or both, in a theoretical or empirical vacuum.

After using a measuring instrument correctly (according to its instructions), checking its validity becomes a measurement of the extent to which the results are *correct* or true. The closer to reality we come, given a certain definition and goal, the higher the instrument's validity.

Because it is so important, even decisive, in the analytical approach to "hit" reality, we discuss specific validating measurements for the analytical approach later in this chapter (see "Some 'specific' groups of techniques" below). At this point we will only mention that, in general, measurement reliability can be controlled *directly* by simply doubling or repeating the measurement. The validity of the measurements themselves, on the other hand, can be controlled only *indirectly*. The only direct way to know whether measurements are true is to compare them to the truth – but if we know the truth, there is no reason to measure it!

Furthermore, as far as the analytical approach is concerned, *validity requires reliability*. The opposite, however, is not necessarily the case (see Figure 7.4).

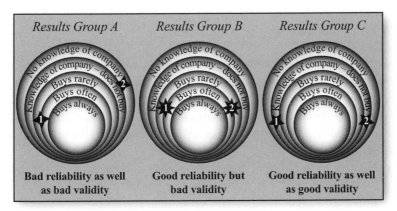

Figure 7.4   Validity and Reliability

Suppose a company, according to Figure 7.4., wants to extend its customer base – reach more consumers – by investing in environmental sustainability. To be sure, they conduct two consecutive tests to find out what potential customers think of their new investment. So, the company is interested in reaching those who *know of the* company today and their invest-ment for the environment, but who *do not* at the moment *have any business with them*. In order to conduct the tests students at a nearby Business school are engaged. The students divide themselves into three groups which each independently set up different *methodical procedures*, including sampling, construction of questionnaires and formulating questions for personal interviews, and respectively establish their *methodics* for the tests. They present the results, where the stars in pairs in Figure 7.4 illustrate the two conducted tests of each the three groups in the study area. As can be seen in the figure, the three groups are not equally good as creators of knowledge. We can also say that the results from *Group C* are not biased. Validity can therefore also be defined as *absence of systematic bias*.

A *decisive* test in the analytical approach of whether measurements are correct, that is, valid, is if they can be used to make good *forecasts*.

The systems approach regards the validity problem somewhat differently. Because of the lower degree of generality and absoluteness of systems theory, the connections among theory, definitions and reality are not as strong as they are in the analytical case. The require-ment is not so much that definitions must correspond with existing theory or be operational, as that they are perceived to be important and relevant to the creator of knowledge as well as to other participants from the real system engaged in the process of creating knowledge. In other words, these people have an interest in and an opportunity to decide whether a mea-surement is correctly made and whether the results are reasonable and correct. Sometimes outside "experts" are *also* asked to make a judgement of the measuring procedure and its results.

A common systems approach procedure for guaranteeing, to the extent possible, that mea-surements are correct is to reflect the real system from as many angles as possible. To do this, creators of knowledge take every opportunity throughout the course of a study to be in the real system as long and as often as possible, to talk to as many people as possible, and to study as much secondary information as they can.

A *decisive* validity control in the systems approach lies in the effects that can be achieved by applying the measurements.

The concept of validity as used in *the actors approach* has a number of different meanings that range from how researchers/consultants/investigators use dialogues to discover whether or not their interpretations are correct, to the "credibility" and "sincerity" of a knowledge report.

The reason there are no concrete validation criteria in the actors approach is due in part to a socially constructed reality being so interactive (in dialectic flux) that the suitability for traditional validation is limited.

Many actors researchers/consultants/investigators have said repeatedly that the only real val-idation is the extent to which the actors *accept* the results and interpretations made. This, however, is a qualified truth. A common sign that an interpretation is "correct" is that the actor reacts *emotionally* and *denies* it. If the interpretation had not been "correct" and therefore had not influenced the actor emotionally, he or she would not have had to *react* emotionally – by denying it – but could instead have presented a well-prepared opinion of the interpretation. In a similar fashion, actors may accept incorrect interpretations that they themselves experience as positive.

Apart from this type of validity check, the necessity of having a *pragmatic* attitude toward validation of results presented by the actors approach is often mentioned. This means that practical usefulness decides the value of the results (compare with similar opinions in the systems approach). This type of validation is questionable, but it can occasionally be used and should not be rejected.

A further way of talking about validation is the extent to which "*dialectic tension*" can be created for a continuing dialogue, that is, whether the results can enhance the dialogue and initiate actions in an understanding, emancipating and innovative perspective.

To clarify somewhat the situation just described, we present a few ideas that can be of help in guiding validation in the actors approach. First, we make a distinction between *validating the process* and *validating the results*. Second, we are of the opinion that validation can take place as either a *scientific* or a *practical* validation.

A practical validation of the process takes place through the *feedback mechanisms* normally present in social contexts among people (the creator of knowledge is not thrown out by the actors; instead the actors show a continued or increasing interest). *A practical validation of the result* can be called the combination of the *pragmatic* attitude and the one to create *dialectic tension* for a continuing dialogue and emancipatory interactive actions.

The scientific validation of the process could be established if researchers/consultants/ investigators show clearly in their reports the basis on which the different interpretive patterns are developed, that is, the *logic* and the *reasonableness* in the *development of these patterns*. Furthermore, the subjective interpretation must be clear, that is, *scientific concepts* must be clearly shown to be *rooted in the first hand expressions* of the actors in the study area. This leads to a further requirement: that the concepts are to some extent translatable into everyday language. The *scientific validation of the result* has to do with the *relation* of the result to existing knowledge, that is, whether the result might be useful in developing the scientific branch (business) as such.

This brings a certain kind of intersubjective testability to the scientific result. The reason we say "a certain kind" is that the result cannot possibly be tested in all aspects. This testability must usually be limited to an interpretation of reasonableness by the scientific community.

In the sense of the *actors approach*, a good practical validity is a necessary prerequisite for a good scientific validity. A good scientific validity, on the other hand, is not a necessary prerequisite for good practical validity.

SOME "SPECIFIC" GROUPS OF TECHNIQUES

The analytical approach and sampling

Most people understand intuitively what a sample is. The basic idea is to select a smaller number of units out of a totality (called a *population* in this context) in order to arrive at a description of the totality from this smaller number. The decisive test of a sample, then, is the extent to which it is *representative* of the population about which the creator of knowledge wants to draw certain conclusions. In measuring terms, we might say that a good sample must have *validity*.

Validity, as we know, means that there are no *systematic* biases. Therefore, a sample has validity if overestimations and underestimations of individual elements in the sample balance each other. We know that no sample completely represents a population in all aspects. But if there is a variation, it must be *random*, not systematic. This random variation is usually called *standard error*, and it is measured by the *sample variance* (or corresponding *standard deviation*). The lower this is, the better, all other things being equal.

The ambitions and assumptions on which the analytical view is based fit sampling theories well. Theories for sampling (and its associated statistical applications) are extensive and quantitative. We know that the analytical approach is happy to use mathematical tools. In order for statistical sampling theories to be used as effectively as possible – for what is called the *law of large numbers* to be valid – it is necessary to be able to select study units from a population, units *that are assumed to be independent of each other*. We know that the analytical view is based on precisely this assumption.

A brief description of some of the most common sampling methods includes:

1. *Random sample*

   o simple random sample
   o systematic sample
   o stratified sample
   o multistage sample

2. *Subjective sample*

   o quota sample
   o judgement sample

A *simple random sample* requires that creators of knowledge have some kind of list of the units that belong to the population. Then they allow probability, and probability alone (e.g. a die, random tables or computer-generated numbers), to decide which units are to be in the sample. A more practical variation, and one that is often used, is to select *systematically* from a list every tenth unit, for example, or the unit at the top of every left-hand page. The creator of knowledge must check the list to be sure that it is not constructed so that the sample contains too many of just one or a few kinds (e.g. systematically selecting all persons whose family name starts with Q, expecting these to be representative of the population at large, is probably not recommended).

A *stratified sample* results from dividing the population into groups, so-called *strata*, from which subsamples are taken. These groups should be as different from each other as possible. For sampling done this way it can be statistically proven that, with the same sample size as for other techniques, an average better representativity (i.e. lower sample variance) will result, or alternatively that one can achieve a certain average representativity with a smaller sample.

Simple random, systematic and stratified sampling require a list of the whole population to start with. This is not the case with a *multistage* sample, which as the name implies is obtained in several steps. For instance, if the researcher/consultant/investigator divides the population into geographic areas and the first step is to be a selection among these areas, only lists of the units that live in the selected areas are needed. In the second step, any of the other sampling techniques can be applied to these areas.

For practical and economic reasons, the creator of knowledge often takes samples through subjective procedures. *Quota sampling* involves taking a sample that, according to predetermined *background variables*, has the same characteristics as the population. A *judgement sample* is made up of units that are subjectively judged to be representative.

As far as representativity (the decisive question for sampling theory as well as for the analytical approach in general) is concerned, we point out two circumstances that are often misunderstood:

A. The representativity of a sample is determined *not* by how large a *proportion* of the population is selected, but by the *total number* of units contained in the sample. In other words, a correctly selected sample of 200 units out of a population of 10,000 units has, in principle, a lower standard error (sample variance) than a sample consisting of 100 units taken from a population of only 1,000 units.
B. It is not possible to determine a priori (in advance) whether a random sample will be more representative than a subjective sample. In random samples, however, the standard error can be calculated. This cannot be done in a subjective sample.

The analytical approach and validation of measurements

The analytical approach wants to chart and measure factive reality. To determine whether this is in fact happening as the research/consulting/investigation proceeds, in other words to *validate measurements*, is considered to be essential.

Considering the way in which measurements are validated, we can talk about three kinds of validity; they should be combined whenever possible:

1. face validity: *acceptance*
2. internal validity (*logical* or *theoretical* validity): *relevance*
3. external validity (*empirical* validity): *consequence*.

Face validity is a subjective assessment of the plausibility of the results and can be done by the creator of knowledge. It is also possible to ask concerned respondents or external experts whether or not they *accept* the results.

Internal validity (also called *relevance*) is primarily concerned with the logical relationship between a study and existing theory in the area. The hypotheses of the study (derived through deduction) should be formulated in such a way that they in fact shed light on the theory the study is based on. When several dimensions of a theory are measured at the same time, the results of those dimensions should be compatible with each other. If, for instance, a study is made of the motivation and the efficiency of a specific factory cell, theory gives us reason to expect that the most motivated people will also be the most efficient ones.

External validity is related to the possibility of generalizing results beyond the actual study area. External validity exists if results can be used in other events or characteristics that are contemporary with, but not of main interest to, the study (i.e. *criterion validity*), or as a basis for making a forecast of future consequences (i.e. *predictive validity*). If a person claims to be very interested in, and at ease with, modern planning techniques, but time shows, perhaps in word and deed, incompetence in this area, we might question the validity of that person's statement. If, on the other hand, we take a sample of political opinions that later proves to fit the actual election results well, the validity of the measurement in question is high. Crucial for external validity, in other words, is the relation (fit) between our measurements and the actual manifestation of other, external (contemporary or future) correlated indicators.

The systems approach and historical studies

The systems approach looks at its real systems as "living" wholes. Such systems often exist long before they are studied and so can be seen at least partly as products of their own history. It is therefore often essential to explain and understand the background of a real system's historical time in order to explain and understand what it is today – and thereby also its ability to face its future.

Being interested in describing the history of a real system, in other words, is not egotistical. History is of interest only to the extent that *its footprints still exist* (cf. Lindqvist, 1978).

Reproducing history and collecting historical "facts" is never simple – it is not like collecting coins or stamps that can be arranged in attractive patterns for public viewing. It is always, to some extent, a question of *interpretation*, either directly through various "relics" such as documents or other manifestations or evidence still in existence, or indirectly through someone else's interpretation – people who can relate the experience of the past at first or second hand.

There are consequently two ways to gain a knowledge of history:

1. various documents (secondary information) or other types of evidence (e.g. a prototype of a company's first product)
2. interviews with those who have experienced (or heard of) the past.

Without going into detail, let us take a brief look at the specific problems connected with reproducing the history of a real system. More specifically, let us assume that we want to reproduce the history of a company. Let us also assume that we as creators of knowledge have access to existing data, be they from public sources or from sources internal to the system (for instance, various kinds of documents and other evidence produced in the course of history), or from contacts with various persons inside or outside the system. Reproducing the history of a real system through access to only *external* material or *interviews* does not lead to specific *methodological* complications, though it does *make the interpretive work more difficult* (something that should not be taken lightly).

First, let us look at secondary information, which is always *selective*. History is never documented (or manifested) in its entirety. The materials, furthermore, can be of *highly differing quality and character*. Secondary information also always carries *a message*, sometimes one that is quite biased (because there is always a purpose behind documentation). Finally, the material may tend to have a *personal* or else an *institutional* character. Personal material can include correspondence, letters to the press and articles written for a newspaper. Institutional material might include reports, minutes, annual reports, various types of statistics, and more.

Similar points of departure are also valid for studying and analysing other (physical) manifestations of history that exist today, like buildings and other constructions, machines, products and trademarks, and so on. One important difference between documents and other historical manifestations, however, is that the latter may not contain words, pictures, and the like. The study and analysis of these, then, should be combined with other techniques for collecting information about history.

A creator of knowledge has reason to be selective about historical material (and manifestations). The material must *first* be assessed for its *usefulness*. *Second*, a creator of knowledge must try to trace *the origin* of the material (which is not always obvious). *Third* is the *interpretive* procedure itself (in the mind of the creator of knowledge). These three aspects are related and interdependent.

Usefulness depends partly on the *questions* the creator of knowledge works with, partly on the *trustworthiness* of the material. Trustworthiness can, in turn, sometimes be verified by other documents and the like – but it is often a matter of finding the *originator*. For example, there is probably a different degree of trustworthiness behind a public annual report or the minutes of a meeting, compared with a letter from the personnel manager to the general manager concerning rumours about a pending strike in one of the company's factories (a strike that may never have materialized). Further aspects of determining origin, apart from the person or persons behind the material, can involve determining whether material is *genuine* or *forged*, attempting to *date* it, and deciding whether it is a first hand source or otherwise. Much can be said about the *interpretation* itself, but space does not permit further elaboration. Let us only say that it is important to understand historical material *from its own contemporary perspective*, which often requires extensive studies of the spirit of the times in the environment of the system being studied.

Another way of gaining knowledge about the not too distant past is, as already mentioned, to ask people who experienced (or heard about) this bit of history to tell their story. This also has special problems. One is that people *forget*. Another is that they may deliberately *lie* (maybe to present themselves in a more favorable light). But even if they really try to remember and do tell the truth, the researcher/consultant/investigator must be aware that such stories are always *fragmented*, open to *reinterpretation* (unless they are about specific facts), and often a matter of *rationalizations*.

So, reproducing history is not an easy task for creators of business knowledge. They must be detectives and be persistent and broad-minded, as well as open and honest. And don't forget that *creativity is a prerequisite for critical thinking and reflection* (see Chapter 2).

The systems approach and case studies

The real systems that the creator of systems knowledge tries to describe, explain and under-stand are often complex both to grasp and to reproduce. One problem is the *historical description*, which we have just touched upon. But there are other problems that are specif-ically related to the systems researcher/consultant/ investigator's method of working with one or a few cases as the area of investigation: that is, *case studies*.

Among other things, we can imagine two very different situations. One is coming to the real system as an *academician*, the other is being invited as a *consultant* (or other type of invited investigator). Access to the real system, the expectations of its members and what they can and will tell rest on very different conditions in each of these situations.

Table 7.1   Expectations

Academicians will	Consultants will
• be matter-of-fact and objective	• be matter-of-fact but subjective
• be many-sided and impartial	• be one-sided and partial
• be theoretical	• be practical
• have plenty of time	• have a time limit
• want to describe, explain and understand	• want to change
• be inexperienced and difficult to understand	• be experienced and professional

Table 7.1 lists differences in the expectations that are commonly held by members of the real system about academicians and about consultants. There are many exceptions, of course, but the patterns described in Table 7.1 shed light on some common differences in the two instances. Further differences between academicians and consultants are listed below.

1. Although neither academician nor consultant will escape the political game that takes place in all real systems, it is a natural part of a consultant's work. This is because consultants normally aim at changing things (for the better) and will thereby disturb existing power balances in the real system. Consultants can therefore expect very different behaviour from those who believe they will gain from change compared with those who fear it. But even academicians will come across expressions of power play and should avoid becoming involved. Both alertness and openness are required to avoid becoming a part of this often com-plicated and subtle play.
2. Consultants are usually required to be confidential. Academicians, on the other hand, want to use their systems knowledge to gain merit, that is, they want to publish their findings and results. It is not uncommon for managers in real sys-tems to oppose publication of certain information (usually financial results and sales figures, but also plans and personal information). Sometimes academi-cians can avoid compromising the scientific value of their publication by disguising the presentation, or by making the real system anonymous (and probably telling the reader that such anonymization has taken place).

3. Experienced consultants usually have a rough plan and model ready after being given their mission. Academicians, though they may want to test a specific model, are often considerably more flexible. Their first goal might be to classify the type of system before proceeding with a more complete description, which may be labourious as well as extensive.
4. Consultants' results are judged by the client in terms of profit, return, new perspectives, or some similar success factor. Academicians' "judges" might include the members of the real system (e.g. for comprehensiveness, impartiality and plausibility), but are more likely to be the scientific community, including the academicians' supervisors and peers who will use more academic criteria.

It is not uncommon today in systems research to place real systems cases in *metaphors*. Metaphors make it possible to look at real systems as something else and therefore raises questions which would not have been asked in explanatory pictures of reality. *Using metaphors* is also a methodical procedure. Using metaphors in order to understand systems and some of the consequences of doing so are treated in Chapter 5 ("Examples of classic systems interpretation").

The actors approach and dialogue

Dialogue was illustrated earlier in Chapter 6, and examples will be given in the more applied parts of this book. But because this section presents techniques specific to each of our three methodological approaches, the dialogue has a place here, too.

Dialogue is different from discussion as well as debate by having completely different intrinsic purposes. This can also be read from the language origins of the different concepts. We bring these differences up in order to deepen the understanding of the central role of *the dialogue* as an investigative and innovative instrument in the actors approach.

As mentioned earlier, *dialogue* comes from Latin *dia,* which means *through* and *logos* which means *words*. The purpose of the dialogue is to clarify *differences* in order to later transgress them toward something new, where differences are conveyed but, as it were, dissolved (synthesized) in a deepened understanding and meaning of life, that is, the parties of the dialogues are looking for a *highest common denominator* (compare *discuss* below). In the dialogue, consequently, *agreement* is to come about through what is *different*. One so-called typical win/win situation.

Discuss comes from *dis* which means *apart* and *cutere* which means *cut* (dash to pieces). The purpose of the discussion is similar to the analytical approach to divide – to cut apart – where the parties of the discussion are looking for the *lowest common denominators* to start from when summarizing. Here, instead, *agreement* is to come about through what is *similar* (compare *dialogue* above).

Debate comes from *battere,* which means *battle*. The purpose of the debate is to beat your opponent with arguments and tricks of rhetoric. Here we get one winner and one loser, and there is no question of coming to an *agreement* through any specific intrinsic principle.

From this we can understand that the opinion of the actors view is to look at *dialogue* as the most important technique for "looking for truth" and groundbreaking acts. It is important to understand that dialogue in the sense of the actors approach is not only about agreeing on a kind of friendly intimacy but also about forging the very master key in the *construction* of *new* social reality.

So, a dialogue in the sense of the actors approach is distinctly different from an interview (see Table 7.2).

Table 7.2   Dialogues contra interviews

	Dialogues	Interviews
Main purpose	To get at meaning and significances in the co-actors' language and culture. To create and emancipate.	To collect data which are facts – to get a mirror reflection of factive reality.
Idea	To create a forum for further co-creation of social reality in a direction of mutual interest according to the knowledge ambitions of the actors view (see Figure 6.2).	To set up a channel in order to transfer objective and subjective facts from respondent to interviewer.
Basic assumption	All meaning is socially constructed. There is no (social) reality beyond this meaning.	There is an objective and subjective factive reality to depict.
The researcher's task	Apart from as other participants in the dialogue, to be an actor (inevitable) and also to be an observer – an "observactor".	Not to influence the interview in any distorting direction.

Below we give a brief summary of some related aspects of dialogue:

- Participating honestly in a dialogue is a difficult *art;* succeeding is the sign of a skilful creator of actors knowledge.
- One must also be honest with oneself as a creator of knowledge in these contexts. The point is to enter the dialogue "without knowing" (in spite of the fact that we always know a lot and have many prejudices, see Chapter 2), and to leave the dialogue feeling that one has in fact grown in capacity and has dared to give something up, not simply had something confirmed.
- A creator of knowledge must be inside and outside the dialogue at the same time. A researcher/consultant/investigator is simultaneously an actor and an observer with ambitions to produce knowledge.
- Participating in a dialogue does not mean using only spoken and written language. As in all social contexts, body language must also be considered.
- Social reality is continuously constructed and confirmed. A dialogue is therefore not a phenomenon that is strictly limited in time. The researcher/consultant/investigator must also be aware of what preceded as well as of what will follow the dialogue.
- Participating in a dialogue as a creator of knowledge can be compared with being a creative and curious artist. An artist "puts pressure" on the present in order to find alternative interpretations, possibilities and openings. Artists are also not only able to shape that which they see, but also to decide which perspective and what aspects of it are to be considered.

Dialogue is essential for the *creation of understanding and meaningful actions* within the framework of a world in which knowledge is created with an *interactive development of understanding* as one of its guiding principles. Kamprad, Ikea's founder says:

> There are too many desks in Sweden and too many people sit at them too much of the time. The obvious risk is that a person loses his contact with reality and with the people he is to serve [...] I would like to make my closest colleagues do what I do, to be out there among people, trying to listen to their everyday problems, learning to understand their thoughts and wishes. You have to live in reality, not isolate yourself from it. (1993: 6; authors' translation)

According to the actors view, this is valid whether it concerns knowledge-creating activities or other activities in business – and elsewhere.

The actors approach and language development

There are many metaphors we can apply to language – reflected image, cultural manifestation, means of communication, guide, entry (or exit) – but no matter how we look at it, language is what makes us uniquely human. Many creatures can communicate, many creatures use "signals", but only human beings can see language as symbols, even talk about language. This uniquely human aspect is the basis of the actors view's interest in language.

What we have words for, we can perceive. It is even likely that if you work in an organization and talk in terms of planning, systems and control, you see planning and lack of planning everywhere, feel that you are part of various systems, and have a feeling of being controlled. If, on the other hand, the environment communicates in terms of service, creativity and solidarity, you probably feel (and act) differently.

This can also be expressed in dialectic terms: we use language as a tool in order to create and sustain reality and to communicate these processes (externalization), yet at the same time language can be said to use us as its tool in order to communicate, create and sustain reality (internalization). Existing language is, at every moment, not only an encyclopedia of all we can see, but also an encyclopedia of all we cannot see. When we think like this we are also able to understand how people are phenomena of language-dependency and also how they reflect upon this dependency of language too seldom.

The same way we use language subconsciously, we can also use it *consciously* to create new thoughts, open up new perspectives, create involvement, etc. It is possible, according to the actors view, to describe a thing almost totally without feelings, but it is also possible to make associations and enlighten the imagination. One may start to think critically and connect thought with feeling. The way in which we work with language and its different varieties of expression is related to those knowledge-creating interests and knowledge ambitions (Figure 6.2) that drive the creator of knowledge to use language in ways that bring understanding about.

As creators of actors knowledge we try to develop procreative concepts which shape and vivify the world for us, but also provide old concepts with new energy and innovative direction, give concepts poetic timbre and depth. It must therefore be of interest to understand one's own and (above all, as a creator of actors knowledge) other actors' finite provinces of meaning in terms of language, and to understand that it is possible to create new finite provinces of meaning and consequently to renew oneself. The creator of actors knowledge can consciously change the finite provinces of meaning held by others, or can at least free others from locked-in frames of reference, giving them new creative power by developing their language.

All kinds of social science language development must, according to the actors view, be based on a relation that focuses on meaning and which relates the actors' *first hand expressions* with the *scientific concepts* in order for a developing tension to arise in the interface between the different worlds. If a creator of knowledge is building his/her language development only on other relations, for instance, previous theories and established clichés in his/her own field, this is, according to the actors view, to be compared with trying to describe summer using the language of winter.

"Procreative words" we call those concepts in language development that have the capacity to catch the creator of knowledge creating him/herself as well as the *knowledge creativity*. These are concepts that are "loaded" by the right kind of energy for the study area and become decisive in the process that makes the *conscious* language come alive. Let us remind the reader of what we mean by "the creator of knowledge creating him/herself". In Chapter 6 we wrote like this: "The actors oriented creator of knowledge is therefore, in different ways searching for the *inner quality* of those micro-cosmoses he/she is meeting. And also, at the same time, he/she tries to re-create this *quality* in him/herself in order to be able to *understand* and to transfer these experiences through '*the emancipatory interactive action*'."

Based on experience we know that this process of transferring these experiences through, among other things, *descriptive languages* and *emancipatory interactive actions* (see Table 3.1) is subtle at the same time as it is very concrete. New words creating culture are introduced in the study area through concrete action! It is through the use of the concepts in concrete situations that the meaning and the relevance are developed. It is a kind of work, which requires feeling and insight about how the *procreative words* arise themselves as carriers of meaning for the creator of knowledge in the interface between the actors' *first hand expressions* and the *scientific* perspectives.

Knowledge creating interface of language development

Nothing can exist or create meaning without its opposite. Light would not be light without darkness, life gets its meaning through the presence of death, change can only be experienced as a background of permanence. An operative and rational language needs a personal and emotional language as its opposite. Different provinces of meaning are each other's productive opposites.

We live and work in a field of tension between a number of opposites and it is in the nodes of these opposites, in their *interface*, that what is interesting and challenging exists. Sea and land meet and create the beach – constantly the same, but always different. Day meets night and delivers dawn, and night meets day in twilight. The day does not destroy the darkness of night and night does not take the light of day – they are instead each other's conditions for keeping the rhythm alive. And so is also the meeting between creators of knowledge and actors – where the *dialogue* is creating an interface of *unexpected possibilities*. It is an interface that in itself contains something more, a power that can broaden and refine our finite provinces of meaning.

It is possible to train oneself (and other actors) to use language more creatively. We can present six principles, in our actors approach, for how to make language understood and developable. They all aim at starting the critical reflective thought and broaden the perspective with the creator of knowledge when he/she develops language in order to give substance to his/her experiences. The language principles below can also be used, of course, in interaction with the actors in the study area.

1. *Language cleaning.* This removes "masking words", reveals established illusions, renders power expressions empty, and more. A few examples can illustrate the principle:

    - In the old days we talked about *unemployment* when we referred to unemployed people. Now we can hear terms like *redundant, dehired* or *terminated.* Why?

    - Why do we say that we *produce* care when we *take care of each other*?

    - Why is *war* referred to as *fighting for peace*?

    - Why do we say *collecting* data when data are *constructed*?

    - Why do football coaches refer to their *players* as *material* and *cogs in a team machinery*?

    By cleaning the language, the creator of knowledge can see the hidden grammar of the concepts that shape our thoughts.

2. *Language reduction.* When we talk about reduction here, we mean the search by the creator of knowledge for the words that are most common in the vocabulary of his/her research (pre-scientific concepts are also included), and the actors' everyday vocabulary, in order to discover what is happening in dialogues and descriptions when these words are reduced in numbers – that is to say, when the creator of knowledge and the actors are forced to look for other words in their expressions of meaning other than those commonly used and taken for granted.

3. *Language polarization.* This sets one concept against its "opposite", puts invisible signs up against visible ones and makes a potentially creative interface become visible:

reflection	proflection
resume	prosume
manufacture	autofacture
insight	outsight
react	proact
official	onicial

4. *Language shift.* This is the understanding of a terminology in terms of a specialized language, such as financial language, hacker language, caring language, sports language, arts language, music language, adventure language or budget language. This means that the creator of knowledge consciously tries to describe phenomena using words and perspectives borrowed from a language field other than the one in which the phenomena are linguistically rooted.

5. *Language subjectification.* This makes language come alive, includes feelings and subjects, increases ambiguity and richness of aspects, and reduces mechanical pictures (metaphors) and the reification of human beings; in short, it includes the full living subject in bureaucratic, business-oriented and scientific languages of description.

6. *Language poetring.* Here the point is to give rhythm and provide metaphors to the describing and procreative language in order to bring it to a kind of poetic level which creates nearness and exactness between experience and transfer of meaning (see "The procreative report" below). Metaphors become here one of the most important forms of substantiating for linguistic/semantic innovation which we, in the name of the actors view, have access to in order to describe and clarify "discoveries" and ideas.

The procreative report

In the same way as an artist or a poet tries to endow substance with that context, those feelings and those experiences he/she is carrying, the actors oriented creator of knowledge tries to transfer his/her experiences. This is often about writing a report of some kind.

Here the creator of knowledge is usually *introducing* the different "empirical" sections of the report by summarizing his/her experiences in *procreating reflections*. These *introductory* reflections ("mini art works") are done in a metaphoric and critical language, sometimes on the verge of surrealistic, in order to deepen and contextualize the human significances – the meaning structures – which then in these "empirical" sections "are allowed to talk" their own language by referring to the *first hand expressions* of the actors. To add the "poetic" dimension here (see language principle number 6 above) is, according to the actors view, also a way to become more *exact* in the knowledge-creating transfer of experiences. To give the *procreating reflection* as many dimensions as possible not only makes the description more rounded but also more precise in the direct meeting with the reader. Because if you neglect the reader's need for meaning being created in the – "poetic" – context of transferring experience, the reader will subconsciously add these dimensions, which might completely disfigure what the creator of knowledge wants to say.

For the reader of a procreative report it then becomes possible in the *borderland* between the *procreating* reflections of the creator of knowledge and the actors' own linguistic description to either experience that "Yes, it is probably so", "This is also a way to think", or argue against and reject. In here it is useful, according to the actors approach, to go beyond the *explaining*, that which is said to be more *generally* valid but which, according to this view, stands as a symbol for what is superficial – what may not concern anybody but still is said to be valid for most. The actors creator of knowledge wants instead to provide a reading which is both intellectual and exciting, where the reader can actively participate, thanks to the *openness* of the text through that dialectics which develops between three *different exactnesses:* (1) the reader; (2) the *procreating* reflections of the creator of knowledge; and (3) the first hand expressions by the actors. The exactness of the creator of knowledge can also be found in those models (see Figure 6.11) that are ending the report. This final *exactness* is then set up against the reader's *freedom* to deliver the potential in the factual. The core of a *procreative report* is consequently a willingness from the side of the creator of knowledge to excite the knowledge-creating *dialogue* at all levels, no matter which way it develops.

The *expression format* of the report, where the creator of knowledge, with creative and scientific precision, is trying to "paint" the picture of complex phenomena using a *procreative* language and the different language models of the actors view (see Figure 6.12), we could call *artistics* – an interpretive pictorial language creating meaning. It is a knowledge-creating expression format that is totally different in kind from *statistics* as a descriptive language (see Figure 6.1).

THE PROBLEM OF OBJECTIVITY

An overview

The topic of objectivity is extensive and touches on several difficult problems in the philosophies of science, ethics and epistemology. In 1916 one could, for instance, in *The Philosophical Review* read the following by Jones: "In classic British or German philosophy, probably no question has been so variously treated, or so differently ranked, as the problem of objectivity" (1916: 778). The issue of objectivity concerns the very conception of science and knowledge in society and the role of creation of knowledge here. Let us raise some questions that can indicate the wide range of ramifications of the subject:

- Is such a knowledge possible that can provide universal and trans-cultural explanations, applicable to all people in the world no matter when? Or are explanations culture, gender and time specific and therefore impossible to apply generally?
- Is such a knowledge possible that can reflect back reality without distortion? Or is knowledge one part of reality itself, such that it can never reflect its own truth? Does what we call "truth" exist in the field of social sciences?
- Does the development of the social sciences mean that knowledge is constantly added to such that insight and understanding continuously create a higher quality of human life? Or does this increase in knowledge take place mostly as an accumulation of information in the scientific society with little importance in a general human sense?
- Has the accumulation of knowledge in social research made us wiser, smarter and more insightful than our ancestors?

All these questions touch upon the problem of objectivity one way or another and are not, as we can see, easy to answer. They also reflect our three methodological views and their ultimate presumptions; so part of the answers could be found in this book.

This section is therefore only a small overview on the topic; it should be seen as an unpretentious attempt to clarify the problem in order to raise somewhat our level of awareness of a complicated issue. People have long debated, both verbally and in writing, whether the *social sciences* can reach objectivity and, if they can, whether it would be worth the effort.

One participant in this debate a long time ago was the Nobel Prize winner in Economics, Gunner Myrdal, and it is starting from his work that we write this little résumé. In *Objectivity in Social Research* (Myrdal, 1969), he raises a number of questions that are still representative of the issues involved:

> The most fundamental methodological problems facing the social scientist are, therefore, what is objectivity, and how can the student attain objectivity. ... How can a biased perspective be avoided? More specifically, how can students of social problems liberate themselves from (1) the powerful heritage of earlier writings in his field of inquiry, ordinarily containing normative and teleological notions inherited from past generations and founded upon the metaphysical moral philosophies of natural law and utilitarianism from which all our social and economic theories have branched off; (2) the influences of the entire cultural, social, economic, and political milieu of the society where he lives, works, and earns his living and his status; and (3) influences stemming from his own personality, as moulded not only by traditions and environment but also by his individual history, constitution, and inclinations? (1969: 3–4)

The presentation of objectivity actually concerns two separate levels, the macro and the micro. We can say that the macro level stands for the value judgements and normative theses that are part of the discipline as such, whereas the micro level centres on the individual researcher/consultant/investigator. It is primarily the micro level that will be taken up here. Myrdal also seems interested in objectivity mainly at the micro level when he asks repeatedly how individual social scientists will be able to reach any objectivity in their profession, and whether there is a method by which they can ensure the highest possible objectivity in their research. Myrdal recommends that science brings its values into the open, making them conscious, specific and explicit, and openly clarifies how they determine theoretical constructions: "I am arguing here that value premises should be made explicit so that research can aspire to be 'objective' – in the only sense this term can have in the social sciences" (1969: 56). These value premises must furthermore fulfil a number of demands:

> They must be explicitly stated and not concealed as implied assumptions.
> They must be as specific and concrete as the valuation of reality requires.
> They must be purposefully selected as they are not, a priori, self-evident or generally valid on the grounds of being founded only on facts or on the "nature of things". (1969: 63)

The numerous ideas that exist in the scientific tradition and the social environment that creators of knowledge belong to, influence, to various extents, their research/consulting/investigations. The fact that the lack of awareness of this is rarely critically discussed led Myrdal to state:

> It is astonishing that this taboo is commonly respected, leaving the social scientist in naiveté about what he is doing. To destroy this naiveté should be the object of the sociology of science and scientists, the least developed branch of social science. This is important, as these influences, if they are not controlled, are apt to cause systematic biases in research and thus lead to faulty knowledge. (1969: 4–5)

Myrdal continues by formulating a number of requirements that may protect us from biases:

1. We clarify the values that actually determine our theoretical and practical research/consulting/investigation.
2. We scrutinize those values from the point of departure of relevance, significance and feasibility in the society under study.
3. We transform them into specific value premises for the research/consultation/investigation.
4. We determine approach and define concepts in terms of a set of value premises that have been explicitly stated (see Myrdal, 1969: 63–7).

The problems that exist when clarifying value judgements are, among other things, related to scientists' fear of explicitly stating evaluations that exist at the micro level. Scientists therefore often try to hide their evaluations by expressing them as conclusions drawn from facts. But making one's value judgements conscious and expressing them explicitly is not a simple matter. Such a procedure will surely lead to new problems of rationalizations and dubious after-constructions.

The first step in improving on this "low level of awareness" might be a sort of inter-reflection among creators of knowledge. They might talk about how values in knowledge creating activities can be *interpreted in terms of reasonableness* and how they might be *legitimized*. As Myrdal points out, it is difficult to claim that one's scientific activities and results are value-free:

> They are always and with logical necessity based on moral and political valuations. … The fact that political conditioning plays such a decisive role in the choice of field for research should make us more aware and apprehensive of that other type of conditioning: namely, of the approaches we choose in research, by which I mean the concepts, models, and theories we use, and the way in which we select and arrange our observations and present the results of our research. That second type of conditioning, though not necessarily the first one, is what leads to biases. (1969: 48–9)

Furthermore, we can be in relative agreement that values also play an important role in choosing and delimiting problems. It seems reasonable to assume this, because behind every such choice there must be certain ideas about what is important to study.

We can conclude this brief overview by saying that the only thing that seems reasonable in this context is both a higher degree of *self-awareness* on the part of researchers/consultants/investigators, and that researchers/consultants/investigators have an *"external" awareness* of the political power systems that implicitly influence their creations of knowledge.

The analytical approach and the objectivity problem

The analytical approach aims at being as objective as possible and claims that this problem, in practical terms, is not as insoluble as is sometimes claimed. It is not possible to be totally value-free when, for instance, choosing problems and selecting methods. But researchers/ consultants/investigators should try to make implicit (hidden) values explicit. In their reports creators of knowledge should declare their own values, and how these might have influenced the results. It is then up to the reader to judge the consequences.

In the analytical approach, creators of knowledge should try to use methods that leave as little room as possible for personal values. Even then, however, they should be explicit about their own values.

Talking about the differences between objectivity at the micro and macro levels, the analytical view believes that *science as such* (macro level) can be *objective*. The scientific tradition (critical attitudes, free and open debate, tolerance for deviant behaviour) is the best guarantee that values have as little impact as possible.

Many analytical scientists refer to *intersubjectivity* rather than objectivity. Intersubjectivity means that there is conformity among the research results reached by different individuals in their studies, given the same circumstances and competence, and applying the same methods. Intersubjectivity can exist without value agreement. Aiming for *reliability* and *validity* can be seen as the analytical approach's means of achieving intersubjectivity.

The systems approach and the objectivity problem

There are only differences in degree (not in kind) between the attitudes of the analytical approach and the systems approach to the objectivity problem in general. In principle, a systems creator of knowledge agrees with what has been said under "The analytical approach and the objectivity problem" above (however, compare the differences between the two approaches' attitudes to the problems of the concepts of reliability and validity). Even when it comes to the problem of objectivity, the systems approach shows its pragmatic attitude. Once again, the results of applied studies are seen as more important than, in this case, the objectivity in descriptive studies or studies that determine relations.

The actors approach and the objectivity problem

Starting from the actors view conception of reality, and in particular the concept of *intentionality*, requirements for objectivity stand out as being absurd and illogical. Humans are subjective beings – they *create* reality out of their own subjective intentions, and they create the objects in the environment from their subjective intentions and then locate them through their senses. How, then, can it be possible for *creators of knowledge* to study *subjectivity objectively*? They are, after all, *objectively* a *part of the subjectivity*. The answer must be that this cannot be done. Not even psychologists studying the behaviour of mice can free themselves of values, because they already have opinions about mice as mice.

Intentionality says that we first, through our egological sphere, create a mental image (a value judgement) and then, through our senses, look for a situation in the environment that corresponds to the image. The final image (the finite province of meaning) is created in the dialectics between our inner images and situations in the environment. Value judgements are prerequisites of our mental experiences. Taking this as a starting point, we conclude that objectivity as normally perceived in contexts of the other two views *cannot* exist. According to the actors approach, the idea of objectivity is based on an "incorrect" ultimate presumption about how social reality is constructed. Ultimate presumptions that require objectivity probably have their historical origins in problems associated with attempts made by the social sciences to legitimize themselves at their inception a century ago. In order to make studies of subjective beings (man/woman, the creative actor) legitimate, social scientists at that time uncritically adopted the objectivity requirements of the highly regarded traditional natural sciences.

The social science interpretation is subjective and should, according to the actors view, be based on reflection of *meaningful data* in near and genuine meetings, where the *dialogue* is the foundation for *relevance*. "The criterion" for its *quality* is not objectivity in the sense of the other two views but something *meaningful* and *qualitative* to reflect on, something that helps others to keep on creating relevant social reality. Furthermore, the more "vividly" expressive the *procreative report* is made (see "The procreative report" above), the higher the degree of *precision* that will be achieved in the overall scientific results. The actors view claims that the more *quantified* something is, the less *precision* the numbers are able to cover and transfer (see Figure 6.1). This thought goes right against the concept of the analytical view in particular. The quantitative form of descriptions does not consider the conscious and subconscious "poetic" need of *meaning* in communication from the receiver's side but is leaving it adrift. The ostensible objectivity of the numbers does, according to the actors view, permit the creation of the meaning of the numbers by the receiver to flutter completely freely.

Taking as its premise that *no* human beings can *free* themselves from their biographic situation and that they can only try to *hide* basic personal values, the actors approach advocates a higher *awareness* and an *open dialogue* about the *importance* of values and their *legitimacy* in different situations. This is especially true of the *micro level*, that is, of researchers/consultants/investigators' more personal values. The more interpersonal level – the *macro level* – contains paradigmatic starting points, that is, normative and stipulative theses for conducting research/consulting/ investigations. Here, too, the actors approach advocates a *higher awareness* of the starting points based in philosophy and scientific theory on which the methodological approaches are based. As far as extra-scientific normative and stipulative factors, like *power* and *party politics*, are concerned, the actors approach advocates an *open* and *critical dialogue* in order to prevent these factors from leading to biases in knowledge creation under the guise that value-neutrality is the same as subordinating oneself to the factors that establish power and party politics.

Figure 7.5 uses a number of key concepts in an attempt to illustrate the outlook on, and requirements for, "objectivity" in the actors approach (please read *objectivity* here as honesty, ethics and high moral standards) in the research/consulting/investigation process and its results. The key concepts are taken from the discussion above, from our discussion of validity, and from Chapter 6.

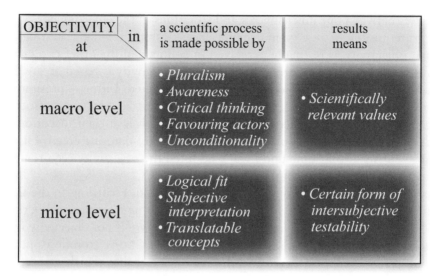

OBJECTIVITY at in	a scientific process is made possible by	results means
macro level	• *Pluralism* • *Awareness* • *Critical thinking* • *Favouring actors* • *Unconditionality*	• *Scientifically relevant values*
micro level	• *Logical fit* • *Subjective interpretation* • *Translatable concepts*	• *Certain form of intersubjective testability*

Figure 7.5   Actors Apporach Requirements for Objectivity

The design process of operative paradigms can be seen as a skill of harmony: how the ultimate presumptions of a view are "playing in concert" with a study area and where the task of the operative paradigm is to make this knowledge developing "concert" sound harmonic. The harmony is a kind of guarantor that those results that are produced are keeping a high knowledge-creating quality. The tools/processes of the operative paradigm for this harmony are methical procedures, which are discussed in this chapter, and methodics that is brought up in Chapter 9. In this chapter a number of techniques, some which the three views have in common and some which are more specific to individual views, have been brought up and related to the opinion of the different views, respectively, as "knowledge creating methods". The different opinions of the views on concepts like validity, reliability and objectivity are clarified by going to the origin of the concepts and matching them with the ultimate presumptions of the views. In this chapter the reader is shown in detail and in depth how the techniques, by being related to a view, become methods for developing knowledge. The process is consequently called "methical procedures".

POINTS OF REFLECTION

1. By the expression *"a lesson in harmony"* the authors want to describe what?
2. What is it that makes an *operative paradigm* look so different in the three methodological views?
3. In this chapter the term *approach* and *view* are used interchangably! Why using both these concepts?

4. What leads a *technique* to be called a *method*?

5. There are *common techniques* that the different approaches use in varying degrees. The main reason for this variation is, of course, that the different views start from different *ultimate presumptions* but give some other reasons for these variations!. (The other reasons are, of course, related to the main reason, but we are after those *reasons* that follow on from that.)

6. If somebody says that a gun when being tested with six shots at a target has *high* reliability and *low* validity, then how have the six shots been positioned?

7. How do you want to describe the concepts of *validity* and *reliability*?

8. The clarification you gave of the two concepts above – from which *view* did you take up your description?

9. In this chapter six *techniques specific to the views* are mentioned – which ones?

10. Give some important *characterics* of the six!

11. *Objectivity* is a concept that has haunted science for centuries. Give some *reasons* for why this has been so!

12. Clarify for yourself how the different views look at the problem of *objectivity*!

RECOMMENDED FURTHER READING

See the end of the Appendix and visit the website below.

Become a worldwide partner as a *knowledge creator* in the development of *Methodology for Creating Business Knowledge* by visiting the website: **www.knowledge-creator.com**. Here you can contribute by asking your own questions and you will also find answers to the most frequently asked questions. The website has been developed alongside this third edition of the book and the questions posted there will be used to provide input for future editions.

8 METHODS IN LANGUAGE AND ACTION

This chapter offers brief examples of what typical reasoning might sound like when parts of studies and other activities that create knowledge are done – in other words, what language and action in methodical procedures might look like in our three methodological views. The examples are from the real world and they are intended to give the reader an extended and improved living background for the theory that has been presented so far.

THE THREE WORLDS OF KNOWLEDGE

The chapter leads the reader (just as did the end of Chapter 2) into three different worlds of creating knowledge (ANAlytical; SYStems; ACTors) at a *practical* level, relating language and action to one world at a time. These worlds will look different from each other in this comparison. The examples are deliberately chosen so that – in their individualities – they will create the contrasts necessary for learning and will offer an extended kind of intellectual feeling for language and action within each of the three knowledge-creating worlds. The examples are not intended to present complete methodical procedures but only to illustrate the actual ways of thinking within the different contexts of the methodological views.

ANALYTICAL PROCEDURES

ANA 1: Professor Peterson on good research

Professor Peterson is an experienced researcher. She has been employed by her university for more than thirty years and has taught business research methodology for a long time. She has three years to go until retirement and wants to leave something for her successors. She has just compiled a compendium that she titled "Business Research Methods". In the first section, she lays out eight criteria for what she believes represents good research:

1. The purpose of the research – the problem involved – should be clearly and sharply *defined* in terms as unambiguous as possible.
2. The concepts used should be *operationalized* as much as possible.

3. The *methodical procedures* used should be described in such detail that it permits other researchers to *repeat* it.
4. The *methodics* of the research should be carefully *planned* to yield results that are as objective as possible.
5. The researcher should, as frankly as possible, *report* flaws in *procedural* design and estimate their effects on the findings.
6. Analyses of the data should be sufficient to reveal its *significance*; the analysis techniques used should be appropriate.
7. Conclusions should be *confined* to those justified by the research *data* and limited to those for which the data provide an adequate basis.
8. *Confidence* in the research is warranted if the researcher is a person of integrity.

ANA 2: The Service Bank questions

Consultant George Carter is asked to assist the new senior management team of Service Bank, the oldest and largest of three banks in a rural district with about 50,000 inhabitants. Its CEO is worried about the slump in the bank's profits and wants to reverse the trend quickly. George thinks that a good start to an ambitious study is to formulate the problem as a hierarchy of questions; he has tried this before and found it useful. The first *methodical procedure* is to formulate the *management question*. In this case, George and the CEO agree that this question could be simply formulated as:

How can we improve the profits of Service Bank?

Admittedly, this question does not specify what kind of knowledge is to be created. First, it is very broad; second, it is oriented only toward the symptom of an existing problem, namely, the lack of profitability. But it does provide a start.

What George wants to do is to reformulate the management question into one or more *research questions,* that is, into a problem of information collecting. Further discussions between the CEO and George indicate that two of the questions have to be answered simultaneously. One problem is a low growth rate in deposits, which seemed related to the competitive situation. Another part of the deteriorating profitability seems to be associated with negative factors within the organization itself. As the client and the consultant discuss the management question with each other, it gradually evolves into two research questions. Both parties finally accept the following formulations:

1. What are the major factors contributing to the lack of a stronger growth rate in deposits?
2. How well is the bank doing with regard to:

    a. Quality of its work climate?
    b. Efficiency of operations compared to industry norms?
    c. Financial condition compared to industry norms?

George knows, however, that he must go further in his formulation of questions. The next step is to develop the *investigative questions* with high validity. After much thinking (and discussion with the bank's senior management) he arrives at the following investigative questions regarding the deposit problem:

1. What is the public's opinion of the bank's financial services and how are these services used?

    a. What specific financial services are used?
    b. How attractive are the various services?
    c. What factors influence a person's use of a particular service?

2. What is the bank's competitive position?

    a. What are the geographic patterns of Service Bank's customers and those of its competitors?
    b. What conclusions can be drawn from the demographic differences between Service Bank's customers and those of its competitors?
    c. How aware is the public of Service Bank's promotional efforts?
    d. What general opinion does the public hold of Service Bank and its competitors?
    e. How does Service Bank's growth compare with that of its competitors?

George starts then to break the *organizational problem* down in a similar fashion, even though he knows that this does not get to the bottom of the hierarchy of questions. He knows that he eventually must formulate several *measurement questions,* that is, questions that will represent parts of questionnaires and will guide direct observations and studies of various source materials. But that has to come later.

ANA 3: A causal experiment

Eve Bacon works in a welfare organization. The organization is short of funds and wants to send out a written appeal to drum up contributions. The organization has approximately 50,000 members; a letter sent to each one should elicit the help required. The only question is whether the appeal should be based on emotion or on logic. In order to resolve this question of *methodical procedure* before the letters are sent, Eve presents a proposal for an experiment that she thinks will give a good indication of which will be the more successful appeal, emotional or logical.

The proposal suggests choosing a sample of 300 names from the membership list and dividing these into two groups of 150. One group will be designated the experimental group (it does not matter which one of the two it is) and will receive the emotion-based letter. The other group will be the control group and will receive the logic-based letter.

Eve knows there are three requirements before a relation can be called causal: (a) *Covariation,* which in this case can be expressed by the percentage of responses. Suppose, for instance, that 50 per cent of those receiving the emotional letter respond, whereas only

35 per cent of those receiving the logical letter respond. It will then be possible to conclude that using the emotional version will increase the probability of getting an answer.

In this case, the (b) *temporal order* between dependent and independent variable does not present a problem. Obviously, nobody answers before they get a letter, so there is no chance that the number of letters with contributions will influence the number of letters being distributed.

The main problem, however, is to ensure that (c) *no other variable* biases the result, that is, that no factor other than the type of appeal will be at work here. For instance, Eve thinks that honorary life members may feel more reason to answer the appeal. *One way* of preventing this factor from exerting influence will be to *exclude* this specific category from the experiment. *A second* way will be to *match* the two groups against each other. For example, there may be reason to believe that age will make a difference. In order to control for this factor, the age distribution has to be the same in the two groups. The *third* way, and the one Eve thinks is best, will be to *randomize,* to let chance determine who receives what type of letter. This means that both groups contain a similar proportion of different possibly influential factors. Every deviation shall be completely random.

ANA 4: How to improve response rates

John Parson, who teaches marketing at university, has a feeling that a piece of the course covering marketing research is missing. He has always warned that a non-response error is to be expected when conducting interviews. He knows that the largest rate of non-response is usually obtained for mailed questionnaires, but he has never in his *methodical procedures* really thought about how to improve this rate. He therefore decides to find out what the literature suggests as possible steps to take. After only a few hours' search he is able to put together a list of steps (reproduced below), but is uncertain about what it means for his future work.

Reminders. Reminders, or a second follow-up, seem generally accepted as a way of increasing response rates. Because every successive follow-up leads to more answers, the very persistent (and well-financed) researcher can potentially achieve an extremely high response rate. However, the value of gaining more information has to be traded off against the cost resulting from further contacts.

Advance Notices. It seems that advance notices, especially by telephone, are effective in increasing response rates. They also lead to quicker responses. However, reminders are probably better investments than advance notices.

Questionnaire Length. Common sense suggests that shorter questionnaires should lead to higher response rates, but studies do not support this opinion.

Sponsorship. There is little research on the importance of who is behind a questionnaire. A few cases, however, suggest that the response rate is higher for official or "respected" sponsors.

Return Envelopes. The few studies that exist concerning the importance of a stamped return envelope point at increased response rates, because the envelopes facilitate the return.

Postage. There is nothing to show that the response rate will increase because stamps are used instead of a postage machine, or because first-day or other commemorative stamps are used instead of "ordinary" stamps.

Personalization. Empirical studies do not usually indicate a significantly higher response rate if personal introductions or individually signed letters are used. A few studies, however, have shown this to be the case.

Cover Letters. It seems logical that questionnaires with cover letters will have a higher response rate, but very few studies have been able to show that this is so.

Anonymity. Experimental studies indicate that promised anonymity does not have a major impact on the response rate.

Size, Typeface and Colour. Here, also, experimental studies have shown no significant differences.

Money Incentives. A number of studies suggest that attaching monetary rewards can be very effective in increasing response rates. However, costs have to be measured against the increase in information.

Deadlines. The few studies available do not indicate a higher response rate if a deadline is given for return; however, deadlines do serve to accelerate returns.

ANA 5: Know and "Don't know"

Bert Lazon wants his research to find an explanation of people's appreciation of their jobs. He has done several studies on the topic, and in this latest survey he tried, among other things, to find a connection between the length of time a person has held a job and whether the person appreciated the job or not.

One question used was: "Do you like your present job?" The alternative answers were "Yes," "No" and "Don't know". What now makes him worried is the high rate of "Don't know" answers. Are these answers from people who really did not know, or is it that many people were not interested in taking a position or giving their opinion? It seems that there is a correlation between the number of years in service and the degree of well-being felt. Because more respondents with shorter service answered, "Don't know", this pointed at many "Don't know" answers really being "No".

Bert can, in his *methodical procedures,* see three ways of handling these "Don't know" answers in his tabulation:

1. keeping them as a separate category in the table
2. excluding the category from the table
3. distributing them among the other answers in the same ratio that the other answers occurred.

Bert chooses the third alternative. He is aware that this means he has to assume that the "Don't know" answers consist of the same proportion of "Yes" and "No" answers as that already found in the distribution of these two answers, but he feels that this is the way failure rates in returned questionnaires – missing responses – are generally handled. Researchers usually assume that those who have not answered would *have* answered according to the pattern established by those who have answered. Furthermore, Bert needs all 950 units in the sample for various calculations (correlations with the answers to other questions that are part of the study, etc.).

ANA 6: Dr Stone's test

This is the eleventh year in a row that Dr Ruth Stone has taught the same course. This year there are twenty-five students in the class, and the average examination result is 64 per cent, with a standard deviation of 9 per cent. The average result for the previous ten years is 61 per cent. Ruth asks herself whether this year's batch of students is better than their predecessors and decides to answer the question by using a statistical test. She does not need much time in her *methodical procedure* to decide what test she will use. The prerequisites for applying a *t*-test seem to be present:

1. The observations must be mutually independent.
2. The observations have to be made in normally distributed populations (Ruth had diagrams of the examination results for each of the past years; they looked like normal distributions).
3. Populations shall have the same variance (these variations had not been large over the years, according to Ruth).
4. The measurement scales shall be of at least an interval type (Dr Stone's school used an interval scale for examination results).

SYSTEMS PROCEDURES

SYS 1: Professor Anholts's introductory lecture

Professor Anholts has a keen interest in research methodology. He is also a devoted user of the systems view in his research and has written several books and a number of scientific articles on this topic. He has, on several occasions, been a member of public investigations commissioned by the government in his country.

Professor Anholts has for a number of years been teaching a course of systems view research for doctoral candidates in his faculty. Below follows some excerpts from the latest introductory lecture to this course:

> The fact that the world is full of systems is known to all of us. Some well-known examples are computer systems, information systems and transportation systems. We are all aware of their existence and most of us use them daily. And I can assure you students that we have a well established and thoroughly tested system in place in this school for measuring and grading your study efforts...

> Why has this word "system" become so popular? The answer is, of course, that we can no longer afford to, and also should not, solve the problems in our society in a one-dimensional and piecemeal fashion. We must provide more holistic solutions in order to be able to sustain our welfare system and have our economy grow stronger...

> We have come quite far in our attempt to explain and to understand how systems are functioning and how we should regard them as researchers. First of all we see them in our *methodical procedures* as *complex* and *comprehensive*. Every system out there in reality should therefore

be searched for facts from many different perspectives and in many different dimensions. Nevertheless, a systems study can never be complete; there is always room for *unpredictability* and every systems study at least partly depends on who is doing it. And because systems can be so complex, we normally have to restrict our studies to look only at a *few cases* at a time and we often have to dig into the history of systems to understand their present…

But I think systems research is thrilling and hope you will too. To dress a situation in terms of *components* and *relations*, *structures* and *processes*, *synergy* and *variety* can be very rewarding…

As part of this course you are to write papers. You are to do it in groups and the objective of the work will be to provide analyses of real problems and to come up with realistic solutions in at least some of the cases. Some examples of topics that have already been suggested to me are:

- An assessment of the system for recruiting new staff to the laboratory of New Bridge Chemicals.
- Clusters in operation in the southwest part of our country – identification and possibilities.
- A survey of opinion among our students on the business incubator system at our university…

I can proudly tell you that the latest doctor who graduated at our school received a Best Thesis of the Year Award for her study "Know-Who Networks in Technology Innovation Systems".

SYS 2: The bank as a system

Vice President Julia Linden has just read a report from a consulting company engaged by her bank two months earlier. Their mission was to make a diagnosis of the corporate culture of the bank. The conclusions from the consultant are, by and large, as follows:

1. The bank contains a mix of different *corporate styles*. This is partly a result of often recurring changes in the market orientation of the bank and partly because of a large turnover of personnel at the top.
2. The bank's *strategic planning* encourages brainstorming and creativity, but, on the other hand, there are no suitable profitability criteria for this. Numerical skills in combination with conservatism tend to put strategic tasks off until tomorrow and foster only marginal improvements. Personnel policies isolate people, reward good news but punish bad, and lead to people both seeking out personal friends and striving for independence. The marketing philosophy is simultaneously to satisfy every customer, to serve all markets, and to observe competitors' moves.
3. The bank's *decision pattern* is reactive and internally focused. Formal decisions are very centralized, and none of the decision processes have a particularly

broad support in senior management. Every person watches his or her turf, and appointed committees can rarely reach constructive solutions. This leads to information and decision requirements flowing down the organization without being followed by any decision criteria.

4. Three subcultures can be identified:

- *Central administration*
  - short-term investment criteria
  - risk avoidance
  - partial assessments
  - make easy decisions first
- *Individual banks*
  - oriented toward reaching agreements with customers on a case-by-case basis
  - guarding one's own turf
  - "fire prevention"
- *Operative areas* (the bank has four operative areas)
  - follow the competition
  - send decisions to the top
  - function "satisfactorily"

Julia reads the report with concern. Interested as she is in the systems view and in methodological issues, she is disappointed that the consulting firm has very little to say about how the bank functions as a system. She is absolutely convinced that to study the bank as a system and make improvements along systems criteria is the only way to move forward. Had she done the study herself, she would have had a holistic orientation in her *methodical procedures*, tried to find a suitable *magnifying level*, stressed *processual aspects* more than *structural* ones and *interviewed* everyone of importance face-to-face. The consulting firm seems to have relied on questionnaires. She knows that a common saying in her bank is to look at it as a "constructive culture of giving and taking in the name of progress", and she would have had all respondents comment on their feeling for, and understanding of, this. Somewhat distressed, she thinks about tomorrow's senior management meeting at which the consulting group is to present its findings.

SYS 3: Calmex Co. as an amusement park

Jon Craig is on vacation. He has brought his whole family on a two-week trip to California. But he cannot completely stop thinking about his research study back home in Sweden, which looks at the connection between how companies are constructed and the degree to which they are successful. He has just been in contact with an interesting case: Calmex Co. The company is obviously very successful and has grown from practically nothing into a dominant force in the special market where it operates.

What surprises Jon to some extent (after having visited the company a few times) is that Calmex Co. seems so disorganized, almost chaotic. It has several special characteristics that he has so far seen only in recent theoretical literature:

- Every department works quite independently. Nobody seems to take orders from headquarters. On a few occasions, however, Jon has experienced that the central management (if "central management" is the right term) has been contacted for advice or ideas.
- Several functions have been contracted out to other, smaller companies. What surprises Jon the most is that sorting and distributing the post is run by an independent service firm!
- Employees always seem engaged in something having to do with customers or suppliers. But that is not all. Customers and suppliers always seem to be present (physically) in one way or another in meetings, at lunches in the company's cafeteria (which is run by one of the restaurants in town), and even in the laboratory. Calmex Co. seems to have no secrets!

Jon is looking in his *methodical procedures* for an *analogy*, a descriptive and developing *metaphor* by which he can place his image of Calmex Co. He feels that such a picture can "put into place seemingly independent phenomena occurring in the company". He feels that an apt simile will give him a "framework" for developing a more "total" understanding of Calmex Co.'s behaviour and its success.

After spending an entire day with his family at Disneyland near Los Angeles, Jon gets such a picture. Calmex Co. can be compared to an amusement park! There are several aspects that "fit":

- One can say that Calmex Co. works in "the entertainment industry," even if the company is not in showbusiness.
- Rather like the different attractions at Disneyland, the several departments of Calmex Co. operate independently and are attractive to their customers in their own right. They are also held together by a common concept and a common theme.
- "Irrelevant" activities are contracted out to other companies.
- The customers (or "the guests", as they are called at Disneyland) are constantly present on Calmex Co.'s premises. In fact, the company depends on their active participation.

Jon is very satisfied with his analogy and looks forward to continuing the work on his study. He has already a number of new questions on his mind triggered by his metaphor!

SYS 4: Rose's final term paper

Rose Campdon has chosen finance as her undergraduate specialization in business, because her father worked in that area. The more she immerses herself in the subject, the more it seems to contain. Her final term paper is to be about financial planning and control in multi-national companies.

Rose has just drawn a diagram of what can, in principle, be the content of financial flows between a mother company and two subsidiaries. Rose's first impression of her own illustration is that there are many more capital flows between companies in an international concern than is at first apparent. But this variety is not the only thing that influences the direction of her work. There also seems to be an endless variety of innovative contracts, terms, options, bonds, stock issues and participants in the international financial world in general.

She wants get a picture of what is going on, as she has written in her research proposal, a proposal that has been discussed in a seminar just a few weeks ago in her academic department. She is not, in her *methodical procedures,* looking for "an average picture" (which she thinks would be quite useless, partly because reality is so complex and partly because participants probably behave so financially differently on the international market compared to at home), but for "a guide to where the international financial world is heading". In other words, Rose wants to study the contexts of these companies that point to the future.

Where should she begin? Words like *models, components, synergy, variety, fit, totality, complexity, relativity* and *mutuality* of *producers* and *products* are rolling around in her head. Finally, she comes to the conclusion to go deeper into the literature to find inspiration for an adequate first systems model to start from.

SYS 5: Technical cooperation

Cooperation is not too good among the H-companies, Alice Coontz soon realizes. She is a member of The Consulting Group and, at the request of the H-companies, has concentrated for the past three weeks on a study to discover "how the different functions relate to each other from a technical point of departure, and to suggest improvements".

Alice has proceeded conscientiously in her *methodical procedures* and used every possible source of information. She has read minutes from meetings and has discovered decisions that contradict each other. She has visited several factories and has studied how they function. In discussions with representatives from all levels of management, she has listened repeatedly to complaints about low morale and lack of information out in the field, about carelessly constructed budgets and about alienation at the middle management level.

She envisions the *systems diagram* in Figure 8.1 (see overleaf) as a starting point for planning the rest of the study. She thinks it is a good model for her to choose which components to approach and which relations to discuss. She thinks she has found a proper magnifying level, that is, a good balance between coverage and content.

SYS 6: The answer is written in history

Mary Leech has been working in a company for seven months. She finds the place very conservative, dull and, frankly speaking, rather unfriendly. She wants to try to explain why she

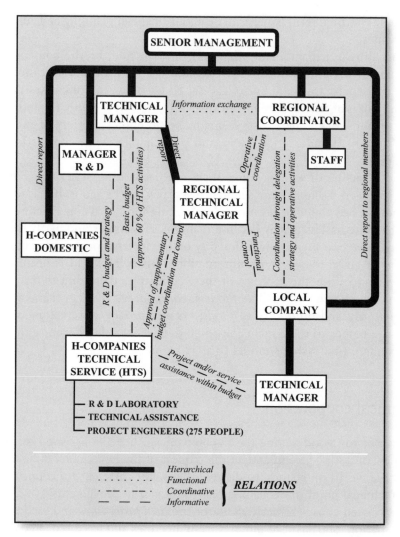

Figure 8.1　A Systems Diagram

has that feeling to her employer. She believes that such an explanation of the company, which has existed for over eighty years, can be traced, at least partly, to its history. By reading all kinds of reports and internal documents, she comes up with the following chronology:

1922:　Johnson (the father) founds Johnson Distribution Ltd, with his wife as accountant. One store-man and one driver (part-time) are also present at the start.

1936:　Still in the same industry and with, by and large, the same line of goods, Johnson Distribution Ltd has thirty-seven employees.

1940:　Johnson Distribution Ltd is engaged for military transport and storage activities, which remain as a smaller branch of the company.

1948:   The company introduces job descriptions for all its employees.

1964:   Johnson (the son, who has been employed in the company since 1938) takes over as general manager. He uses major portions of his first year as general manager to put together on paper the company's established routines. This becomes a written manual, which Johnson (the son) gives to every employee. Johnson updates this manual annually.

1968:   Johnson Distribution Ltd has forty-three employees.

1982:   Johnson Distribution Ltd has forty-four employees (thirty-seven of whom have been with the company since 1968).

1989:   The company buys its first computer system; it includes one standard package for inventory management and one for accounting.

1993:   Johnson (the grandson) takes over as general manager.

When reading this list, Mary says to herself: "Nothing has really happened for the past fifty years here!" However, she is still not satisfied with this alone as a credible explanation. In her *methodical procedures* she thinks that she also has to talk to a number of her colleagues on an informal basis about how the effect of this picture of history can be seen in the daily life of the company today, and in this way she might come up with a modified history of the company. But she has to be careful and tread warily in order not to offend anyone. She has, on the other hand, a rather determined opinion about which people she would like to speak with first.

ACTORS PROCEDURES

ACT 1: Professor Wild on research as an innovative idea

Professor Wild, who always tries to encourage young researchers to develop their creative talents when doing their *methodical procedures* for their master's or doctoral degrees, delivers the following appeal to new graduate students: "Before you started school you had 100 languages. By the time you arrived here your schooling had done away with ninety of them. If you aren't careful, your further studies will take away a few more." What he means by this is that the graduate students ought to find their own directions, search the backyards of science, and not let themselves be enticed by narrow-minded supervisors who, out of a fear of philosophy and all new thinking, point out only the established main roads of research.

Professor Wild, therefore, unlike several of his colleagues, always recommends to his graduate students that they do not start by studying previous research. "They say", Wild points out,

> that if you don't, you run the risk of re-inventing the wheel. But I claim that the real danger lies in the established wheels. You see, the risk is just the opposite; that when you start your discovering process by reading what others have researched, your thoughts will probably follow the same tracks, and those tracks may be so firmly established in your head it is almost impossible to leave them. Therefore, I prefer philosophy and free reflection in the very beginning of a research process.

For this reason, Wild always encourages his graduate students to reflect first on their own inner drive for doing research, place this in relation to their inner vision, and then start right out to create knowledge by *interactive development of understanding* in the study area. As part of this process, Wild recommends that his graduate students use every means they can – film, sound, pictures, art, even other "languages" – to poke holes in their own perspectives, to discover the potential in what is factual, and to relate this to the various *metatheories* of the construction of *social reality*. The professor says that when this phase has reached a stage that can be articulated with the help of the written word, it will be time for his graduate students to find out what other researchers have written about the phenomena they have found, that is, it will be time to study the research field they have entered as it was expressed by others. In other words, Wild sees the study of earlier research as the final phase in his students' research, whereas his colleagues assert that it ought to be the platform from which research is launched. To Professor Wild, research is mainly a question of breaking away from established patterns and not, as he says, "pouring more concrete into already established forms".

ACT 2: Jones and Jones on uniforming methods

Jones and Jones, both researchers, are asked to help the top management of the major daily newspaper, *The News*. The problem, as the managers tell them, consists of an increasingly diminishing circulation over the past two years, while at the same time questionnaires and interviews in several statistical studies cannot give a clear explanation of readers' lack of confidence in the newspaper. The researchers ask now to be allowed to take an unbiased walk around the newspaper's headquarters and then to come back to the managers. At the next meeting with these managers, the researchers raise two important starting points for their *methodical procedures*, which they describe as follows:

1. Methods chosen to study the problem so far are, by and large, the same as those used by the competitors. Because of this, everybody competing in the field runs the risk of constructing an objectified "newspaper reality" that will converge. Unique profiles are wiped out. Knowledge about their own problems will, by means of *self-reference* in these statistically *uniforming* methods, lead toward business decline. Methodologically, this can be described by the metaphor: "if your only tool is a hammer, everything you see in your surroundings will look like nails". The real problem is, so to say, *a problem of methods*. If we only look for similarities in what is different and regularities in the irregular and not the other way round, we will surely get a business problem.
2. Furthermore, if the study is not also combined with internal development, the most important *questions* about the market cannot be posed, at the same time that *answers* coming from the market cannot be fully used as development tools. This is a *dialectical* process of pressure and counterpressure that can free (emancipate) *the potential in what is factual*. And the potential – the business venture – is situated in the tension between creation/production and market.

After presenting their two standpoints, researchers Jones and Jones describe to the management group how they intend to start internally as well as externally.

Externally, they want to conduct repeated *dialogues* with what they call eight "ideal-typified readers", several of whom will not be said to represent the majority of the newspaper's present readers – what could be called a *problem/ opportunity-oriented selection.*

Internally, the researchers want first to develop a historical diagnosis using longer dialogues with three retired journalists and two former editors-in-chief. Through a *recommended selection* of other employees, the researchers intend next to continue to get an understanding of the structure of company jokes combined with each of the employees being allowed to select photos, drawings and works of art that, in their opinion, describe the present situation and what they personally want to achieve in the future, both for themselves and in their work at the newspaper.

The researchers justify the last part by wanting journalists, editors and others to express themselves in a *language* other than the written one; that, according to the researchers, is where most of the present problems are stuck: in the actual, well-established *language game* of problem solving. Jones and Jones claim that the structure of jokes is important because "in this objectified language of description, which is supposed to entertain, many problem pictures are hidden for which there is no legitimate company language". The management team, not being used to actors research, fears its own inability to understand what the researchers are really aiming for with their somewhat different methods, but at the same time management is curious and full of expectations.

ACT 3: The number of rejects must decrease

The senior management of Fix Production Ltd has asked consultant Sara O'Brien whether she wants to conduct a survey of job satisfaction among those who are directly related to production. Sara, however, immediately expressed her hesitation about the project as framed by senior management. They want a conventional attitudinal survey in order, as they said, "to be able to derive the steps to take to increase the motivation among personnel to decrease the seemingly ever-increasing costs of the number of rejects".

Consultant O'Brien raises in her *methodical procedures,* as an antithesis to the senior managers' opinion, that they should probably first make themselves understand the totality, develop a vision, and look for the metatheories on which their opinion is based. The senior management team thinks that Sara's discussion sounds a bit too loose. But Sara asserts that an alternative to the law of causality does not have to be either "loose" or random. Instead, Sara says, humbly, it can signify meaningfulness. After this first dialogue, a question arose about whether the problem is embedded in a tension field. Consultant O'Brien draws a model (adapted from our book) for the senior management team to consider (see Figure 8.2 and compare with Figure 6.3).

Out of the *quantitative accumulation* created in the field of *dialectics* – meaning – between work and everyday life, the *quality* that this accumulation becomes seems to be rejects as *externalization* and gloominess as *internalization.*

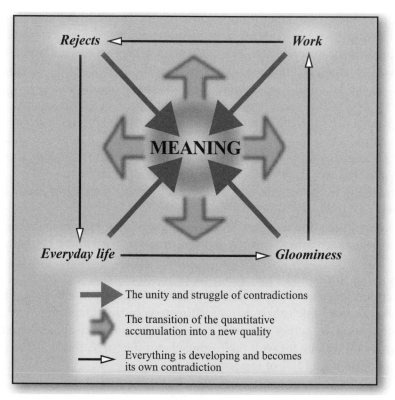

Figure 8.2   O'Brien's Model for Senior Management

Starting with this construction of an image of everyday reality, and together with the senior managers, Sara is assigned to interact with the people concerned to develop something that will transform the situation, something that can show how the *potential exists in what is factual*. Everything contains its own contradiction, according to O'Brien, who is a devoted user of the actors view in her consulting work. Therefore, the opposite of the rejects shall exist within the frame of the rejects themselves. *Dialogue* is Sara's "weapon" and *action* her "strategy". By working with the people concerned to develop a creation that will be run by meaning, like a seed that creates its own flowers, this should in its quantitative accumulation turn into another quality: *meaningfulness* and fewer rejects.

In the creative activities of the *emancipatory interaction*, Sara, again with the people concerned, develops an interesting plan in which – among other things – a major portion of the profit resulting from the reduced number of rejects is transferred to children's and young people's organizations that directly benefit the children of Fix Production's employees. After this interactive study those who participated feel a dramatically higher meaning in what they now are doing – to the extent that both the number of rejects and the gloominess have virtually disappeared, and at the same time the quality of the products has improved and discussions about ideas and visions have gone sky-high. According to Sara O'Brien, the company has received a vital injection in the form of tangible proof that the alternative to causality questionnaires and motivational steps is *understanding* and *meaning structures*.

ACT 4: An experiment in organization and leadership

Patrick Nelson is a researcher. His interest is in how medical service is managed and organized. He has for several years conducted different variations of *interactive development of
understanding* in the study area. He has presented his results as *descriptive language (process
models)* and *ideal-typified language (models of typified cases)* in *procreative reports* as well as
in *direct acts*.

At the moment he is conducting a knowledge-creating experiment in which around 100
persons are participating. All of them have some kind of leadership position. They are representing everything from care centres, small, medium-sized and large hospitals and
university hospitals, to central administrations in different county councils. A broad spectrum of experience and different life-worlds are represented, in other words. Patrick lets all
of them, individually as well as in groups, bring up issues of, for them, important organization and leadership themes. These issues are then mixed and spread among the participants
and this allows them to use the issues themselves as the basis of interviews/conversations with
specially invited guests, everything from actors and authors to senior business managers.

The idea behind this *methodical* reasoning is that the participants are to have their urgent
issues reflected as the complex phenomena they are, from several different perspectives and
language areas, beyond their own operative service. The interviews/conversations are filmed
and the actors are then to edit the material, in other words decide what they feel is more or
less meaningful. This way every "interview" is "cut down" from about 40 minutes reasoning
to about 15 minutes, which is the target Patrick has set up. In these 15 minutes, problems
and answers are now condensed/qualificated as *first hand expressions* by the actors, where
the editing criteria are the study area's own measure of the degree of urgency.

In other words, the participants in these kinds of experiments are themselves to decide
how the material is to be condensed and what they feel to be the urgent issues and meaningful reflections of the same. When editing, the participants are also asked to reflect on their
reasoning with the guest in question and write down their reflections.

Using these edited films and written materials and his own *interactive development of
understanding* in the experiment, Patrick then presents a *procreative report* where the experiment is described using different kinds of descriptive languages. The different sections,
where the experiment is treated in the actors' own words, Patrick usually introduces with a
procreative description. In this description he often uses *language poetring* as a principle to
make language intelligible and developable (see Knowledge creating interface of language
development in Chapter 7).

ACT 5: Graduate paper on the concept of quality

When Mary, Philip and Mike (all students) meet for the third time to work on the
methodical procedures of their graduate paper, they decide that it will deal with questions
of quality in industry in the context of quality itself. The paper will not merely take into
consideration product quality but will focus on different *meanings* of the concept of *quality* in business in general. After a pilot phase of *interactive development of understanding*

and of searching for meaning, the students come up with an idea about how to structure their work, in which different kinds of actor selections will be made in the course of the study.

Mary, Philip and Mike (for quality reasons) decide to limit their study to two cases; these are seen as the basis of a number of *ideal-typified descriptions* of the concept. From the introductory interactive stage they hope to be able to "strike" a few areas of typified phenomena that can be related to different levels of *structural meaning*. The students feel this is important because in the course of the study it will enable them to formulate more precise questions as *antitheses* to the everyday denotation of the quality concept that at the time control the *language games* in the two company cases. The hope, then, is based on this so-called counter pressure to generate the background of the *descriptive language* and the *ideal types* they intend to create, starting from the denotations of conceptual meaning in the study.

ACT 6: Knowledge creating and examination

Lecturers Cathy and Bryan are in the process of constructing an examination after teaching a course on entrepreneurship and business ventures. They intend, in their *methodical procedures,* to give the exam the highest possible *content validity*. Among other things, they want the arrangement of the exam itself to conjure up a picture of the content of the course. Cathy and Bryan are absolutely convinced that there is no neutral way of examining students; instead, all exams, one way or another, reflect a certain outlook on people as well as a conception of reality and a vision of knowledge. What Cathy and Bryan want to achieve is an exam that, through its very structure, not only openly articulates the *ultimate presumptions* upon which it is built, but also condenses the learning and the content portions of the course.

Finally they come up with a 24-hour-long exam that is divided into four-hour sessions in which the students themselves, in six different groups, are given the responsibility of achieving high content validity in every session of the course.

After assigning the sessions among the students by lottery, part of the time allocated to the course is used for the groups to plan their exam exercises. Each of the six groups, then, in its four-hour session at the time of the examination, is supposed to assess other students on the basis of their exam activities, *and* at the same time will be assessed on the merit of whether they can achieve a format and content that reflect the content of the course. All points are then to be weighted together into a traditional exam result.

Under the motto "Put your courage and theories on the line", this 24-hour exam is carried out as a bus trip. Altogether, 300 miles are covered in the 24 hours, and the allocated four-hour intervals and sections of road are very creatively used to present various situations to test the course content. It was very much an entrepreneurial and venturing project and it succeeded so well that the students later claimed that they had never before studied and been examined on a course with such joy and with such a learning effect.

Cathy and Bryan were very satisfied and felt that through their efforts they had been able to show partly that examination and teaching are not *value neutral*, and partly that the learning effect is very high if education is based on *creating meaning* and if it is able to reveal the *potential* in what is trapped in the *factual*.

In this chapter, 3 x 6 different examples have been provided of how argumentation, thinking and application of different investigative efforts and consulting assignments, etc. may look in our three methodological views. Here, everything from the criteria for good research in the analytical view, non-response to questionnaires, introductory professorial lectures and experiences from a visit to Disneyland, to how to treat the number of rejects and the construction of a final student test in order to reach high validity according to the actors view, has been presented. By different examples it has been possible to follow how thinking and language is growing depending on which view we start from. Alongside this, illustrations have also been provided of how the ultimate presumptions in the different views will be expressed in different everyday behaviour and action within the domains of creating knowledge.

POINTS OF REFLECTION

1. Take any of the examples provided in this chapter and discuss in another *methodological view* than the one used originally.
2. Many of the above examples are methodological stories which provide sections of some study for creating knowledge, often the beginning of that study. *Choose* your favourite example from some of the views and *continue* to tell the story as you think it might go on.
3. One of the professors gives the advice that a creator of knowledge, as much as possible, should *describe in detail* his/her methodical procedures in order for other creators of knowledge to be able to *repeat as exactly as possible* that research which has been done in the light of these procedures. What types of ultimate presumptions are contained here and what is this advice based on?
4. Another professor asserts that research is mainly a question of *breaking away from established patterns* and not, as he says, "pouring more concrete into already established forms". What separates these two professors (in points 3 and 4) more than that they obviously start from different methodological views? We ask you to have a bit of imagination to answer this question, because there are no immediately obvious answers here.
5. When it is about *"exactness" in presenting results* (the report) two of the views are on a direct path of colliding with each other as far as the value of quantifying is concerned. You know already which these two views are. We want you now, using what has been brought up in Chapter 7 and what has been described in this chapter as a background, to try to clarify to yourself what "exactness" can mean in the two contexts of creating knowledge.
6. What is meant by *causal experiments*? Try to come up with such an experiment of your own where you are careful about considering possible intervening and background variables. By the way, what does "intervening and background" mean in this context?

(Continued)

(Continued)

7. A metaphor is a linguistic picture that tries to describe something by using something else – using some kind of an ideal case. In one of the examples Disneyland is mentioned as a possible business *metaphor*. If you associate this picture of Disneyland with business, what possible *perspectives* seem to come up in your opinion?

8. To *envision* a systems diagram, as Alice Coontz is doing in one of the examples, as a starting point for planning a study, might be a good idea in a systems oriented study. To create one *metaphor* might be another good idea. Try to bring up some positive aspects that might arise if these two good ideas were *combined*.

9. In one of the examples there are two researchers who claim that when competitors use *similar knowledge-creating methods*, there is an obvious risk that *competitive advantages are diminished*. Since these methods, according to the researchers, are indirectly aligning the companies to each other they will also increasingly perceive the market in a similar fashion. What is your own opinion on this issue after having, by now, taken part of a number of worlds of creating knowledge?

10. Sara asserts in one of the examples that *an alternative to the law of causality* does not have to be either "loose" or random. Instead, Sara says, it can signify ...? What?

RECOMMENDED FURTHER READING

See the end of the Appendix and visit the website below.

Become a worldwide partner as a *knowledge creator* in the development of *Methodology for Creating Business Knowledge* by visiting the website: **www.knowledge-creator.com**. Here you can contribute by asking your own questions and you will also find answers to the most frequently asked questions. The website has been developed alongside this third edition of the book and the questions posted there will be used to provide input for future editions.

9 METHODICS

We have devoted one chapter to methodical procedures in theory and one chapter to examples of language and action based on such procedures in our three approaches (methodological views in application). It is now time to put this into context, to consider and arrange the techniques-made-into-methods in a study plan and to look (in principle) at the way in which a researcher/consultant/investigator conducts a study in practice. This is what we call methodics. The chapter also introduces a few central concepts for excellence in knowledge-creating work.

THE ANALYTICAL APPROACH

In general

We know that the scientific prototype for the analytical view came from the natural sciences. And it is from the natural sciences that analytical creators of knowledge have borrowed techniques, methodical procedures and methodics. This is important to our continuing discussion:

- Both the natural and the social sciences aim at exploring, explaining and predicting the factive reality, even if the two are looking at different parts of this reality.
- Great formalistic demands are made of those who use techniques by the analytical approach.
- How data are collected, arranged and analysed is decisive for success. There is no room for metaphysics.

Methodical procedures

The methodical procedures in the analytical approach have to do with *choosing* the right technique in relation to the characteristics of the study area. Although it is sometimes necessary to modify a technique, developing a technique does not happen often, and totally new techniques are extremely rare.

The guarantee of a good result for the creator of knowledge lies here with choosing the right techniques and applying them correctly. The analytical approach has, as we know, an extensive collection of *rules* for choose and design techniques.

Methodics

The goals of the approach

The levels of ambition when creating knowledge within the analytical approach are:

- to determine (a problem)
- to describe
- to explain
- to forecast
- to guide.

These goals are developments of each other. A problem cannot be described until it has been determined. It cannot be explained until it has been described. A good forecast is based on explanation (and consequently a description as well). A guide is useless if it does not refer to the future – if it is not based on a forecast.

A study plan for determining problems

To determine a problem means to formulate a problem for further description, explanation, forecast or guidance. In order to have the best possible determination of a problem, it is important to use all available sources (see Figure 9.1).

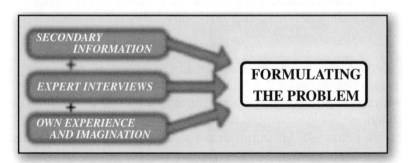

Figure 9.1   A Plan for Determining Problems

Secondary information consists of diverse documentation, which can be essential for breadth (see "Secondary information" in Chapter 7). For example, it is important for researchers to study what other researchers have achieved or concluded in the study area in question. *Expert interviews*, or discussions with those who know about the problem, can, in principle, lead to a deeper perspective. A consultant's client is a kind of "expert" in directing studies for determining problems. The *personal experience and imagination* that the creator of knowledge brings to bear him/herself can be based on work or on lived events of interest to the present problem.

The extent to which these three sources are used will *vary* strongly from case to case, depending partly on the degree to which the problem area is already researched and *explained*, partly on whether the job is a research task, a consulting mission or an investigation, and on the interests and experiences of the creator of knowledge.

Another name for determining a problem is *exploratory* studies.

It can be useful to ask which *criteria* were used to choose a study area (i.e. if there was a choice). Ideally, a *researcher* choosing study area should be able to say "Yes" to each of the following five questions:

- Is the study needed?
- Do data and a method exist?
- Can I do it in the available time?
- Do I have both a knowledge of, and an interest in, the study area?
- Will it be personally developing and useful?

Consultants may of course be partially governed by other criteria when choosing an area for their mission. Consultants' freedom of choice is usually somewhat restricted. An *investigation* is commonly made based on guidelines provided by the commissioner of the study.

The way a problem is formulated (the outcome of formulating a problem) varies primarily with the type of problem, that is, whether it is descriptive, explanatory, and so on. We will come back to this.

A study plan for analytical studies

Studies for generating knowledge by the analytical approach need to pass through a number of steps. These steps in all cases in this approach can, in principle, be summarized in one figure (Figure 9.2). However, as we can see in that figure, which steps are to be included and what their content will be will vary according to whether the study aims to provide a description (D), an explanation (E), a forecast (F) or a guide (G).

D: A study plan for descriptive studies

Formulating the problem. Problem formulations in studies that have "only" a descriptive purpose amount to *defining* the following:

1. the population
2. the characteristics and/or behaviours to be measured in the population.

The *population* encompasses the group of units for which the creator of knowledge intends the description to be valid.

The formulation of a problem (when describing as well as when explaining, forecasting and/or guiding) can, of course, be the result from a previous more or less extensive study for determining the problem.

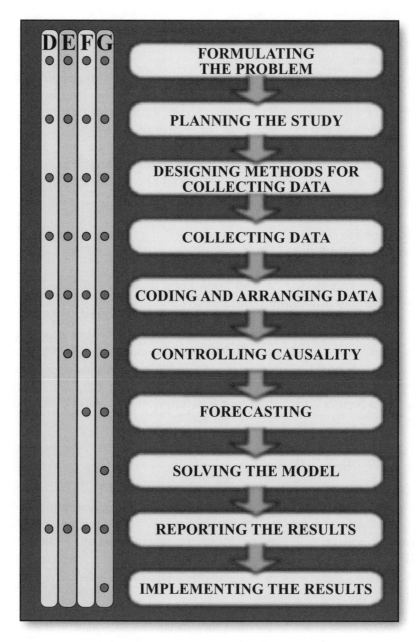

Figure 9.2   Plans for Analytical Approach Studies

Planning the study. The first important decision is whether to conduct a *census* or to take a *sample*. Be aware that planning a study means planning all of the steps from "Designing methods for collecting data" to "Reporting the results", that is, all of the remaining steps in the study.

Designing methods for collecting data. In the context of descriptive studies there is reason to use only secondary information and/or to collect data by means of direct observations, interviews or both. Because the purpose of an experiment in the analytical view is to provide a direct basis for explanations – the step *after* descriptions so to say – experiments are not of interest for descriptive studies. The details of how the methodical procedures are used to design various methods for collecting data depend on the nature of the study area and on personal circumstances, e.g.:

- access to data already collected
- the population at hand
- the characteristics that are to be measured, the behaviour to be observed, or both
- the time frame and budget.

Collecting, coding and arranging data. The content of these two steps in Figure 9.2 will be largely determined by the results of previous steps or stages. We point out, however, three things that are valid for our methodological approaches and for all arrangements of studies within the approaches – though they may be valid to a lesser degree in the analytical approach than the systems approach, and most valid for the actors approach:

1. It is often difficult to draw a line between where one step of a study ends and the next begins.
2. Nobody is perfect, not even the best researcher/consultant/investigator. A creator of knowledge may discover, through faults or deficiencies in later steps of a study, that earlier steps must be supplemented or even repeated.
3. Circumstances can change or turn out to be different than originally believed, which may lead to the continuation of the study following a revised plan. These exchanges can, of course, also mean that the researcher/consultant/investigator will have to go back and repeat or supplement previous steps.

So, there may be *substantial* differences between a *study plan* and the *study itself*.

Reporting the results. The quality of the report of created knowledge results can be of major importance to the opinion which readers or listeners may have about the quality of a study. A creator of knowledge should therefore take seriously the importance of communicating what he/she has been doing clearly and convincingly.

The content of reports on created knowledge varies substantially. Research reports often emphasize the formulation of the problem, the background analysis and the methodology. Consultation reports and public investigations place more stress on the results.

The author of a report should be guided by four questions:

1. What is the report's purpose?
2. Who will read the report?
3. Under what circumstances and limitations was the report written?
4. How will the report be used?

Reports should be clearly structured, physically appealing and easy to read. Report writers can reach these objectives if they are careful with technical details, style and intelligibility. Particular importance should be placed on communicating statistical data.

Oral briefing and presentation are common and should be conducted within the existing practical communication circumstances. Oral presentations usually have a time limit, so a good delivery requires preparation and organizational ability. Audiovisual means are of special importance in such cases, but are often neglected or used poorly.

Whether written or oral, a poor presentation can destroy what was otherwise a splendid effort towards creating knowledge. A good presentation, on the other hand, brings life to the results and a good reputation to the creator of knowledge.

E: A study plan for explanatory studies

An analytical explanatory study consists of the steps that are labelled E in Figure 9.2. However, there are similarities as well as differences in the content of the steps compared with descriptive studies.

Formulating the problem. Formulating the problem for an explanatory study means two things:

1. draft the hypotheses
2. define

   • the variables and concepts that are part of the hypotheses (including possible background and intervening variables)
   • the population

The *population* for an explanatory study encompasses the group of units for which the researcher/consultant/investigator intends the explanation to be valid.

Drafting the hypotheses at the beginning of an explanatory study is necessary for gaining control of the study.

Planning the study. Again, a decision must be made about whether to take a census or a sample. Also, the groundwork for the proper execution of the study's remaining steps – including *verifying* or *falsifying* its hypotheses – must be made.

Designing methods for collecting data. In explanatory studies, data can also be collected through experiments (in the analytical sense of the term).

Controlling causality. To control causality means to test the suggested cause–effect relations that were proposed in the form of hypotheses at the beginning of the study:

a. Test for a connection between the variables representing causes and those representing effects.
b. Check the temporal order between the two groups of variables.
c. Check the importance of background and intervening variables.

The creator of knowledge should, early in the study (see "Formulating the problem", above), be aware of potential influential background and intervening variables, in order to collect data on them as well as on the hypotheses themselves.

F. A study plan for forecasting studies

In Chapter 3 (see Box 3.3) we introduced the concept of *models* in the analytical view as deliberately simplified pictures or prototypes of pieces of reality. All analytical creators of knowledge endeavour to construct such pictures or prototypes.

Such models can contain variables and the relations between them. A set-up of a number of adequate variables may be enough for a descriptive model. However, in the case of good explanatory models, the relations between these variables must be included as well.

Forecasting means to assign assumed or derived "values" to variables in the model, values that *represent the future*, in order to describe or explain a reality that has not yet taken place.

It is possible to differentiate among models based on their *purpose*, whether they are descriptive, explanatory, and so on. Three other categorizations of models are a, b and c below:

a1. *static* models, which do not have any time variable.
a2. *dynamic* models, which have a time variable.
b1. *qualitative* models, which do not contain numerical variables.
b2. *quantitative* models, which have variables that are capable of assuming numerical values.
c1. *scalar* models, which are physical, simplified pictures of prototypes of a piece of reality. The scale of the model can be miniaturized in relation to reality, such as an architect's proposal for a new factory building. The scale can also be enlarged, such as a drawing for a new computer chip.
c2. *analogue* models, which are physical and constructed so that some of their characteristics are analogous to an aspect of reality. Imagine, for instance, liquid being pumped through a construction made of pipes and containers. If the construction is dimensionally correct, the flow of liquid could be analogous to, say, the flow of capital in an economy.
c3. *symbolic* models, which are made of "construction elements" that consist of words, figures, diagrams and/or mathematical symbols and numbers.

Although there are other kinds of models, analytical creators of knowledge claim that those most suitable for forecasting are the dynamic, quantitative and symbolic models.

The design of forecasting studies does not need any further discussion. They simply include an extra step inserted before "Reporting the results" in the methodics of the descriptive and explanatory studies already described. As will become clear, "forecasting" is a necessary step in guiding studies.

G: A study plan for guiding studies

In the analytical approach, a complete guiding study follows all the steps shown in Figure 9.2. However, as before, the content of the steps contain unique aspects.

Formulating the problem. In analytical approach guiding, this is a question of transforming a decision maker's problem into an investigative problem. This requires that the following components of the decision problem (the one we intend to guide) are mapped out:

1. the interested parties, that is, the decision maker and others concerned, including their relations to each other
2. the objective that the decision is to satisfy
3. the possible alternative actions
4. the problem's environment, that is, the factors that cannot be controlled by the interested parties but that may none the less influence the result of the decision.

Mapping out or clarifying these aspects may be fairly complicated, depending on the nature of the decision. If, say, the interested parties are members of a large organization in which there is plenty of both contrasting knowledge and contradictory opinions, then classification of the decision to be made may require extensive effort.

Formulating the objective that a decision is to satisfy and generating possible alternative actions will not be discussed; this is covered in other literature and is too extensive to include in this book. The principle for formulating decisions in the analytical approach is – while considering the interested parties (see item 1 above) – to find the suitable factors in a *decision model* (consisting of items 2, 3 and 4 above), a model that the study is to construct, to forecast the position of, to solve and to implement.

An analytical *decision* model can *in principle* always be formulated in the following fashion:

$$V = f(Xs ; Ps)$$

where:

V is the objective (also a kind of effect)
Xs are the factors to be decided on (the controllable causes)
Ps are the environmental factors, the parameters, the value of which are to be forecasted (also a kind of cause)
f is the format of the model

Thus, a decision model is an *explanatory* model that causally relates the controllable causes (Xs) and the environmental factors (Ps) to an objective (V).

Example. Suppose we are consultants and looking at a problem of high absenteeism in a company. The senior managers in that company claim that they have as an objective to reduce absenteeism by half, from the present situation, where on average every 10th person is absent, to a new situation, where on average only every 20th person would be absent. In other words:

V = Absenteeism down to 5% of the workforce (on average)

After having talked to the great majority of the workforce in the company, and having put together opinions from various open sources, like textbooks and articles on the subject and the Internet, and after having discussed the situation with our own colleagues in our consulting firm (compare "A plan for determining problems", Figure 9.1), we have come up with the following causes on which we have should concentrate in our assignment:

Controllable causes (Xs):

⇨ salary
⇨ other financial compensations
⇨ working environment
⇨ management style
⇨ composition of the workforce

Environmental factors (Ps):

⇨ relevant laws in the country
⇨ norms and traditions in the industry
⇨ the geographic location of the firm

In other words, the problem (formulated in a decision model) in this case can be presented as the following question: "Given the relevant laws of the country, norms and traditions in the industry and the geographic location of the firm, what should we do about salary, other financial compensations, working environment, management style and composition of the workforce in order to reduce absenteeism to 5 per cent of the workforce (on average)?"

Much more could be discussed in this example and many more details could be brought forward, but we believe it will serve its purpose as an illustration.

Forecasting. To make a forecast means in this context to come up with an opinion of the position of the three non-controllable factors (*Ps*) in that period in the future during which the decision is to be valid.

Solving the model. To solve a model means *in principle* that, while considering the interested parties, the creator of knowledge determines the *Xs*, given the *Ps*, which yield the desirable *V*.

To go back to our consulting example, it could, for instance, be so that we suggest a numbers of actions that the company should take under each of the five controllable causes. We might claim that, if this is done, the problem is solved, that is, the company will reduce absenteeism by half.

Reporting and implementing the results. It is important to keep in mind that no matter how carefully various factors and interested parties are considered, complications (minor or major) often arise when implementing the results of a guiding study. This is because, among other things, the researcher/consultant/investigator has (in accordance with the rules) constructed deliberately simplified pictures and prototypes – models – that necessarily neglect aspects that may later turn out to be of importance. Also, as we know, models in the analytical view are formulated *ceteris paribus* ("other things being equal"). Other "things" may not turn out to be equal.

THE SYSTEMS APPROACH

In general

In the systems approach, the purpose, in general, is to explain and/or understand a reality, which consists of objective and subjective facts. However, the high level of formalism demanded in the analytical approach is not asked for here. Using the various techniques "correctly" does not guarantee success in the systems approach: success is associated with imagination, flexibility and awareness when facing the complex reality postulated by this approach.

Methodical procedures

It is significantly more difficult to choose and to develop techniques in a study area using the systems approach. This is partly because the analysis of real systems is very much a matter of trial and error, which means that, to some extent, techniques have to be chosen and developed into methods only when the creator of knowledge has gained enough knowledge of the real system to make a correct and progressive choice. Also, systems reality is presumed to be multidimensional and complex enough to complicate knowledge-creating work. Finally, there are several alternative designs to choose from for systems studies.

Methodics

The goals of the approach

As we did for the analytical approach, we list the objectives of the systems approach in five levels:

- to determine the type (of system)
- to describe
- to determine finality relations
- to forecast
- to guide.

But a complication is added here. From a *methodological* point of view, "determining the type", "describing", and "determining finality relations" cannot be completely separated from each other. This is because the systems approach starts from the presumption of a reality that is constructed of various totalities, each of which contain numerous connections (had these totalities not contained connections or relations, they would not have been called systems).

In some cases, researchers/consultants/investigators are satisfied with a superficial study of certain external (and/or very stable internal) characteristics and behaviours of systems. In these cases, it is sometimes practical for creators of knowledge to disregard the fact that they are working with systems. A descriptive study of this kind can be designed as if it were using the analytical approach.

But when the assumptions of the systems approach are respected and we enter "deeper" into the system (or systems) being studied, we know that by definition they contain finality relations. Looking at systems as systems *requires* that we include these relations in our picture. So, whether the primary ambition is "to describe" or to "to determine a type", the most fundamental possible level of ambition in systems studies is *to determine finality relations.*

A study plan for determining finality relations

A plan for a study to determine relations according to the systems approach might look like the one presented in Figure 9.3 overleaf. However, in the figure we note several differences compared to the analytical approach:

1. Formulating a problem by the systems approach is more extensive than by the analytical approach. In seriously designed systems studies it is wise to proceed cautiously and to avoid determining the problem too soon. A good way to express this is to say that a knowledge creator has captured *the problem* (which is still subject to revision) when he or she feels a connection backward as well as forward: *backward* in the sense that the researcher/consultant/ investigator has a general sense that he/she has done what is possible under the practical restrictions to come up with the results, and *forward* in the sense that the knowledge creator thinks that he/she can, in confidence, report the results. Therefore, formulating the problem is, in the systems approach, the whole of the box A. This contains what it is necessary to say: "*Now* I can explain/understand the real system"!

2. Apart from explaining, the ambition of understanding can enter the systems study. This is done, as we have seen, by introducing concepts, models and even whole metaphors that, in a sense, do not "belong to" the real system, but which are used by the creator of knowledge to get a somewhat "deeper" comprehension of what is going on in the real case. Such understanding additions will generate new questions, which in turn will complicate the whole process of creating knowledge.

3. Determining the type of system goes on "in parallel" with the rest of the study (in box B). This determination of type can "be finished" at any time as the study proceeds, but because possibilities for revisions and refinements are always present, Figure 9.3. shows the process running throughout the study.

4. A study to determine finality relations implies ongoing interactive contact with "representatives" from the part of reality being studied (in one or a few real systems) in order to increasingly clarify the finality relations that exist. A number of feedback mechanisms therefore exist among the various stages of the study plan. Explicitly mentioning these feedback mechanisms in the systems approach (as opposed to the analytical approach) should, to be fair, be seen as a difference in degree rather than in kind. We have said before that analytical creators of knowledge also often have reason to go back and repeat previous stages in their studies.

Differences from the analytical approach also exist regarding the content of several of the stages.

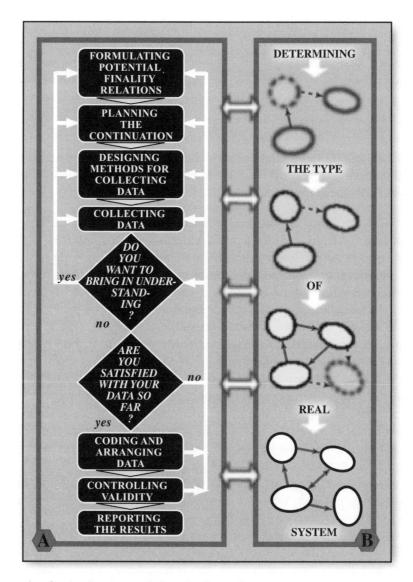

Figure 9.3   A Plan for Studies Determining Finality Relauons

Formulating potential finality relations. A creator of knowledge cannot start a systems approach study for determining relations by formulating hypotheses, as is done in the analytical situation. We remind the reader of the difference between analytical theory and systems theory. In analytical theory, hypotheses (potential causal relations) are often deduced, and an explanatory study is conducted in an attempt to verify or falsify them. Systems theory, however, is a source of ideas about how certain characteristics and behaviours of real systems might be formulated. It is not until real systems *are contacted and studied in detail* that the concrete finality relations that are to be studied can be stated.

So, studies for determining finality relations always contain aspects of induction (studies in the field of real individual cases with the intention of finding real relations). As mentioned before, creators of knowledge using the systems approach are not as dependent on existing and established theory as creators of knowledge are in the analytical approach. Therefore, the best a creator of knowledge can do in the beginning of studies for determining finality relations is to formulate *potential* relations.

Planning the continuation. The study should be planned, even if only roughly. Yet the plan should not be so rigid that a researcher/consultant/investigator is cut off from new signals from the real system.

Designing methods for collecting data. The idea is, of course, that the creator of knowledge shall think of available techniques for collecting data and designing them according to the basic requirements of the systems view and of possibilities in the study area in question. As we know, all techniques for collecting data (except setting up experiments) are available in the systems view.

Collecting data. The content of this step follows naturally from the previous one.

Do you want to bring in understanding? In some systems studies, the creator of knowledge may feel that he/she does not get a good comprehension of the real system(s) in the study area by simply studying it (them) as it (they) is (are). Therefore, he/she might add his/her own ideas in terms of intellectual constructions like models or metaphors to intensify his/her imagination. This will most likely add at least another round of formulating potential finality relations and its consequences (compare the arrows in Figure 9.3). We have talked about this kind of understanding earlier (in Chapter 5).

Are you satisfied with your data so far? The systems approach lets the creator of knowledge's personal judgement play a more decisive role than is the case in the analytical approach, a point we also made in the discussion of validation techniques in Chapter 7.

Coding and arranging data. The idea here is that the creator of knowledge is to look for patterns in his/her data according to the five basic principles in the systems view, that is, the principles of totality, complexity, relativity, mutuality and unpredictability (compare Chapter 5).

Controlling validity. Recall that the relations that are found according to the systems approach, that is, relations between producers and products, are neither necessary nor sufficient. This means, above all, that these relations should be seen as fully valid for only the real system(s) that the creator of knowledge has actually studied. Furthermore, the *finality* relations found in a group of real systems (or in a single one) cannot always be considered sufficient or necessary either. This follows from the assumption of how real systems are built up.

To control such finality relations, therefore, means using different methods to find out whether the discovered *producers* can provide the discovered *products*. The analytical three-stage division (below and above under "E: A study plan for explanatory studies – *Controlling causality"*) is, as we know, *not* possible for the systems approach because (b) and (c) are not applicable to finality relations:

a. Test for relations among the variables.
b. Check the temporal order between these variables.
c. Check the importance of background and intervening variables.

Although finality relations that seem to be present often should be considered as only "preliminary", they can, however, be included in systems theory as an inspiration to future systems construction of knowledge.

We cannot go any further with finality relations in a systems study at this step for determining relations because of the nature of the approach. It is not until these relations are tested in an *applied* study (a study with a guiding ambition) that there is a "definite" settlement of the value of the relations.

Reporting the results. From the assumptions behind the systems approach it follows that real systems are not usually completely comparable with each other. One might draw the conclusion from this that very extensive studies are always necessary to arrive at valid results. For practical reasons, however, creators of knowledge must often limit a study to a few objects in the study area (maybe a single real system). After describing this limited selection, creators of knowledge cannot safely draw conclusions about any other real systems outside those that have actually been studied. This is *not* in any way a reduction of the level of ambition compared to representative samples in the analytical approach, but a consequence of the systems approach presumptions about the way reality is built up. Case studies are therefore, as we mentioned already, very common in the systems approach.

This characteristic of conclusions within the framework of the systems approach should be reflected when reporting a systems study.

A study plan for forecasting studies

As in the analytical approach, a detailed discussion of systems approach forecasting study plans will not provide any major contributions to our *methodological* discussion. We only point out again that forecasts based on the premises of the systems approach rest on "shaky" ground because of the presupposed interactive and complicated reality of this approach. As we stated earlier, there is a definite limit to forecasting the future course of a real system. Good forecasts are therefore not as crucial for determining the validity of research/consulting/investigation results as they are for the analytical approach. (Recall the five principles of the systems view; see above and Chapter 5.)

A study plan for guiding studies

Sometimes, systems studies go as far as to give advice. This means, in general, to continue *after* the end of Figure 9.3 (commonly as a consultant, sometimes as an investigator and even, occasionally, as a researcher) to tell the participants in the study area how problems they face could be solved. This could generally be seen as a *systems construction* (compare Chapter 5 on this topic), because of the fact that the real system as it is functioning now is in trouble. You have to build a new one.

The way this is done, that is, how advice is given, depends, of course, on what you see a system to be, what mechanisms are holding it together and what it aims for. There are so many models (and interpretations) available and suggested that it is practically impossible to list them all. However, there are, in principle, three common situations here:

- *Unfitness of specific components.* A system is supposed to, if it is working well, operate as a system, that is, all components are to be aligned and in co-operation, supporting each other. If a specific systems component contradicts and does not fit the rest of the system, it has, in the name of systems perfection, to be corrected or, if this is not possible, be eliminated.
- *Systems totally out of place.* Business systems are open. Their environment is changing. Many real systems are organized to solve problems that no longer exist. Something has to be done to that system as a whole.
- *Systems are no longer a system.* There are situations, in reality, which have ceased to function as systems, that is, there is no common mission, no values and beliefs which are shared and even no common language in understanding the problem and what should be done. Serious steps are necessary.

All of the above three, and other problematic systems, give their own hints to creators of knowledge of what to search for to find remedies.

THE ACTORS APPROACH

In general

Actors creators of knowledge consciously work under the assumption that they not only change the actors, but also are, at the same time, changed by the actors – they both create new social reality together. This situation constitutes *the basis* of how *growth of knowledge* in the actors approach ought to take place (a process of mutual development that creates *meaning*). In this process, creators of knowledge intend to develop insights that make it possible for them to look at the situation from new perspectives, which in turn changes the initial prerequisites of the study. This is what we previously referred to when we stated that the actors approach is the *least* formalistic of the three approaches; this is apparent in that study plans are usually not complete until the study is finished. This might sound strange at first, but we can compare the conduct of an inquiry to a single act (or a series of acts). An *act*, according to the actors approach, is based on a purpose, but not on a purpose that is *definite* and completely conscious in advance because the act also realizes the purpose, which does not take full shape until the act takes place, so that it is this dialectic process that reveals the purpose.

From this it follows that when the study is finished (the last act in the series) the purpose is revealed, in this instance the plan for the study. A study composed according to the actors approach is of course not entirely "unintentional". It is controlled by what we might call *background visions* that become more and more concrete (more goal-oriented) as the study proceeds.

In the actors approach, this openly declared connection between purpose and action is a guarantee that a study can start with the least number of prejudices and become realized with the greatest possible innovative influence. The actors approach attempts to practice what it preaches at the same time that it preaches what it practises. This *state of affairs is also the direct reason why every serious actors researcher/consultant/ investigator allocates considerable time and effort in the scientific report to describing the process of creating knowledge as such.* The report is an important contribution to other actors creators of knowledge as well as a must for assessing the created knowledge in an actors study.

If we consider the synthesized relation between action and purpose just described, we also realize that problems arise when we try to illustrate the course of a study in the actors approach. The description below should therefore be seen as an *ideal-typified case* for the course of a study. This also means, of course, that the applied example in Chapter 12 cannot be completely reported within the framework of the course of the typified case below.

Methodical procedures

The methodical procedures within the framework of the actors approach relate mainly to how the *dialogue* and the *act* are to be *varied* in relation partly to other techniques, like the experimental activities of the actors approach (see Chapter 7 "Traditional techniques for collecting data" and Chapter 8 "ACT 4"), which always have a dialogical basis, and partly to the desired *degree of* information, *character of* information and its *cost*. The information developed via dialogue should provide answers to what things mean in a company or in a wider perspective. The actors creator of knowledge can ask other questions, too, in order to *broaden the framework for* what something means; for instance, how often, when, where and to what extent do these things appear? *Techniques* other than the personal interview and the dialogue, and consequently another form of methodical procedure, is then needed for these matter-of-fact questions. It is important to remember that the questions do *not* then refer to denotations of *conceptual meaning* – like how often a specific *conceptual meaning* appears. This cannot, according to the actors view, be depicted in the sense of a *quantitative* perspective (see "*the Arbnor Uncertainty Principle*", Figure 6.1). A *denotation of conceptual meaning* is based on a human *qualification* created in the dialectics of *first* hand expressions and can therefore *not* be reduced to *second* hand expressions in a questionnaire. In such a case, other methodical procedures provide for adapting selective procedures and previous experiences to the character of the study area.

Concerning the discussion under "In general", we *again* point out the difficulty associated with describing methodical procedures without a connection to a specific study area. Furthermore, in the actors approach, *the methodical procedures* of the ongoing process stand in a *dialectic* relation to *the methodics,* which makes it even more difficult.

Methodics

The goals of the approach

A basic goal of creating knowledge using the actors approach is to *denote the conceptual meaning* of social phenomena, which can be:

- actors-based
- structurally based
- dialectically based.

Over and above this, we want to remind the reader of the different knowledge "interests" and "ambitions" guiding the creator of knowledge. We have previously called the *interests*:

- understanding
- emancipative
- innovative.

The knowledge *ambitions* are to be found in Figure 6.2.

The creator of knowledge can operate within the framework of the actors and the structurally based denotation of conceptual meaning, as well as the dialectically based denotation, with one, two, or all three of the above *interests* in mind according to the *ambitions*.

The principal course of a study is not changed in any tangible way by the kind of denotation of conceptual meaning, and the interest and ambitions, which a creator of knowledge chooses. What is changed is the level of procreative feedback in the results and the design of the *emancipatory interactive action*.

The reason the actors view talks about "emancipatory interactive action" is related to what we have described as the dialectical connections between language and existence. The *creative act* encompasses the final "artistic" development of language. The concrete participation of creators of knowledge in practice – such as creating businesses, starting ventures, transforming organizations – constitutes the *direct act*. If the knowledge ambitions of the actors view (see Figure 6.2) and the potential in what is factual are to be made visible, intelligible and believable, emancipatory interactive action in the form of *creative* and *direct acts* out in the field is necessary (see Figure 9.4 overleaf).

A study plan for actors studies

The course of a study in the actors approach is characterized by *interaction imagination*, and *non-prejudice*, with simultaneous and *diagnostical* development. In this development, the creator of knowledge achieves an ever higher diagnostical certainty that finally enables coordination of the continuous conceptual development with a coherent and procreative language. Figure 9.4 illustrates the dialectics between different "stages" of an actors approach study in progress, in which problematization and the development of the diagnosis and the opportunities run through all stages in an interplay of *engagement* and *dissociation* (see Chapter 6 under "Diagnosis").

This is a kind of knowledge creation process where metatheory, empirical reality and ultimate presumptions are up against each other in a spiral fashion, where dialogue and action as "interactive development of understanding" are inside and outside of the same helix.

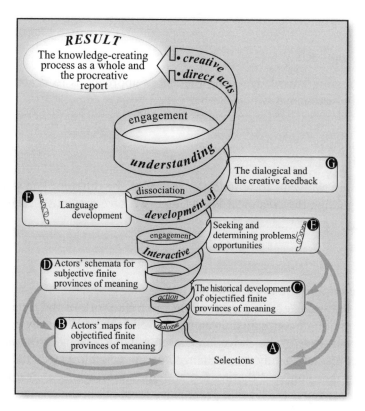

Figure 9.4   The Dialectics of an Actors Approach Study

Figure 9.4 illustrates, therefore, the mutual development of *methodics* and *methodical procedures* during the process. The arrows in the figure show how, in one stage, the researcher/consultant/investigator may discover, for example, that further selections (A) (as recommended, understanding and/or problem/opportunity oriented) are necessary, or that revisions of actors' maps (B) must be made because of something brought up under actors' schemata (D); this in turn may necessitate a revision of the determination of the problems/opportunities. It becomes apparent that the development of knowledge is a *dialectic process* involving the various stages, methodical procedures and methodics.

The small helix inside stage F illustrates that language development is a gradual development of descriptive elements made clear in all the previous stages; they become a language in stage F. In a similar fashion, stage E, "Seeking and determining problems/opportunities", collects contributions from the problematization in all of the previous stages.

The helix in the centre of the figure illustrates that the course of a study is characterized by a number of rounds through the stages.

In Chapter 6, we separated the diagnostic process into the three phases of preunderstanding, understanding and postunderstanding. If we look at Figure 9.4 and assume that the boundaries are not fixed, we can match stages A, B and C to preunderstanding, stages D and E to understanding, and stages F and G to postunderstanding.

We now discuss dividing the several stages into *engagement* and *dissociation* phases. Keep in mind that there may be several techniques under specific items from the previous general description in Chapter 7 – such as "experiments" under the actors approach – that are not included in the discussion.

A. Selections

Engagement 1:   Selecting strategically important actors starting from some initial problem area; *recommended* by other significant actors.

Dissociation 1:   What do these recommendations mean and what *significance* do they hide?

Engagement 2:   New actors are selected based on a *new understanding*. Further selection of actors takes place based on actual/factual data (see "Traditional techniques for collecting data", Chapter 7), such as age, position in the company, and the like. Discussion concerns only what important actors *do* and what kinds of *information* they can provide to denote conceptual meaning and establish significance.

Dissociation 2:   *Interpret* the recommendations – see if it is possible to distinguish *groups of actors*. Why do people make the recommendations they do?

Engagement 3:   *Control* the groups of actors. Do the assumptions made seem to be applicable?

Dissociation 3:   *Evaluate, interpret* and *develop* a conscious but unprejudiced expedition to construct actors' maps for objectified finite provinces of meaning.

B. Actors' maps for objectified finite provinces of meaning

Engagement 1:   *Study* to determine whether *dominating ideas* exist (previously conducted actors studies have described that such ideas exist and are common). What are they and who are their proponents?

Dissociation 1:   *Interpret* to see if there are *specific patterns* – is it possible to distinguish any *topology* for actors' maps?

Engagement 2:   Control and *interpret* possible topology in the maps among different, possibly existing, actors' groups. Are actors' groups changing?

Dissociation 2:   Compile maps and groups for a structural starting point for a study of the *historical* development of objectified finite provinces of meaning.

C. The historical development of objectified finite provinces of meaning

Engagement 1:   *Documentary analysis* – consider institutionalization processes and objectification. Determine whether there are special *externalizing actors* and if there are any *special legitimization factors*.

Dissociation 1:   *Interpret* the *historical* processes using previous diagnosis of the *present* and possible *future* states as a background.

Engagement 2:   *Dialogue* in larger actors' groups – some feedback and control.

Dissociation 2:   *Interpret* the above with the goal of designing a *plan* for developing *actors' schemata*.

D. Actors' schemata for subjective finite provinces of meaning

Actors' schemata are meant to serve as a means for the creator of knowledge, a manageable means for obtaining a compilation of the subjective conceptions of the actors participating in the study; that is, some kind of descriptive instrument in which the subjectivity of the information is maintained (first hand expressions). The descriptions in the actors' schemata must not be seen as a final form of presentation for the information being developed. Every actor's schemata, beyond the basic schema for each individual actor, has a connection to some specific phenomenon; therefore, a single actor may appear in a number of schemata. The combination of different schemata is therefore important in the development of understanding.

Engagement 1:	*Dialogue* with important actors – *diagnosis* of *subjective finite provinces of meaning* – whereas *actors' schemata* are constructed.
Dissociation 1:	*Interpret* actors' schemata using possible actors' groups, actors' maps, the historical development and *power-politics* as starting points.
Engagement 2:	*Feedback* and *control* the interpretations – new *dialogue*.
Dissociation 2:	*Interpret* the individual actors' *finite provinces of meaning* – develop an *understanding* of their *actions* based on these (reproduce the subjectification process).

E. Seeking and determining problems/opportunities

At this stage, previous problematizations and experiences gained earlier during the process are interwoven according to the diagnosis below. It is possible to discern the three starting points for denotation of conceptual meaning (actors, structurally and dialectically based) in the development of language in the actors approach (see "The goals of the approach" above, and "The objective of creating knowledge" in Chapter 6).

Diagnosis:

1. Prescribe the meaning of *actors based* phenomena.
2. *Relate* actual/factual data *structurally* – general restrictions and subjective data.
3. Interpret the meaning of the *dialectics* and the way it is expressed – the general in the specific and the specific in the general.

F. *Language development*

Language development means the development of a coherent pattern of communication for the problem/opportunity area or company concerned in the study (see "The actors approach and language development" in Chapter 7). Different *elements* that are descriptive and that make an understanding possible are gradually generated in and through the interactive process as knowledge is created. This stage in Figure 9.4 should therefore be seen as:

1. *a diagnosis* in which the different *elements* are related
2. the different *languages* (descriptive and ideal-typified languages) with models *constructed by* gradually reducing the influence of the situational factors
3. *the language development* that contains any of the previously mentioned *interests* and the above-mentioned *knowledge ambitions*.

G. *The dialogical and the procreative feedback.*

The dialogical and procreative feedback refers to the creation and presentation of knowledge results in a way that makes it possible for the recipient to exist "in" a *dialogue* with the material being presented; that is, the language should show as the *second* in relation to the *first* (statements and language of the actors).

The dialogical feedback (see Chapter 7 "The procreative report) of the description (post-understanding) is the very end phase of the *dialectic trinity* (thesis–antithesis–synthesis) that the creator of knowledge has entered into along with the actors in the field. This aims at gradually establishing a *language commonality* between the creative act and the direct act (see "Action" in Chapter 6) in order for the actors to understand the premise on which the creator of knowledge has *diagnosed* and *condensed the statements*. Creators of knowledge relate to *existing theory* in order to broaden further the perspective on that which is being formed. This *dialogue* between the actors and the creator of knowledge should function as an incentive to further emancipatory and innovative dialogues and to direct actions between various actors in the company and the creator of knowledge. *Our principal description, therefore, can refer to a finished totality as well as to several parts of the total process of creating knowledge.*

Finally, all knowledge results should be documented so as not to create more of the same knowledge. In the actors approach we can, for instance, make a distinction between research reports and consultant reports, as far as documentation is concerned. Research reports *require more* description of the knowledge creation process itself and of the creation of the dialogical character of the descriptive language. Consultant reports require this to a lesser degree, partly because consultants are always expected to participate personally in the feedback process, and partly because the feedback has a time limit as well as space limit.

EXCELLENCE IN KNOWLEDGE-CREATING WORK

Before we illustrate the applications of our three views, we want to shortly present Arbnor's conceptualization of excellence in knowledge-creating work. As a scientific concept we want to introduce his *"crealiability"* as an overall notion of quality and credibility in researching/ consulting/investigative work. The concept is a compound of *creativity* and *liability* and the prefix "crea" denotes, in this context, to be creative, to have imagination and ingenuity. This is connected to the suffix "liability" in the sense of responsibility, obligation and duty. It can be read in many different ways, which is also one of the basic ideas with the concept. For example; a creator of knowledge has an obligation for being creative, an obligation, which also means a responsibility, but also a duty in relation to the study area, as well as to the chosen methodological view, to act stringently and consistently. Our notion of excellence in knowledge-creating work is therefore to be assessed against the concept of *crealiability* according to Figure 9.5.

The relative importance to place on the four different core elements of crealiability when planning and assessing knowledge work must be done on a view by view and on a case by case basis, but the essence is that excellence means the highest possible *crealiability*.

APPLYING THE THREE METHODOLOGICAL VIEWS

In Chapters 10, 11 and 12, we will demonstrate applications of our three methodological views, applications that have been used in practice (methodological views in

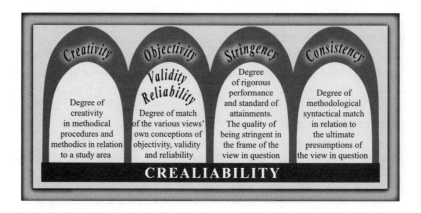

Figure 9.5 The Cores of Crealiability

application are called *methodological approaches*). We keep the same order as before, that is:

Chapter 10: The Analytical Approach
Chapter 11: The Systems Approach
Chapter 12: The Actors Approach

Two illustrative and more extensive examples of application will be provided in each of these three chapters. Applications of research, consulting as well as investigation will be presented. The differences between the three are not as distinct as one might think. If they are all conducted ambitiously and handled by methodologically aware creators of knowledge, they have many characteristics in common within any given approach. It is not unusual in the subject of business for research, consultative works and investigations to use each other's results and knowledge, if they are in the same field and based on the same methodological approach (and if, in the case of consultations, they are publicly available).

The presentation of the different applications follows the structure of relevant parts of Chapters 7 and 9. It is our intention to offer the reader an opportunity to follow these methodological ways of thinking closely in longer sections than was the case in Chapters 2 and 8.

The descriptions in Chapters 10, 11 and 12 are, on the whole, structured around direct accounts from the reports that originally presented the studies in their entirety. These accounts are, for pedagogic reasons, presented and labelled somewhat differently than in the original versions. Also, of course, the studies are not presented in full, and do not in all respects follow the principles for the methodics of the approach in question which have been provided in this chapter. If readers have acquired the level of understanding that we, as authors, intend for them, they should have no problem situating themselves in the thinking behind the design and accomplishment of the actual studies.

The two of us participated in most of the studies presented in the rest of this book (see Chapters 10, 11, 12 and 14). Whenever that was not the case, we have been granted explicit permission from the original creators of knowledge to use their material.

No story is finished until all of it is told. This chapter has provided the framework, called methodics, for what is necessary from certain presumptions to put techniques, theories and previous results by methodical procedures into practice. We have seen methodological similarities, but mainly differences, in how our three views are to be applied in general, that is, are seen as operative paradigms (see Figure 1.10). In this chapter we have accordingly introduced three different study plans; one for analytical studies, one for systems studies and one for actors studies. At the end of the chapter we presented our conceptualization of excellence in knowledge-creating work using our concept of "crealiability" and its core elements.

POINTS OF REFLECTION

1. Think back to how this book started. What consequences from Chapter 1, according to the *language of methodology*, can you see in what is said in this chapter?
2. Formulation/determination of a *problem* has been discussed on several occasions in this chapter. Which are the differences in the three methodological approaches to this? Are there any similarities?
3. What does "*planning*" mean in the three approaches? Similarities? Differences?
4. Give one example of why the three approaches will come to different *results* concerning a "given" problem. What do these differences really mean – in practice?
5. In the chapter we gave a description of how the views look at methodics. This description has contained different degrees of *formalism*. What is meant by this? Try to provide some telling descriptions of why it looks as it does and do this by trying to put yourself in the place of how an analytical, a systems and an actors creator of knowledge could describe it, respectively. When playing the role of different creators of knowledge, how do you think they would look at each other's formalism and lack of formalism in this respect?
6. One of the views talks about both *problems* and *possibilities* to try to determine and start from. Why are possibilities of central importance to this view?
7. All the views talk about "*the report*" as the end of a knowledge-creating effort. Can you provide some important differences and similarities as to the very design and function of the report?
8. One of the views starts from the assumption that *prediction* is a *goal* of less relevance in creating knowledge. Which one? And why this attitude here? Another view asserts that the belief in possibilities of forecasting is not in line with *humanistic* values? Why? In a third view the *goal* of prediction is stated *explicitly*. What is the basis of this idea?
9. This chapter has been about methodics. How would you describe the three concepts of *methodical procedures*, *methodics* and the *operative paradigm*? Try also to describe how the three concepts are related to each other.

(Continued)

(Continued)

10. Three different *study plans* have been described in the chapter. If you had to describe them in pictures to somebody who has not seen them, which pictures would you then use (consider pictures of, for instance, nature as well as of urban environments for all the plans)?

11. Excellence in knowledge-creating work can be described as reaching high *cre-aliability*. Which are the core elements of this concept? How would you describe the elements in relation to the different methodological views?

RECOMMENDED FURTHER READING

See the end of the Appendix and visit the website below.

Become a worldwide partner as a *knowledge creator* in the development of *Methodology for Creating Business Knowledge* by visiting the website: **www.knowledge-creator.com**. Here you can contribute by asking your own questions and you will also find answers to the most frequently asked questions. The website has been developed alongside this third edition of the book and the questions posted there will be used to provide input for future editions.

PART IV
APPROACHING METHODOLOGY

10 THE ANALYTICAL APPROACH

This chapter provides two examples of the analytical view in application. The first is a public investigation commissioned by the Ministry of Industry in a single European country. The other is an annual study that provides information about entrepreneurial activities in different countries in the world.

INTRODUCTION

The analytical view has a long and solid history. Its operative paradigm is also the most formal among our three views, which means that there is more "to hold on to" for creators of knowledge in an analytical approach than in a systems or an actors approach.

Two examples of analytical approaches are provided in this chapter. Their topics are:

1. business bankruptcies
2. entrepreneurial activities in different countries.

CASE I: BUSINESS BANKRUPTCIES

The Ministry of Industry in a certain European country commissioned a university researcher to find out the *factors* that could explain business bankruptcies in that country and to come up with suggestions for how to reduce the number of bankruptcies in the future. More precisely, four main purposes for the study were agreed upon between the ministry in question and the researcher:

1. to describe bankrupt companies and company bankruptcies statistically
2. to determine the factors that are likely to cause bankruptcies
3. to estimate the importance of the factors causing bankruptcies
4. to use the results of the study to suggest steps to influence the development of bankruptcies.

This is the story of how this study was done.

Broad outline

The operative paradigm was divided into three partial studies in orders to let the results of the first guide the methodical procedures and the methodics of the second, and to let the result of the first two guide the methodical procedures and the methodics of the third. A brief overview of the three partial studies is given before they are presented individually.

Methodics

1. Initial orientation study (descriptive purpose). This partial study includes a description of the institutional conditions related to bankruptcy. Legal processing of bankruptcies, the organization of creditors and the way in which this organization operates are the focus here. The main part of the initial orienting study consists of two extensive empirical studies that statistically define all finalized company bankruptcies between 1996 and 2000. Information is also collected concerning the structural aspects of the insolvent company, such as size, legal form, industry orientation and the distribution of the insolvent cases in different types of bankruptcy, who initiates the bankruptcy, final financial outcomes for the creditors, bankruptcy costs, the functions of solicitors and receivers, and the causes of the bankruptcy based on the judgement of the receiver.

2. Resources and transformation of resources by the bankrupt company (explanatory purpose). In the second partial study, the focus is on investigating the causes of bankruptcy that were provided by the receivers. This partial study consists of five clearly defined field projects. These empirical projects are oriented primarily toward describing the human, material and financial resources of a bankrupt company, as well as the results of how these resources were used.

3. Evaluation and suggested remedies (guiding purpose). The third and final partial study contains an evaluation of the result of the total study and suggests steps to influence the development of bankruptcies.

The case and the analytical approach

We recognize typical characteristics of the analytical approach in the design of the study of business bankruptcies, such as:

a. The study's starting point is to find facts in one part of the society: bankruptcies and their social and economic consequences for the parties directly concerned as well as their ethical, political and economic impacts on society.
b. An objective measure of the problem's significance is the fact that the number of business bankruptcies is seen as large in the country in question.
c. The goal is to quantify as far as possible.

d. The idea was to study a factive reality that is constructed summatively. This, in turn, is shown in several ways:

⇨ the research mission is divided into partial studies
⇨ the five different projects in partial study 2 (explanatory purposes) were completed independently of each other
⇨ various potential causes were treated *ceteris paribus* (see Figure 10.1)
⇨ the more causes one finds, the better the explanation one gets (this, in fact, is a major part of how the concept of analysis is treated here)

e. The knowledge to be produced must be independent of individuals (observers). Conclusions will be made public in the hope that various legislative and executive offices will react. The organizational reality in which these power holders operate is not discussed in the study.

f. Besides quantification – see (c) above – the goal is also to arrive at invariable results. There is no point in studying just one or two persons in one or two bankruptcies, but rather the goal is to achieve generalizable results that will apply to as many bankrupt companies as possible.

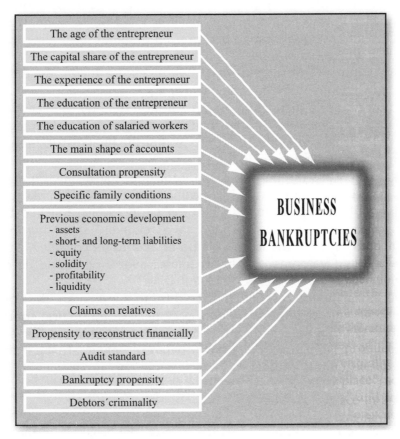

Figure 10.1   Potential Causes of Business Bankruptcies

Further aspects of the analytical approach will be clear as we discuss the partial studies one by one.

Orienting initial study (descriptive purpose)

Methodical procedures

The orienting initial partial study was governed by the first of the four main purposes, to describe bankrupt companies and company bankruptcies statistically.

A study of business bankruptcies concerns mainly companies that no longer exist. When considering the methodical procedures behind considerations of what to record, the researcher decided therefore to base analyses on the *measurement* of consequences of bankruptcies rather than on the bankruptcy processes in themselves. Methodical procedures in the initial study were further based on the following considerations:

- In order to obtain a background for discussing the concept of bankruptcy, the researcher decided *early* in partial study 1 to go through the bankruptcy literature. The researcher then decided to concentrate on works written during the preceding ten years.
- The researcher wanted the study sample to be as large as possible. If a census proved practically and economically possible, it would be done. The researcher then intended to get quantitative background material for the rest of the partial studies of business bankruptcies.
- Several definitions (and thereby delimitations) were made. By *business bankruptcies*, for instance, was meant bankruptcy in connection with practising a trade. Furthermore, a distinction was made in the study between *decided* and *finished* bankruptcies. A bankruptcy is decided when the bankruptcy application is approved. It is finished when the proposal for the final distribution to creditors has been set up and is legally in force.
- The researcher chose the period of study for both the decided and the finished bankruptcies such that the large increase in the number of bankruptcies, which began during 1996, was included. The time during which finished bankruptcies were to be studied was also limited to a relatively small number of years (1996–2000), because of the large volume of data to be collected. The necessary overview of the development of bankruptcies over time would be obtained by analyzing decided bankruptcies (1994–2004).
- Whenever possible, the researcher should try to supplement the collected data through other sources if there are non-responses from the first source.
- Reliability was to be assessed with consideration to what the researcher called *congruency, precision, objectivity* and *constancy*. Only internal validity was seen to be of interest in this context.

Methodics

The purposes behind the main part of partial study 1, the depiction of the extent of the development of bankruptcies in the country, were formulated as follows:

- to register the development of bankruptcies on the basis of decided personal bankruptcies and business bankruptcies between 1994 and 2004
- to study the structure of the bankrupt company with respect to company size, legal form and type of trade between 1996 and 2000
- to study the structure of business bankruptcies with respect to the initiation of the bankruptcy, final distribution to creditors, and the information from the official receivers about the causes behind the bankruptcies from 1996 to 2000
- to measure the life span of the bankrupt company.

Also contained in the first descriptive partial study was a *literature survey* (mentioned above) and a brief description of the most important steps in legal handling of bankruptcies.

The study population consisted of 6,673 completed business bankruptcies. Information about these was collected by questionnaires sent to district courts in the country, that is, courts that had handled the bankruptcies from a legal point of departure.

No repeat measurements were made to control for reliability. Nevertheless, reliability was considered to be good, mainly because the study was based on secondary material throughout. Its internal validity was also judged to be good.

Table 10.1 shows an example of the results from the initial descriptive partial study. As can be seen in the table, the number of completed bankruptcies increased from approximately 800 in 1996 to 1,800 in 2000.

Table 10.1 Finished Bankruptcies 1996–2000 Distributed in Different Ways to Liquidate the Business

Year	Finished bankruptcies	Final distribution bankruptcies		Poor man's bankruptcies		Other ways	
		Number	Percentage	Number	Percentage	Number	percentage
1996	808	456	56.4	346	42.9	6	0.7
1997	1,091	576	52.8	508	46.6	7	0.6
1998	1,355	694	51.2	651	48.1	10	0.7
1999	1,621	813	50.2	785	48.4	23	1.4
2000	1,798	832	46.3	951	52.9	15	0.8
Total	6,673	3,371	50.5	3,241	48.6	61	0.9

The extensive material that was collected in the orientating initial study could be divided in several ways. In the actual case, distributions were made on company size, company legal form, type of trade, initiation of the bankruptcy, time to liquidation, estate inventory, final distribution and on the causes for the liquidation given by the district courts. This final distribution is of interest because it becomes part of the foundation for the next (explanatory) partial study.

We pointed out in Chapter 9 that a study plan for a *descriptive* study in the analytical approach contains six steps (see Figure 9.2). The initial descriptive partial study followed this model exactly.

Resources and resource transformation in the bankrupt company (explanatory purpose)

As mentioned previously, the second partial study, which was of an *explanatory* nature and consisted of five limited projects with dissimilar content, investigated the bankruptcy causes given by the public receivers. These projects were conducted relatively independently of each other, even though they were methodically quite similar. They result in a number of hypotheses that provide the background for the guiding partial study 3 in this study. As authors, we do not consider it pedagogically worthwhile to discuss all five projects and so choose to discuss the first reported project, called "Project and accounting standards", and to finish this section on the explanatory partial study by summarizing its results – which are needed for the discussion of partial study 3, the guiding study.

An *explanatory* study designed according to the analytical approach should follow seven steps as set out in Figure 9.2. In every step there are methodical procedures to put in place.

Formulating the problem

The following purposes were formulated in this project:

- to study the business leaders in bankrupt companies with respect to their number, age, capital share, educational level and professional experience
- to investigate the level of education of salaried employees in bankrupt companies
- to provide a picture of the internal and external accounting procedures in bankrupt companies with regard to extent and standard
- to investigate consultation propensity among bankrupt companies, chiefly in the area of accounting
- to study to what extent business leaders in bankrupt companies have marriage settlements or judicial divisions of the joint estate of husband and wife
- to show bankruptcy frequency related to successive generations.

These purposes provided the background for a number of hypotheses to be tested in the study:

Hypothesis 1: That there is no difference between the number of principal owners in bankrupt companies and living companies, whether these be:

1. limited companies
2. sole proprietorships.

Hypothesis 2: That there is no difference between the bankrupt companies and operative companies with respect to the age of the company leaders.

Hypothesis 3.1: That there is no difference between bankrupt companies and operative companies with respect to the capital share of the business leaders.

Hypothesis 3.2: That there is no difference between bankrupt companies and operative companies with respect to the professional experience of the business leaders.

Hypothesis 3.3: That there is no difference between bankrupt companies and operative companies with respect to the education of salaried employees.

Hypothesis 4: That there is no difference between the education of the business leaders and the salaried employees in the companies being studied.

Hypothesis 5: That as great a share of the bankrupt companies as of the living companies have accounts designed so that they provide:

1. monthly reports of results
2. quarterly book closings
3. profit/loss of products and services
4. profit/loss from retail
5. timely invoicing
6. timely customer payment
7. budgeting for action and control
8. comparison between budget and outcome.

Hypothesis 6: That as great a share of the bankrupt companies as of the living companies use consultants for:

1. current accounting
2. annual closing of books
3. filing tax returns
4. budgeting
5. planning of purchases, manufacturing and sales
6. other.

Hypothesis 7: That the same share of married business leaders in bankrupt companies as in operative companies have marriage settlements and judicial divisions of the joint estate of husband and wife, whether this concerns:

1. limited companies
2. sole proprietorships.

Some *definitions* of concepts were the same as those presented earlier in the descriptive partial study; other definitions were added during the course of the study. Some concepts were left without definition because their meaning was considered to be generally known.

The population consisted of all companies in the country. The researcher looked for characteristics of bankrupt companies that might explain their development in contrast to characteristics that were common to both bankrupt and living companies; in other words, characteristics that were not unique to bankrupt companies.

Planning the study

The researcher realized that collecting data from every company in the country would not be possible and asserted that some kind of *sample* was necessary. For practical reasons, therefore, the study was here limited to companies in the southern most judicial district of the country. This judicial district was chosen because the researcher was employed by the university in that particular region. The researcher wanted to be within travelling distance of the bankruptcy debtors.

To *simulate* an experiment, the researcher decided to take a sample of bankrupt companies, which became (by personal judgement) all of the companies in the region operation had been discontinued due to bankruptcy during 2000. In addition, a sample of still active companies was needed for a *control group* as a basis for drawing *causal* conclusions. The researcher decided here to choose 204 companies (the same as the number of bankrupt companies) from among those that were active in the region during 1999.

The specific units for the control group were chosen from the value-added tax file at the regional government office. This control group consisted of a simple random sample based on the computer files of companies.

Designing methods for collecting data

Data could be collected either by means of a mailed questionnaire or through personal interviews. The researcher argued that a *mailed questionnaire* would be *less costly* – respondents would have the opportunity to answer at their convenience and they would not be influenced by any interviewers. The disadvantages of this method of data collection include a low percentage of responses, the risk that a person other than the selected respondent provides the answers and the possibility of misunderstanding one or more questions.

Personal interviews are relatively costly and resource intensive but usually result in fewer non-responses and internal dropouts (*answers which are not codable*). They also allow the presentation of the question to be less structured.

After discussing these considerations a mailed questionnaire was chosen, mainly because of the size and geographic dispersion of the study group. It was later found that the mailed questionnaire had to be supplemented by personal interviews.

Using only case studies was deemed to be inadequate. Case studies cannot provide the necessary information to test the hypotheses in a *statistically* reliable way.

The questionnaire was to consist of questions with relatively fixed alternative answers. The language used in the questions, the number of questions and the degree of detail were influenced by the respondents' expected qualifications for providing answers.

The questionnaire was tested in a *pilot study* that consisted of twenty-seven bankruptcies in a local government area neighbouring the study region. It was concluded from this pilot study that the respondents would have no difficulty interpreting and answering the questionnaire.

Collecting data

Data collection followed the working order below:

1. questionnaires sent through the mail
2. reminders on the telephone

3. reminders through the mail
4. personal visits (interviews) to the respondents.

Collecting data turned out to be both complicated and time-consuming. A debtor could have moved away, sometimes to an unknown address – or even abroad – or have died. Many of the respondents were hesitant or unwilling to answer the questionnaire. The end result was a response rate of approximately 70 per cent in both the *study group* and the *control group* (see above under "Planning the study").

Coding and arranging data

An important part of coding and arranging (and analysing) data is *clarifying non-responses*, that is, trying to discover the characteristics of those who do not answer and the reasons for their refusal. Non-responses and dropouts were therefore studied regarding type of company, number of employees, district court and trade orientation. The conclusion was that the response rate among responders and non-responders was not related to any of these background variables. This was taken as a sign of *good representation*.

The companies (business leaders/debtors) classified as "not available" could not be traced through the registrar's office, post office, telephone directory services or other means.

Where given, among the reasons stated for being a non-respondent were:

*   lack of time
*   fear that information being provided would not stay confidential
*   heavy duties as far as the requirement to provide information to central or regional government offices are concerned
*   dissatisfaction with the economic conditions for small companies.

The material was assessed with respect to *coverage mistakes* (i.e. whether answered questionnaires were part of the pilot sample but not part of the study population), non-response errors, measurement errors, codification errors, reliability, validity and representativity.

Controlling causality

In explanatory studies, controlling causality means testing the proposals formulated as cause-effect relations that were presented as hypotheses at the beginning of the study. As we know, this involves three requirements:

1. finding out whether there is a connection between the variables that represent causes and those that represent effects
2. checking the temporal order between the two groups of variables
3. checking the importance of background and intervening variables.

In this study, temporal order was of no concern because bankruptcy is an end stage and it was the characteristics of the companies prior to bankruptcy that were studied.

Controlling the influence of background and intervening variables was not seen as necessary. The design of the study and the set up of the study and control groups were considered sufficient to allow the researcher to draw the conclusion that he had found "factors that are likely to cause bankruptcies".

Statistical χ^2 tests were applied to all hypotheses; several of them were rejected:

- *Hypothesis 3.2* (that business leaders in bankrupt companies have less professional experience than business leaders in living companies)
- *Hypothesis 4* (that business leaders in small companies have clearly less education than their salaried employees – this is valid for both bankrupt and living companies)
- *Hypotheses 5.1, 5.3, 5.4 and 5.6* (that there are differences in accounting standards between the two company groups, to the disadvantage of the bankrupt companies)
- *Hypotheses 6.2 and 6.3* (that fewer consultants are used by bankrupt companies)
- *Hypothesis 7* (that business leaders in bankrupt companies are more likely to have marriage settlements or judicial divisions of the joint estate of husband and wife).

Reporting the results

The project led both to reports provided to the different stakeholders and to several research papers.

Assessment and suggested steps (guiding purpose)

The analytical approach to a *guiding* study requires formulating the problem as a *decision problem* (compare Chapter 9):

$$V = f(Xs;Ps)$$

where:

- V is the objective
- Xs are the factors to be decided
- Ps are the environmental factors, the parameters
- f is the format of the model.

In this case:

V = fewer bankruptcies
Xs = societal steps (new legislation, various rules, advice and directives from the public, etc.)
Ps = examples of factors that society should consider when applying corrective steps:

- business establishments
- the state of the economy
- credit restrictions
- existing legislature
- (and so on)

f = not provided in the actual case

The societal steps suggested by the study presented here were:

1. Steps directed at actions to prevent bankruptcies or to initiate them at an earlier stage:

   a. development and formalization of business advice
   b. voluntary business reorganization
   c. qualification test for business leaders in some cases
   d. extension of the requirement for auditors
   e. demand for higher qualifications of auditors
   f. future-directed information
   g. revised rules for collecting taxes.

2. Steps for more effective bankruptcy procedures:

   a. provide expert help for official receivers
   b. shorten time for handling major bankruptcies
   c. abolish the right to demand that debtors pay remaining claims in a business bankruptcy.

3. Steps for taking legal measures against debtors' crimes:

   a. improve reporting procedures for debtors' crimes
   b. increase investigative capacity.

4. Selective societal steps:

   a. consider small companies when imposing credit restrictions
   b. offer financial support for voluntary reconstruction.

The four groups above are presented in order of priority. Several of the suggested steps were implemented by the authorities and offices concerned.

CASE II: ENTREPRENEURIAL ACTIVITIES IN DIFFERENT COUNTRIES

Introduction

The Global Entrepreneurship Monitor research programme is designed as a comprehensive assessment of the role of entrepreneurship in national economic growth. Initiated in 1998, the GEM research programme provides the required fundamental knowledge by assembling relevant *harmonized* data on an annual basis. This has been done since 1999. The conceptual model used is, according to the analytical view, reflected in a wide range of factors associated with national variations in entrepreneurial activity and their major contextual features.

The data has been assembled to facilitate cross-national comparisons at the level of national entrepreneurial activity, to estimate the role of entrepreneurial activity in national economic growth, to determine the factors that account for national differences in the level of entrepreneurship and facilitate policies that may be effective in enhancing entrepreneurship.

Much of the discussion of this research programme follows Reynolds et al., 2005.

Overview

Empirical advances on the GEM programme objectives, to explain the relative impact of entrepreneurship on national economic development, required the development of an explicit statement of the relevant *variables* and their role in *causal processes* affecting economic growth. In addition, any complex initiative involving a huge number of national teams and hundreds of individuals is facilitated by a formal focus to guide the coordination of multiple disparate elements. The challenge of *harmonization* is also exacerbated by considerable language diversity (compare with the discussion under "The problem of objectivity – An overview" in Chapter 7). Early in the development of the research programme an explicit model of the process was developed; the diagram in Figure 10.2 opposite presents the 2001 version. The major dependent variable (the major *effect* to be explained) is national economic growth; the diagram represents the causal mechanism considered to represent the impact of entrepreneurship on growth.

The cause–effect relations in the figure are a result of what is seen as *existing analytical theory* in the field of entrepreneurship and by using *representative cases*, the goal is to come up with an ever better explanation of what is causing the growth of an economy (compare Table 3.1).

The country is considered to be the basic unit of analysis for the GEM initiative. While there are over 200 countries in the world, the financial support for GEM is largely provided by individual national teams. Hence, the countries to be included in the project reflect the emergence of groups of researchers that can raise the required funds to participate in the project. The "GEM countries" represent a sample of self-funded volunteers and consist of the G-7, most OECD countries, and an increasing number of developing countries in Latin America and Asia.

Empirical tests of the many relationships in the GEM model requires four major data collection activities:

- adult population surveys
- unstructured interviews with national experts
- self-administered questionnaires completed by national experts
- assembly of relevant standardized measures from existing cross-national data sets.

The most complex, expensive and visible aspect of the data collection effort are the GEM Adult Population Surveys. They are completed in each participating country to provide *harmonized estimates* of the level of entrepreneurial activity there. These surveys involve locating a representative sample of the adult population to create national measures of entrepreneurial activity. The indicator, the Total Entrepreneurial Activity, or TEA, Index reflects the prevalence of individuals that are (1) currently starting a new business or (2) the owner

Figure 10.2 GEM Conceptual Model

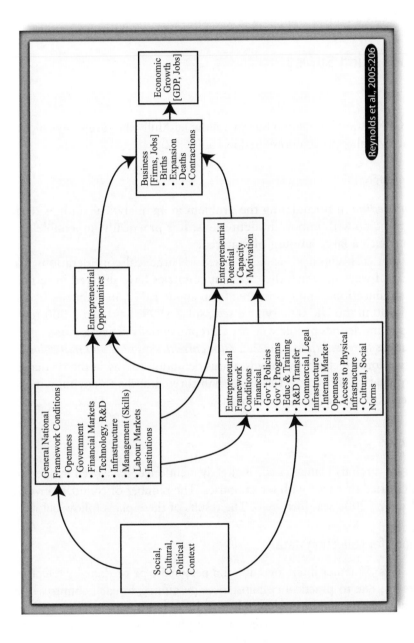

Source: Reynolds et al., 2005: 206. Reprinted with kind permission from Springer Science+Business Media: Small Business Economics, *Global Entrepreneurship Monitor: Data Collection Design and Implementation 1998–2003*, Volume 24, Number 3/April, 2005 pp. 205–231, by Paul Reynolds et al. © 2005, Springer Netherlands.

and managers of a young firm. The Total Entrepreneurial Activity Index can be interpreted as the number per 100 adults 18–64 years old actively involved in the initial stages of the entrepreneurial process. This is the most recognized and publicized activity in GEM studies and our discussion will be limited to this. This is more than enough to show that GEM studies are examples of a typical analytical approach.

GEM Adult Population Survey

In general

The stages in the GEM Adult Population Survey follow faithfully the seven steps of an explanatory study in an analytical approach presented in Figure 9.2.

Formulating the problem

The methodical procedure in formulating the problem in an analytical study is to decide on *sampling* and to come up with important definitions. It is practically impossible to come up with a census from such a large amount of material.

The sample size in each country has been based on practical considerations taking into account the variety of ways in which the different countries have differed in terms of infrastructure and communications, and has ranged from about 1,000, in countries like Thailand, to up to about 55,000 in the UK. The typical size, since 1999, has been 2,000 respondents.

The GEM programme defines people who are entrepreneurially active as *adults in the process of setting up a business they will (partly) own and/or currently owning and managing an operating young business.* More precise breakdowns of this definition follow in the text later on.

Payment of any salaries and wages for more than three months to anybody including the owners is considered to be the "firm birth event".

Planning the study

The GEM studies are carefully planned and, as already mentioned, have been in operation annually since 1999. It started that year with ten countries. The number of countries involved in the latest report concerning 2006 was forty-two. The results of these plans follow below.

Designing methods for collecting data

Methodical procedures: Whether interviews are of a personal type or done by telephone varies, as mentioned already, due to practical circumstances pertaining to each country. In advanced countries where the majority of the population lives in households with landline phones, the surveys are completed by phone. In most cases landline phone numbers are to be generated at random and a phone call placed to a household on a weekday night or during the day on a weekend. In countries where a small proportion of households have landline phones, a geographically stratified sampling procedure is to be used to locate households and respondents for face-to-face interviews.

Methodics: The survey firms or organizations in each of the countries are responsible for providing the descriptions of the business activity reported for the start-ups, new or established firms as well as firms receiving investments of informal investors. They are provided in both the original language and translated into English. Each year the coordination team develops and supervises a coding staff to ensure that a single procedure is used to classify business activities from all countries.

Once the separate individual datasets are checked and harmonized, and all individuals have been assigned the appropriate final weights, the files are consolidated into one single master file by a coordinating team. This team then processes the consolidated, harmonized dataset to locate respondents that could be considered entrepreneurially active.

All kinds of measures to harmonize and equalize the structure and content of data sets are made.

Collecting data

Methodical procedures: There are three basic elements of the development to the GEM measures of national entrepreneurial activity: the sample of respondents; the interview schedule used to collect individual level data, and; the creating of indices and measures that reflect entrepreneurship as a national attribute.

An overview of the interview schedule used is provided in Figure 10.3 overleaf.

The questionnaire contains ten initial items for all adults interviewed. These include six statements, provided in Table 10.2, relating to several kinds of individual involvement in entrepreneurial activity; for each there are four possible responses: "yes", "no", "don't know", or "refused".

Table 10.2   GEM Adult Population Survey: Items Related to Individual Involvement in Entrepreneurial Activity (Reynolds et al., 2005: 213)

(1a)	You are, alone or with others, currently trying to start a new business, including any self-employment or selling any goods or services to others.
(1b)	You are, alone or with others, currently trying to start a new business or a new venture for your employer – an effort that is part of your normal work.
(1c)	You are, alone or with others, currently the owner of a company you help manage, self-employed, or selling any goods or services to others.
(1d)	You have, in the past three years, personally provided funds for a new business started by someone else, excluding any purchases of stocks or mutual funds.
(1e)	You are, alone or with others, expecting to start a new business, including any type of self-employment, within the next three years.
(1f)	You have, in the past 12 months, shut down, discontinued or quit a business you owned and managed, any form of self-employment, or selling goods or services to anyone. Do not count a business that was sold.

Reprinted with kind permission from Spinger Science+Business Media: Small Business Economics, *Global Entrepreneurship Monitor: Data Collection Design and Implementation 1998–2003*, Volume 24, Number 3/April, 2005 pp. 205–231, by Paul Reynolds et al. © 2005, Springer Netherlands.

The remaining four initial questions relate to attitudes to entrepreneurial activity. If a respondent answers yes to any of the first set of six items, 1a to 1f, they are asked to respond to the items in both Groups A and B in Table 10.3. All remaining respondents are randomly split into two groups of equal size, groups A and B. Group A is asked questions that relate

Figure 10.3 GEM Adult Population Survey: Schematic of the Interview Structure.

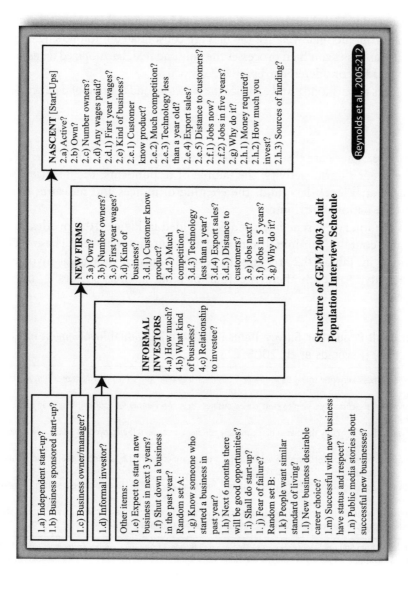

1.a) Independent start-up?
1.b) Business sponsored start-up?

1.c) Business owner/manager?

1.d) Informal investor?

Other items:
1.e) Expect to start a new business in next 3 years?
1.f) Shut down a business in the past year?
Random set A:
1.g) Know someone who started a business in past year?
1.h) Next 6 months there will be good opportunities?
1.i) Shall do start-up?
1.j) Fear of failure?
Random set B:
1.k) People want similar standard of living?
1.l) New business desirable career choice?
1.m) Successful with new business have status and respect?
1.n) Public media stories about successful new businesses?

INFORMAL INVESTORS
4.a) How much?
4.b) What kind of business?
4.c) Relationship to investee?

NEW FIRMS
3.a) Own?
3.b) Number owners?
3.c) First year wages?
3.d) Kind of business?
3.d.1) Customer know product?
3.d.2) Much competition?
3.d.3) Technology less than a year?
3.d.4) Export sales?
3.d.5) Distance to customers?
3.e) Jobs next?
3.f) Jobs in 5 years?
3.g) Why do it?

NASCENT [Start-Ups]
2.a) Active?
2.b) Own?
2.c) Number owners?
2.d) Any wages paid?
2.d.1) First year wages?
2.e) Kind of business?
2.e.1) Customer know product?
2.e.2) Much competition?
2.e.3) Technology less than a year old?
2.e.4) Export sales?
2.e.5) Distance to customers?
2.f.1) Jobs now?
2.f.2) Jobs in five years?
2.g) Why do it?
2.h.1) Money required?
2.h.2) How much you invest?
2.h.3) Sources of funding?

Structure of GEM 2003 Adult Population Interview Schedule

Reynolds et al., 2005:212

Source: Reynolds et al., 2005: 212. Reprinted with kind permission from Springer Science+Business Media: Small Business Economics, *Global Entrepreneurships Monitor: Data Collection Design and Implementation 1998–2003*, Volume 24, Number 3/April, 2005 pp. 205–231, by Paul Reynolds et al. © 2005, Springer Netherlands.

to *individual* attitudes towards entrepreneurship in questions 1g–1j as shown in Table 10.3. Group B is asked about several *national* attitudes towards entrepreneurship. These respondents indicate if they agree (or not) with the statements 1k–1n in Table 10.3. This split-half procedure is done to reduce the cost of collecting information in countries with less than adequate funds.

Table 10.3   GEM Adult Population Survey: Items Related to Individual Attitudes and Perceptions Regarding Entrepreneurial Activity (Reynolds et al., 2005: 213)

Group A

(1g)   Do you know someone personally who started a business in the past 2 years?
(1h)   In the next six months, will there be good opportunities for starting a business in the areas where you live?
(1i)   Do you have the knowledge, skill and experience required to start a business?
(1j)   Would fear of failure prevent you from starting a business?

Group B

(1k)   In your country, most people would prefer that everyone had a similar standard of living.
(1l)   In your country, most people consider starting a business a desirable career choice.
(1m)   In your country, those successful at starting a new business have a high level of status and respect.
(1n)   In your country, you will often see stories in the public media about successful new businesses.

Methodics: As mentioned above, thousands of individuals in the member countries have been interviewed about their participation in, and attitudes towards, entrepreneurial activity.

All items in the questionnaires have been tested in minor pilot studies. Also, research seminars are held at several places in the world annually to improve the questionnaire techniques.

Coding and arranging data

Methodical procedures: The national teams are to supply weights for all data, developed such that proportions of different subgroups (gender and age, for example) will match the most recent official data providing descriptions of the entire population of the country. The basis for weighting varies somewhat among countries. Gender and age are always involved, but other features might be used, including geographical distribution, ethnic background, educational attainment, household income or a range of other factors considered appropriate in a specific country.

Almost every data set provided requires some adjustment or correction.

The individuals represented by the TEA Index form a very heterogeneous group of entrepreneurs; motivations for participation may vary among those involved. One possibility might be, for instance, that they they cannot find a suitable role in the world of work. Therfore, creating a new business is their best available option. The GEM study identifies both groups by asking all those in start-ups or with an existing business one item related to their personal motivation.

Over 90 per cent of the respondents answer this question and the majority of those that give a brief commentary are classified as motivated by either opportunity or necessity; all but 3 per cent are classified into these two motivational categories.

New firms created in all countries may have a substantial impact in several ways. First, they may grow in such a manner that they increase the total numbers of jobs for those that choose to work. Second, they may introduce new goods or services that will substantially alter the structure of the economy. Some firms may actually do both – grow to create jobs for others and alter the economic structure with new goods and services. Measures related to both types of impact are made based on answers given in the interviews.

Controlling causality

Methodical procedures: Attempts are made to measure what they call "accuracy" in the GEM studies. "Accuracy" is seen as reflecting validity and reliability. In three of the countries involved in the studies, measures of the rate of start-ups have been made independently of the GEM programme. In all three cases, the levels of start-up activity estimated independently were not statistically significantly different from the GEM estimates.

It is also, according to the study, possible to compare the results of the GEM procedures on the same countries from year to year. The year-to-year correlations of the overall TEA rate have been very high.

Statistical tests are made to control the causal results that have been found. The coordinating group of GEM thinks that after so many years they have secured the causal mechanisms with some certainty.

Reporting the results

The numbers in 2006 can be presented as in Figure 10.4 (Bosma & Harding, 2007: p. 5). This is generally seen by the participants as the "crown" of the GEM efforts. The results are

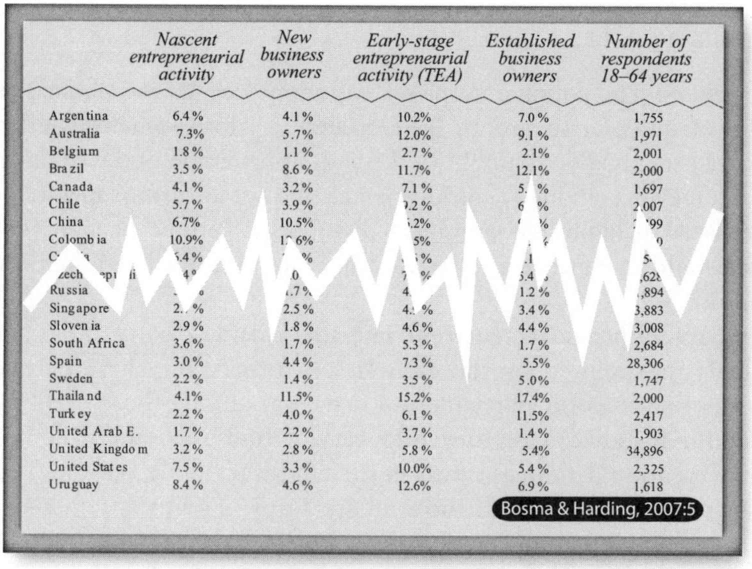

	Nascent entrepreneurial activity	New business owners	Early-stage entrepreneurial activity (TEA)	Established business owners	Number of respondents 18–64 years
Argentina	6.4%	4.1%	10.2%	7.0%	1,755
Australia	7.3%	5.7%	12.0%	9.1%	1,971
Belgium	1.8%	1.1%	2.7%	2.1%	2,001
Brazil	3.5%	8.6%	11.7%	12.1%	2,000
Canada	4.1%	3.2%	7.1%	5. %	1,697
Chile	5.7%	3.9%	?.2%	6. %	2,007
China	6.7%	10.5%	.2%	%	?,?99
Colombia	10.9%	1?.6%	?5%		?
C... zech ... i	4	0	? %	.1	5.
Russia	?	.7%	4.	1.2%	,894
Singapore	2. %	2.5%	4. %	3.4%	3,883
Slovenia	2.9%	1.8%	4.6%	4.4%	3,008
South Africa	3.6%	1.7%	5.3%	1.7%	2,684
Spain	3.0%	4.4%	7.3%	5.5%	28,306
Sweden	2.2%	1.4%	3.5%	5.0%	1,747
Thailand	4.1%	11.5%	15.2%	17.4%	2,000
Turkey	2.2%	4.0%	6.1%	11.5%	2,417
United Arab E.	1.7%	2.2%	3.7%	1.4%	1,903
United Kingdom	3.2%	2.8%	5.8%	5.4%	34,896
United States	7.5%	3.3%	10.0%	5.4%	2,325
Uruguay	8.4%	4.6%	12.6%	6.9%	1,618

Bosma & Harding, 2007:5

Figure 10.4   Prevalence Rates of Entrepreneurial Activity Across Countries in 2006
Source: Bosma & Harding, 2007: 5. Reprinted with permission.

as quantitative as can be (all according to the operative paradigm of the study) and they are widely spread in various publications.

> This chapter has presented two examples of the analytical view in application. Aspects such as formulating the problem, planning the collection of data, controlling causality and reporting have been foregrounded in two cases, one on bankruptcy in a specific country and one on business start-ups worldwide. It is clear that the analytical approach follows a rather strict operative paradigm, which is, of course, a result of its basic presumptions.

POINTS OF REFLECTION

1. What in the *presumptions* of the analytical approach makes its *operative paradigm* so strict?
2. Why are *definitions* so important as early as possible in an analytical approach, for instance, the definition of "bankruptcy" in Case I and the definition of "entrepreneurship" in Case II?
3. Looking at a selection of theories and previous research results in relation to the intended study area is important as a start for the creators of knowledge. Why is this generally seen as so important to the analytical view? The two cases consequently use this *methodical procedure* (to adapt theories and previous results as a starting point for their own studies), but with what purposes is this applied in Case I and in Case II?
4. What can be learnt from so-called *"pilot studies"* that can be of particular interest to the analytical approach (in both cases in this chapter, such tests were made)?
5. In Case I the researcher comes up with seven different *hypotheses* at the beginning of his study. How will he ever come to know whether he has "missed" any hypothesis?
6. Would you add any *hypothesis* to the seven suggested by the researcher in Case I? If you do, why?
7. In Case II so-called *harmonized data* are used as a starting point (which is not unusual in the analytical approach). Give some advantages as well as some disadvantages with such a procedure!
8. Both cases presented in the chapter are *extensive* and require major resources. Are there aspects or stages of the studies that you are *critical* of? Are there any steps of either of the two studies in which you would like to have been involved? Why? Why not?
9. Look hard at Tables 10.2 and 10.3. Are there any items that you would like to include over and above those which are there already? Why?

RECOMMENDED FURTHER READING

See the end of the Appendix and visit the website below.

Become a worldwide partner as a *knowledge creator* in the development of *Methodology for Creating Business Knowledge* by visiting the website: **www.knowledge-creator.com**. Here you can contribute by asking your own questions and you will also find answers to the most frequently asked questions. The website has been developed alongside this third edition of the book and the questions posted there will be used to provide input for future editions.

11 THE SYSTEMS APPROACH

This chapter provides two examples of the systems view in application. The first is a consulting assignment to try to get an explanation and understanding of some organizational problem in a specific company and to come up with some solution. The second is a research study in order to trace the business culture of a specific ethnic group.

INTRODUCTION

The systems view holds to certain ultimate presumptions of reality as (imperative) *prerequisites* for the efforts of the systems creator of knowledge in general:

1. Reality is assumed to consist of "units". These units are called "systems".
2. The units consist in turn of components that are fairly intimately related to each other.
3. Each unit usually has connections to other units, and is then called an "open" system. Open systems have no natural boundaries.
4. Reality is seen as filled by objective and subjective facts. From a methodological point of departure, the two are treated the same.

Some specific consequences of this for systems approach in business are:

- The units of the business reality are seen as open systems, which mean that they must *be placed in context* in both time and space before they can be explained and/or understood.
- Business activities are simultaneously *rich in aspects and in relations*. Systems creators of knowledge must, for practical reasons if no other, focus their aspect orientation and limit the scope of the systems relations being studied. The *aspects* of a company that are to be considered are ideally governed by the interests and goals of knowledge creators and, in the event of a *guiding study*, by the practical problems at hand. *In practice*, in guiding studies, the interests and ambitions of the creators of knowledge of course influence how the problem is formulated and how the study progresses. As far as the *delimitations* of studied

systems connections are concerned, knowledge creators must decide on a particular *magnifying level*. Which magnifying level is chosen is *ideally* determined in a guiding study by the practical problem, and in all studies by the *aspects* that will be focused on. *In practice*, however, there are always restrictions of both time and resources that must be considered.

- Under these circumstances, it is natural that information collected according to the systems view comes from a few *real cases* that are studied relatively extensively and intensively. Furthermore, because real systems may contain unique aspects, the systems creator of knowledge should be rather sceptical about using existing systems theories *in detail*.

These are relatively strict *basic prerequisites* for creating knowledge according to the systems view. At the *practical level* the situation is different. Here, the systems creators of knowledge are encouraged to be both versatile and imaginative, something that comes naturally because the view claims to deal with a very multifaceted reality.

In other words, the *operative paradigm* for systems creators of knowledge is *relatively fixed in forms, but has a highly varied content*.

This chapter presents two cases that offer illustrations of how the systems view functions in *application*. One concerns consultancy work, the other a research study. When reading these cases, the reader should know that both come from what is called the developing world. This means that many aspects that are taken for granted in the so-called developed world are not in place, for instance, strict laws, long traditions of modern business, democracy at the work place and reasonably high wages and salaries.

CASE I: ELECTRONICS LTD

The start

Stewart Grant was employed as a visiting professor of Business Strategy at a university in southern Asia. One day his good friend Bob Stevens (who was executive director in a subsidiary of a major multinational corporation, a subsidiary that had manufacturing facilities in the same town as Stewart's university) called him on the telephone and asked him if he would consider getting involved with Bob's company as a consultant. He suggested that they should meet over dinner to discuss the matter, which they did. During dinner with his friend, Stewart was given more information about the history and present situation of Bob's company, Electronics Ltd.

Electronics Ltd had been founded at the end of the 1920s as the result of a merger of several smaller manufacturers of radio tubes and related products. The merger was successful and sales expanded in spite of heavy competition. The company specialized in radio transistors during the 1950s and 1960s, but technical developments forced them to "change horses" and move increasingly into electronics, which led to the adoption of its present name.

Electronics Ltd soon became a multinational company with sales representatives in several parts of the world. During the 1980s, however, as a response to the excellence of the Japanese electronics industry, the concept of quality became the company's top priority. This led to two developments on the manufacturing side of the company:

1. Manufacturing became more and more automated, including the introduction of robots.
2. Major portions of the company's subcontracting – manufacturing for other companies/customers who in turn used Electronics Ltd's products (Electronics Ltd was relatively big in this respect) – were moved to "low-cost countries", mainly to south Asia.

Just such a subcontracting company/subsidiary had been established eighteen years ago in the city in which Stewart Grant worked. Bob Stevens had been its local manager for the past two years. He was, in fact, recruited from another subcontracting company among those that during the twentieth century, in increasing numbers, had established themselves in this part of the world.

Bob's company, which is the one we will mean whenever we refer to Electronics Ltd henceforth, dealt only in subcontracting – to be more precise, in assembling integrated circuit boards ("chips") based on nanotechnology that were in turn used in their customers' manufacturing of computers and electronic control systems.

Bob showed Stewart the organization chart of Electronics Ltd (illustrated in Figure 11.1), with its mix of local and expatriate personnel among the senior managers.

When Stewart asked what CCM and TCM stood for, Bob said that CCM stands for Consignment Contract Manufacturing, which means that all material is provided by the orderer at no cost. The task is to assemble these "kits". The margin is low but stable if the manufacturing is kept rational. TCM stands for Turnkey Contract Manufacturing. Here the subcontractor is responsible for purchasing all components – which must meet the orderer's drawings and specifications.

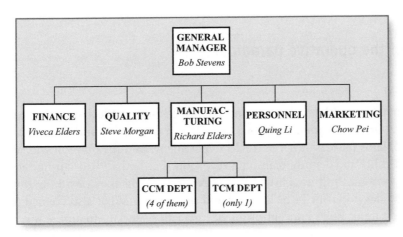

Figure 11.1   Organization Chart

Bob said that the CCM departments ("4 of them") and the TCM department ("only 1") are organized in generally the same way. Every department has a departmental head that oversees those who are responsible for planning, purchasing, assembling, testing, packaging and delivering. Each of those five departments has about 50 employees, all of them local personnel.

Bob also claimed that the "problem child" was the TCM department. It had been set up in 2002 and since then had lost about US $2.5 million annually on its operations. Bob did not have much hope for its future development. The CCM departments, on the other hand, did well, and he saw no immediate problems there. Bob put a direct question to Stewart: *What is wrong with the TCM department?* As we will see, it became Stewart Grant's mission as a consultant to answer this question.

Stewart asked Bob if he could tell him what was so special about the TCM department, apart from it being the latest offshoot in the growth of the company, being based on a different manufacturing concept than the other departments and being unprofitable. Bob answered that the situation in the TCM department was "completely different" from that experienced by other departments. The industry it served was in a state of flux and growing very rapidly, a growth directed by both technological progress and more sophisticated demands from customers. Customers consisted mainly of computer manufacturers who used companies like Electronics Ltd as subcontractors for components for specially designed, automated and robotized control systems of various kinds.

The customers/orderers, therefore, gave very precise specifications for what they wanted. Yet these specifications – as Bob expressed it – changed "seemingly at random and from one day to another. When we think we're about to get our manufacturing in shape and start to make money on a board, it's time to change it."

In the course of the evening, Stewart had more and more interesting ideas about the company and how he wanted to approach its situation. Bob told him that he could talk to anyone he wanted to and spend as much time as he needed "to get an understanding of the company's situation".

The evening ended with Stewart promising to submit a proposal and study design in the near future.

Planning of the operative paradigm

Methodics

Stewart understood that he had not been asked to consult at Electronics Ltd just because he knew Bob. Stewart had made a name for himself as a consultant and the company obviously had some problems (at least with its TCM department) and his opinion was wanted.

Stewart based his initial study plan on a suspicion that he had had during the evening with Bob. When Electronics Ltd established the TCM department they obviously saw it as natural considering the development of technology and the market. What also seemed to be regarded as natural – in spite of Bob's concept of the department's special situation – was to *manage* the TCM department in the same as the other departments, which had been part of the company for some time. In other words, tradition was allowed to take over without any further reflection. Was the administrative management of the TCM department an outmoded historical product that in its present shape was more of a burden than an asset to the department?

To test this, Stewart planned to adopt a mainly *structural perspective* in his study and then concentrate primarily on *the administrative aspects of the TCM department*. The latter aspect would be Stewart's *external systems delimitation*. The internal systems delimitations, that is, the *magnifying level* best suited to the study, would be revealed as the study progressed.

Stewart envisioned a three-stage study like the one illustrated in Figure 11.2.

The problem would be formulated in the study's first stage (*systems analysis*). Based on the formulation of the problem, in the second stage (*systems construction*) he would work – mainly on his own – to provide a new systems proposal, and in the third stage he intended (if possible) to participate in the *implementation* of this new systems proposal.

Stewart also had definite ideas about how the systems analysis was to be done. We will come back to this shortly.

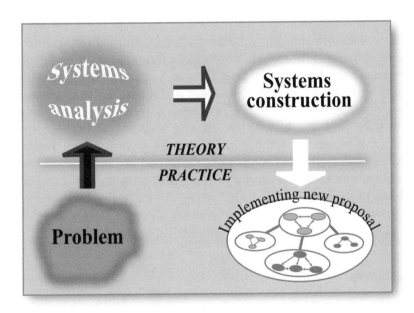

Figure 11.2   Grant's Three-Stage Study

Stewart's ambitions

Based on a suspicion that the TCM department was run the same way as other departments in Electronics Ltd (and on his conviction that this department needed its own, at least partly unique, form of planning and control), Stewart decided first to *determine finality relations* (compare Figure 9.3) in this department from an administrative point of departure. This would require that certain determinations of finality relations be made in other departments for comparison.

With this background, Stewart intended to come up with an improved proposal (*guide*); a *systems proposal* that he hoped would be a part of the implementation and application.

Stewart's *guiding* ambitions included coming up with a proposal for improvements within six months, at the most. During this period he intended to spend half his time at Electronics Ltd and the rest in academic work.

Stewart presented his preliminary ideas and goals to Bob. They were approved without any reservations.

Let us note certain systems *methodical* characteristics of the study before we go on (see "The systems approach" in Chapter 9):

- The present situation at Electronics Ltd can, to a great extent, be explained by its history.
- Stewart wanted to look at the TCM department as *one* system and the CCM departments as *other* systems. These systems are open, that is, they have *connections* with *each other*, with *other parts* of the company and with the *external* world. This is the *external* delimitation of Stewart's study.
- Stewart knew that determining a system's type and describing and determining its *finality* relations are intimately connected. Even so, he found from a perspective of *prerequisites for determining type* of both the TCM department and the CCM departments, that they were different as far as their manufacturing technology was concerned and probably required a partly different orientation and design, but they could all be seen as having a similar structure and administrative focus. One *potential finality relation* was that they all (apart from their manufacturing technologies) were dependent on the central business management of Electronics Ltd as a whole and on the markets and buyers relevant for the two types of department.

Systems analysis

Methodical procedure

Stewart had conducted several consultative studies before and he had based them on his general understanding of the meaning of systems theory, an understanding that he felt very comfortable with. This theory told Stewart that he could look at a company (or any of its parts) from a *structural perspective*. In such a perspective, in order for a system to function well (so that a positive synergetic effect could arise), all its components had to interact to support each other – *they should fit each other*. And all components should individually and together promote the business of the company/system.

Stewart had three components (levels) in mind in terms of Electronics Ltd or any of its departments:

1. the level of the organization of the company (or any of its departments) at large
2. the level of interaction in groups in the company (or any of its departments)
3. the level of individuals working in the company (or any of its departments).

If these three levels fit each other, with the business of the system in mind, the system would function well. If any of these levels did not fit the others, the business of the system could not be achieved satisfactorily.

The groups and the individuals could be called the *social* aspect of the system.

Methodics

Stewart intended the first stage of the study, the *systems analysis* stage, to provide a more definite determination of finality relations, a more detailed description and a more thorough determination of the type of system (i.e. the TCM department and one CCM department) than what he had so far.

Stewart and Bob selected one of the CCM departments for comparison with the TCM department. For practical reasons, we will refer to this as *the* CCM department.

The systems analysis – formulating the problem – was not conducted in *conscious* steps that were *planned in detail*. Stewart by and large lived at Electronics Ltd during this intensive, introductory stage of the study. During this time he *gradually* reached a better understanding of the types of systems concerned, their existing relations and the problems the systems had (compare the B-side of Figure 9.3).

We now present the working procedures, how methodics was done, in two sections. The first contains a number of quotations from various interviews, interviews that might rather be characterized as discussions. Only quotations that are relevant to Stewart's formulation of the problem are included. The second section contains Stewart's own developed analysis (formulation of the problem) set against the background of these interviews.

We hope that the reader will get some sense of the systems insight that Grant gradually reached, as well as a sense of his methodical considerations in the meantime, even if the presentation does not follow strictly the chronological order in which the process went on. Keep in mind that Stewart intended to: (a) *analyse two systems*, the TCM and the CCM departments; and then (b) focus mainly on their *differences*. Behind all this was the previously mentioned *theory of managing on three levels* (organization, group and individual) *towards a goal (a business) in a system*.

Discussions with senior management

In one of his visits to Electronics Ltd, Stewart became interested in how Bob Stevens cooperated with other senior managers. He confirmed that cooperation had increased among various senior managers since Stevens had joined the company. In fact, Stevens spent considerable time in discussions with different people – he said he had an "open door policy". He was also happy to call for meetings. Stevens said:

> I believe in talking to my team and in following their advice. There's no sense in having a staff if you don't use it.

The rest of the company had become accustomed to senior management spending a great deal of time in meetings. Senior managers had much in common. Most of them were university graduates and they spoke very much the same "language". The manager of finance, Viveca Elders, spoke of relations with the mother company:

> We have strict guidelines and demands from above. We also have to make quarterly reports on where we stand. So far, we've been able to hide the disappointing results of the TCM department in our total figures. But we can't do that for ever. They've started to wonder at home why our profitability here these days doesn't reach the same level as most of our other subsidiaries in the world.

They had no personnel problems in the company according to Quing Li, the personnel manager:

> My task is mainly to recruit personnel to our assembling departments. But people stand in line to get in! As you might be aware, there is a lack of paid working opportunities in this country. And we have virtually no personnel turnover.

Marketing was a tough task according to its manager, Chow Pei:

> Most of our jobs are arranged by our mother company – but, on the other hand, they are not our customers. I have to be out there all the time, both here and abroad. My contact work goes on around the clock, seven days a week. Most of our clients have representatives and even their own manufacturing in this country, and they see the possibilities here and often seem to play us subcontractors against each other. We can't relax for one second. An unsuccessful delivery from us with unacceptable quality can spoil that customer relation for all time.

Steven Morgan, the manager of quality, also had something to say on this issue:

> Quality is the be-all and end-all. And that our deliveries stick to the schedule. We have often had problems with the TCM department in this respect. I don't know if they're too inexperienced or butter-fingered in there or what!

Discussions with the TCM department

Stewart visited the TCM department for the first time together with the manufacturing manager, Richard Elders (married to Viveca Elders, the manager of finance). Stewart and Richard Elders walked through the department together with its head, known to all as Mr Tan. Stewart noticed that offices were arranged for the administrative handling of planning, purchasing, assembling, testing, packaging and delivery; he would speak with representatives of these functions later. Mr Tan, too, had a private office, but he claimed that he was never there: he was "always out among the girls", as he expressed it.

Those who actually did the direct assembly work were, in fact, all women (this was not an unusual situation in such contexts, according to Richard Elders). They wore uniforms and each sat at her own workstation. The stations were spaced along rectangular tables. Each table completed one type of integrated circuit board – each person attached certain components to a board and then sent it on to the next station for further assembly. Each workstation had a mounted soldering apparatus, and in front of each worker was a drawing that indicated what they were to do. The fully assembled integrated boards ended up at one end of the room where several testing stations were situated. Packaging and preparation for delivery took place in another room.

The assembly work was consequently relatively simple and of a repetitive nature. The only people who moved about in the room (except for Mr Tan) were those who, from time to time, rolled in small carts filled with components for the different stations. This took place according to a predetermined schedule, not on demand from the stations.

Later on that first day, both Richard Elders and Mr Tan told Stewart about their problems with the TCM department. The result of this discussion, together with several others that Stewart later had about the TCM department, can be summarized in the following points:

- The TCM department, unlike the CCM department, had to buy its own components for assembly. In spite of an intensive input of work from the purchasing office, the department often had problems with the quality of these components. To make matters worse, this inferior quality did not show up until the final testing stages, which periodically led to a large number of rejected boards.
- Because of frequent changes in the specific products to be manufactured, it was often necessary for the workers to relearn their assembly work. This entailed new drawings and new assembly steps – even having to rearrange the workstations.
- Those employed in assembly were paid by the week; their pay did not exceed the minimum payment rate stipulated by the government of the country (this weekly pay was not much more than worker in the West might be paid per hour).

After collecting this background information, Stewart concentrated on the human aspects of the TCM department. He talked with most of the people employed there. Mr Tan said about his department:

> We have the best group of girls in my department, but if anybody comes from another department or from outside they don't like the job at first. Then they sit in the cafeteria and talk about their job and say that the TCM department has a bunch of slave drivers. We don't drive our girls particularly hard, but we do expect them to do what they're supposed to, and we are the only department that uses production standards.

On another occasion Mr Tan said:

> Last Friday, I told Huan Sing [one of the assembly workers] that she might as well start getting used to producing by next month, because the manufacturing programme next month will put a higher demand on her results. I told her that if she was now making 240 [per day], they would ask her to make at least that many next time – if not more. So she should take it easy and give it a try.

When Stewart spoke with the assembly line employees in the TCM department, he was particularly interested in picking up comments about the departmental head, the job itself and the workers' relationships with each other. The following was a typical statement about Mr Tan:

Tan is OK. He always tries to treat me fairly and if he does, I have nothing to say about him. All my friends here like him. He doesn't worry us. Yesterday, Tan told me to do another job as good as the one I'm doing now, but I told him to go to somebody else. He did. He's good in that way. He also helps you if you want him to – I have always liked him – and my job, too, for that matter.

A typical statement from an assembly worker about attitudes towards company standards and her own productivity:

The standard on my task is 420 a day but I've never been able to reach it. I don't worry too much about it. I suppose I like to talk much as I am doing now, for instance. One day I really tried to reach it but didn't make it. We used to work harder when there was a lot to do, but right now there's not that much, so we're not exactly overdoing it.

One point of departure on the tasks of the assembly workers and their attitudes towards each other:

This is all I know. When they taught me the job they explained nothing about how the [soldering] machines work. The board I'm working on now didn't function at all well in the test yesterday. But I was not told until afterwards. They want us to come up with 83 correct boards per hour, but how can we do that when half of them will be rejected?

Steven Morgan (who manages quality in the senior group) made the following remark concerning the TCM department:

I did a lot of work at the department when I came here two years ago. Some people in that department have the idea that they're not going to manufacture more than they decide themselves. Employees have been promised major changes in our long-term programme, including pay rises, if they can improve their results. But nothing has happened.

Discussions with the CCM department

Stewart also visited the CCM department on several occasions (we remind the reader that "the CCM department" is one of four similar departments). Space does not permit any quotations, but Stewart's impression can be summarized as follows. Superficially, the department looked the same as the TCM department. The atmosphere, however, seemed much more peaceful and harmonious (this was confirmed in Stewart's discussions in the department). The carts of assembly components did not roll in, as often as in the TCM department and the tables were shorter, that is, each station performed more operations (or the table worked on a less complicated integrated circuit board). In short, work was even more repetitive in this department.

Stewart's formulation of the problem and his new systems proposal

From the quotations and the observations presented above, our aim is to show some of the foundation Stewart built on when he eventually made his *systems analysis*. This stage of his study lasted about three months, which underlines that the quotations above should not be seen as more than examples.

The following results are based on the report Stewart presented to the senior management group after having been at Electronics Ltd for about five months.

Reporting the results

I have studied the TCM department and one of the CCM departments in detail. Furthermore, I have repeatedly had discussions with all of you. As you know, this has been aimed at trying to explain why the TCM department is unprofitable and problematic but the CCM departments are not. All departments are similar in several aspects; for instance, the products are designed by the customers/orderers, the same demand on profitability is asked by the mother company, and they are exposed to tough competition (and, as a consequence, required to be technologically up-to-date and business oriented). But more to the point in this discussion of how they are to be administered and controlled, are the differences:

TCM	*CCM*
• *The contract manufacturer is responsible for purchasing all components*	• *All components are provided by the orderers without cost (a straight "assembly kit")*
• *The price is of lesser importance; the important thing is that the products are delivered at a guaranteed quality (specified by the orderer)*	• *Prices are under pressure; marginals are low but stable – provided that production is rational*
• *Short-term planning only; replanning is frequent, as is rearranging of work stations; changes are frequent, sometimes abrupt; new products unlike old ones*	• *Long-term planning possible; changes are minimal; stable, more long-term customer relations*

One can say that the two departments ought to be guided by different business demands:

TCM	*CCM*
• *Alert to changing demands, quick to give customers what they want, no matter what*	• *Reliable and consistent with what customers want at unbeatable prices*

Bob Stevens once asked me a direct question: *What is wrong with the TCM department?*

I would like to respond: *That it has been organized, administered and run as a CCM department!*

Because of their predictability and lower degree of change, CCM departments can continue as they are, that is, keep to their repeatable sequence (see Figure 11.3).

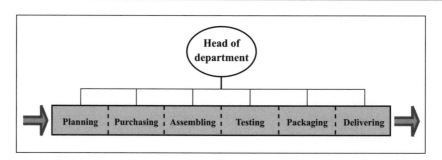

Figure 11.3   Work Sequence in a CCM Department

But in the TCM department, frequent contacts with the customers are decisive. Furthermore, the purchasing function is more important than it is in the CCM departments. Also, every assembling contract may lead to a partly different set-up for assembling and testing. Therefore, I propose that the TCM department be organized in terms of process teams. Every such team is built up according to the systems proposal in Figure 11.4., where no component is seen as more important than the other and they all co-operate as a true system.

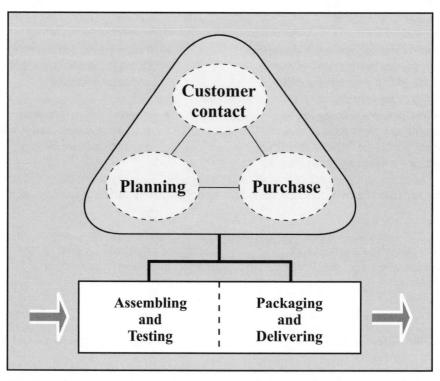

Figure 11.4   Systems Proposal for the TCM Department

Team management consists of people responsible for contacting customers, purchasing and planning. The manufacturing procedures themselves are allowed to have different courses from one process to another. These teams are established in connection with a contract being awarded by an orderer (in many cases even before that), and the teams are dissolved when the order has been delivered and approved.

This means that a person could, at one and the same time, be part of the leadership of several process teams. However, this can be an advantage as far as communications and learning are concerned. The department head becomes responsible for more strategic customer relations and coordinating the process teams.

The present arrangement has led to several occasions of *lack of fit* between various levels of Electronics Ltd in reference to the TCM department and in reference to its business demands. I would like to summarize the most essential aspects of these deficiencies in fit in Figure 11.5. I think the figure speaks for itself!

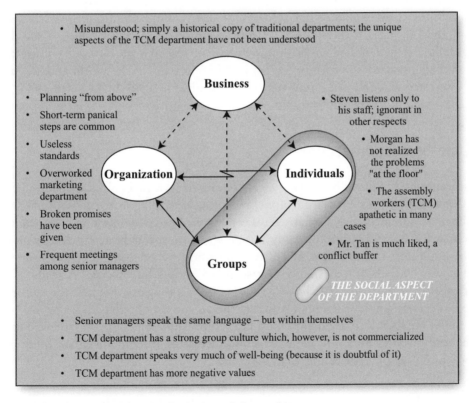

Figure 11.5   Stewart Grant's Formulation of the Problem

I suggest that Electronics Ltd immediately appoint a task force to make the TCM department more purposefully organized according to my principles. I would be glad to be part of that force.

And then?

The discussion at the meeting in which Stewart presented his *formulation of the problem* and his *proposal for improvements* (the new systems construction) was both lively and enthusiastic. As Stewart wished, a work group to change the TCM department was immediately appointed. Also at his request, this group included two representatives from the assembly workers and one representative from the more frequent customers/orderers.

CASE II: CHINESE BUSINESS CULTURE

How it started

A researcher was working as a visiting research fellow at a university in Southeast Asia throughout almost the whole of the 1990s. One day two old friends, a professor in a university in the US and a professor in a European university contacted him. They told the research fellow that they had raised funds for doing research on business cultures among small and medium-sized enterprises (SMEs) in different parts of the world and asked him if he was interested in doing the Asian part of the study. He agreed, but before he could do some field research, he started to think.

Initial methodical procedures

The researcher had to begin by making clear to himself how he could do what he promised to do. Coming up with such clarifications, including providing initial definitions and conceptualizations, are included in what we refer to as *methodical procedures*. He realized first that there was no way for him to study business culture throughout the whole of Asia. It would be a hopeless task, but it would also be meaningless, he thought. The reason why he thought it was "hopeless" was simply that so many people live in Asia. A study of such a number would be impossible. But he also thought it "meaningless" because the cultural variety is so large among people living in Asia that there is no meaningful "average" or "typical" culture there. He therefore decided to limit himself to Chinese people – a large group whose economy and business methods were attracting increasing interest. Even so, he decided to make two more restrictions, A and B, in his study.

A. Study overseas Chinese only. The researcher had a feeling that overseas Chinese had been allowed and able to develop their specific business skills more than those Chinese who lived on the mainland. The researcher furthermore decided to study only those overseas Chinese that lived in Asia and who were generally understood as dominating business and economic activities in seven Asian countries outside China (for practical reasons, he excluded the small number of overseas Chinese who lived in less accessible countries outside those seven, like Vietnam and Myanmar, from his study). He later found out that the number of overseas

Chinese living in these seven countries was estimated to be about 50 million (Lasserre & Schütte, 1995: 100) according to the figures below:

Malaysia	*6 million*
Indonesia	*8*
Philippines	*1*
Taiwan	*21*
Thailand	*6*
Singapore	*2*
Hong Kong	*6*
Total	*50 million*

B. Limit himself to study SMEs only. The reason why the researcher made this delimitation was that he believed that big enterprises often more or less lose their cultural identity and might not reveal any specific ethnic cultural pattern the way SMEs would. Furthermore, the *number* of large overseas Chinese businesses was obviously very small at the time.

When the researcher wanted to come up with a common definition of SMEs in his seven countries, he soon realized that the public definition differed among the seven; for instance:

- Hong Kong limited the number of employees in SMEs to 100 in manufacturing and to 50 in non-manufacturing firms.
- Malaysia limited its public interest in SMEs to manufacturing only and preferred to talk about "small and medium-sized industries" (SMIs) to stress this fact.
- The Philippines divided enterprises below 200 employees into "medium" (those with 100–199 employees), "small" (with 10–99 employees) and "cottage enterprises" (1–9 employees). If the value of a cottage enterprise's assets fell below a specified amount, it was called a "micro enterprise".

Realizing that every definition is leading its user in a specific direction, that every definition may have a specific purpose and that he wanted a definition which was flexible enough to be used from country to country in his study rather than coming up with harmonized quantitative results, so the researcher adopted the following definition of an SME to use in his study:

> A small or medium-sized enterprise is one which is independently owned and operated, which is in business for profit and which is not dominating its field of operation.

One important *methodical procedure* was, of course, to come up with a *conceptualization* of what he would mean by *culture*. He spent an essential time studying the literature on the topic and came up with the following.

Culture seems to mean almost anything – and so could become virtually meaningless! Sometimes culture stood for "the ways in which we function in this place", sometimes for "programmed behaviour", sometimes for "our slogan and our logo" and sometimes for "what is right and what is wrong". And it seemed sometimes possible to excuse any behaviour by simply saying, "Well, that's our culture". However, there were some commonalities.

No matter how culture is understood, it seems to be generally seen as being based on the following:

- Culture is something that unites a certain group.
- Culture is something that one learns as a member of a group.
- Culture is related to values.

> Of those more than 160 definitions of culture analysed by Kroeber and Kluckhohn, some conceive of culture as separating humans from nonhumans, some define it as communicable knowledge, and some as the sum of historical achievements produced by man's social life. All of the definitions have common elements: culture is learned, shared and transmitted from one generation to the next. Culture is primarily passed from parents to their children but also by social organizations, special interest groups, the government, the schools, and the church. Common ways of thinking and behaving that are developed are then reinforced through social pressure. Culture is also multidimensional, consisting of a number of common elements that are interdependent. Changes occurring in one of the dimensions will affect the others as well. (Czinkota et al., 1994: 264)

In spite of this, one can ask how extensive culture is. It cannot be almost anything or everything. That would not give any focus to a person, a researcher like the one in the present case, trying to devise a map of it.

The researcher found that *various ways of characterizing culture* could be classified along two dimensions:

1. One dimension is to ask whether culture is *behaviour*, alternatively what is influencing and regulating behaviour, that is, different kinds of *values*.
2. Another dimension is to ask oneself whether culture is something one is *conscious* of or whether it is something deeper, that is, something *unconscious*.

Along these two dimensions, the researchers could see, in the subject of business as well as in many others, four different ways to look at culture (alone or in a combination) according to Figure 11.6.

One definition in category I in business is the following:

> ... the way we do things around here. (Deal & Kennedy, 1988: 4)

CULTURE AS	*Something conscious*	*Something unconscious*
Behavioural	I	II
Non-behavioural (values only)	III	IV

Figure 11.6 Various Ways to Look at Culture

One definition in category II in business is the following:

> An organization's culture can be described by its management in terms of the way their tasks are typically handled in the context of key relationships (in a take-for-granted fashion). (Schwartz & Davis, 1981: 36)

Two definitions in categories III and IV in business (where from the definition it is hard to say whether values are conscious or not) are the following two:

> As knowledge and belief, culture exists only as thought and is nonmaterial and nonbehavioral (therefore, behavior is guided by and reflects culture but is not the thing itself). (Dredge, 1985: 412)

> Organizational culture is that pattern of beliefs and expectations shared by the organization's members which powerfully shape the behavior of individuals and groups within the organization. (Byars, 1987: 48)

The researcher thought that the most interesting and intriguing aspects of a culture would be its unconscious parts, that is, categories II and IV. He also chose to use a definition that would fit his systems research interests and came up with the following *conceptualization of culture* for his project of tracing the business culture of overseas Chinese:

> CULTURE = Basic values, assumptions and beliefs (which are mainly unconscious) and everyday behavior (which is mainly taken for granted), which are, as related components in a value-laden system, developed interactively in a specific systems environment.

The operative paradigm

Potential finality relations

Now, if culture is something which is mainly unconscious and by and large taken for granted, how can you get a picture of it, how can you map it in all its relations? It cannot be directly observed and it cannot come out directly in interviews! The researcher came up with five perspectives for his study – see Figure 11.7 overleaf.

The basic logic of Figure 11.7 is the following. As stated above, the researcher looked at *culture among overseas Chinese* (his study area) as something, which is more or less unconscious and implicit (almost hidden). It is therefore only possible for a researcher, for instance, to reach indirectly, through an *analysis* of what might be *finality relations* behind the way it manifests itself in all aspects of life. As also mentioned above, culture develops *interactively* in a specific *systems environment*, in this case among overseas Chinese. And this is done over a long time, in fact, over several generations as far as overseas Chinese are concerned.

Overseas Chinese culture, so the researcher thought, should manifest itself in all the five perspectives (1–5) in Figure 11.7. It should manifest itself, for instance: in action and thinking among power holders in the seven countries in question (perspective 1); in the economy and small business in the region (perspective 2); among what other researchers had found out about the Chinese way to do business (perspective 3); and in stories and material from real

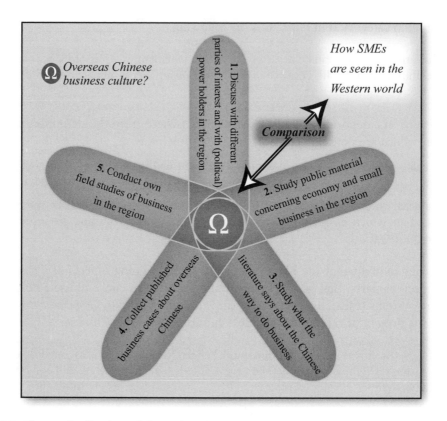

Figure 11.7 The Methodic Plan of the Cultural Study

overseas Chinese business practice (perspectives 4 and 5). Then the *common denominator or the core of the value-laden system* (Ω in Figure 11.7) could be read between the lines as *overseas Chinese business culture*!

In the language of Figure 9.3, this planning of the study would be, as *methodics,* like going five rounds in the loop at the top of the A-side of it, that is, from "Formulating potential finality relations" to "Are you satisfied with your data so far?", even if, in practice, much of these five rounds would, of course, take place in parallel. (We will have something to say about the step "Do you want to bring in understanding?", which is part of this loop, at the end of Case II.)

We could express it such that the researcher looked at overseas Chinese culture as a *deep systems structure.*

As seen in Figure 11.7 ("How SMEs are seen in the Western world") and as we can read in the beginning of this case, the whole study aimed at providing results that could be used as a comparison of SME business cultures in other parts of the world. From a methodological point of departure, according to the systems view, such comparisons would be very interesting to discuss, but it leads in this case beyond our aims and will therefore not be taken up again in this chapter.

Designing methods and collecting data

The researcher was designing methods and collecting data from his five different perspectives for about one and a half years. Below there follows a general presentation of the *methodics* and the sources used by the researcher in the five different perspectives and also some examples of the results from these five. This may not lead to very many *general* methodological additions to Case II, but as *specific* methodological comments, we think that this presentation may serve two purposes for the reader:

- It may provide an idea of the extensiveness of the research that was actually done in this case. We said early on in this book that systems research, due to its presumptions of a complex reality, requires a large effort in almost any study area it approaches. This was certainly the case when, as here, studies were made of culture as *contextual manifestations* in *different* systems environment in a large geographical part of the world.
- It may provide a foundation with the reader of the systems structure for an acknowledgement of the analysis that was made by the researcher and which is presented at the end of this case.

1. *Discuss with different stakeholders and with (political) power holders in the region.* The researcher visited the seven countries several times to discuss his research interests. He concentrated on three types of institutions:

   a. governmental institutions involved in SMEs
   b. universities
   c. SME interest groups, employers' confederations, industrial associations and the like.

All the seven countries had (a) governmental institutions with names like the Ministry of Industry and Trade (Malaysia), the Industrial Development Authority and the Agency for Development of Small Industry (Indonesia) or the Bureau of Industrial Promotion Policy and Planning (Thailand). All of them had public material that was given to the researcher. However, most of this material concerned what *they wanted to do, not what they had actually done* and *very little concerned the SME sector* in the country. Also, very few university departments (b) showed any interest in small and medium-sized business at the time. SME interest groups and industrial associations (c) existed in all seven countries, but in none of these cases were they specifically (or at least not openly) concerned with Chinese business merely. The only *methodical procedure* the researcher did *before* he met all these institutions and organizations was that he had armed himself with a list of themes, all more or less related to the Chinese way of doing business, which he wanted to focus on in his discussions with various representatives and his reading of the varied material handed to him. He wanted, apart from this, to keep his mind as open as possible.

Some examples of results from discussions and readings from perspective 1 are:

- All the seven countries, with the exception of Hong Kong, had very interventionist governments. Two of them, that is, Singapore and Taiwan, had been "designed" by public policies more than the others.

- Due to this, SMEs had been crowded out in many industries in the seven countries.
- As a result of the former two points, it was no surprise that the proportion of SMEs was highest in Hong Kong among the seven countries.
- There was no support until very recently for SMEs in any of the seven countries.
- Most of the seven countries had developed a dualistic national structure with a relatively rich and prosperous (or at least active in terms of various kinds of businesses) capital and a very poor countryside. Exceptions were Singapore and Hong Kong which had no agricultural business worth mentioning.

2. Study public material concerning economy and small business in the region. There turned out to be a rich body of material concerning the economy of the seven countries in general, but very little material concerning their SME sectors. Most material was attained by the researcher from APEC (Asia Pacific Economic Cooperation – a supranational institution with an office in Singapore). They provided the researcher with several comparative studies of countries in the Asia Pacific region which the researcher studied critically and methodically and chose information from. As *methodical procedure* here the researcher conducted different systems analyses of the material to make sure that the results matched his conceptualization of culture (see above). Some examples of results from perspective 2 are:

- The countries varied from very rich (Singapore) to rather poor (Indonesia and the Philippines).
- All the countries had moved from being commodity-based to becoming manufacturing-based – and some even further to becoming service-based.
- There is no way to understand the Southeast Asian boom without understanding the overseas Chinese.
- If the overseas Chinese were an economy of their own, they would probably be the third largest economy in the world.
- The overseas Chinese started as traders and, to some extent, as contract workers. Many of them left their homeland because their lives were impoverished there and they were often treated harshly and as outsiders in the communities where they settled.
- Overseas Chinese, when entering business, concentrated on family businesses in order to keep themselves together by ties of blood, geography and business procedures.
- The overseas Chinese run an extremely efficient opportunity-seeking machine and were moving funds around in networks.

3. Study what the literature says about the Chinese way of business. The researcher studied the Chinese way of business through about twenty major works and about 100 articles, most of the latter in so-called recognized scientific journals. Within the framework of this perspective the researcher also conducted *methodical procedures* at the general level of the methodological view as well as at the level of its operative paradigm. This related to the source material that he had been able to retrieve before it was used as part of the results from his study.

Some examples of results from perspective 3 are:

- Overseas Chinese are very secretive about what they are doing.
- Overseas Chinese (as Chinese in general) are very superstitious, fatalistic and intuitive.
- The businesses of overseas Chinese are often a second-generation business as part of the inheritance from the first-generation patriarch.
- The businesses of overseas Chinese can survive in an industry with a very small margin as long as the turnover of sales is reasonably high.
- Long-range planning rarely exists in an overseas Chinese business.
- The manager/owner of the overseas Chinese business is a natural networker.
- If an overseas Chinese business is growing, it is often split in several units, the sizes of which are not larger than can be controlled by a family.

4 and 5. Collect published business cases about overseas Chinese (4) and *Conduct own field studies of businesses in the region (5).* (These two sources are combined here, because they came up with very similar results.) The researcher found forty-three published case studies that told the stories of overseas Chinese businessmen (no women) – a surprisingly low number. In order to come up with more stories he paid consulting companies to go to small business people for them to tell their stories in their local language and to translate those stories into English for him. Six such field studies were made in Malaysia and eight in Indonesia. These were two countries not represented among the forty-three published cases mentioned earlier. The consulting companies had a directive to find "what in their opinion were typical companies in their country". They were also given an interview guide to follow as far as possible. They had three months to do the job. They were provided with a large list of generally formulated questions and issues that the researcher wanted answers to, but, otherwise, for practical reasons (only the researcher and one assistant were involved in this large project), the consulting companies were left by and large to themselves until a one-day discussion was held individually with each of them when they handed over their material. These discussions were aimed at achieving a better comprehension and greater clarification, on the part of the researcher, of what the consulting companies had been able to come up with. The researcher used the same list of issues and questions when analysing the forty-three published cases previously mentioned. These fairly unstructured *methodical procedures* hopefully led to an open-ended array of answers.

Examples of results from these two perspectives are:

- Overseas Chinese SMEs are commonly in subcontracting.
- Management is based on person-to-person transactions to minimize bureaucracy and paperwork.
- Very few standard procedures exist in overseas Chinese businesses.
- Overseas Chinese SMEs may be personally influenced by the founder/owner to the extent that it may lead to confusion among employees.
- Promotions among employees are made from inside in overseas Chinese businesses.

- Overseas Chinese SMEs give priority to manufacturing.
- The meaning of marketing in overseas Chinese SMEs does not include advertising, sales promotion or public relation activities.

Do you want to bring in understanding?

There is one component in Figure 9.3 on the A-side, which is called "Do you want to bring in understanding?" The researcher thought for a while that he would improve his picture of overseas Chinese business culture by doing so through arranging its components in a metaphor as *a hierarchy of values, beliefs and assumptions*. It was quite obvious that, in Figure 11.8. below, for instance, "seniority" could be seen as a *product* of "family orientation" and that "good contacts" could *produce* "trust when needed". However, he came to the conclusion that his knowledge of his study areas would not be improved to any major degree by doing this and therefore never went any further here.

Coding and arranging data

On the B-side of Figure 9.3, we can read: "Determining the type of the real system." This meant here that the researcher gradually improved his knowledge of overseas Chinese business culture as a systems structure as the study went on. It is impossible to say exactly when specific insights came to him, but in our systems language we can say that he came to the following conclusions when he was coding and arranging his data (compare "A 'common' systems language" in Chapter 5):

- *Systems, subsystems and components.* Overseas Chinese business culture is rather old and has changed very little over time. The researcher found no differences of importance between overseas Chinese business cultures between the seven countries he studied. He therefore decided that it was possible to talk about overseas Chinese business culture as *one* system, that there were no subsystems of interest here and that the components could be seen as "basic values, beliefs and assumptions" (compare the researcher's definition of "culture").
- *Open and closed system.* In one way, overseas Chinese business culture is a very closed system. It has developed on its own premises and has been very little influenced by other business cultures. Also, the overseas Chinese keep very much to themselves and are quite secretive about what they are doing.
- *Systems environment.* On the other hand, overseas Chinese business culture has an environment in the sense that it is operating in a given economic context. This context, which in this study consists of seven different countries, varies from quite poor, like the Philippines, to rather rich, like Singapore. The researcher found the overseas Chinese business culture extremely flexible and adaptive *in its daily operations*.
- *Real systems vs. models and interpretations of systems.* The real overseas Chinese business culture is filled with facts. However, as mentioned earlier, the researcher concentrated on coming up with an analysis of this real system and bothered very little about modelling all the factive details of it.

- *Magnifying level.* The researcher, for practical reasons, used different magnifying levels in his five perspectives (compare Figure 11.7), from very high when studying public material and the literature, to very low when conducting his own field research, studying individual overseas Chinese in their daily operations.
- *Systems relations.* As mentioned earlier, the components in the researcher's systems analysis consisted of "basic values, beliefs and assumptions". He did not specify the relations between these components further than simply talking about "influences". So, the relation between, say, component (a) and component (b) is to be read as that the components *mutually* influence each other, without clarifying what this influence consists of.
- *Structural and processual perspectives.* The researcher took the overseas Chinese business culture as a *structural* given without studying in any detail how it has developed and continues to develop interactively (compare the researcher's definition of "culture"). The result of the study was, from the start, always meant to provide a structural basis for further comparative studies of SME cultures in different parts of the world.
- *Systems analysis, systems construction and systems theory.* No new system was constructed in this case. The purpose of the study was to come up with a picture of overseas Chinese business culture by analysing it as a system.

Controlling validity

No control of validity was made apart from the fact that he made sure that the results from the five different perspectives, as far as overseas Chinese business culture was concerned, corroborated each other. This was enough, according to the researcher, to have confidence that he had traced and presented a valid picture of *overseas Chinese business culture seen as a systems structure.*

Reporting the results

The results of this research led to a major report and an article in a so-called recognized scientific journal. The researcher came up with a concluding systems model of overseas Chinese business culture as illustrated in Figure 11.8 overleaf.

Figure 11.8. should be read such that every *component*, that is, every "basic value, belief and assumption" influences every other component in a complex pattern of finality relations. The common core Ω becomes the symbol for what is not possible to directly touch and see, but what exists as the glue of the system. In that way it keeps all the components together as well as becoming its external borderline against the environment.

When the researcher reported his results, he made sure that the reader could comprehend that it was impossible to come up with just *one* picture of overseas Chinese business culture from such a huge amount of data being collected. At the same time he pointed out clearly that his conclusions could not be applied outside his own study area, seven countries in Southeast Asia. This is all in line with the systems view, as we have seen earlier in Chapter 9.

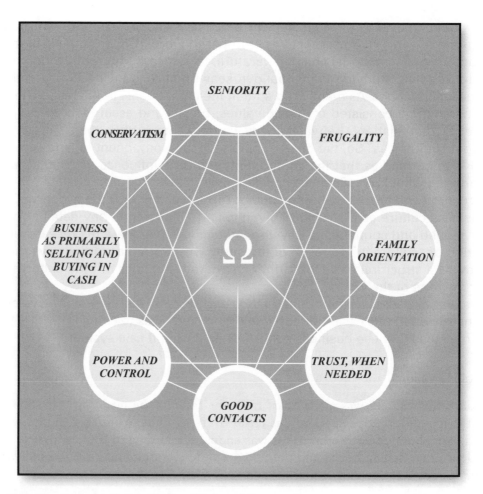

Figure 11.8 The Business Culture from a Structural Perspective

This chapter has provided two examples of systems applications, one regarding a consulting assignment concerning an organizational problem, the other concerning to map the business culture among overseas Chinese. Both cases provide an insight in the intricacies that are sometimes associated with doing systems research. However, it is clear from both cases that doing systems research means, above all, to make sure that all the steps in an operative paradigm fit each other and that conclusions can be drawn often only very late in the process of creating business knowledge using the systems approach.

POINTS OF REFLECTION

1. In Business systems are normally seen as having *no fixed boundaries*. What are the "no fixed boundaries" in the two cases in this chapter and what lies outside these boundaries?

2. As far as formulating the problem in a *guiding study* with a systems approach we can note what?

3. Try to come up with some explanation of when a *definition* of "culture" (compare Case II) should be restricted in business and not in, for instance, Social Anthropology.

4. Reality in the systems view consists of *objective* and *subjective facts*. Please provide examples of objective as well as subjective facts in the two cases in this chapter.

5. Both cases in this chapter are taken from the so-called developing world. Would the *operative paradigm* have been different in either of the two cases if the study area had been the so-called developed world?

6. In Case I, the consultant Stewart is applying a *structural perspective* on the problems of the company, which means that he will focus on aspects like …?

7. At the end of Case I, Stewart suggests a *task force* be appointed. What would you suggest if you were member of this group?

8. In Case II, the definition of an SME is "A small or medium-sized enterprise is one which is independently owned and operated, which is in business for profit, and which is not dominating its field of operation". Would any other definition of an SME make a difference to the study and, if so, what?

9. In Case II, the researcher starts by conducting a methodical procedure, which aims at focusing in on the study area. Provide some typical characteristics of the researcher's thinking at that point and reflect how you might have done it in another way.

10. The researcher in Case II uses five different perspectives in his methodic plan. What was the basic logic behind this plan?

RECOMMENDED FURTHER READING

See the end of the Appendix and visit the website below.

Become a worldwide partner as a *knowledge creator* in the development of *Methodology for Creating Business Knowledge* by visiting the website: **www.knowledge-creator.com**. Here you can contribute by asking your own questions and you will also find answers to the most frequently asked questions. The website has been developed alongside this third edition of the book and the questions posted there will be used to provide input for future editions.

12 THE ACTORS APPROACH

> This chapter provides two examples of the actors view in application. The first provides an action-oriented, explorative experiment around organization and leadership in business development. The second is a historical diagnosis of the building materials trade in Country S for the purpose of denoting conceptual meaning in order to create an understanding.

INTRODUCTION

It has already been pointed out that the explicit ambition of the actors approach is to function as a creative and reorienting field of knowledge. Furthermore, the actors approach, with its ultimate presumption of human nature and construction of reality, encourages an experimentally searching attitude toward both how knowledge is developed and how it is formed in relation to actors in the study area, as well as to actors outside the area. So, within the actors approach there may be studies that create knowledge with highly varied characteristics as far as their immediate forms of expression are concerned. In the mediating – reflective – forms of expression, on the other hand, the ultimate presumptions of the approach become apparent.

The applied examples we describe here provide two informative knowledge-creating cases for the reader because they are quite different from each other but are both research oriented within the framework of the actors approach.

We want to point out at this stage that this practically oriented chapter, like Chapter 6, contains a number of so-called synthetic concepts, such as dialectics, process and totality. These concepts cannot be expressed in extensive descriptions, such as the criteria for determining what dialectics is and what it is not. In other words: if, in the presentation, an attempt had been made to create analytical concepts out of these synthetic descriptive tools, the attempt would probably have been on the wrong track – at least as far as the actors approach is concerned. What we have attempted is to determine the meaning of this type of synthetic concept in a number of different contexts. This led to allowing the concepts to keep their position as intuitive reality concepts.

CASE I: DEVELOPMENT OF BUSINESS AND ACTIVITIES

Starting point

In order to discover possible interest in a *common research project*, one researcher contacted a number of key persons in an international major corporation operating in the engineering industry. The idea of an action-oriented project was developed during those conversations. The idea was that a knowledge-creation integrated in work should be combined with an explorative activity around the organization of the corporation and its leadership for business development.

The knowledge interest was innovative and *the knowledge ambition* to inspire the actors to an explorative and experimenting way of working of their own as far as R&D and the and development of business and activities were concerned, and to try to replace the company's technocratic language of modelling with a more entrepreneurial and artistic – vivifying – approach.

In all, thirty-two project leaders in charge of business development were participating together with their senior group for R&D in the corporation.

The *first phase* of the project was completely based on the premise that the researcher together with the senior group in an unconventional way were to develop the framework of an action-oriented, explorative experiment on the theme of the development of business and activities. The researcher had earlier chosen to call these kinds of meeting "production philosophical" in order to stress that the meetings were about production as well as reflection. (Compare the two mutually dependent elements of a dialogue: reflection and action. See "Dialogue" in Chapter 6.)

In the *second phase*, separate dialogues with the project leaders were conducted, this in order to illustrate the problems and possibilities of creating something in an ordered fashion.

In the *third phase*, the senior group (nine people) was confronted with the result of the second phase, this in a new so-called production philosophical meeting, in order to develop one proactive *flow* of business renewal for the future, where what is potential in what is factual could be released.

In order to catch the soul and what is qualitative in this purpose, the researcher chose to develop a *methodics* that in itself should be a mirror of this *flow*.

Operative paradigm as experimental flow

The purpose that the researcher and the senior group agreed upon was consequently that the actors should research themselves and their own life-world by going outside the conceptions in the established language of the corporation. By this they should be given the possibility in a creative and language-developing way to come up with proposals to different types of development programmes for their own activities; programmes which were based on the passion, creativity and commitment of the participants. The project was christened "Luminous power", because the seniors had asked what could happen if the present business concept started to totter. At the same time they experienced the feeling, as it was phrased, "that the embers of the developers of the corporation do not glow as strong as before".

The whole thing resulted, as mentioned above, in two production philosophical days and nights (meeting 1) as well as two days and nights six weeks later (meeting 2) plus dialogues in between with twenty-three colleagues (project leaders) to those nine who were members of the senior group. The researcher summarized this in a *procreative report* to be used in a summing-up meeting in the corporation a few months after meeting 2 (see Figure 12.1).

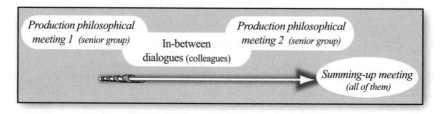

Figure 12.1   The Flow of Experimental Acts

The work up until the summing-up meeting with the procreative report can only be described in broad outlines. The "real flow" was, of course, much more multifaceted and filled with content than a summary can convey. It entered, for instance, the life of every actor in a unique way.

From a methodological point of departure this case can be called a typical case of how *experiments* can be done with the actors view as a guiding star. The *methodical procedures* take place in a dialectical play with *methodics* and constitute as such an *operative paradigm* as a *flow* of experimental acts. By trying to describe parts of the researcher's way of thinking and acting, and by concretely illustrating some of what is created in this flow, it is our hope that the reader explicitly, as well as by reading between the lines, shall be able to interpret the creative play that has taken place between the methodical procedures and methodics.

Production philosophical meeting 1

The questions

The *methodical procedures* of the first meeting were composed by the researcher with the intention of letting participating actors begin by reflecting on how they interpreted their own metaphorically formulated project title "Luminous power", and to relate these denotations of conceptual meaning to three aspects of existence: *life itself*, *work* and *leadership*. (With *the idea of flow* as a guiding star, the composition – methodics – of the second meeting had to wait until later.) The nine participants, therefore, were told – as a "ticket of entrance" to this first meeting – to bring along three questions. The researcher had formulated his request like this: "Three questions You – from the bottom of Your soul – would like to put to a person with 'Luminous power'." The first question is to touch on *life itself*, the second *work* and the third *leadership*.

The deeper undercurrents of business development

At the meeting the actors, divided into three groups, were looking, as a first step (and with possibilities to relate to a number of distributed novels and textbooks around life and passion), for *undercurrents* in typed out copies of all the questions (referred to as 'entrance tickets'). It was important to the researcher that the actors here should meet their own *first hand expressions*, that is, those expressions that were the same as the experiences when the questions were formulated. This first step also meant that every group came up with common condensations of their denotations of conceptual meaning of the project title *Luminous power*, starting from those three aspects of existence mentioned earlier, that is, life itself, work and leadership, using the following new questions and reflections.

About undercurrents of life itself:

- Is Luminous power an internal power which is beaming outwards?
- Deep feelings, human values and lively imagination – are they the power source of the luminosity?
- Where is the dividing line between being Luminous and being possessed?
- Is to be possessed to want nobody else to beam?
- Is Luminous power infectious on its own?
- Is the condition to be "infectious" that one has a relationship?
- Can Luminous power extinguish the beaming power of others?
- Is it possible for me to give light to and to extinguish my own beaming power?
- Can I exercise my own beam?

About undercurrents of work:
In order to reach the 'ultimate' state what is required, according to the actors in question, is a mix of the following feelings and values,

engineering skills	inclination	brilliance
joy	freedom	creative
realization	commonality	searching
shared joy	presence	echo
belongingness	courage	curiosity
love	internal energy	flow
succeed/success	ecstasy of joy	longing

About undercurrents of leadership:
Leadership is the way/method to make a group of people reach a certain purpose. But is then *leadership* a work method or a colleagueship? Is it covering all these extremes: order giving,

"the stick" – afraid – punishment, and total wooliness: nobody cares? In these interfaces we can find the following important characteristics of successful leadership: *vision, image, beauty, participation, commitment, inspiration, ethics, politeness, empathy, improvisation* – which it takes time to realize.

Qualification in cultural meeting

One further intention with the first meeting was to give participating actors the possibility to search "the roots" of their own and their colleagues' reflections and to further widen the conceptual framework around "Luminous power" in dialogical meetings with some external and well-known cultural personages with strong Luminous power (one actress, one artist and one author).

In three completely new groupings the participants were holding dialogues with these guests around the undercurrents of *Luminous power* described above. The purpose by changing groups, here as well as later, was in a deep sense to promote a variety of thoughts in a thesis–antithesis–synthesis relationship. The *complexity* that the group had to make sense of was consequently to be illuminated from the point of departure of a large number of angles with the purpose of creating something new and coming up with an *understanding* (not explanation!) – as regards complexity, see "Social science knowledge" in Chapter 6.

The interpretations of the "entrance tickets" (and the following qualification together with invited guests) can also be seen as a process of constituting language – as a part of the creation of *procreative words* that can shape "what is pregnant", and which in an action-oriented fashion is able to create a leadership and an organization where *Luminous power* is something central for all in their activities.

Finish

After some more reflection around the epistemological and linguistic roots of the participants' own texts the production philosophical days in meeting 1 finished with a plenary conservation. In this conversation, by the researcher's request, the following questions were brought up:

a. Which questions are relevant to ask in a "pilot study" around *Luminous power* in the corporation if one wants to take a new step towards a union between knowledge-creation integrated with work and future business development projects?
b. With which actors in the corporation are dialogues to be held? Can a recommended sample be chosen?
c. What does the senior group want the second production philosophical meeting to contain?

In a scheduled meeting between the researcher and the senior group the following week it was decided that the senior group should create a number of questions and choose the first group of actors with whom the researcher should hold *dialogues*. These actors should then, in their turn, recommend other interesting persons to hold dialogues with on the theme in question. The researcher wanted, with these dialogues, to further widen the conceptual framework before the second production philosophical meeting with the senior group. The intention was also that the result of these dialogues should form a knowledge-creating and challenging platform for meeting 2.

In-between dialogues

The questions and shape of the dialogues

During ten days the researcher held dialogues with twenty-three actors in all, all of whom had been chosen through what was, in principle, a recommended sample. The dialogues were held around those ten questions that the senior group had created after meeting 1 (see below). It was important that *the meaning* of those questions, which should *act as a starting assistance* for the dialogues, had its home in *the life-world* of the senior group, a world that had been deepened through meeting 1. The questions from the senior group were the following:

1. When you have experienced something meaningful in your work, which factors have then been influential?
2. Have you ever lost your commitment? What has influenced it?
3. What in your work has given you a real kick?
4. How do you feel when persons around you get a kick?
5. Do you show feelings in your work? If not, why not?
6. In which situations have you felt that you want to go on because of your commitment?
7. What brings you zest for life?
8. Do you admit to yourself and to others when something has not functioned as it should?
9. Do you experience that developing work is a kind of creation?
10. Is it allowed to "play" at work?

All who have held consecutive dialogues with many people – *creative and confidential meetings around a specific theme* – know that it is demanding but also that it can be very enjoyable and informative. The knowledge ambition of the actors view in this context is not in any way to yield to that logic where terms like "interview", "respondent" or "interviewing object" exist. According to the researcher this ambition was successful. In holding dialogues a confidential atmosphere should rule. In the case of the researcher this was manifested, for instance, by the fact that the actors could have the short "conversation guide" with the questions of senior group in front of them.

All dialogues were recorded on tape. All answers from everybody to, and comment on, the ten questions that the senior group had formulated were typed out verbatim. From this material the researcher chose a manageable number of quotes (fifty of them) as a basis of meeting

2. The only guiding star for the selection, apart from condensing and looking for an appropriate number, was to illustrate/give examples of the variety of statements. The statements were then to be used as subjective "fuel" for further creativity together with the senior group during the second production philosophical meeting.

For several reasons it is, of course, tricky for a researcher to *diagnose* and *summarize* the phenomena, or rather types of phenomena, which can be read in fifty statements. Apart from possible perspective blindness with the interpreter there is a risk of bias in that the type of phenomena which the researcher's actors brought up in the dialogues had been given a temporary legitimacy through the form of the pre-formulated questions and by the fact that it was known to everybody that they had been formulated by the senior group. Here, however, an actors oriented researcher should stop for a while!

Those arguments you just read about bias, etc. rest on another conception of knowledge and another methodological view than is the case in this project. The main point of holding a dialogue, and not an interview, was, according to the researcher, to look for *what is potential in what is factual*. If what has been said is not representative of what the actors in their everyday life say together with their colleagues or with their seniors, from the point of departure of an action and knowledge-creating perspective, it is irrelevant in this case. According to the actors view the researcher is, in and through his very presence, always participating in a continuous construction of reality – the researcher cannot stand outside. An argumentation according to the analytical view does not, therefore, belong in that social reality which the researcher is stipulating here and tries to deliver together with the actors – *Luminous power* – as something potential in what is factual.

Production philosophical meeting 2

An explorative methodics

The explorative *methodics* for the second production philosophical meeting were developed by the researcher after the dialogues and an extensive work of structuralization. The number of statements which were to be handled as inflow to the process in meeting 2, being fifty, as mentioned before. The intentions of the researcher included that, in the extensive material, he should methodologically look for *differences* rather than similarities and bring up quotes with a certain *theoretical* connection.

One intention with the second production philosophical meeting was that the senior group should not only meet the reflections from their colleagues and the comments to those questions they had formulated themselves, but the purpose of the researcher was rather to let the quotes participate in a knowledge-creating process, as a real development project, with what is potential in focus – a process where the feelings of the actors for *Luminous power* could get an ever clearer form.

Another intention was that the process as such should deliver creative thoughts around that development which the project had as a purpose as well; to come up with suggestions for different forms of work-integrated, but personal, development projects in the corporation, where the passion, creativity and commitment of its staff should constitute a base.

Back to the fifty quoted statements from the dialogues. In three new groupings of three actors each, the senior group met every quote on a card which had been prepared by the researcher. All the three groups had consequently fifty quote cards as explorative "production material".

In a first stage every group of three members created a "main thread" which included those twenty cards that in their opinion best described this thread, which was derived from the *diagnosis* of the material. The three groups also gave a name to their "main thread". The researcher noted with great interest how the different groups reacted to the quote cards. In spite of the fact that they had *exactly the same* text on their fifty quote cards and that they together consisted of a senior group with some shared life-world, there were clear qualitative differences between the reactions to the quotes. (Please compare with earlier reasoning in Chapter 6 about the possibility of quantitatively comparing and measuring experiences.)

- *Group 1* saw the quotes rather as an expression of a positive and enjoyable attitude among the colleagues.
- *Group 2,* on the other hand, said that "it was profoundly tragic that reality looked this way" as reflected by the texts on the cards. The group also became noticeably depressed.
- *Group 3* thought that the quote cards reflected how important it was for the corporation at this stage to discuss commitment, passion ... "Luminous power" – "where there is a will there is hope", as somebody expressed it on behalf of the group.

In order to increase the dialectical tension as the creative process went on the researcher had every group start by condensing their own "main thread" from the chosen twenty cards *taking away* those ten which they thought described the "main thread" the least, without, however, reducing the variety.

Then the creative work of the three groups was integrated. In a *simultaneous* circular movement, with the ten cards that had been taken out in hand, the group then visited each other's group room. By this explorative movement the researcher did not only want to illustrate, but literally vivify the structure of thoughts and feelings in *dialectics*. The researcher wanted, for instance, to let the participants *carefully* and with *empathy* try to *understand* the intentions of the group that had created the "main thread" they now visited. This was also a prerequisite for the development which was later to take place. This was made concrete by adding five of those ten cards excluded from their own thread to those ten that were already in the room when they entered.

With *understanding* follows also a responsibility. The responsibility of the visiting group was to handle and create a new order among *all* the fifteen, which were now in the visited "main thread".

A further methodical intention was to let the participating actors experience the liberating antithesis, sometimes as a surprising insight, that those cards which had been taken out by their own group because they did "not fit in" among the ten which finally were allowed to condense the own "main thread", may not only fit in but may also bring up another totality in another context.

The circular movement of the groups between the group rooms was carried out in further steps. In the next step every group was handling its five remaining cards (of the ten taken out) in the same way with the next group as above. At the third stage the groups were back to their own "main thread", now with twenty cards laid out again (ten of their own + five + five from the other two groups) – and in a completely new order.

No group was now allowed to change the look of its "main thread". The intention of the researcher was here, among other things, to vivify that experience which consists of being able to accept the fact that somebody else re-creates something which was previously seen as one's own creation, – and then perhaps to discover that the re-creation might very well be as ingenious as one's own ... even if perhaps in another way than one originally thought. The *emancipating creativity of the dialectic reinterpretation*, using the rapture of facing something unknown, was allowed to be delivered here, in the same way that must be done in the real development projects which the corporation had going on, with many developers involved. But now it was about "processing" the human experiences and feelings which otherwise lie as an implicit *undercurrent* to what takes place in the flow of the technical development projects.

In order to further enrich the flow with other experiences, the researcher let the participating actors also listen to musical interpretations of the fresh "main threads", accompanied by verbal interpretations. A concerto was created, where the notes were the different quotes in the three main threads of the groups. A flautist went from room to room with the actors in her wake. She played quote card after quote card, or rather her feeling for their meaning, at the same time as she slowly moved along the main thread on which the cards were now hung.

Afterwards she also *verbalized* her feeling of the three works she had interpreted. That is, that feeling which is created at the same time as she played them as a kind of *first hand expression*.

The words of the musician around the thread of the first group were:

Zest for life, imagination, inspiration ... Poetic!

About those cards that hung on the thread of the second group, she expressed herself as follows:

Inspiration, time, "kicks" are repeatedly asked for. Commitment, but very much about time ... moments of stress – no peace. This was about something that seems to be difficult or wrong. Sad!

The cards of the third group she commented on like this:

Much thought, deeply philosophical. "Kicks". Attempts to show feelings and a willingness to develop ... move on. But a feeling that "we are not getting anywhere" or that "it stands still". Searching!

Compare the interpretation of the flautist with how the three groups had first reacted on seeing the quote cards (see above) and how these came to influence their work, in spite of the fact that the groups in a flow had participated in developing all three main threads. That imprint made by the original group was consequently alive as an active undercurrent and pointer of direction, even when the other groups were to condense the message with their cards. *That is the way it can also be in real projects!* This became, according to the researcher, an important eye-opener for all the actors (compare the experiment at MIT under "Seeing and thinking" in Chapter 2).

In his procreative report the researcher wrote among other things:

> The fact that interpretation of texts and undercurrents of linguistic expressions appear with such a variety in what seems to be a homogeneous group (the senior group) and the fact that these then can point out the direction for other developing thoughts should be an eye-opener for all that research which is working with questionnaires. And where the researcher assumes the right from an outside perspective to ask the questions and interpret the answers. This also concerns, of course, personal surveys and traditional market research studies.

Business artistic creation

After this interpretive experience the groups were given the task of *giving names to* their "main thread" in the form that it had now been developed by the other groups. The task was then to choose the three cards which in their opinion contained the *essence* of what they saw in the depth of their "main thread" (see "Denotation of conceptual meaning and scientific language" in Chapter 6).

Because now there was the time to let the quotes be part of a process, where creation of art and knowledge was to be synthesized – a process to continue to create a language, which could give a shape to the procreative concept *"Luminous power"*.

The intention was materialized as an offer from the researcher to the three groups to create a work of art in a dialectics between their imagination, the name they had chosen for their "main thread" and the three quotes. The only physical prerequisite that the researcher gave was that the three quotes should be part of the final work. As tools each groups was given one canvas with a frame, one set of paint and brushes and an easel.

So, in a "chaos" filled with passion three procreative forms with great future potential power of thought were born. All actors saw how their way to create businesses related to personal development, which all, in some inscrutable, way had directed their intentionality during the whole process, and which now in an unpretentious and self-evident way had shown its form in the three works of art. They also saw that the works symbolized a plain order in an intentional future developing flow. The dialectical interpretation of the quotes and the sorting of the cards, which the researcher had developed as one of his methodical procedures, had given a *language created in a spirit of community*. Starting from the insights that had been won in this explorative experiment, a deep concretization of thoughts had taken place around future R&D and business development, where procreative activities not only are to be taken advantage of, but also used to guide the future.

The production philosophical work was now finished. The researcher had by then shown that creating knowledge and creating art are difficult to separate. During the vernissage where the three works of art were shown, participating actors were amazed by their own creative power: by the powerful – and understandable – symbolism, by the aesthetics they were able to create during such a short time, by how fast time had passed. They were also amazed by how the whole process in itself vivified precisely what they wanted from the company – the ability to deliver what is potential out of what is factual in a provocative organization where all actors are offered the opportunity to establish their own personal imprints.

The procreative report

The researcher wrote, in this procreative report, as follows under the four headings below:

The embryo to businesses

> The fact that the R&D activities in the corporation had long since stretched themselves far beyond the industrial *metaphor* as a kind of component in a system – which develops physical products and technical solutions to a network of individuals who then develop embryos of businesses – became ever clearer in the exploring experiment. In successful companies, construction, production and customer value are so interwoven in thought and action that only an *artistic* way to proceed – in the sense of a continuous, creative way to proceed throughout the whole value chain – is able to take on this dialectic challenge.
>
> Into the arena then enters a language which does not traditionally belong to the systems oriented world that is inhabited by engineers and economists. That language, which is used by, among others, inventors, entrepreneurs, culture workers and visionary business people, insists on being given space. Such a language is used by persons who often – in a symbiosis with other aspects of life – are literally shaping and living with their own creation. A kind of master quality as an idea for life! A quality which shapes meaningful cultural totalities, out of which creativity, vitality, feeling and passion collect their power of brilliance.

With the disposition of the master

> Is not the disposition of the *business developing research* deceptively similar to the creator of culture? The Artist's, the Musician's, the Author's ... ? The constant exploration towards ever-higher quality, where the passion to express and shape – the right of all of us to create our own audience/market – is our genuine creative fuel for creating knowledge. A disposition where we are allowed to genuinely be ourselves and are allowed to place this, our own subjectivity, as personal imprints in what is created.

Enriching the encounter with the audience/customer/market

"Let me with some examples sharpen the eyesight for the work of creating culture and arts as a metaphor for creating businesses, and then provides a few such examples. "

There have been many attempts to clarify that mysticism and magic which arise in the genuine meeting with art. It is commonly designated with words like "meaningful", "qualitative", "inspiring" and "enriching". *It is a common opinion as well* that one has to *want* to feel empathy – feel its enjoyment from just embarking upon experiencing a qualitative meeting.

There is also an opinion that knowledge of an artist, an author or an opera composer provides a ground to grow from. A ground where to plant the work in order for it to grow in scope. A further idea, which is related to the first, is that if one knows how the artist thought and felt when he made his painting, how the author experienced his own writing or how the situation of life was for the opera composer when he composed his work, that *understanding* in some incomprehensible way is fused with the experience of the work.

Can we use the analogy/art metaphor to open for another, more genuine and vivifying customer and research perspective? Can we think of this art analogy as a vision for a description of the experience of the brand of the corporation?

Business embryos as works of art

If we let business embryos of the R&D activities take place on the stage of the art metaphor, we would put up a number of *requirements* to create vital *conditions* for their growth processes (given that the metaphorical idea above is ingenious). These conditions will widen the framework for what we call development near the customer. They also unite this development with the legitimate right of the creator of knowledge to passionately create his/her own audience – create the need of others – and open up for new eras.

One *first* condition would be: *The power and courage* in small as in large to look for the unknown business situation, to deliver what is possible out of what is factual and to go beyond the customer-specific normal distribution of normally distributed differences.

The *second* would be to *meet an audience* which does not only *want* to face the possibility of a future business, but which at the same time *can* give the Business and themselves creative nourishment, which can enjoy just to see the business (relationship) develop – listen and look at it again and again.

The *third* condition of the business embryo would be that its artistic creators – the engineering artists – are provided with rich possibilities to enter a *dialogue* with the "customer", both around the very creative process itself and the intentions of its future life. One could even be able to reach future dialogical and *qualitative* forms such that the creators now and then would be able to meet their "work in reality", to generate new impressions from the external variety, where the works are creating productivity or enriching joy, that is, processes far away from the *quantitative* cooperation in questionnaires which many companies offer their customers – or what the workforce is offered in surveys of personnel – and instead

(Continued)

(Continued)

work with genuine and near encounters (as production philosophical meetings), for instance, with a limited number of actors (customers), where developers, constructors, fitters and sellers under creative forms similar to social gatherings are able to meet their "audience" for *dialogical* developmental leaps. What would not such annual meetings, where the personal imprints are put into process and product, mean for personnel as well as for customers, not to forget future businesses! And then I mean not test panels or focus groups, but something completely different!

CASE II: A LINE OF BUSINESS WITH ADAPTATION PROBLEMS

Introduction

The study has a knowledge interest oriented at understanding, but it could also, according to the two researchers who conducted it, have had an emancipatory interactive action as a starting point for later stages of the study, so that in creating changes in the building materials trade the knowledge of both the actors and the researchers is developed. This did not occur within the framework of the project reviewed here; the researchers chose instead the feedback of their descriptive and ideal-typified languages and a model for synthesization as an antithesis. The ideal-typified presentations in the case provided a means of capturing and vivifying the specific character of what was studied. What is general and what is specific are synthesized in order to stress what is *essential*. "Ideal", therefore, has nothing to do with ideal in the sense of the best, the most ethically correct thing to do, or the like. The reader should therefore be aware that the methodical procedures and the methodics (the operative paradigm) cannot be presented as they were gradually (dialectically) developed, but are shown in a reconstructed form.

The following presentation will be constructed mainly around direct abstracts from the report that originally presented the study. These abstracts are, for pedagogic reasons, structured and classified somewhat differently from the original version. What might be most interesting – the researchers' thought processes during the development of the diagnosis – is not explicit. Implicitly, however, diagnostic thinking exists in the very presentation of what has been the basis of the development of the descriptive and ideal-typified languages.

History

Until the end of the l9XOs, trading in building materials in Country S was characterized by a notable passivity as far as renewing the distributional channels was concerned. During this particular decade, the great majority of all wholesale/retail sales of building materials was distributed through lumberyards. These points of sale generally had their historic roots in the firewood industry, which also dealt in building materials because their seasonal demand resulted in a more even utilization of capacity throughout the year. In the south of the country, it was common to combine selling building materials with the sale of grain; and in the north, building materials were often combined with the sale of iron.

At the end of the 19XOs, a building materials trader with a full range of products would act as wholesaler, retailer or both, with such main products as carpentry, timber, boards, bricks, cement, ceramic products, and so on. By the end of the 19XOs, nearly 1,000 traditional building materials traders shared a market worth US $4–$5 billion dollars. Approximately the same amount was delivered outside the building materials trade industry, directly from building materials manufacturers to the building construction industry. This latter share, which continued to increase, was noticed with a great amount of dissatisfaction by the traditional building materials traders. These traders saw their opportunity to supply building materials for new buildings under construction being seriously restricted. Furthermore, they saw the most attractive parts of their product range being sold by building materials departments in hardware and building supply stores and supermarkets.

A diminishing share of sales of supplies for new construction, along with tough competition from hardware and lumber supply stores and supermarkets for an attractive portion of the product range for craftsmen and the increasingly important do-it-yourselfers, are only two examples from a whole problem complex that the traditional building materials trade faced at the end of the 19XOs. It was also clear that the building materials trade, in comparison with most other businesses, was characterized by a definite passivity in important functions like marketing, the layout of their premises, the development of a product range, the education of personnel, and so on. The distinct structural change that took place in the building market in general – especially during the 19XOs – consequently confronted the building materials trade with difficult adaptation problems. One type of adaptation took place during 19X8 to 19X9, however, when several building materials traders put their money into hardware and building supply stores specializing in building materials. But this step later proved to lead to a completely new set of problems.

The starting point for the study

The problems described above could be seen as the starting point for the present study. The study was conducted as a research project in which the researchers wished to bring about an understanding of the *denotation of conceptual meaning* that was built into the *historic* developmental pattern of the business. Through such research it was the researchers' hope that the actors in the business in question would be better able to understand their situation and, as a consequence, be in a position to develop a better harmony with the market (the researchers used the concept of *harmony* in a dialectical sense – synthesization – that should not be confused with the definition of harmony as fitness in the systems approach (see "Some important concepts of classic systems models" in Chapter 5).

Problem and purpose

From the point of departure of research, consulting and other investigative activities that are presented by the actors approach, it follows that problem formulation and purpose are developed gradually as the researchers/consultants/investigators become dialogically connected with the actors. This means, of course, that an actors creator of knowledge must refrain from presenting detailed problems and specified purposes too early.

In this study, it was clear from the start that the idea, based on a *dialectic denotation of conceptual meaning,* was to develop a model for *constitutional ideals* (that which constituted the business in question), in order to be able to put a *synthesization model* together, constructed as an example of *typified cases.*

The development of the operative paradigm

Operative paradigms as a continuity

An operative paradigm is, as we know, the instrument for a consistent and constructive experiencing of a study area, using a methodological view as a base. An *operative paradigm,* in the sense of the actors approach, is therefore *developed gradually* during the research/ consulting/investigation process, as a process of searching for harmony between the methodological view and the finite provinces of meaning of the actors (i.e. the study area).

The description of the development of the operative paradigm that the two researchers provided *a posteriori* in their research report contains sections that are of importance to the development of *understanding* by the reader. These are presented below.

Historical development and description

Studying the past – the history of an organization – places the researcher in a different relationship to the study area, both as an observer and as an actor, than studying current activities and events. When studying the past, the interactive situation is limited to the traces left by history and the traces that can be generated. As an actor, the researcher cannot, of course, influence events in the history being studied. The future characteristics of the organization in question can be influenced, however, because a historical description may improve understanding and consequently the possibilities for handling and changing the organization as well.

In order to construct an *operative paradigm* that takes this into consideration from the point of departure of a *dialectic* denotation of conceptual meaning, three *methods* were developed (based on a number of techniques for collecting data). The methods were made up of *the actors intentional method, the actors constitutional method* and *the organizational documentary method.* The background for these methods will be described below, along with techniques for collecting and arranging data that can be of relevance.

Because statistically based techniques for collecting data are considered less relevant in actors studies, a *procedure for recommended selection* was developed and will be described below. During the course of the study, it was found necessary to *classify* the companies that were part of the building materials industry. The methodical design of this classifying procedure will also be reported.

The description of these parts is designed in such a way that it will differentiate *methodical procedure* from *methodics.*

Actors intentional method

Methodical Procedure: This method is called the actors intentional method because of its purpose: to focus on *subjective* elements and *everyday* conceptions. It is therefore aimed at an understanding of the social reality from a *dialectical* thought process. A study aimed at *dialectically denoted conceptual meaning* in a wide research field – such as the adaptation problem facing the building materials trade in Country S – must not, according to the actors approach, exclude the *subjectively given conceptual meaning of the dialectics.*

If overall structural phenomena are to be understood, they must include an actors *intentional* dimension as a basis for that understanding. As creators of knowledge then place this in a wider dialectic context, they will usually be better able to interpret and to understand the actors concerned. This means that this method will provide *one* part of the dialectic interpretation: the collection of "live" subjective finite provinces of meaning.

The data collection techniques of interest are those that have a *dialogical* status. By the phrase "dialogical status" the researchers pointed out that data collection techniques that do not allow the actors to correct themselves and the researchers were not acceptable. Depending on information requirements, they wanted to use everything from very informal talks to more structured face-to-face or telephone interviews. The ongoing combination was meant to prevent the researchers from taking certain starting points for granted and, as a result, fixing their attention in certain directions, something that is common in studies based on other approaches where that which is unstructured is given the epithet of "pilot study or generating hypotheses".

Using methods in which dialogue is central always entails being particularly attentive to the resource side. To resolve this, the researchers chose a methodical development of their most dialogically based technique for collecting data, which they called "Talks and informal deliberations", with an eye on resources, from their own point of departure as well as that of the actors. These talks were divided into two groups, *planned* and *unplanned*. "Planned" talks meant only that they were to be conducted in a separate and undisturbed place at work and recorded on tape. "Unplanned" talks were those that might come up spontaneously, such as in coffee rooms or when walking around in the company – in other words, all the talks that did not take place in separate rooms and were not recorded.

Both the planned and the unplanned talks were divided, according to their mode of accomplishment, into *planned unconditional* and *interview-like* talks. A planned unconditional procedure was an attempt on the part of the researchers to arrange an unstructured planned talk with actors in a problem area in order to initiate a narrative style that would make explicit to the actors that their experiences were important. As far as unplanned talks were concerned, it was only a matter of initiating a talk within some problem area. The planned and unplanned interview-like talks were intended to provide answers to more detailed questions that appeared as the study went on.

Methodics: The above-mentioned classification of the talks, related to the methodics of data collection, is illustrated in Figure 12.2.

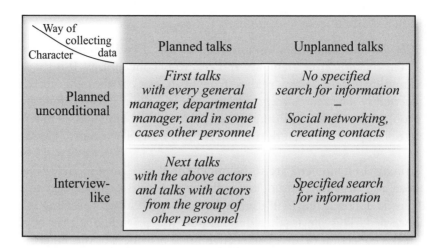

Way of collecting data / Character	Planned talks	Unplanned talks
Planned unconditional	*First talks with every general manager, departmental manager, and in some cases other personnel*	*No specified search for information – Social networking, creating contacts*
Interview-like	*Next talks with the above actors and talks with actors from the group of other personnel*	*Specified search for information*

Figure 12.2   Groups of Talks and Informal Deliberations

Actors constitutional method

Methodical Procedure: The primary purpose of the actors constitutional method is to activate important actors in an independent assignment in which they have the opportunity, during a longer period of peace and quiet, to consider the questions the researchers want to highlight. The idea behind this procedure is that the researchers – partly through descriptions made in the actors' *own descriptive language* (an authentic language as first hand expressions) and partly through descriptions made within *a given frame of reference* provided by the researchers themselves – improve their chances for seeing the totalities and parts the same way the actors do.

These descriptions must have a *subjective* character in order to reflect how the actors perceive the structure of the organization from their own position, partly through the frame of reference provided and partly in their own *descriptive language*.

The collecting and constructing procedures are related to questions like the following:

- To what organization does the description refer?
- What in the organization should be highlighted?
- What is the organization's environment?
- What time period is the description to cover?
- What is the educational level of the actors?

From these ideas, two different techniques for collecting data were constructed that correspond to (1) a description in the actors' descriptive language, and (2) a description based on a provided frame of reference. The former was called a *history-critical phase description* and the latter a *history-periodic organizational description*. (The actors constitutional method requires that a good relationship be established with the actors concerned, as it is rather demanding in terms of work.)

Methodics: Both techniques required a long explanation, so assignments were presented in person. The history-periodic organizational description, which was to be given based on a provided frame of reference, was accompanied by an introduction to the research problem and instructions for what was to be done and how, plus preprinted templates to draw and write on. The other technique (history-critical phase description) had *only* an introduction to the research problem (the same as for the history-periodic organizational description); additional information was provided on delivery. This information is briefly summarized as follows:

> Try to think back in time and try to remember what things were like ____ (individually, depending on number of years employed in the organization) years ago; then move forward in your own mind and try to describe how you have experienced the critical events that have hit the building materials trade during this period. Try to place this in relation to different phases in the building materials trade and its environment. You will have about three weeks to write this down; we will contact you by telephone in the meantime.

Organizational documentary method

Methodical Procedure: The organizational documentary method aims at capturing the historical process starting from documentary material. This is doable if the material covers aspects that illuminate what is wanted and potentially *possible* as well as *actual/factual* aspects that illuminate the problem from different phenomenal angles. In the actors approach, the *secondary data method is based on phenomena rather than on subjects.*

This means that the area of phenomena, not subjects, should broadly indicate the search of the organizational documentary material. The data that must be collected for each, ever more extensive study consist of the organizational documentary material that considers the general historical background – the development of society in general.

Methodics: The organizational documentary research was conducted in accordance with these ideas. After a *planned unconditional* phase, the documentary material crystallized in a way that made it possible to draw up a specific plan. This led to the scheme depicted in Figure 12.3 overleaf, which shows the organizational documentary material divided into categories and sources.

Selection

Methodical Procedure: Figure 12.4 illustrates how representatives of the structure were to recommend other representatives inside the structure, as well as individual building materials traders.

Figure 12.4 also indicates how building materials traders recommended some from within the structure as well as other building materials traders. The researchers' own selection was added to this (see "Methodics" below). The methodological point was to minimize the risk of

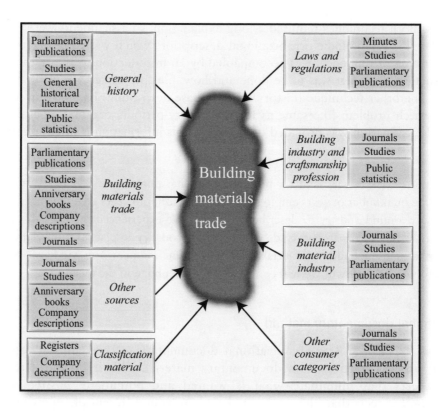

Figure 12.3   Categories and Sources of Organizational Documentary Material

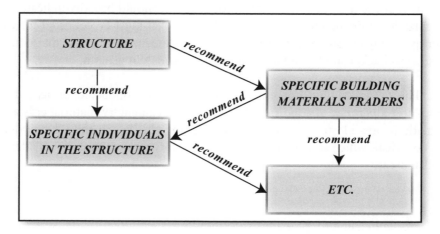

Figure 12.4   Recommendation Procedures

ending up with everybody discussing the same problem, from the same angle and proposing the same solutions; this can easily become the consequence of talking only with those who are recommended.

Methodics: The organizational documentary work, together with experiences from previous interaction phases and telephone interviews with all of the representatives of the Wood and Building Material Traders Central Organization in Country S (SWB), eventually gave an indication of the organizations from which it would initially be appropriate to select representatives for longer talks (real dialogues) according to the *actors intentional method.*

The *initial* selection from each organization consisted of those who had at least fifteen years' experience in the industry and who were also in a position to have an overview of the entire picture. During this introductory work, recommendations were always given in accordance with the previously outlined idea. This procedure, when later reviewed, proved to be very rewarding as far as the selection of important actors was concerned, both those important to the organizational change and those with considerable experience. The strength of the selection procedure also lay in making selections that were based on *understanding.*

Classification work

Methodical Procedure: As the project proceeded, it became more and more obvious that a classification of the building materials trade in Country S was necessary for a more comprehensive understanding. Besides, it was considered valuable to supplement the classification with information from the public records to get an idea of the activity in, for instance, the types of ownership from 19X8 onwards. The registers referred to seven national organizations.

The purpose was to find some kind of basis for classification, to discover whether this varied by geographic location and to establish the companies' backgrounds in the operations from which sales of building materials originated. Companies that were to be included in the classification had to meet the four demands listed below, which were developed in cooperation with two representatives from SWB and three building materials traders. The qualifying criteria were:

1. product range: some building material group apart from wooden products and products based on wood
2. warehousing: having the product range in item 1 in stock
3. terms of payment: both cash and credit
4. an expressed policy of selling to private persons – do-it-yourselfers

In order to apply the classification, a scheme with classification variables, which was to be completed by each major organization in question, was constructed in cooperation with one representative from SWB and two other actors in the organization.

Methodics: In order to contain the total population, of all those satisfying the above demands, the sources were divided into two groups:

a. registers from all of the seven national organizations
b. telephone directories: all of them (a total of 24).

Because the information in the several registers and the phone directories overlapped, it had to be checked for duplications. The seven registers were then approved in a presiding meeting of SWB and a clear signal was given that the regional representatives *(n = 19)* were to ask the companies for the information and complete the diagram. Other organizations also gave their go-ahead for this.

This completed the design of the classification work with "the register companies"; only "the telephone directory companies" remained. These were later classified by means of telephone information and with the assistance of a representative of SWB.

The total methodics of the study

By means of the methodical procedures just described, the researchers created a *harmonious* combination of methods for studying the problem the line of business had had and was still experiencing. We have also been able to see the methodics used for the different methods. The total methodics of the study, then, amounted to nothing more than the researchers' ways of combining the different methods in order to achieve the best possible combination effect from an *understanding* point of departure. Furthermore, the selection procedure provided an essential opportunity for the researchers to ask themselves what the various recommendations meant (why do people recommend the way they do?).

The combination being sought was based on the idea that the actors *constitutional* method would function as a certain indicator for selecting and collecting organizational documentary material, and the actors *intentional* method as a verification of these selections. Moreover, the pure combination of the methods and the selection procedure based on the recommendation method was intended to give an understanding that permitted specific other selections of data to be undertaken.

Two case studies of building materials trade companies, thirty-one "dialogues" and informal deliberations, eighty-eight personal interviews, sixty-two telephone interviews and five seminars were conducted in accordance with *the actors intentional method*. In *the actors constitutional method*, nineteen actors were engaged. *The organizational documentary method* eventually consisted of approximately 10,000 pages of data. A total of 762 building materials trade companies were *classified*.

Through this combination of different methods with its wide variety of data sources and the total amount of data in each source, the researchers could be sure of a good volume of collected *historical* material. The methods and the varying character of associated techniques for collecting data also gave a good coverage of the material.

Feedback and the continuing dialogue

In this research project the developed languages were fed back through a kind of *descriptive dialogue* among the researchers (the written text), the actors in the building material trade, and the scientific community (the readers). As a result, the researchers did not enter the business in a continuous dialogical feedback phase in which the *direct act* could be expressed. Within the frame of some of the substudies – among others, in relation to the two case companies – some continuous dialogical feedback and actions took place with the actors in the study area.

Feedback as a *descriptive dialogue,* which the researchers as a whole chose as a means of feeding their results back into this project, is a common way of feeding back results in the actors approach.

Descriptive dialogue as feedback

The researchers' project had been oriented to visualize and to create an *understanding* of the *denotation of theme* that was behind what was visible on the surface. By going back to the basics and creating an understanding based on the egological sphere, the creators of knowledge can shake off their responsibility in relation to the research/consulting/investigation field, knowing that changes/transformations that take place as a result of various knowledge-creating projects are based on the actors' meaning context.

The gradual emergence of the *descriptive* and the *ideal-typified* languages (dialogue – first hand expressions – diagnosis of situation) was presented in this project's research report in a way that made it easier for the readers (building materials traders and other researchers) to follow how everyday – quoted – forms of expression are refined and shaped and thereby given a distinctive character around which the learning of new attitudes can take off.

Through the *essential* character of the ideal-typified language, the changes that this language can lead to will depend on the situational circumstances in which the language is placed and who places it there. This means that the language and its procreative concepts can function as a *self-diagnostic* instrument and initiate *change-generating* interpretations of the potential in what is factual (the objectified reality).

In this chapter we have been able to follow two different cases with the actors view as a guide for methodical procedures and methodics in real research work. Operative paradigms illustrated show several similarities in their basic formations, but also several methodical differences, which can be directly related to the study area. Through this the cases also clarify the relation between a methodological view and a study area as an operative paradigm is designed as a way to create harmony between the ultimate presumptions of a view and the nature of the study area. Case I illustrates the essence of an experiment according to the actors view, while Case II illuminates the demand in extensive research work for variation and richness in methodical procedures and methodics.

POINTS OF REFLECTION

1. In Case I the researcher introduced something he called "production philosophical meetings". What did he mean by this? Please relate your answer to the *concept of a dialogue!*
2. What is meant in Case I by: *methodical procedures* take place in a dialectical play with *methodics* and constitute as such an *operative paradigm?*

(Continued)

(Continued)

3. Why does the actors creator of knowledge think that it is so important to work with *first hand expressions?*

4. The researcher in Case I is working with several different *methodical procedures* in order to make the senior group deepen and condense as well as broaden their conceptualization of those different linguistic expressions which had appeared in both their own questions and answers, and in those answers that were given in the dialogues between the researcher and their project leaders. So, for instance, the senior group had their own "tickets of entrance" brought into a dialogue together with some well-known cultural personages. What was the researcher's *methodical idea* in all this?

5. Another way that the researcher in Case I used to give perspectives to the work in the senior group was to let a musician in *tones* interpret their "main threads". What was the researcher's *methodical idea* with this? (Compare with the music analogies provided in Chapter 6 under "Denotation of conceptual meaning and scientific language".)

6. As the project went on and as all the participants are deepening their perspectives in Case I, the researcher and the actors in the senior group discover those large differences which existed in the beginning in the linguistic/meanings oriented understanding of the different quote cards, in spite of the fact that the group is supposed to share the same professional life-world. What conclusions can the researcher draw from this as far as *questionnaires* are concerned as a research technique? (Compare with Figure 6.1 *"The Arbnor Uncertainty Principle".*)

7. In the researcher's *procreative report* in Case I, an analogy is drawn with the help of a metaphor of business development – which one? The researcher also relates back to what he earlier referred to as the "production philosophical meeting" and compares with, for instance, focus groups, but asserts that he himself expresses this as "something completely different". No doubt this statement diverts from the ultimate presumptions of the actors view. Give some examples of how the researcher might have been thinking here.

8. In Case II the researcher has developed the following three methods: *the actors intentional method, the actors constitutional method* and *the organizational documentary method*. Describe briefly the intentions behind this methodological development.

9. Case II is a rather extensive study and here there is a *sampling procedure* that also exists in Case I. Which one? Describe briefly the advantages and the disadvantages you can see with this procedure.

10. In Case II the researchers are, as they move on, developing a *descriptive* and an *ideal-typified* language. Describe in a few words the differences between these two (compare also Chapter 6).

11. The researchers in Case II also bring up in their report this matter of *"first hand expressions"* meaning that they are fundamental in developing *language* and *pro-creative concepts* that can function as *self-diagnostic* instruments and initiate *change-generating* interpretations of the potential in what is factual. Describe what the researchers mean by this, plus how in the report they have illustrated – vivified – the connection between the actors' first hand expressions and the language development being done.

RECOMMENDED FURTHER READING

See the end of the Appendix and visit the website below.

Become a worldwide partner as a *knowledge creator* in the development of *Methodology for Creating Business Knowledge* by visiting the website: **www.knowledge-creator.com**. Here you can contribute by asking your own questions and you will also find answers to the most frequently asked questions. The website has been developed alongside this third edition of the book and the questions posted there will be used to provide input for future editions.

PART V
METHODOLOGY OF COMPLEMENTARITY

13 THE VIEWS AS TRANSFORMATIVE OPERATORS

> This chapter is the first of three chapters that conclude this book. One part of our methodological grammar remains. This final part will make our methodology more extensive at the same time as it will make it more advanced. We call this a methodology of complementarity, and it is about how we can, as creators of knowledge, reconcile those methodological views presented previously in this book. This chapter presents this methodology of complementarity and in doing so also introduces some central concepts in this type of knowledge-creating work.

AN INTRODUCTORY SUMMARY

In the twelve chapters so far, we have tried in different ways to illustrate the basis of what might be included in a methodology for creating business knowledge. Some more important subjects of our methodological grammar remain to be discussed. Before treating these subjects, we briefly recapitulate what has been said so far in order to provide a natural transition to the book's conclusion. This is because the three chapters that constitute the *finish* of this methodology for creating business knowledge also, in a way, make the *beginning* of a more personal, conscious application of what has been said so far. Here we present the prerequisites that give creators of knowledge plenty of opportunities to develop our methodological grammar as well as their own activities of knowledge creation, all within the framework of what we have chosen to call a *methodology of complementarity* (Part V).

Chapter 1 laid the foundation of our *language of methodology* with a description of our attitude towards *research methodology*. We claimed, among other things, that conscious development of knowledge in business is far from "just" collecting data and making statements. To be aware of, and reflect upon, the theory of science and the content of methodology is an important task for anyone who wants to understand knowledge-creating studies, and what that knowledge is knowledge about. We made a distinction between *tools, techniques* and *methods*. We also presented the concept of *paradigm* and *ultimate presumptions*. This led to *methodological view* and our conception of an *operative paradigm*, which contains the two main tools/processes: *methodical procedures* and *methodics*.

Methodical procedures refer to how creators of knowledge *arrange, develop and/or modify* techniques into *methods* in the frame of different methodological views. To adapt and possibly modify previous results, theories, or both is also called *methodical procedures*. How creators of knowledge relate and arrange those techniques-made-into-methods logistically in *study plans* and conduct these planned activities for creating knowledge is called *methodics*.

Box 13.1

Methodology in Theory and Practice

When we are talking about methodical procedures and methodics in *theory* we call the methodological point of departure "view". When we are applying this view in *practice*, with its procedures and methodics, we denote it, as said before, "approach". Hereby we also have a distinguishing language for evaluation and discussion of knowledge-creating works in terms of methodology in theory and practice.

Methodical procedures and *methodics* are two very important methodological concepts in the book.

Chapter 2 paid attention to the fact that *critical thinking* is associated with *imagination* and *perspectives*. Such real situations of critical thinking are based on deepened thinking as well as on a creative attitude, this in order to build a serious foundation to the "adventure" that is offered by investigative work in general, and by research in particular. In order to illustrate this, we chose a *practical theme* of entrepreneurship for the chapter. At the end of Chapter 2, *our three methodological views* were introduced and briefly illustrated in relation to this theme of entrepreneurship as a study area.

In Chapter 3, we discussed the *basic conditions* for the three methodological views, their similarities and differences. We compared some of the *ultimate presumptions* of the views; such dimensions as, conception of reality, prerequisites, ambitions and results were illustrated. We also described how the views are focusing *relations* in reality and how they differ. As the analytical view chooses to look at these relations as *causal*, the systems view talks about the relations in terms of *finality* and the actors view sees them as *dialectical*.

Chapters 4, 5 and 6 presented our three methodological *views in greater detail*. Their order of presentation is arbitrary. We chose to consider them in chronological order, but this is in no way meant to be an evaluation of their quality. Please keep in mind that there are no objective and general criteria for choosing among methodological views. There are criteria, but these are valid only *within* a methodological view. It is, to be sure, not uncommon for proponents of the different views to claim that "ours is best", but this can only be supported philosophically and speculatively. What we tried to show above all in Chapters 4, 5 and 6 was the meaning of the most important *basic concepts*, their relation to their *paradigms*, and the *goals* and *ambitions* of the views for creating knowledge.

In Chapter 7 we took an additional step toward practical fieldwork. That chapter was devoted to *methodical procedures* and a number of different *techniques* were presented, which by the methodical procedures for the different views can be designed as effective *methods* for creating knowledge. Presented here were also some techniques that are *specific* to different methodological views as well, techniques that in several respects characterize these different views and their actions in the study area. The different opinions of the views about concepts like *validity, reliability* and *objectivity* were clarified by going to the origin of the concepts and matching them with the ultimate presumptions of the views.

Chapter 8 provided 3 x 6 different examples of arguments and activities that are part of the methodical procedures *applied* in *language* and *action* in our three approaches (please remember that methodological views in application are called *methodological approaches*). By the different examples it was possible to follow how thinking and language was growing depending on which view we started from. Alongside this, illustrations also were provided of how the ultimate presumptions in the different views were expressed in different every-day behaviour and action within the domains of creating knowledge.

In Chapter 9 we introduced *three different study plans*, one for analytical studies, one for systems studies and one for actors studies. The chapter contained a brief description of the way our approaches look at issues of *methodics*. We saw methodological similarities, but mainly differences, in how our three views are to be *applied* in general, that is, are seen as *operative paradigms*. The design process of operative paradigms can be seen as a skill of harmony between ultimate presumptions of a view and a study area. The harmony is a kind of guarantor that those results that are produced are keeping a high knowledge creating quality. The tools/processes of the operative paradigm for this harmony are *methodical procedures* and *methodics*.

Chapters 10, 11 and 12 showed 3 × 2 different examples of how researchers/consultants/ investigators have *applied* the methodological views in various studies, as well as the different techniques and study plans that were discussed in Chapters 7 and 9. The reader could see that methodical procedures and methodics are constructed differently for each of the three methodological approaches.

The design of the methodical procedures (discursive arguments, etc.) was to a large extent given earlier in the *analytical approach*. This meant, for example, that for the two studies reported in Chapter 10 which discussed the application of the analytical view, we referred to a large part of what the view stipulates. Apart from this, we discussed briefly the extent to which the character of the *study areas* might *influence* methodical procedures and methodics. This is a natural consequence of the character of the analytical approach because, as has been made clear, it is based on a model borrowed from the traditional natural sciences where the objects under study are considered to be equal in their essential bases and their nature; so the techniques given earlier are also assumed to be *generally valid*. Then the main point is, by and large, to *choose* the right technique in relation to the knowledge problem at hand. In the two other approaches the situation is more or less different.

The *systems approach* is happy to talk about systems boundaries and magnifying levels (sometimes called external and internal delimitations) and a holistic perspective within the systems framework. A fundamental stage for creators of knowledge is to position *them-selves* in these matters of system environment and magnification. Systems creators of knowledge assume that the factive world consists of complex relations and treat the world as if that were true. They therefore regard all limits as arbitrary but know that they have to be present for practical reasons. There are no *generally valid* rules given a priori for external and internal limitations of real systems that are being studied. When the choice of the extension and content of study objects is made, however, certain rules for designing methodical procedures and methodics are given. These rules are based on a somewhat different *conception of reality* than in the case of the analytical approach.

The *actors approach* is the least formalistic of the three. It is also the approach that most points out the importance of *shaping and creating* methods according to the character of the study area (within the framework of its paradigm). Readers unfamiliar with the actors approach will find that it contains many difficult concepts, such as dialectics, intentionality, externalization, ideal-typified language and constitutional ideals. Because the *conception of reality* of the actors approach is so different from that of the other two, it is necessary for this approach to use a "special" terminology. Otherwise it would be like trying to perform a Beethoven symphony by beating on a drum. On the whole, the actors approach proceeds in a "flow" that allows the study itself gradually to point out possible roads. Although the knowledge creator is in control, this control is not based on the possibilities and limitations of various techniques for creating knowledge, but on a number of metatheories and what is called the creator of knowledge's preunderstanding – that is, his/her acquired experiences from the construction and ambiguous meaning of social reality.

What has been described so far in this book has been deliberately given in terms to emphasize exactly what *distinguishes* each view/approach from the others. This point of departure has several advantages:

- There are greater possibilities for showing what is specific to the view/approach in question.
- The presentation becomes clearer.
- It is possible to discuss the view/approach on its own premises.
- The understanding of what the view/approach stands for is increased.
- The possibility of developing the view/approach further is increased.
- The possibilities for going deeper into the view/approach, philosophically as well as practically, are improved.
- If the ambition is to supplement an approach, the constituents will stand out more clearly; this leads to a more conscious result.

There are also disadvantages:

- The differences among the views/approaches may sometimes be exaggerated.
- The way to supplementation or reconciliation may seem more complicated than necessary.

We have seen in Chapters 10, 11 and 12 that there are creators of knowledge who perform investigations by keeping more or less strictly, inner-paradigmatically, to *one* of the methodological approaches. It is also common in *practice*, however, to approach what we refer to as "a view as transformative operator in a methodology of complementarity". This is because it is possible when creating knowledge to let the three methodological views as approaches creatively supplement each other and *exceed* themselves. In order to see how this can be done, what it means, and how we look upon it, we have developed a methodological grammar, which we will return to later in this chapter. First we want to present some notes about the continuation of the book and some of the ongoing polemics among the proponents of the different methodological views, as a *complementary criticism* that the views level against each other and how they respond. We believe that this provides a further contribution to understanding different methodological positions in business.

The continuation

Four more subjects that are a part of our methodological grammar as a whole remain then to be treated:

1. some of the *complementary criticism* that the different views have addressed against each other – and still do – at both the paradigmatic and at the operative paradigmatic level
2. our *reconciliation* of the three views to a *methodological principle of complementarity* as *transformative operations* (see Figure 13.2 further on)
3. an illumination of this methodology of modifications and possible creative supplements in *practice*. We denote these *view-operations* in application "an approach as transformative operator" in line with our earlier statement: "methodological views in *application* are called *methodological approaches*"
4. methodology as the ultimate business-creating tool in a society based on knowledge.

These four subjects are interconnected and are treated in the remaining three chapters of the book. By and large, the first two subjects are the concern of this chapters and the remaining two are the concern of Chapters 14 and 15 (see Figure 13.1 overleaf).

Quality and complementarity

We have clarified in this book that we do *not* think it is possible to straight off *combine* our three methodological *views*, because that would lead to an eclectic maze – a lack of consistency, stringency and credibility when creating knowledge. Unfortunately, there are still too many theses, dissertations, public and consultant investigations, papers, and more in which it seems that the creator of knowledge has taken, depending on the taste of the day, one concept from here, another technique from there, and a further model from over there. Being confronted with reports in which a creator of knowledge attempts to prove statements by using results arrived at through methods based on ultimate presumptions that only a few pages back were criticized and refuted as untenable does not feel good.

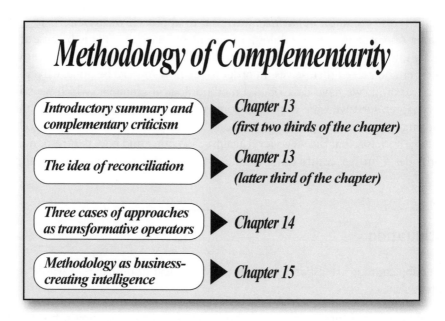

Figure 13.1   An Overview

However, by using our *methodological principle of complementarity* as a concept for a conscious and creative use of methods, all within the framework of one *methodological base approach* (using some of our three approaches as a *transformative operator*), from which we can pick out and use techniques/methods from other approaches (we will return later to how this will be done), we are convinced that *Methodology for Creating Business Knowledge* offers a foundation for the sustainable creation of knowledge.

Box 13.2

The Arbnor/Bjerke Methodological Principle of Complementarity

The potential interdependency in opposite methodological opinions of similar problems is to be used for excellent explanations and/or understanding of them. The principle implies that there are many such problems with this kind of inherent interdependency, which cannot fully be treated by only one of the approaches, in question. Therefore, it is possible and desirable to use complementarity in studies faced with multifaced problems.

Let us start this final phase of our methodological grammar by more firmly clarifying the position of our three methodological views/approaches. This is done by looking at the criticism they have levelled at each other over the years and still do.

COMPLEMENTARY CRITICISM

As the reader surely understands, it is possible to present only a few fragments of the (often heated) debate that has been, and is still, going on between our three methodological views (and in consequence also between our three approaches). What will become quite clear, however, is that there are *semantic complications or a lack of common language* among the three, and we do not mean a minor terminological difference of opinions, but a deep grammatical conflict.

What will be confirmed from the polemics that will be illustrated here is that it relates to the ultimate presumptions on which it is based. This means that the full content of concepts like "operationalization", "finality" and "ideal-type" can only be understood in the context of the paradigm to which each one belongs. In Chapter 8 we tried, with several shorter examples in which *language* and *action* constituted each other's prerequisites, to bring these different worlds of knowledge creation to life. In those practical examples it was possible to follow the deeper grammatical differences that are referred to here.

Based on these insights, one of the things we have attempted in our *Methodology for Creating Business Knowledge* is to present a *methodological language commonality* aimed at making a kind of overarching communication possible among proponents of the different views. We call this overarching methodological language commonality *thematic*. In order for methodology as such to progress, it is important that a thematic language commonality is both established and improved (see **thematic language of methodology** in the Glossary at the end of this book).

Back to the future

A critical polemic among proponents of different scientific thoughts shows most clearly, according to Thomas Kuhn and his description of scientific revolutions, when "conceptual argumentations" run the hottest; that is, before the thoughts are mixed with each other, before they have refined their defense for the sake of refinement alone, and even before they have gained broad experience from participating in theoretical scientific discussions. In the case of our three methodological views, the conceptual argumentations were the clearest in business when the methodological thoughts behind our systems view were "teenagers" and the methodological thoughts behind our actors view, "children".

So, at the end of the 1960s and throughout virtually all of the 1970s, the systems view levelled serious criticism against the analytical view. Yet at the same time, the actors view levelled crushing criticism against both of the others.

The criticism among the proponents of our three different methodological views continues today, though in a less aggressive form. This criticism is equally important, but not equally obvious because most experienced creators of knowledge have learned the rhetoric and the arguments. We think, however, that the reader benefits the most if we, in a fashion similar to the presentations of our methodological views, present the criticism that the views level against each other in a kind of purified, absolute form. This is best achieved by reporting on some of the criticism "already" levelled when the conceptual argumentations were started within business as argumentation among these opposite schools of thought. Besides, it is also our experience and conviction that it is not possible to fully understand any of our views – analytical, systems or actors – without tracing the history of the polemics between them.

It is our hope that the reader, through the reported criticism from "the old days" (which can often still be heard today), will assess the present with an inquiring mind, to unmask, if possible, fellow-travellers lurking, not only in the margins of most study reports, but between the words and the lines of the reports, consciously or unconsciously to hide ultimate presumptions.

A warning for the road

What follows should be seen more as an "invitation" to one's own work than as a "menu" for a comprehensive description of the polemics that has continued for decades (sometimes for centuries), a polemics that is still kept alive by proponents of the three methodological views. When reading on, it is important to appreciate the fact that in this matter, nobody, including the authors of this book, can place him/herself outside him/herself. We have said this before and we say it again. There is no neutral position, no fourth methodological view from which we can objectively scrutinize the other three described in this book. We consequently cannot remain "neutral" and cannot "objectively balance" the criticism. An attentive posture from the reader is therefore in order here.

Criticism of the analytical view

In general

The general criticism that is usually levelled against the analytical view is related to what has come to be known as "dataism" and determinism. *Dataism* is characterized by a reduction of all knowledge to only that knowledge that can be codified and placed in more or less pre-constructed categories of data. It becomes a "naive" empiricism for classifying what is observable; in it, definitions of problems are based on existing techniques for collecting and arranging data. Because the orientation of the analytical view is to reproduce only what is *factive* but not what is *potential*, its critics say it conserves and extrapolates what exists.

This goes hand in hand with *determinism,* which is a philosophical concept of nature and human behaviour and action where every event is causally determined by a chain of cause–effect relations. This scientific thought will reduce human beings' freedom over their future to a question of dependency on the present and the past.

According to some critics, this is reinforced by the fact that analysts look for *general* knowledge without situating this knowledge in time or space or in the idea of human freedom.

Criticism from the systems view

The systems view claims that a basic mistake is made by the analytical view when it tries to isolate a number of variables (parts) from several different (larger) contexts in which these variables – because of the different composition of these contexts – mean different things.

The systems view is therefore critical of the alleged objectivity of the creator of knowledge within the analytical view, because he/she in reality is the one who gives the variables their empirical content. This is consequently not determined by the *complexities* and *totalities* from which they are taken, which would have been the case if empirical relevance were the goal.

By means of the analytical view we do not, according to the systems view, reach real knowledge of the parts in their *temporal* and *spatial* context, a knowledge that is necessary for solving, say, problems in various businesses. The systems view claims that the analytical view, due to its idea of additivity, is not able to handle the complexity and the interconnectedness of modern business. According to the systems creator of knowledge it is necessary to analyse the characteristics of companies as systems in order to be able to *explain* and *understand* serious aspects of problems in industry that are easily neglected when analysing them by the analytical approach.

An analytical creator of knowledge might claim that such procedures would not develop general and objective knowledge. The systems creator of knowledge, however, would respond that organizations are unique and should be studied as such. To reduce organizations and social phenomena to superficial generality by general concepts and ideas is no better as an excuse for the analytically oriented creator of knowledge than the drunk in the anecdote who looked for his watch under the lamppost where there was light instead of in the dark alley where he actually lost it (based on the general theory that the better the light, the more we can see).

Criticism from the actors view

Because the actors view is placed "further away" from the analytical view than the systems view is, its criticism is more comprehensive. The following seven statements about what studies conducted according to the analytical view really mean can summarize the general criticism from the actors view:

1. Things are studied in *isolation* and not in their *meaning context*.
2. What *exists* is studied, but not its origin and its disappearance, that is, not its history and not what is *potential*.
3. Things are studied at *rest*, not in a *dynamic state*.
4. A *distinction* is made between knowledge subject and knowledge object, instead of studying them as a *given* meaning context.
5. The individual is *deprived of free will*, by thinking in terms of causality, instead of having the potential of being *emancipated*.
6. There is an inherent *guarantee* of being right even if one is wrong, by formulating conditions under which a result is valid but which may never have existed in social life.
7. There is no *awareness* of the phenomenon of *self-reference* that exists in all forms of social science studies. That means the a priori *representation* of existing social science knowledge of generality, normality, clichés, uniformity, etc. in individual human beings.

The actors creator of knowledge asserts here, as in other contexts, that there is a decisive difference between *explaining* something statistically (causally) and *understanding* something dialogically (dialectically). Statistical pictures are not the ambiguous courses of events out of which social life forms itself. This perception of social life is like understanding a text by studying its individual words and analysing the frequencies with which they are related to each other, but without considering the fact that the text in its entirety (social life) is an expression for a *meaning context*. By looking for explanations of various social phenomena – not for understanding – we make ourselves outsiders. We do not admit that as creators of knowledge we are actually an active part of the flow of life. The analytical view, then, by means of its statistical method, presents the future as a repetition of the past instead of as a transformation of the past.

This is related to the presumption of reality made by the analytical view and what follows from it: never waver in the ambition of discovering unambiguous and general relations. The opinion of the actors view is that this is completely wrong and that it leads to a distorted understanding of social reality, an understanding in which people are presented as deterministic and totally objectified, and in which they become things in the conceptual hands of the analyst. The actors view sees this as giving birth to knowledge that attracts and is attracted by alienation, passivity, emptiness and meaninglessness in social life and business, instead of being attracted by needs and wants to attract nearness, engagement, creativity and meaningfulness.

In the analytical view, what might be called a totalization has taken place. By this the actors view means that the connection between, (a) a person's (a creator of knowledge or not) inescapable interest in interpretations (e.g. based on previous knowledge – view of life, people, business and society – as a living individual in a social context), and (b) the result of the process of creating knowledge as such, has been lost, has vanished. The techniques are applied in a manner that is taken for granted. They justify their own existence. The actors view therefore claims that the result of the analytical view's process of creating knowledge cannot be anything but trivial – and consequently without subjective (actors-based) meaning; in other words, it is meaningless.

Presuming that "reality is what it is", that is, factive, can, according to the actors view, have very unfortunate consequences for the development of society and business. This is because the analytical view, precisely because of this presumption, is, and remains, unaware of how its procedures for creating knowledge produce in self-reference its own reality instead of the one which is meaningful to us as human beings in everyday life.

The response of the analytical view to this criticism

Creators of knowledge dedicated to the analytical view would be bewildered by the above criticism from the systems and actors views. They would definitely claim that it gives a completely misleading picture of the analytical view. This is because the criticism presented is based mainly on the specific premises on which the other views are based; an analytic creator of knowledge can therefore not answer in the same language. This is a natural reaction, something that will also apply later when we look at the reverse situation (compare with our previous statement that it is not possible to find criteria for choosing the best view – we are reduced to using a philosophical and a speculative reflection).

The analytical view would reject most of this criticism as *metaphysics* and would respond in its own language. A devotee of the analytical view would claim that all science starts with finding out how things really – causally – are related; then theories can be constructed. These theories can then be refined at the same time that new ones are constructed. The best way to find the truth of the factive reality is to quantify and operationalize as far as possible. Facts are important because reality in itself is basically factive and independent of our thoughts about this reality.

Based on the analytical view it is not enough, as it would be in the systems view, to be satisfied with only describing and analysing various mutually related processes and then using this to classify social phenomena against the background of their construction, course and external situation. This does not *explain* anything. Certainly, no science can progress without using categorizations only, such as systems. Science also needs general theses concerning the relations among these classes and categories, because without such theses no *explanations* are possible. Creators of knowledge should not quit after putting different behaviours in various theoretical pigeonholes. The analytical approach maintains that if the mutual connections and finality relations that systems creators of knowledge operate with are broken down, it will be discovered that they are basically related causally – and explanation is placed in the causality.

The talk about complexity and totality from the systems view is no problem for the analytical view to deal with. If one *breaks down* the factive reality's complexity into its parts the opinion of the analytical view is that this will enable the creator of knowledge to study even systems complexity in *general terms* of cause/effect.

To the criticism from the actors view, the analytical creator of knowledge would answer by brushing most of it aside as "nonsense" that has nothing to do with a science of the factive world. To try to incorporate subjective meaning, ambiguity and various life-philosophical and artistic ways of expression, which the actors view does attempt, is not compatible with a knowledge that tries to *explain general* relations. In order to do this, science must instead resist what the actors view wants to do. As a matter of fact, this is just what the analytical view for its entire existence has worked hard to keep outside its domains, in order to become a respectable science. It would therefore be senseless, according to the analytical view, to enter this kind of metaphysics, arbitrariness and unclear relations.

Criticism of the systems view

In general

The criticism most commonly levelled against the systems view is that it "cannot see the trees for the forest". Through the spread of the systems view, expressions like "you are a victim of the system" have become common. This may in turn lead to a tendency for people to *experience themselves* as "systems components in the process of solving problems, having information relations among themselves", that is, being defined by the system. This is reinforced, so the critics say, by the fact that the business concepts and operative ideas of organizations are often formulated in systems terms, which define possible actions among individual members of the system. People may believe that the *systems that exist* on paper exist as such *in the factive reality*.

Another general criticism of the systems view and its holistic thinking is that a concept that in itself tries to include everything at one and the same time, will finally become empty and void of content, or, alternatively contain so many conflicting conceptions that it becomes useless as a methodological view.

Criticism from the analytical view

According to the analytical view, systems theorists have in no way shown what is *operational* in the concept of synergy. The concept is not uniquely "systemic", so the analysts say. It is easy, using analytical techniques like mathematical set theory or statistical covariance analysis, to present situations in which "the totality" deviates from "the sum" of its parts. The analytical view claims that the concept of synergy is just a polemic expression that creates confusion among creators of knowledge. The systems view does not contain anything new just because it talks about "synergy".

The goal of science *cannot* be to look for what is *specific* and in all situations to emphasize differences in order to maintain the image that everything can be described as systems. Its goal, instead, must be to look for *general* statements, to determine the *similarities* among various phenomena and the relations among the parts of these phenomena. Where would science be if it had not, by using the means of the analytical view, aimed for (and found) general statements and causality relations? The fact that it has succeeded less well in social science contexts is only because the phenomena being studied there are so much more complex in nature. Its proponents say that this does not in any way reduce the value of the analytical view. The analytical methodological view asserts that systems theories are too loose and that their analogical discussions are misleading, and that too much is left to the gullibility of the creator of knowledge.

Furthermore, to claim that everything can be seen as systems brings as little analytical edge as claiming that everything has a relationship with everything else. Many proponents of the analytical view therefore claim that systems researchers/consultants/investigators basically are analytics (in the sense of the analytical view) even if they (probably without knowing it) try to deny this in order to appear as something in their own right.

Criticism from the actors view

The actors view claims that the actions of the actors *cannot* be derived starting from the system. The systems view contributes, by its focus on systemic characteristics of human activities, to developing theories that tend to force upon the individual act more and more of the logic derived from the system. In all fields of life, from systems companies to systems soccer, the systems view employs its systems eye – a one-eyedness in which individual operators (and the entrepreneurs) are given *ever less space of action*. According to the actors view, the systems view fits the "bureaucratic constructors of industry" like a hand in a glove when they, lacking imagination of their own, claim that they are "developing business by structuring the economy", something that usually means merging companies into larger units with less innovative vitality. The proponents of the systems view never ask which forces they support through the use of their theories. In this respect they are of the same old stamp as the proponents of analytics, this according to the actors view.

This thing about explaining an individual's way of functioning as *conditioned* by external circumstances is just as *objectifying* as the analytical view's reduction of the individual to a few measurable variables. To claim, say, that "business concepts or the psychological needs of the members *determine* their behaviour" or that "the system reacts to the changes in the environment" leaves no room for the *meaning* and *significance* that individuals place on their own fields of knowledge creation. Yet this meaning and significance are the source of all acts.

So, the actors view asserts that we cannot develop any real knowledge on the basis of systemic principles. Instead, we must understand aspects in our environment in terms of the *meaning* that we bring to them. Otherwise they will become, in the right sense of the word, rather *meaning-less*.

Basing our business models on knowledge generated by the systems view leads, so the actors view claims, to actors becoming strangers to models and therefore unable to act accordingly. The logical base is wrong. Basing our understanding of an organization on the functions that it (as an organization) fulfils in its environment would mean that the "organization" has a "life" of its own, which is reification. This excludes not only those finite provinces of meaning by which the actors of the organization orient themselves, but also the opportunities (and the interest) the actors have in developing the real *potential* of the organization.

The response of the systems view to this criticism

The proponents of the systems view would claim that the supporters of the other two views have completely misunderstood the ultimate presumptions, the design and the ambitions of the systems view. They would claim that history has proven the systems view right. The development that took place after its launch was that more and more creators of knowledge adopted this view. It has been successfully implemented in an increasing number of areas. Its terms have even become part of everyday language.

Systems proponents, furthermore, would take the pragmatic stance as usual. They would assert that not all problems need to be solved by the methodical equipment of the systems view. Many social problems can also be solved without looking at them in terms of systems. There is also room for analytical explanations.

In one respect, however, they would claim the advantages of the systems view. When a researcher/consultant/investigator faces a complex problem, it might be *dangerous to simplify* things (both for the understanding of the problem and the usefulness of developed solutions) by trying to *reduce* it to what it is not. Sometimes one has to consider *unique aspects*, deny the possibility of going for representativity, and sacrifice generality in favour of specificity.

Responding to actors creators of knowledge, they would further assert that systems creators of knowledge do not in any way deny that the people in an organization must be considered. They would also state that there is sometimes a reason to look at systems at such a low level of *magnification* that individual, subjective conceptions enter the picture, but sometimes not. They would claim that approximations are deliberately made in their models; this claim is made by all constructors of models. These approximations often mean that organizations/companies are seen as "living" systems; actors creators of knowledge can call this "objectification", "instrumentalization" or "reification", or whatever they like.

Criticism of the actors view

In general

If we can formulate the general criticism of the systems view as "not being able to see the trees for the forest", then the reverse would be valid for the actors view: that this view "cannot see the forest for the trees". The actors view tends, so its critics say, to look at all social phenomena starting from the subjective conceptualizations of individual actors. This can bring only subjective knowledge, which is of lesser value for solving more complete problems. How is something like scientific knowledge supposed to be taught under such circumstances?

The criticism claims, among other things, that it is not worthwhile to engage intimately with single actors when we need more *general* knowledge. Of what use is it that individuals become aware of their situations, if they are subordinate to structural systems conditions that their "conscious" acts cannot change?

Criticism from the analytical view

The analytical view opposes the actors view on a number of points:

a. Actors creators of knowledge can never provide *general* results. All actors creators of knowledge can do is to collect a lot of data and then not know what to do with them. They have neither real *theories* nor logically formulated *hypotheses* in which to place these data and treat them in a process of scientific *quantification*.
b. Actors creators of knowledge are not nearly as unconditional as they claim. Under the pretext of being "like a sponge", they absorb everything that comes their way. Analytical creators of knowledge can instead come up with facts by *deducing* their starting points from *established* theory, using well-known *techniques*, and conducting thorough *validity* controls.
c. If dialectics is broken down into its single *variables* (i.e. analysed), one can find *causal relations*. Causal relations, furthermore, do not exclude contemporaneity between *dependent* and *independent* variables.
d. Besides, why should something be good just because it's a little bit newer?

Criticism from the systems view

The systems view, by and large, supports the criticism that the analytical view levels against the actors view. The systems and the analytical views are, as we know, similar in several respects. As far as the criticism in point (d) above is concerned, the overlap is total. On points (a), (b) and (c), the systems view lowers its voice a bit. The systems view talks rather about analogies than "real theories" and "logically formulated hypotheses"; it does not rely that much on deduction, the value of techniques in themselves or the control of validity; and it does not speak of causal relations.

Furthermore, the systems view asserts that it really is possible to *speak* of *totalities* and their *lives*. This is a deliberate and useful approximation. It is often impractical to go down to the individual level. It is of course true that the goals of a company are formulated by its members, not by the company per se, but this does not mean that the goals of a company are identical with those of its members. The most important *perspective* in social studies of complex organizations is therefore that of *totality*, and here we also find the most obvious weakness of the actors view.

The systems view also claims that the actors view tries to establish delimitations that do not exist. The systems view has also not been standing still. Several of its followers assert that the systems view really does consider (for instance) dialectic relations, and that there is no sub-jectivity that cannot be situated within the systems view. It is even a common method in organization theory (for example) to work with subjective ideas held by (for instance) business leaders and to be part of modifying these to make them more purposeful, as seen from the point of what is best for the total system (and consequently best for "the actors"). That something is "factive" and includes subjective facts. The actors view just complicates the discussion by trying to establish artificial boundaries. "Actor's conceptions" (if it is necessary to operate with single individuals) are often transferred to a systems frame of reference.

The response of the actors view to this criticism

An actors creator of knowledge would probably respond spontaneously to this criticism by saying:

> No answer is really necessary. The two other views have, entirely on their own and in an elegant way, shown that they do not make understanding possible. They do not know the deep difference between *explaining* and *understanding*. They try to understand by explain-ing. They treat and try to explain the actors view in the same way they treat and – under the pretext of "science" – try to explain social phenomena. First the phenomenon is objec-tified so that it fits into well-known categories, then an attempt is made to explain the objectification as a result of "scientific" activities.
>
> The actors view does not even have to answer the criticism from the analytical view, because analysts choose to criticize the actors view because it does not use techniques that will legitimise their conception of reality.
>
> The systems view talks about totality and the occasional need to consider dialectic rela-tions, but at the same time it is completely incapable of seeing the development of the actors view as a dialectic totality. It is very revealing to hear that a view that claims a holistic approach seems to reduce another view (or another conception of the world) to what it calls "actors conceptions" – that it also claims to consider in its own view.

After this, the actors creator of knowledge would probably, as a second thought, take up the so-called "scientific quantification" by the analytical view, and this view's, according to the actors view, almost religious faith that the truth is resting here, in the quantification of social life.

> Trying to measure on a cardinal scale, for instance, the *intensity* in a *feeling* or an *experience* is not possible on the whole, according to the actors view. The reason is that the intensity of

this human life feeling/experience is then seen as equal to a tone, which might become stronger or weaker. But our emotional life is richer than that. Its intensity is not even the same as a tone rising in pitch; its *intensity* is rather comparable with a whole symphony, where one instrument after the other comes in. The *qualitative* complexity is here continuously rising. If we would measure music as the analytical approach measures human experiences, knowledge and emotional life, it would be reduced. There is something in the interface between tones and instruments that could be called *the inner quality* of music and can be compared with our emotional life. So if the quality of music is reduced by measuring it – which few people would deny – what would then happen to our emotional life if it were exposed to the same simplification?

Furthermore, to look at the *qualitative complexity* of different people's emotional life on a par is not only illogical; it is unethical as well. Somebody grading his/her experience as a four does not in any way include somebody else grading his/her experience as a three and, somebody grading his/her experience as a four does not mean twice as much as somebody grading his/her experience as a two, which is the very idea in the world of numbers – that every higher number includes the lower ones. Our experiences are in *content* as well as in *intensity completely different*. Even if two persons put their numbers on the same grading, so the feelings will remain *different* for each and every one of the participants, except for the analytical knowledge creator who treats them as *equal*.

Finally, as the actors view looks at it, if we claim that statistics has proven its ability to describe, explain and forecast human life, this might consequently be a result of the fact that the population – the lonely crowd – has been reduced to becoming Xerox copies of each other as a "factive" matter through the *self-reference* phenomenon. The question is whether we can oppose the thesis: the simpler mind, the easier it is to describe, explain and forecast for an analytical view looking for the *regular* in what is *irregular* and for *similarities* in *differences*. Maybe we can, according to the actors view, look at statistically good explanations and forecasts of human social life as a proof of human flight from the values of freedom in thoughts and life?

THE IDEA OF RECONCILIATION

After this cannonade of criticism among proponents of different methodological views, we can, in spite of everything, realize their mutual potentiality of complementary opportunities (see Box 13.2). We need to reconcile them, that is, getting these opposing thoughts to correspond in one way or another.

As mentioned earlier, it is also common in *practice* to approach what we, for our further methodological development in this book, refer to as "a view as transformative operator in a methodology of complementarity". Does this mean that the views in application, i.e. as approaches, in their "pure" forms, are of value to only "ascetic creators of knowledge" (such as those presented in Chapters 10, 11 and 12), and, apart from those scarce situations, that the approaches can be combined without any extra complications? *In our opinion, this is not the case!* Compare with Chapter 3 and the discussion on criticism above and our opinion will become obvious.

Just as an example, what would it look like if a researcher/consultant/investigator combined belief in a *factive reality* that is independent of the observers and built up by, say, *causal* relations, with belief in a *socially constructed reality* built up by *dialectic* relations? Even if there are some researchers, consultants and investigators who without further ado pick concepts, models, techniques and ideas from different methodological orientations, the creator of knowledge (the conscious researcher, consultant or investigator, for whom this book is written) maintains that this is not possible. The serious choice of any methodological view is associated with *ultimate presumptions* that create knowledge in the community as well as among separate individuals. This not only has a bearing on, but also an importance for, all methodological activities.

To claim that different methodological approaches can be easily combined is, in the meaning of methodology proper, not only naive but directly misleading. Going back to our metaphor about whether the Earth is a sphere or a disk, it cannot be reasonable for one and the same person to claim at one moment that Earth is round like a globe and that we can travel around it in all directions, and at the next moment to claim that the Earth is flat like a disk and that we run the risk of falling over the edge. We are convinced this way of thinking is logically unreasonable and not compatible with efforts to create knowledge.

For example, it would make no sense in the presentation of the results of a study to put *causal* relations into a system – that is, to let the system no longer be a system; or to place producer–product (*finality*) relations in the finite province of meaning of an actor – and not to allow this finite province of meaning to be based on *dialectical* relations, in other words, no longer be actors-based. Even worse, when presenting the results of a study, would be to come up with, say, a conception of a company as three parts, one of which is explained causally, one described in terms of finality, and the third understood as dialectic.

On the contrary, we would like to claim that, starting from a view as *transformative operator*, based on concepts proposed earlier in this text (which then could be seen as thematic), it is not only possible, but in many situations desirable, to let the different views be included in our *principle of complementarity* (to paraphrase the physicist Bohr, 1928); that is, no language in itself and by itself can capture reality in its entirety. According to Bohr, the richness of reality is too great and too sensitive to be captured in a single logical structure.

No matter how hard we try with words to *describe* a musician and his/her instrument, that description is unlikely to come even close to audibility. Nor can we *find* the piano music through searching around in the piano. And how are we going to answer the question: does the music exist if no one is listening? Yet, by means of a complementarity among the methodological approaches, aspects like those above can be researched and made figuratively visible (audible).

Like Bohr we don't use the term "complementarity" in its ordinary everyday meaning of two different parts of an entity that make up a whole. Bohr gave "complementarity", according to Stent (2002: 244) "a special, esoteric meaning, namely the relation between two rationally irreconcilable … descriptions of the world whose factual irreconcilability no experiment can ever demonstrate. Bohr's prime example of complementarity was the description of electrons in terms of *both* waves and particles."

To be able to comprehend this we present the idea of *reconciliation* through our methodological principle of complementarity (see Box 13.2). The whole concept of complementarity is illustrated in Figure 13.2 and will be thoroughly exemplified below, especially by the three research cases in Chapter 14.

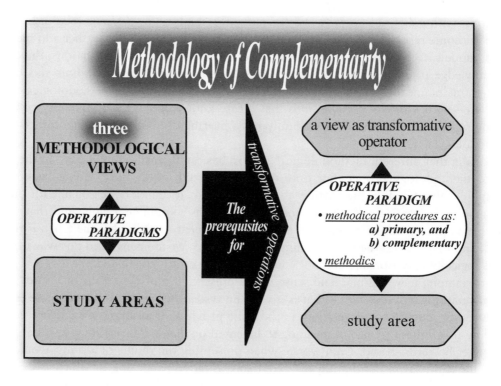

Figure 13.2   Methodology of Complementarity

To summarize, thinking, concepts and techniques/methods in one methodological approach can be used in another methodological approach, but they are *reshaped* on the way, they *change form and content with* context. They are, in a term we want to use, *transformed*. What takes place (and should take place) is that one view is then used as a *transformative operator*; that is, the creator of knowledge confesses to *one* of the *methodological views* and its ultimate presumptions. Some methodical – *primary* – procedures (and part of the methodics) are conducted accordingly. Within the framework of the view as transformative operator, techniques, methods, results, etc. from other methodological views can be used at the same time and as the study proceeds. What happens is that a *special form* of methodical – *complementary* – procedure is used, one in which researchers/consultants/ investigators try to consider circumstances based on the point of departure of another methodological approach, against their *own ultimate presumptions*. What do the circumstances mean, where do they lead, what are the consequences for the creation of knowledge as a whole, and more. The circumstances will then be *creatively reshaped and reconfigured*; they will take on another character and meaning. The view/approach as transformative operator thereby *exceeds* itself, so to speak.

Through this form of *thematic language* of methodology, we claim that it becomes possible, again using our illustrative example from Chapter 1 and above, to "navigate" with methods that are based on the perception that "the Earth is flat" after a reshaping/reconfiguring – a contextual transformation – when travelling around a "sphere", and vice versa. This requires, however, that we truly know the *presumptions* on which these "methods of navigation" are based; otherwise we can run into trouble. The same thing goes for using our methodological views as *transformative operators*. If the creator of knowledge does not know the overall ulti- mate presumptions on which the views in question are based, the risk is obvious that the researcher/consultant/investigator will sally forth and fall over the edge – he/she will not come up with a good outcome by approaching the view as a transformative operator in an attempt to create knowledge (see Figure 13.6 on page 347).

A view as transformative operator, in the meaning of methodology, *does not lead to a sep- arate and independent methodological approach* but is instead seen as *excellent knowledge-creating work* and another set of thematic concepts alongside those that already exist inner-paradigmatically.

The difference between *primary* and *complementary* procedures is that the "material" to be treated by complementary procedures must be *transformed* (reshaped and reconfigured) against the ultimate presumptions of the methodological view used as transformative opera- tor, in which the primary procedures are naturally arranged.

Some principles of complementarity

We will thoroughly illustrate the language and action within the frame of *complementary procedures* with three extensive illustrations in Chapter 14. Below, we will give the neces- sary background for comprehending these examples. The starting point is always the same: that we examine a *study area* with a *methodological view as transformative operator*, as in Figure 13.2.

We can find complementarity possible in three areas:

A. adapting existing concepts and theories
B. collecting data
C. modeling and interpreting data.

Let us look at these three, when moving from one methodological view to another, illustrated by a few examples. We start with the principal case A.

Adapting of existing concepts and theories

In principal case A (Figure 13.3) we may for example imagine that a systems creator of knowl- edge borrows the conceptual idea of *subjective denotation of meaning* from the actors view.

Maybe he/she wants by this to deepen the systems own conceptual meaning of a specific systems structure. The transformative operator in this example is the systems view, and this means that the *complementary procedure* has to deal with the questions: what will happen with the traditional systems language when doing this conceptual displacement, and how

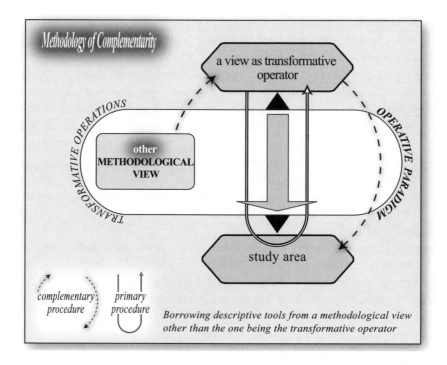

Figure 13.3   Principal Case A

should the borrowed conceptual idea be interpreted/treated in its new *context*. All this has to be examined also in relation to the *study area* in question.

These different kinds of questions and thoughts and their concrete answers are what we call a "complementary procedure". The total amount of such procedures, including the primary, in connection with the methodics will form the *operative paradigm*, and the overall concept for all these operations is thus *transformative operations*.

Collecting data

In principal case B (Figure 13.4) we may for instance envision how an analytical creator of knowledge tries to run an actors-based experiment in order to get material for hypotheses before an extensive survey.

In line with the discussions according to principal case A above, we can ask ourselves quite a lot of questions here. This case will be a very complicated project, as it has to reconcile two of the most opposite directions of thinking. Probably, the analytical creator of knowledge will take advantage of the normally *processual* and *creative* approach of the actors-based ideas of experiment and *transform* these into a model of cause–effect relations and then try to explain by that, the human actions in the experiment. Out of this he/she will formulate hypotheses and questions for the questionnaire.

The knowledge creator may even, as a possible *exceeding* result of the complementary procedure, test the *self-reference* of the survey in the sense of the actors view.

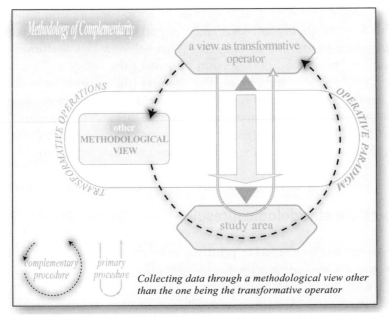

Figure 13.4   Principal Case B

Modeling and interpreting data

In principal case C (Figure 13.5) we may, in line with the two others, imagine, say, an actors creator of knowledge analysing data through the analytical view.

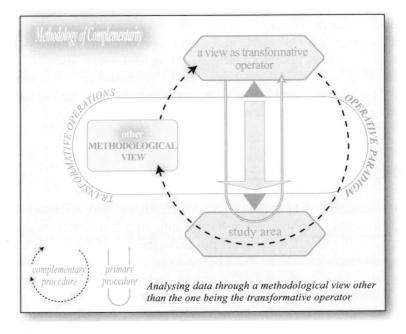

Figure 13.5   Principal Case C

He/she wants perhaps to collect a large number of actors' opinions on a specific theme in order to be able to contextually interpret some important actors' proceedings. The actors view is the *transformative operator* in this case. What will now be transformed in a complementary procedure? Presumably, the selection process of the actors will become a creative mix of the two views' selection techniques. The *operator* (the actors view) will also influence the questions and the construction of the questionnaire. Perhaps, every question in the questionnaire will have an attendant question about the actors' (respondents') conceptual meaning of it. This will then affect the statistical treatment in a way we don't know before the result is available – all in accordance with the operator's dialectic process of knowledge creating.

Exceedance as a methodological result

We have now presented three separate principal cases that can exist within the framework of a methodology of complementarity. *Combining all of our principal cases into a single study will not create any obstacles* (see Chapter 14). What has to be done, in each case, is simply to make use of a complementary procedure in relation to one's methodological base approach, used as a transformative operator.

The ever-present question about complementary procedures is: What happens? How will data be changed (reshaped, transformed), when something is placed in a construction of explanation/understanding that is different from the methodological approach through which it was developed, analysed, and so on? All methodological procedures are *contextual*, but in the case of complementary procedures it is particularly important to reflect on how form and content are changed by the context (as determined by the area under study and the ultimate presumptions of the operator).

The most interesting methodological issue in this kind of creating knowledge is that the transformative operator must also constantly *exceed* its own proper limits. This means that there will be an inherent seed of development in the methodology. Methodology of complementarity is thus, over all, the idea about how to continuously take the methodology of creating business knowledge to new levels of excellence.

CREALIABILITY OF COMPLEMENTARITY

Having a methodological insight does not guarantee a high quality of knowledge, however, because without *creativity* any insight can harden into an instrumentalism as simple as the construction of rules in general, which does not make the *exceedance* possible.

Excellence in knowledge creating is an act of ingenious pregnancy in maintaining an eligible mix of the four core elements of *crealiability* during a whole process of conducting a project. In Chapter 9 we introduced this concept of *crealiability* (see Figure 9.5) and now we want to supplement it and make it even a little bit more sophisticated (see Figure 13.6. and compare with Figure 9.5), in order to make it suitable for assessing knowledge of complementarity.

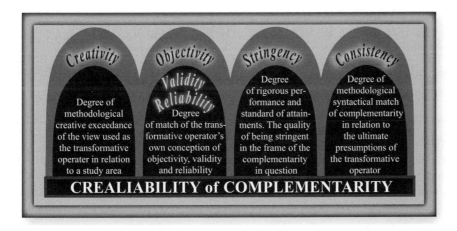

Figure 13.6   The Cores of Crealiability of Complementarity

The relative importance of the four different core elements of crealiability of complementarity must, when planning and assessing knowledge work, be launched on a case by case basis, but the essence is that excellence in work of complementarity means the highest possible *crealiability of complementarity*. The substantial thing in the concept is the intrinsic "conflict" between the core elements, which will secure the inherent seed of development in our methodology of complementarity.

THE THEMATIC LANGUAGE OF METHODOLOGY

Our intention throughout the book has been to develop what we call "a thematic language" that we hope will make it possible to bridge some of the problems in the various contexts of knowledge creation and will allow an ongoing discussion on methodology and the quality of knowledge. These thematic (or generic) concepts are intended to be "neutral" themes in the sense that proponents of the methodological views can use them – even in dialogues between them.

In our Glossary we briefly bring together the most important concepts in this thematic language (see "Thematic language of methodology").

This chapter has presented the final part of the construction of our methodology for creating business knowledge. It started by further clarifying the position of our three methodological views by summarizing the criticism they level at each other. We continued by providing a possibility for reconciliation between these three views. In order to visualize this possibility we drew up three different principal cases of complementarity. At the end of the chapter we presented our conceptualization of excellence in knowledge-creating work by using the concept of "crealiability" and its core elements in a new configuration of complementarity.

POINTS OF REFLECTION

1. We make a distinction between methodological *view* and methodological *approach*. Why?
2. Give two good reasons why it may be a really *bad idea* to straight off *combine* our three methodological views!
3. What do we mean by our methodological *principle of complementarity*?
4. Try to find a situation in your own learning life of *business*, where the above-mentioned principle may be *applied* successfully.
5. In the text we have mentioned the concept of "operationalization", "finality" and "ideal-type" as examples of *concepts* which can only be fully *comprehended* in the *context* of their alleged own *paradigm*. Come up with three more concepts in the same situation!
6. Do you find any *criticism* of our three base methodological views more *interesting* and/or *worthy of note* than any other? Which one(s)? Why?
7. We have told the reader to have an *attentive posture* when reading the *criticism* presented in this chapter, which the different methodological views level at each other. To what should the reader have an attentive posture?
8. If somebody asked you to clarify what you mean by *transformative operations* and *complementary procedures* when conducting a study, what would your answer be?
9. Give some examples of what a creator of knowledge must keep in mind when *applying* a view as *transformative operator*!
10. Excellence in knowledge-creating work can be described as reaching high creali-ability. How would you describe the elements of *crealiability of complementarity* in relation to *crealiability* in Figure 9.5? Which are the essential differences?

RECOMMENDED FURTHER READING

See the end of the Appendix and visit the website below.

Become a worldwide partner as a *knowledge creator* in the development of *Methodology for Creating Business Knowledge* by visiting the website: **www.knowledge-creator.com**. Here you can contribute by asking your own questions and you will also find answers to the most frequently asked questions. The website has been developed alongside this third edition of the book and the questions posted there will be used to provide input for future editions.

14 THREE CASES – KNOWLEDGE OF COMPLEMENTARITY

In this chapter we present three different applications of the methodology of complementarity, all related to research. We follow the same order as earlier in the book, which means that we start with the analytical approach as transformative operator, then continue with the systems approach and finish with the actor approach. The different cases enlighten very clearly the complex structure that exists in this kind of methodology. They also illustrate the solid need for critical and creative thinking from the researcher/consultant/investigator. Conducting projects of complementarity with high crealiability commonly provides unexpected and rich, as well as exceeding, answers.

INTRODUCTION

To approach complementarity in knowledge creating work requires, as shown in Chapter 13, a knowledgeable combination of creativity and methodological awareness. To reconcile opposite techniques, methods and so on under one methodological approach as a *transformative operator* is not an easy task. When this is done in a study, it means that the creator of knowledge must not only have a good knowledge of his/her own view but also of the other two.

Because, what is happening in transformative operations is that one's own base approach *is exceeded* in a complex and positive way, which at the same time asks for responsibility. The creator of knowledge takes on a *responsibility of development* in relation to the different methodological views as well as to the study area to create a transformative edge, guided by *consistency*, *stringency*, etc. (see Figure 13.6), which, from a complexity perspective, goes beyond the skills that are required when he/she carries out the study without complementarity.

Below we present three different studies, where all of them show high *crealiability of complementarity*. The three cases, where each of our three methodological approaches acts as a transformative operator, are naturally of a very different character, not the least for reasons of complexity just mentioned. We have, as much as possible, without violating the material, tried to come up with pedagogically interesting narratives related to our methodological grammar. In a similar fashion as it is not possible to describe the views with the same structure and content, precisely because they represent different ways of looking at reality, it is also not possible to follow one given design when presenting research done which further-more uses the principle of complementarity and which touches upon completely different study areas. We have therefore focused on bringing up the *methodologically interesting* issues, which are rather extensive in themselves because all our three *principal cases* from Chapter 13 are used in each of the three studies.

CASE I: THE ANALYTICAL APPROACH AS TRANSFORMATIVE OPERATOR

Background

This case is based on a thesis and a consulting report where the doctoral candidate, through his supervisor, came in contact with a company which wanted ideas around improved business and product development as well as production management for one of its depart-ments. The company had no objections to letting the work be a section in the empirical part of an academic product. The doctoral candidate decided to say "yes" and travelled, together with the supervisor, to the company to discuss the project, which was to be conducted as a *combination* of consultation and research in business.

First meeting with the study area

The company FoodEx Co. is in the food industry and has a department that develops, produces and markets poultry products for different kinds of consumption. Already at the first meeting the company makes clear the relevant circumstances for the project and what is required:

- The poultry department is a rather separate part of the company. Poultry prod-ucts are, however, seen as strategically important to the range of products of the company and have a key position in launching and marketing food.
- The profitability of the department is not considered as satisfactory; it is seen as a contribution margin compared with the rest of the company.
- The department is also not generating enough new product ideas and has bad contacts with the market.
- The purpose of the project is to be seen to "develop a model for business and product development in the poultry department of the company, which makes it possible to cost-effectively develop and produce profitable products with better contacts with the market".

Consequently, the doctoral candidate accepts the task and sees possibilities to combine his ambi-tions of writing a doctoral thesis with gaining experiences from industrial development work.

Our description below combines results from what we might call "*the consulting part*" of the doctoral candidate's project with the more extensive "*research part*", as both contain inter-esting complementary methodological aspects.

The researcher's thoughts in the beginning

From the background of his knowledge of business theory as well as of knowledge-creating *analytical* methods the doctoral candidate sees several interesting possibilities with the project:

1. He sees a challenge in learning how to work with biological material in an industrial process as well as in production development and customer contacts.
2. He perceives the project as a good platform for focusing on *best practice* in innovation, which is his research interest.
3. He sees possibilities in one and the same project to take into consideration a whole spectrum of methodological issues, which also touch upon other methodological views than his own, which is the *analytical* one. He knows that this is called "creating knowledge of complementarity" and is happy to develop and illustrate such a conduct as an essential part in his struggle for academic qualifications.

Determining the problem

As a first step in the design of an *operative paradigm*, the doctoral candidate begins by *determining* the empirical *basic problem* in the project that he aims to start from. He does this by first walking around at FoodEx Co. (the company) for a couple of days and, in an unbiased fashion, talking with the people concerned. Through this introductory probe he gets a relatively good picture of what people want and what they do not want. Some products are not attractive enough and some processes are not cost-effective enough. However, above all, people are disturbed by all those demands which are directed at the department, and dissatisfied by the existing creative climate which is not generating new product ideas to the extent asked for.

He then continues with *expert interviews* and studies of *secondary information* (see Figure 9.1). After the first fourteen days he is more and more convinced of the need to conduct the research part of the study as a larger investigation of several other companies and looking there for *common variables explaining* "best practice in innovation". In the consulting part he intends to present a decision and explanatory model for FoodEx Co. to work with. As one of his first *methodical* (primary) *procedures* he is drawing the following simple model of possible influencing factors for the poultry department (see Figure 14.1 overleaf).

After probing interviews and discussions with experts and after studying secondary material he has come to experience more and more that the department he is studying is under all sorts of pressure. He looks at these pressures as partly direct *causes* of the low level of achievement in the department. The consulting problem appears clearer to him as a *problem of reaction*. The department in question is lacking, as he sees it, suitable *tools* with which it can respond to all the different sorts of pressure to which it is exposed. According to that theory and those expert discussions which the doctoral candidate has taken part in, the result of such a strong pressure overall (the *effect* of several *causes* working together) is widely spread passivity and lack of creativity.

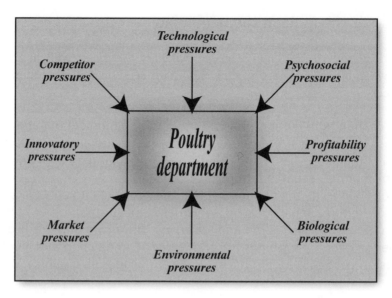

Figure 14.1   External Pressures

He can now clearly see how the combination of the consulting and research part will enrich each other. Starting from his hypothesis about lack of tools to manage different pressures, he believes that he, by, in the research part, focusing on *best practice* in innovation, shall be able to supply those response tools which the department is lacking today. He also believes that he can mitigate the effects from several different pressures by, in the consulting part, developing a decision and explanatory model that in a clear fashion illustrates various cause–effect–conditions ruling. His idea is that this model then is to be *implemented* in FoodEx Co. after he has finished the project.

Transformative operations

The study area in theory – primary procedures

Beginning by studying and adapting earlier *theories* and *research results* to one's own study area is one of the most basic *methodical procedures* contained in the analytical approach. As this case is about methodology of complementarity, these procedures are referred to as "primary" in order to differentiate them from the complementary ones.

For a few weeks the doctoral candidate searches through that literature which he sees as relevant for the project. He does not intend to read it all before he starts as he has already made himself a preliminary picture of the research object "best practice". As an orientation, we present below, very briefly, some short extracts from what became his relatively extensive mapping of the research object in theory. He writes and quotes from some selected works in relation to his literature study:

From the book cover of *The R&D Workers: Managing Innovation in Britain, Germany, Japan, and the United States* by Shapira (1995) we can read: "Of critical importance is how these R&D workers are selected, trained, and managed, and how their activities are linked to other aspects of production."

There are seven categories in the Baldrige award of relevance for best practice, writes Zairi:

- *Leadership*: senior executives' personal leadership and involvement in creating and sustaining a customer focus and clear and visible quality values.
- *Information and analysis*: the scope, validity, analysis, management and use of data and information to drive quality excellence and improve competitive performance.
- *Strategic quality planning*: the planning process and how all key quality requirements are integrated into overall business planning.
- *Human resource development and management*: the key elements of how the company develops and realizes the full potential of the company's quality and performance objectives.
- *Management of process quality*: the systematic process the company uses to pursue ever higher quality and company performance.
- *Quality and operational results*: the company's quality levels and improvement trends in quality, operational performance and supplier quality.
- *Customer focus and satisfaction*: the company's relationship with customers and its knowledge of customer requirements and the key quality factors that determine marketplace competitiveness. (1998: 460–1)

Under the head of "Benchmarking innovation management for best practice," Zairi continues: "Despite the thousands of publications, research studies, books and reports that have been written on innovation, there are still big differences in the levels of understanding among companies managing innovation and the activities surrounding it" (Zairi, 1998: 132).

According to Ashworth (2005: 256): "Best practice is the adoption and development of ideas, systems or methods in a way that measurably improves a business or enterprise so that it continually offers or secures best value for money."

One real interesting observation is the following from Matheson & Matheson (1998: 75): "One of the important findings of our survey is that the best practices are the same across industries. ... This finding supports what many understand; R&D decision makers face the same types of issues in many industries; thus the best practices for addressing them are similar. ... The fact that the best practices are the same across industries means that a company can adopt a practice being successfully applied in a completely different industry."

If we relate this assertion by Matheson & Matheson to the following statement from Mertins et al. (2003: 282) we get some very important research issues to reflect upon: '... current approach in 2000 to best practice exploitation is balanced on recognizing that sharing ideas and creating new knowledge is as much about behaviours and cultures as it is about process and databases".

Back to Zairi again we can read in his book *Best Practice: Process Innovation Management* (1999: 88) the following: "Every team that is created must be developed according to its own characteristics. They must play to their strengths and think through how they are going to build this strong sense of team identity ... To facilitate this, there are some best practice rules which should be considered by any team."

At the same time as he is studying the very research object "best practice" the doctoral candidate also runs into critical analyses which lead to deepened methodological thoughts. When he reads in Kunde's book *Unique Now – Or Never* (2002), for instance, that "Companies have defined so much 'best practice' that they are now more or less identical", he gets the following methodological eye-opener which he formulates in his report like this:

> When I read this in Kunde's book and think of Matheson & Matheson and their findings "that the best practices are the same across industries" and relate this to what is referred to as *self reference* in actors view – that is, that social science studies also indirectly study the result of one's own influence on society – then I start to think whether these findings may be a result of such influence as well. The global spread of research results and consulting activities in this area may also have such consequences. Or may this possibly be hidden in the ultimate presumptions about the factive world in my methodological view as well?

As he also has a number of other theoretical references as well where, like in Zairi's later work, there is talk about development teams and their possibilities from having *unique* and not just *general* characteristics, it becomes, as he writes himself "clearer to me that the road to success in this study goes through a methodology of complementarity".

The study area in theory – complementary procedures

In the same way as the doctoral candidate earlier selected literature in the area of "best practice"; he now starts more actively to look for complementary research results and critical views in order to broaden his base of methods. However, in principle, he follows his own analytical methodology view's plan for studies.

What is starting to interest him more and more is how, in his planned study of what characterizes particularly successful cases of so-called best practice projects, he is able to pay regard to what is *specific,* at the same time as coming up with what is *general*. He therefore starts to study *the case study method* of the systems view and *the selection methods* and the *ideal-typified descriptions* of the actors view as a way to collect information also from the unique characteristics of the factive reality in order to come up with general conclusions in the sense of the analytical view. We present below, only as a short orientation, some few excerpts of what became the relative extensive mapping by the doctoral candidate of complementarity in theory. Here are two direct quotes from his study:

> According to the Foreword by Day in Blumer's (1979, p. xxxii–xxxiii) *Critiques of Research in the Social Sciences* we have to be aware of the fact that there are certain qualities we risk to miss by general selections: "If one is studying the formation of social action, the data that one needs have to refer to how the actors approach, see, define, and handle the situations in which they have to act. The representativeness of the data yielded by human documents has to be determined by considering the question of whether the data cover what is involved in the formation of the given action; representativeness must be sought, not in getting a representative sample of a given demographic population, but

instead, in making sure that the authors of the human documents were knowledgeable about the formation of the given action under study. Half a dozen individuals with such knowledge constitute a far better 'representative sample' than one thousand individuals who may be involved in the action that is being formed but who are not knowledgeable about that formation."

In *The Handbook of Information Systems Research* by Whitman and Woszczynski (2003: 217) we can read about something that, perhaps, may be regarded as a thought of complementarity. The researchers call this a constitutive analysis: "Constitutive analysis is necessary to discover how social systems and the variables and relationships that compose them are constructed through human interaction. Constitutive analyses reveal the interpretive processes that figure in the operation of causal relationships. For example, task is commonly used as a causal variable in systemic studies of work. However, it may not be task per se, but *actors' interpretations* of work tasks that influence organizational processes. These interpretations may be included in a functional analysis as 'perceived task,' but this transforms an interpretive process into a static variable. It does not fully capture the role of interpretation in the actor' approach to their work. Underlying every variable and relationship in a causal analysis is a process of social construction responsible for making it an active force in the social system. A constitutive analysis takes the functional analysis as a starting point, shows how the system operates in terms of actor-structure interaction, and then adds additional rich detail from the actors' viewpoints about these processes. A constitutive analysis is a useful supplement to functional analysis because it reveals the 'whole picture' behind seemingly deterministic facts."

Note that the doctoral candidate in the latter reference writes "perhaps, may be regarded as a thought of complementarity" about those thoughts which Whitman & Woszczynski present around what they call "Constitutive analysis". And the question is whether we can call their analysis complementary. They mix here a number of methodological conceptions with directly contradictory paradigmatic references without clarifying these relations in some *transformative operation*. Then it is easy to run the risk of losing *scientific stringency* in a kind of eclectic maze. Some examples of contradictory concepts in relation to the context in Whitman & Woszczynski's short text above are: constitutive, variables, discover, interpretive, causal relationships, system, actor–structure interaction, social construction and deterministic facts. All of these concepts are discussed in this book and have then been related to their scientifically relevant ultimate presumptions (see the Glossary).

The doctoral candidate shows, however, *awareness* as well as *self-reflection* in this connection but is nevertheless inspired to find his own interesting reconciliations which can present methodologically stringent, valid and reliable results within the framework of the *analytical view as transformative operator*. He is now planning to conduct a major survey of several companies around best practice as a study of a limited number of cases, where he knows that they have, as far as best practice is concerned, a representativeness according to Blumer above. Now he aims to use some of the *selection procedures* of the *actors view* in combination with the *case study* thinking of the *systems view* within the framework of an extensive survey study.

The study area in practice – primary procedures

Starting from those experiences he gains in FoodEx Co. and what he learns in his literature studies of best practice, he comes up with a questionnaire containing sixty-five
questions in total. In his construction he is also using some well-tested surveys measuring
leadership style, cooperative style, innovation culture, suggestion activities and customer
relations. His purpose is to use the questionnaire answers to get a quantitative base material for his development of theories around best practice. This research ground he aims
himself to concretize in different consulting proposals to the poultry department. His
ambition with the survey he describes like this in a research report: "The questionnaire
aims at providing analysis material for what are the characteristics of successful – so-called
'best practice' – projects/ways of working. The objective is to look for *common* factors
explaining excellence." In the *research part* of the project the doctoral candidate uses some
more analytical *techniques,* which through *primary procedures* are made into *methods* in
his relatively extensive study. Furthermore, he is combining these with specific techniques-
made-into-methods for the problem at the company in question. As part of his *consulting
part* he develops a number of well-structured *interviewer guides* in order to depict those
cause–effect relations he is looking for to be able to construct a decision and explanatory
model for FoodEx Co.

His purpose is, within the consulting part, to *explain* as well as to provide material for a
decision as far as the very complicated technical and biological conditions that dictate the
material flow of the poultry department are concerned. As a mathematical basis to build an
optimization model for this flow he starts from the following formula: $V = f(Xs;Ps)$, where V
(the objective) is the "highest possible contribution margin", Xs (the decision variables) are
to be the points in time for slaughtering different broods of poultry being raised and Ps (the
parameters) are to be different factive circumstances.

Via new *work conditions* (best practice) in the poultry department, his idea here is to make
it possible through product development and market contacts to *unite* the different requirements from the *marketing* and *productions sectors*. These thoughts lead in turn to the
reflections of the doctoral candidate on presenting some kind of a model where the often
irreconcilable demands from the decision makers' point of departure can be illustrated. His
thoughts go here complementarily to the *guiding principles* from the systems view about
totality, *complexity* and *relativity*.

The study area in practice – complementary procedures

As the first and most important complementary procedure, the doctoral candidate comes up
with a kind of bifurcated criteria for selecting those case study companies which are to be asked
to participate in the *research related* study of best practice. He establishes a number of *factors* as
such criteria for the selection process. These factors include concepts like: "leadership/leadership
style", "way of project planning", "controlling resources", "creativity methods", "principles for
coordination" and "type of technical aids".

Starting from a selection technique taken from the actors view – *recommendation selection* in combination with a *problem/opportunity oriented selection* – he aims at coming up

with some twenty different case companies with interesting and different connections to best practice. He wants with this to try to reflect what is *different* in what is *similar.* He is very clear about the fact that his questionnaire questions will look for what is similar ("to look for *common* factors explaining excellence" – see above). At the same time, in his research report he wishes to be able to *explain* the importance of difference for excellence, even if he is using the questionnaire to look for similarities – hence his interest in the methodology of complementarity for exceeding his own analytical approach.

He also intends to incorporate the actors view's *idea about ideal types* in order to create those *developmental tools* that he wants to come up with. This he plans to establish in *dialogues* with some leading person in each of the case companies in combination with a larger number of concerned actors in the poultry department of FoodEx Co. As he has not used dialogues before as a method he enrols in a methodology course in order to learn about dialogue in the sense of the actors view.

In order to interpret the results of those irreconcilable demands among decision makers in the poultry department, and to be able to illustrate the consequences of this for the decision makers in question, he constructs a systems model, as shown in Figure 14.2.

The doctoral candidate looks at the decision system as consisting of three subsystems: the Marketing system, the Production system and the Finance system. Their relations to each other he describes in terms of information and trust (or lack of it). The formula in the center symbolizes a kind of mechanism for reducing conflicts.

In order for the decision system to work the best way, according to the doctoral candidate, the different subsystems must consider each other's demands, adapt and fit each other and, by this, create synergy.

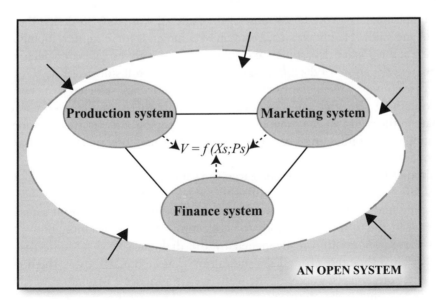

Figure 14.2   The Decision System

The demands (partly irreconcilable) that the different subsystems wanted to satisfy were:

Production

- To produce poultry from a purely biological point of view so that it is possible to slaughter all those units of poultry which are one brood at the same time (broods are called "feeding sites" and constructed in a large number in the neighbourhood of the poultry department of FoodEx Co.; for rational as well as sanitary reasons all poultry units in one brood have to be slaughtered at the same time).
- Even and full employment at the slaughter house (which was owned by FoodEx Co).

Marketing

- To come up with poultry products in the sizes and qualities that the market wants.
- To come up with new varieties more often.

Finance

- To have as few days as possible without poultry on the "feeding sites".
- Not to let the "products" grow too big.
- Increase the speed of breeding and use "the waste" from poultry as much as possible.

Methodics

After the doctoral candidate had initially probed the study area, determined the basic problem with which he was to work and conducted a large number of transformative operations (primary as well as complementary procedures) most of the material was ready to design the rest of the methodics of the study. He chooses to create an exciting and, for him, developing interaction between being at the poultry department and being involved with the case companies, one by one from, the point of departure of the *selection techniques,* he has transformed from the actors view.

At every case company five persons related to best practice are selected to answer *the questionnaire* containing sixty-five questions. In total, twenty-three middle-sized companies are to participate in the study. At the same time as the five persons answer the questionnaire, the doctoral candidate is conducting a longer dialogue with somebody in a senior position in the chosen company.

The methodics that follows is by and large the same as that logical flow which was presented in Figure 9.2, "Plans for Analytical Approach Studies".

When coding and arranging data the doctoral candidate notices several interesting connections between the different methods for collecting data, for instance, how parts of the answers to the questionnaire are deepened by the dialogues, and in some cases he even *changes* his original thoughts around that definition that he himself, using the literature and well tested questionnaires (see above "The study area in practice – primary procedures"), had come up with in some of the questions.

Results

In his reports the doctoral candidate is describing best practice as well as those tools that are a result of his study. He is providing a number of common factors, which are direct causes of successful and innovative business actions in project work. Below we can see some of the factors on his long list with notations to indicate with what frequency they existed in the twenty-three studied companies.

- Effective coordination (18)
- Well established objectives (16)
- Integrated team (15)
- Proactive thinking (12)
- Leadership (12)
- Good communication (12)

From working with his statistics he established a number of personal characteristics for best practice in innovation. He transformed these in his consulting reports to a number of typical individuals of importance in best practice. Part of the transformation was "spicing" them further with favourable characteristics, which he found in his dialogues in order to create an even higher degree of excellence.

At the same time he constructs a few different systems models in order to illustrate, as he writes in his report, "all those different relations that exist in a kind of mutual dependence". He also solves the optimization model for the material flow, which is the basis for his decision and explanatory model (the mechanism for reducing conflicts – see Figure 14.2).

To the FoodEx Co. senior management group he later hands over, for subsequent *implementation* in the poultry department, the different models and tools for best practice in innovation.

CASE II: THE SYSTEMS APPROACH AS TRANSFORMATIVE OPERATOR

Introduction

In this case we will take look at a research project where the researcher was approaching the systems view in a project of methodological complementarity. The project was very extensive and only central parts of the study's transformative operations will be commented on briefly.

As the construction of public housing continued in Sweden, more and more voices were raised for a direct user influence on the construction process. It was claimed that the *consumers* of public housing should be part of making decisions as early as the *planning* stage. In the same way that customer focus was increasing in other parts of the business world the time was ripe for such a focus in the relatively conservative construction industry. Yet this co-determination demanded, at least in part, a new kind of technology; experiments of some sort would therefore be necessary to develop both the technology and the planning. A number of such experiments had taken place over the years. One such experiment – or rather, a small part of an investigation that studied and assessed such an experiment – is described below. The study was conducted by an independent researcher.

Transformative operations

The independent researcher's evaluation study is an excellent example of a constructive creation of knowledge based on a methodology of complementarity. A large number of procedures, both primary and complementary, were made using techniques and earlier results from the analytical approach as well as from the actors approach. These techniques-made-into-methods were *reconciled* during the course of the study and were subordinated to a *methodics* that, by and large, tried to "live" its own "life" based on conditions set down by the planners, the building constructors, the architects and the users. The researcher remained true to the systems approach as her transformative operator. Being true to a methodological *base approach*, as we have pointed out, is the most *fundamental* prerequisite for a methodology of complementarity to lead to good quantitative as well as qualitative results.

Several of the discussions that the researcher recorded in her report often contained, for purposes of formation, actors concepts placed against a systems base. In this way, the researcher hoped to create a feedback mechanism for the *language games* that took place in this specific study area (planning public housing; building public housing) of the factive reality in Sweden, and to combine systems and actors concepts within different forms of holistic discussions. Examples of how the researcher conducted discussions and acted in a complementarity sense when she constructed a questionnaire and placed actors concepts against a systems base are given below.

Primary procedures

The researcher's *primary* procedures are directly related to the five principles of the systems view: *the principles of totality, complexity, relativity, mutuality and unpredictability* (see Chapter 5). Consequently her knowledge interest is related to trying to describe this experiment in a *structural* overall construction-technology *perspective,* as well as in a *processual perspective* close to the *user.* Through this combination of systems perspectives she wishes to reflect *the totality* and *the complexity* at the same time as the shift between the *magnifying* levels would point out *the relativity* in this kind of systems descriptions (see "Systems view in the twenty-first century" in Chapter 5). By systems models she wanted to illustrate how the activities of the different subsystems are intimately *interrelated* and at the same time almost impossible to *predict*.

After some introductory interviews the researcher attempts to clarify the overall purpose with the experiment in question around user influence. Through a first *primary* procedure she illustrates the *study area* in a systems model where *existing* and desirable relations between what is *social* and what is *technological* are described, that is, between the two systems "Social (user) system" and "Technology system" (see Figure 14.3).

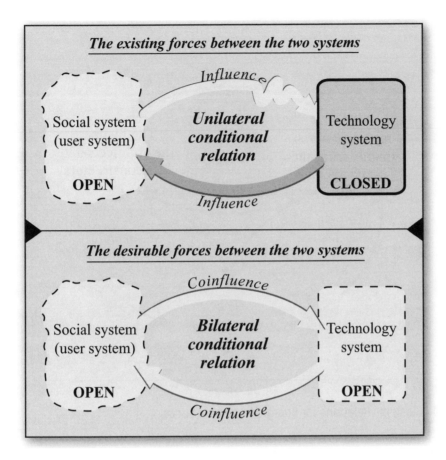

Figure 14.3   Systems Relations in the Experiment

The researcher notes at the same time that the *study area* consists of another dominating system – "the bureaucratic system" – that may come to play a decisive role. It is the local representatives, mainly from the estate agency, which are to approve the plans and the processes in the experiment. She makes the assumption, however, that it will not cause any problems, as the bureaucratic system has taken the initiative on the whole thing. The only aspect that is added is another open system involved in what she refers to as *mutual conditional relations*. A preliminary outline of this wanted and ideal *systems condition* is shown in Figure 14.4.

As a systems oriented researcher she tries in this project to *explain* important factors at the same time as creating an *understanding* for them. In order to deepen this *understanding* in the *metaphoric* meaning of the systems view, the researcher chooses, furthermore, to supplement this with central concepts from *the actors view* (see below). The researcher also wishes, early on, to be able to follow the whole experimental group of users out of a *processual perspective*, and within its framework, through questionnaires, to conduct a census of all 260 participating users. She wants in connection with these questionnaires to conduct an *analytical* quantification and testing of hypotheses (see below).

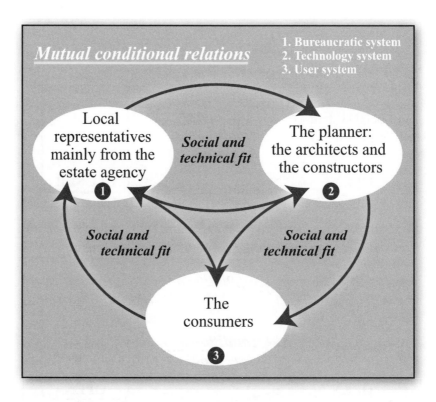

Figure 14.4   Systems Relations for Energizing the Processes

Complementary procedures

After an introductory problematization the researcher is formulating the following two *hypotheses* of five all together, which she intends to *define quantitatively* and test in the study using an *interval scale*:

1. A real user influence requires that every planning and construction issue in the process starts from the *everyday level* of the actors in order to be relevant and create meaning for them.
2. User influence requires extended flexibility in the planning, as well as in the construction process in order to also include the users' *learning* as the process goes on.

In order to test these hypotheses the researcher must also be able to *quantify* the results of her planned surveys. In order to create as *valid* results as possible she is of the opinion that her questionnaires, as an instrument, also must satisfy what she has written herself about creating meaning and about relevance in the first hypothesis above. For the purpose of coming up with relevant questions creating meaningful *finality* relations, the researcher goes beyond traditional analytical ways in her construction of the questionnaires. Here she turns *transformatively* to the idea in the actors approach about *first hand expressions* as a point of departure for relevance and creating *meaning*. In a number of *complementary procedures* she develops what became her *method* in order to *test* the hypotheses and also, partly, to contribute to *evaluating* the process. Before every new survey (4 of them over time) she applies the following *three steps procedure*:

1. *Dialogues* with a varying number of four to six users in order to come up with *structural and process oriented phenomena,* which are felt to be important to them.
2. A *random sample* of twelve users out of the total experimental population containing 260 users, to whom she presents the phenomena. *Together* with these twelve she *develops the questions* to the actual questionnaire.
3. At moments where all the users participate in order to be informed about the project managers' plans and acquaint themselves with site descriptions, the researcher is given an opportunity at the end of these occasions to present the coming questionnaire and to *denote the conceptual meaning* of the questions in a plenary meeting *together* with all 260 users.

After this three-steps procedure all 260 users are given the actual questionnaire, which is then answered. Beginning with a *quantitative analysis* of the questionnaire answers, the hypotheses are tested, and the researcher writes in her report: "Through actors-*complementary procedures* at these questionnaire constructions I wished to reach beyond superficiality and approach profundity."

Besides these complementary procedures the researcher is working with *basing* her systems descriptions with the *actors*. She thinks this is the best way to *compound* and *energize the five principles* of the systems view (see below), which she is not leaving behind during the project but uses as her platform here and in other projects, being a systems oriented researcher.

Some results

The project, which the researcher followed and evaluated, did not become exactly what the involved local representatives (bureaucratic system), the planners (technology system) or the consumers (user system) had in mind. The desirable forces between the two systems (user and technology) were never realized. The relation was rather tightened between the bureaucratic and the technological systems to such a degree that the users were left outside without these two systems noticing it. The researcher's two hypotheses above were also strongly confirmed, but unfortunately then in a negative direction for the experiment. The users never entered, so to say, any relevant interrelationship with the *dominating forces* in the different processes where meaning was intended to be created.

The researcher starts one of her systems descriptions in the report like this: "The 'one-dimensional' theory states that bureaucracy and ordinary technology develop according to each other's conditions. The user – consumer – system finds itself on the outside, which means that the connection to consumer influence is crashing" (see Figure 14.5).

In the experiment discussed here a systems constellation was constructed – on a local level – in which the bureaucratic and technological systems should open themselves and establish *bilateral conditional relations* with the user – consumer – system.

So, what is the content of these conditional relations? In the interest of developing a descriptive edge in the systems language, *conditional relations* will refer to the conditions for a social and technical *fit* (see Figure 14.4). It is therefore with these conditional relations that the *actors* who are part of the systems constellations aim for a technical and social fit.

Now that we *understand* how relations were constructed in this particular experiment, it is no longer, according to the researcher, appropriate to talk *only* about systems as such (i.e. the "bureaucratic system, technology system and user system"); we must also talk about their representatives: the *actors*. For this reason the systems *denotations* are changed to actors denotations.

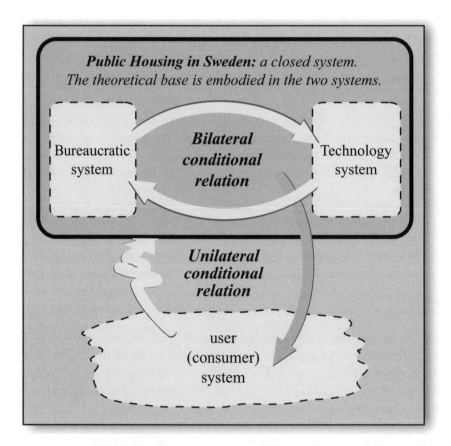

Figure 14.5   The Codetermination Act as a Crash

Now that there are "living" actors in Figure 14.5 it is, according to the researcher, natural to look at the development of conditions for a social and technical fit as a *language game* (language game relations). The reason it is more appropriate to talk about language game relations as a kind of investigating instrument is because the actors in the experiment use everyday terms to express their opinions about the conditions for the social and technical fit. Nevertheless, the contents of these terms – the concepts – must be continuously reinterpreted so they suit the situation in which an actor is placed at any given moment.

A magnificent language game takes place. The researcher provides the following example in her report:

> At the start of the project the head planner directs his version of the story to (representatives for) the local authorities to gain their interest. The authorities in question formulate objectives, and invite users/consumers. The architects present the conditions in a way that interests the users. The users become interested, but find out later that the conditions were not as they had perceived them. Now the head planner explains to the users that they must somehow have misunderstood, and the conditions are reinterpreted. The local authorities then find it necessary to change their opinion about the conditions, at least partly. Now, the users begin to ask questions and the local authorities ask why. This explanation is relayed to the building constructors, who, in turn, specify some conditions and changes others. And then ...

An institutionalizing and legitimizing pattern is established in this continuous process of externalized reinterpretation, which means that some aspects of the experiment within the systems constellations become cemented; that is, they become accepted and no longer questioned. As the experiment continues, more and more aspects are cemented until, at the end, we can talk about the specific *factive reality* to the experiment. Put together, this makes it possible, according to the researcher, to better describe the construction of the systems and their relations to the experiment; this is done based on *the conditional relations* for a social and technical fit interpreted as language game relations (the constitution of actors).

In order to assess this experiment it is important to keep this aspect in mind. To be able to *understand* the social game and to translate the experiences into planning instruments, *the conditional relations mentioned above must be anchored in the different meaning constructed contexts of the systems.*

A comment on complementarity

One important aspect of this description is how the researcher used actors concepts within the framework of the development of illustrative languages in the systems approach, to be better able to communicate the phenomena that she attempts to make explicit. The researcher also sometimes deliberately used actors concepts (not illustrated above) in her description in order to "puncture" what she referred to as "the planner's levelling systems-eye". The planner and the representatives of the local authorities usually spoke in fairly extreme technological/bureaucratic systems terms to the users, who, on their side, usually picked up their language images from totally different social contexts. On some issues, especially among the planners, this led to seeing the participating users/consumers as nothing but *components* of the system, lacking meaning contexts of their own, in relation to the *totality* as defined by the planner.

Another important aspect of the researcher's investigation is how she, *actors-wise*, created meaning around the *construction* of the questionnaires and the *analytical testing* of hypotheses. The result of these complementary procedures strengthened the evaluation and gave further material to the researcher in giving weight to her critical systems descriptions and language comments. The researcher proceeded as mentioned and looked for *under-standing* (see Figure 9.3) by introducing a number of *metaphors,* out of which we have here reported what is possibly the most important one.

The researcher's critical *metaphor* – "the planner's levelling systems-eye" – and certain systems concepts surrounding it were consequently used in the report to make visible the problems that arose through the very real difficulties the planners and people from the local authorities had in overcoming their superior and patronizing attitude, in which the other "actors" (users) were constantly to be helped and formally placed in a *technological system for co-determination. The metaphor, in this context, is built around the middle concept of "leveling". The first phrase (the planner)* indicates the active part, and the final word *(systems-eye) is* the tool for the activity. *Levelling* means dominating, ruling and controlling the context, based on the fact that the word is taken from the planner's own technical vocabulary and refers to the activities that planners normally engage in – levelling the terrain's natural broken ground and thereby rationalizing the technical fit. In a transferred sense, therefore, "levelling" stands for the social insensitivity that constantly "levels" the users' personal ideas about how they want to live. In spite of the fact that this was only an experiment, the planners often experienced the users' subjective plans as just as hopeless and disturbing for the expansion of the technical – industrial – construction of the housing, as the hard formations of the terrain for a rational allocation of foundations and roads in the physical area.

So researchers, in their studies, frequently use various systems concepts and, furthermore, do so for varying reasons. Sometimes systems concepts are used to create a higher level of understanding for various *holistic* discussions. Sometimes they are used in order to criticize what they think is an exaggerated use of these concepts. Overuse of the concepts can lead to the construction of a systems-eye – an eye that looks at everything in terms of systems, subsystems, relations and components – that, according to the researcher in this experiment, leads to "fitting like a glove those individuals who want to plan and structure other people's lives".

What we have seen in this example is how the construction of questionnaires and testing of hypotheses, together with actors concepts, are used creatively and consciously by the systems approach as a transformative operator. What made this exciting use possible is the fact that the techniques and concepts are placed against a base other than their own; this, in turn, led to their *transformation* in an interesting way in the process of creating knowledge. Yet our presentation shows only one of several sections of a study based on a methodology of complementarity.

CASE III: THE ACTORS APPROACH AS TRANSFORMATIVE OPERATOR

Starting point

This case is an action-oriented research case (in future called the research project) where the actors-oriented researcher has been given the mission, in cooperation with a world leading multinational firm, to develop new forms of work for its machinery development for the firm's company for research and development (R&D).

The firm wants employees in its R&D company, more trans-functionally on a *dialogical* basis, to match different professional skills against those problems that are at hand in various research and development projects. At the time, for this research project trans-functional dialogues were rare. The researcher therefore chose, at an early stage, to call his project "an industrial jam session". This *metaphor* for creative development work he picked up from a book by Kao, *Jamming – The Art and Discipline of Business Creativity* (1997). With the metaphor he wanted to illustrate the improvisation's demanding exercise to empower a person to *emancipate* himself/herself and reach higher creative levels in trans-functional cooperation. That cooperation which the firm wanted was, after all, to take place within an existing relatively strict control system, which the senior management of the firm did not want to waive.

In his first contacts with the firm's R&D company the researcher quickly found out that present work was organized completely linear-functionally, and *trans-competent* contacts were seriously obstructed. People consequently worked almost completely within their own professionally homogenous departments. When some specific competence was missing in their own group, they passed well-defined problem specifications to other equally skill-homogenous groups. The constructors called this way of working somewhat jokingly "the container model", which also pointed at how they looked at the existing lack of trans-contacts between people themselves. This way of working was in operation in spite of the requirement that most projects at that time demanded cross-boundary work from a cost effective as well as from a conceptual perspective. As a *dialogical multiprofessional* "creative jamming" did not exist in the firm to the extent asked for, in spite of the strong need for such a way of working, the researcher was asked to come up with proposals for new forms of organization of, and work in, a new *innovation system*: forms which could satisfy the senior management's desires, but which could at the same time function within the present control system. Furthermore, the firm had previously engaged consultants, the outcome of which had been rather pouring more concrete into already established forms.

The work of these consultants had, for instance, resulted in a number of project management programmes being set up to handle what was already there (= already known). In order to reduce the costs for developing new machinery, the consultants had recommended that this should, to an increasing extent, be done by assembling already known "building bricks" (technical solutions). The innovation process had therefore been divided into phases with strict rules for moving from one of these phases to the next. There were also carefully developed technical specifications for these moves. "Key technologies", "docking in" and "process flow" were key words in this innovation system. The goal of the consultants' model was to use that knowledge which already existed, and minimize the risk by auditing at every phase.

Some of this had made the innovation process to substantially lose creative height compared with the competitors. The senior management of the firm at large, therefore, experienced to an increasing extent that its R&D company was characterized by *reactive* behaviour and that it was no longer the *proactive* company it had once been.

The senior management of the firm at large had self-critically asked itself if it would be possible, with the existing *innovation system* of the R&D company, to come up with a world leading multinational firm similar to the present one, which had been built on those basic innovations which were generated eighty years ago. Its answer had been a clear "no".

It would not be possible: Present working order was designed to take care of a mature system, not handle radical innovation and high-risk projects.

Another major problem was how new projects *were initiated*. The researcher also discovered early in his *dialogues* how the present way of working reinforced "the container model". From their own range of competencies the project managers chose that competence they thought was needed in the different phases of the course of innovation. This resulted in too narrow *perspectives*. The problem was, furthermore, that they had little knowledge of what skills were actually obtainable (almost non-existing knowledge of what skills other colleagues had) or even what skills might be necessary. The senior management of the R&D company was here of the opinion that their project managers were very little aware that it was not only about knowing where the competence was; the real problem, as this senior management saw it, was that the project managers often did not even know which *general* competence was needed to find out what *specific* competence was lacking. "The container model" and the formalized innovation process were in fact effectively de-organizing an effective initial and chaotic *cross-competence search* (jamming) when starting a project. This was also quickly discovered by the researcher in his introductory *problematization*.

The complementary ambitions of the researcher

The researcher saw early in the project a possibility to develop a theory for MultiProfessional Dynamics (MPD) in *innovation processes*, containing *descriptive language*, *models* and concrete *instruments* for this MPD work as innovative *structure* and *process*. He realized after a number of exploring dialogues with actors from both senior management groups (the firm at large and the R&D company) as well as with individual researchers/constructors, that the project could also offer exciting possibilities for *complementary* methodological creations.

Using the actors approach the researcher takes on the project. As a first *instrument* he is thinking of putting together a new kind of *personality test*, which is focuses on the personal characteristics that are necessary from an MPD perspective. Using *analytical* tests and questionnaires of this type is not something that is normally part of the actors approach. Nor is it common to use *systems* terms, as these, according to the actors view, do not consider the *dialectics* of being a creator of relations and an *actor* as an inviolable whole. These thoughts are triggering the researcher to *transform* analytical techniques, as well as systems oriented terms, to become *methods* in the project in question.

So, for the researcher, it is about developing a personality test (MPD test) which is based on the basic idea of the actors approach to search for *first hand expressions*, which cannot normally be caught in questionnaires and personality tests. Through these latter exercises, *second hand expressions* are obtained instead, that is, *expressions about expressions* around experiences which somebody has already given *expression* to in the very moment of experiencing. The researcher also has to try to describe the innovation process in a systems model which builds further on the jamming *metaphor* and which can show that multidimensional complexity which the actors view attempts to *vivify* through its *structurally and dialectically based denotation of conceptual meaning*. The researcher is consequently *applying* his methodological view *in practice* (*approach*) as a *transformative operator* to achieve a, for him, desirable *complementarity* in his project.

Transformative operations

Primary procedures

The researcher is planning, as *primary procedures,* to conduct a number of *dialogues* and draw *actors' maps* on those he conducted initially in order to understand the actors' *intentions* with the project. In these dialogues he aims, as an antithesis, to bring up his own ideas as well around how he looks at what previous consultants have done.

He is looking at the *selection* of actors as a *recommendation selection* as well as a *problem/ opportunity oriented selection.*

Through *experiments* and personality tests (MPD tests) of a complementary nature (see below) he wants to create a research foundation, which can later be condensed, in order to come up with a number of *ideal types* in the *primary* meaning of the actors view. These are to focus the *essences* in a theory of multiprofessional dynamics (MPD) as an innovative process on the vision of an industrial jam session as a *metaphor.* The researcher wants to show that multiprofessional development is not only about mixing different professional skills but increasingly about using the personalities of participating actors in relation to their creating of meaning in inventive group processes. This whole thing requires keeping in mind the different actors' finite provinces of meaning in all aspects of the social reality's dialectical process structure of subjectification, externalization, objectification and internalization.

Complementary procedures

The researcher is interpreting the present senior management's description of the innovation system of the firm and is converting, with the actors view as operator, important systems concepts in their present model. He is trying to create an alternative more *dynamic* and *process oriented* model where the relation-searching *actor* is put in the centre. The systems model also builds on those *first hand expressions* that the senior management team in the firm has used when describing the R&D company innovation process. Through this the researcher is able to catch the leadership's intention in a *systems language* which they recognize, at the same time as it is shaped so that it shows itself, in a dialectical sense, as the second in the relation to their first, that is, as an antithesis (see "Dialectics" in Chapter 6). The researcher's *knowledge ambition* (see Figure 6.2) is, in fact, to let this model (see Figure 14. 6 overleaf) participate as a step in *a field of procreative tension* – a field that he aims to establish as an experimental research basis for his theoretical development and modelling of an *MPD-oriented innovation process.* In this field of procreative tension a vital interplay is to take place as seen in living processes and the imaginative triggering of ideas. He is very anxious to use his *operations* to deliver what is potential in what is factual as one part of his own theoretical development around MPD. At the same time he wishes to illustrate this theory in an action-oriented way.

The next extensive *complementary procedure* he is facing is how a personality test of an MPD type is to be constructed. This is not done by simply focusing the personal characteristics that according to different theories are prominent in similar developmental contexts. He has to create a test which is based on the actors principle of *first hand expressions,* while at the same time creating one that it is possible to *quantify* to a certain degree. The researcher, therefore, cannot just use some analytical test (technique) which asks the actors questions

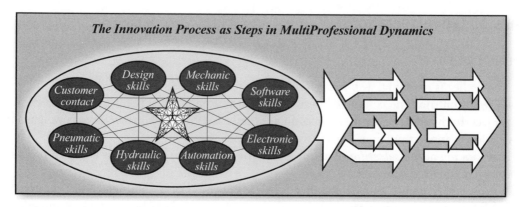

Figure 14.6   The Innovation System

about how they have acted or believe they would act in a specific situation, he has to develop an *action-oriented* test which in principle lets the actors arrive at their answers through their own first hand expressions of what they have been exposed to. That is to say, instead of asking the actors how they think they would act facing a specific situation they are now to assess for themselves how they did act in such situations.

Consequently, he is exposing, for an experimental purpose, chosen actors (forty-eight selected researchers and constructors from the firm's R&D company) to a number of *development situations*. All these situations are related to the present systems model as well as to the new one, built on the metaphor of an industrial jam session as *innovation process*. The development situations initiate in different ways actors oriented subjectifications and externalizations as direct first hand expressions, which then immediately provide the actors with answers in the MPD test to questions about how they act in a specific situation. The actors are only to read how they just have acted and provide that answer. A number of questions and situations with cross-references are created to increase the *validity* as well as the *reliability* of the test (see "Methodics" below). The test material then provides a basis together with conducted dialogues for his condensation of the results to those different *ideal types* that are mentioned above under "Primary Procedures".

Methodics

That *methodics* which the researcher designs as a kind of *logistical flow* of those activities he intends to implement is planned in detail – almost as an analytical project would proceed. It is, however, supposed to be really chaotic within the different partial steps in order to vivify what the researcher sees as decisive *constitutional factors* for creative innovation processes. Another basic actors principle with which the researcher is working is that research/consulting/investigation and implementation are not to stand in a kind of before–after relationship, which is often the case within the systems approach where new systems solutions are implemented at the end of a knowledge-creating process. The researcher has seen this leading to problems too often. He therefore wants to show that it is possible, as with *practical* (approaching) *methodics* in research and action oriented projects, to let implementation be a part of the *on-going* experimental process of *thesis–antithesis–synthesis*.

The researcher's initial round of dialogues leads into a first session of three days of experiments (*the main thesis*) where personality tests of the MPD type are conducted. Those *development situations* that the researcher has designed are based on a large number of *realistic* and on-going *real development projects* in the firm. In the main thesis the constructors are now in *traditionally* composed groups according to the so-called "container model", confronting those realistic and on-going real projects mentioned according to the R&D company's way of working – also *traditional*. The actors are to provide as individual answers to the test questionnaire that was constructed how they react personally and express themselves in such situations. After analysis of personalities and a condensation of these into a number of *ideal types*, which the researcher asserts is supporting the dynamics of multi-professionalism according to the *metatheories* of the actors view (see Figure 6.7), he feeds back the results to the senior management of the firm.

After one month the researcher confronts the forty-eight researchers/constructors again in a three-day session of activities (*the main antithesis*). *The development situations* are the same as before in the main thesis, but now the actors are divided into MPD teams. They are composed by skills as well as by how the individual actors match those different ideal types which the researcher has condensed out of the test material. The researcher is, so to say, composing *ideal MPD teams* as a starting point for this main antithesis. Here the chosen actors are now to meet different *ways of working* as well (see under "Results" below) which match the *metaphor* of an industrial jam session. This means that the researcher in experimenting action is presenting what he sees as the road to a new *innovation system*. This time the actors are once more answering questions in the constructed questionnaire as a *reliability* control of the MPD test being developed.

Furthermore, the researcher conducts a number of dialogues after these tests and experiments to come up with a deepened *understanding* around how the groups have attacked the problems in the first format ("container") and in the second MPD format. All this had as a purpose to make it possible as a *main synthesis* to give shape to the whole experimental process through a *model* and a *language* for a new *innovation system*, a *system* where all *actors*, through creative actions, have been allowed to give their personal prints as complete and authentic human beings. *The synthesis* then becomes the natural *implementation*. Which means, in turn, that no implementation is needed, as the new system, *materially* as well as *intentionally*, has been delivered by the actors themselves as what is *potential in what is factual*. The actors have, through their creative actions, in experiments and dialogues externalized a new social reality together with the researcher. The researcher illustrates his dialectical methodics in the Figure 14.7:

Please compare Figure 14.7 with Figure 3.15. Here it is possible to see how the researcher's *applied methodics* follows the basic principles for the *dialectical thinking* in the actors view.

Results

Having come to the result of this *operative paradigm* with the researcher's *procreative report* as its end product (see "The procreative report" in Chapter 7), we want to point to some

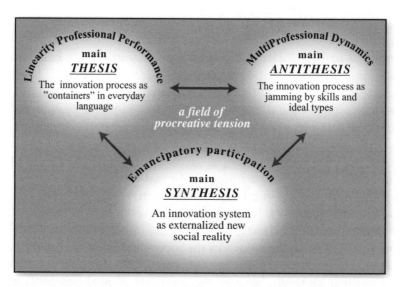

Figure 14.7   The Dialectic Methodics of the Actors Apporach as Transformative Operator

important matters from the researcher's *complementary* perspective. Within the framework of this book it is, however, not possible to describe those theories and ways of working for MPD processes which the researcher developed. Nor is it possible to illustrate all those different parts that went into the new *innovation system*. This is outside the methodological ambitions of this book.

The basic idea of the researcher, as presented in his report, was the importance of *procreative tension* to combine and confront different skills with different ideal types in one and the same MPD team. And in order to do this he constructed an MPD test, which made it possible for him and management to get a good picture of the profiles of the participating actors from an ideal typified *perspective*. He also presented a putting together of this for the whole participating group. We are, below, examine, in a shortened version, some of these *ideal type descriptions* and parts of that *descriptive* and *symbolic language* developed by the researcher. He started his report with the following:

MultiProfessional Dynamics as an innovation system is not a new collection of boxes, arrows and models to learn for cooperation and construction in the engineering sense. MPD is a multicomplex *totality* and by this a way of *thinking* and *acting* as researcher/constructor. The moment somebody attempts to describe and bring *analytical order* to such a totality, the *totality* easily *disappears*. A work of art is not presenting itself to the person who *attempts* to separate and describe it in terms of colour chemistry, construction of forms or size and weight. Complex phenomena (such as your machinery and like a work of art) have the peculiarity to lose their *construction potential* identity at such *analytical* attempts. These phenomena are like pictures – genuine wholes. MPD should therefore be reflected out of a large number of aspects, which is enriching the insight of *the potential totality in what is factual*. Otherwise it becomes as if one is tearing a picture into pieces, and by that act, hoping to see what it represents.

The researcher condensed ten different ideal types out of the material and chose in his feedback to every individual actor to denote that ideal type which was most prominent with him/her – their "dominant ideal type" – and characteristics of others as "secondary ideal types". He also presented a quantified picture of the collected group's profiles in relation to *dominant* and *secondary* ideal-typified characteristics. The reason was that this was necessary as a basis for being able to match suitable MPD teams in relation to the different projects of machinery that the firm's R&D company was working with. Before the researcher presented his different ideal types he reminded the individual actors of the meaning of the ideal type as a notion "loaded with energy", with procreative words as follows:

No single actor represents any of the ideal types in full. Rather a person is seen as "gliding" somewhat between them in his/her ambition to create technological development. However, the ideal types have a meaning by enlightening what can be seen as necessary triggers (instruments) in order for an MPD team to start "swinging". All the participants in such a team are informed of this necessity, and that no ideal type is worth more than any other. It is therefore possible to act safely within the framework of these ideals in one's conviction that *the intonation, the sensitivity, the dialogue and the dialectics* between them all create synergy of an unexpected kind. Without this insight the process runs the risk of ending up in too much of a "solo play", which will not entice that improvisation which is a quality of a "jamming" MPD team. "Ideal type" therefore becomes a *metaphor* for delivering what is potential in what is factual.

When an MPD team is put together one has consequently to see to it that the group has the necessary professional set-up as far as the mission is concerned and that the members of the group have personal qualities that are matching the different ideal types for an ideal MPD team.

In a reduced version we reproduce six of the ten ideal types that the researcher presented:

The down-to-earth project maker
The practical creative seeker (technically/economically/marketwise), who easily loses the totality and the overriding objectives. An "inventor" who understands the importance of listening but who is at the same time exclusively focusing on each part of a creative process in isolation.

The process guide
The empathical leader who understands the group process on its own terms. Tries to create preunderstanding and "tone up". Has understood that leadership for technical development is about leading human development in multi-professional teams, with the differences in the ideal types as an inspiration.

The development therapist
The methodically constructive person who asks questions rather than generates answers and ideas. Is able with his/her questions to point at similarities and differences. Is no direct leader, however, rather a kind of development therapist, which is keeping the "safe" rhythm in the MPD team.

(Continued)

(Continued)

The visionary project maker
The imaginatively creative seeker (technically/economically/marketwise), who is focusing on the totality and the overriding objectives. A visionary who understands the importance of listening but who is, at the same time, devotedly focusing on the major issues in an MPD process.

The equilibrist
The actor who is technically structuring the process as it moves on. Brings a necessary aspect of structure/analytics into the MPD process and contributes by this to strategic balance/feeling of objectives. Is the person who continuously and purposefully is running a project toward completion and production.

The image interpreter
The actor who is likely to see technical solutions as images without any limited technical look. Is experimental and lively with his/her own thinking, as if it was a collage of images which can be cut and pasted in any combinations.

The researcher also designed a complete *systems language* with symbols for the whole innovation process. This *constituted* the foundation of the company's new *innovation system*. Some shortened examples of this work of language and symbols are illustrated in Figure 14.8.

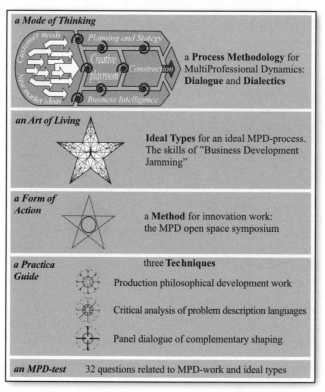

Figure 14.8   MultiProfessional Dynamics

We have in this chapter, with pedagogic care, tried, in a practical way, to illustrate the potential interdependency in opposite methodological opinions of similar problems which is described in Box 13.2 "The Arbnor/Bjerke Methodological Principle of Complementarity". With high crealiability in knowledge-creating work we can reach surprising and highly interesting results – that is, when research/ consulting/ investigation is at its best. The three different cases described also show clearly that it is not only possible to conduct studies using this methodology of complementarity but that it is also very desirable.

POINTS OF REFLECTION

1. What is it that the doctoral student in Case I is doing as a *first step* in designing an *operative paradigm* with the analytical approach as a transformative operator?
2. The *ultimate presumptions* of the analytical approach, for example, that knowledge is seen as something cumulative, is quickly shown in Case I. Give two examples of this!
3. The doctoral student in Case I chooses to combine his consulting mission with a research oriented study of so-called "best practice". In this *way of searching* (looking for "best practice") there is an important starting point for the analytical approach. What is it?
4. The doctoral student also makes a discovery in Kunde's book which makes him deepen even further his *complementary way of* thinking. What was it that he started to reflect on?
5. In order to, through complementary procedures, compensate for those shortcomings the doctoral student thinks he can see with "best practice", he brings up, inspired by the actors approach, what he refers to as *"typical individuals"*. Point out in which way his treatment here *exceeds* normal analytical/statistical acting by what he refers to as "typical individuals".
6. With respect to one of the literature references which the doctoral student in Case I is using he feels hesitant about whether it concerns *complementarity*. Study the quote he leaves in the report and come up with your own opinion of what is said by Whitman & Woszczynski (2003).
7. In Case II the researcher is conducting a number of *primary procedures* in relation to the *five principles* of the systems view. These principles you know from before (Chapter 5), together with those *two perspectives* that might exist in systems studies. How does the researcher think concerning the issue of perspectives? And why?
8. In Case II with the systems approach as operator, the researcher is conducting complementary procedures in relation to the actors approach as well as to the analytical approach. Point out the two most central *concepts/techniques/methods* that she is looking to use as complementary.

(Continued)

(Continued)

9. The systems oriented researcher in Case II is conducting a *questionnaire study* in three steps using *complementary methodology*. Apply this thinking to an optional business case where you perceive that it would provide added interesting aspects and results.

10. The researcher in Case II is also talking about a *language game, which* she wants to illuminate. What does this mean and how does it come out in the case, and from which view does it originate?

11. In Case II there is also talk about creating *understanding* in the meaning of the systems view. Among other things, the researcher presents a critical *metaphor*. Why does she refer to it as "critical"? And in what way is she constructing an eye-opener in the metaphor?

12. Case III starts from an actors oriented researcher who is developing a new type of mode of working for the R&D activity of the company. Early on the researcher is setting up a *metaphor* of "an industrial jam session" as a kind of prototype. What is the idea behind having a metaphor as a *guide* in a project like this one?

13. When the researcher in Case III is to find out what the consultants have done earlier, he discovers that the company, instead of having increased its comparative creative height, has actually lost it. If you *study* how the consultants *were thinking,* can you conclude which *view* they started from when they talked in such terms as "key technologies", "docking in", etc.?

14. If you had worked with *Competitive Intelligence* and run into something similar, that is, if a company had organized its *innovation activities* in the same way as the researcher faced in Case III, what would you then have reported to your employer about the competitive position of this company?

15. The systems oriented researcher in Case II is using, through a complementary procedure, the concept of *first hand expressions* from the actors view when conducting a questionnaire study. In Case III, which starts from the actors view as a transformative operator, this is a logical outcome. But here a *transformation* in relation to the analytical approach is taking place instead. What is the researcher aiming at then? And how does he solve this problem of testing personality in a creative way?

16. In Case III the researcher is presenting his view on *implementation* and creates, according to the dialectical methodics of the actors view, an "implementation process" which differs completely from the one in Case I. Describe the *difference* and how this difference can easily be *derived* from the ultimate presumptions of the various views.

17. The researcher conducts a reliability assessment of his MPD test in Case III. What is he assessing then?

18. In a fair way judging the degree of *crealiability of complementarity* in the different cases is not possible, of course, with the material that has been presented here. But for the sake of a pedagogical exercise we want you independently, but at the same time as others, to make an evaluation of the three cases. After having done so, compare your evaluations and argue for how you have weighted the different core elements and why, as well as how you have actually judged the cases.

RECOMMENDED FURTHER READING

See the end of the Appendix and visit the website below.

Become a worldwide partner as a *knowledge creator* in the development of *Methodology or Creating Business Knowledge* by visiting the website: **www.knowledge-creator.com**. Here you can contribute by asking your own questions and you will also find answers to the most frequently asked questions. The website has been developed alongside this third edition of the book and the questions posted there will be used to provide input for future editions.

15 METHODOLOGY AS BUSINESS CREATING INTELLIGENCE

> In this chapter we examine in what way our methodological grammar can be an important and decisive part of a larger field, which is about how creating knowledge has become an overall production factor for business. The chapter also illustrates briefly how the methodological theme of the book can enrich and deepen what we associate with business and competitive intelligence. We introduce the concepts of knowledge audit and knowledge intelligence here as a conceptualization of methodology as business creating intelligence.

CREALIABILITY OF COMPLEMENTARITY IN FOCUS

To learn how to think and act in terms of methodology of complementarity is a strength in all types of knowledge-creating work. It also provides the absolutely necessary circumstances to be able to assess and develop *the knowledge-creating resources* of a company with a high *crealiability,* that is, the very foundation for a company's present and future power as a business culture for *development* and *renewal* of their operations.

This way of *thinking* and *acting* not only provides opportunities to create one's own competitive advantages by honing one's knowledge-creating resources to the highest possible degree of *crealiability of complementarity* (see Figure 13.6); it also provides unique possibilities to *decode* the competitors' ways of thinking and acting. Through such an ability for *intelligence,* using a well developed methodology for creating Business knowledge, the best possible business abilities are created in a global economy where knowledge is a *production factor* of superior value.

The point is that a well developed methodology provides the possibility of acquiring competitive advantages of *immaterial excellence.* The skill in a business context of being able to interpret and see what others do not see is perhaps the largest immaterial success that one can achieve. It also makes it possible to perceive what is going on in a market before others do. With competitive advantages invested in knowledge-creating resources, one can acquire a sustainable and innovative lead.

KNOWLEDGE-CREATING AS PRODUCTION FACTOR

The growth of new institutions/organizations for allocating *production factors* has historically varied with the importance of these factors in development. In the course of industrialism, a number of institutions have emerged to make the allocation of *raw materials*, *capital* and *labour* more effective. This has often resulted in *lower transaction costs* for necessary economic development, dispersions and exchanges.

Delivery routes, trade structures and marketplaces have been developed and improved to facilitate an ever more effective allocation of raw materials in industrial society.

In the meantime, banks and other financial facilitators have become effective institutions for allocating capital between people willing to save and people willing to invest in what they consider to be profitable projects.

The labour market has also developed and has recently gone through drastic changes, with the appearance of both public and private institutions for facilitating the linkage of labour with available and suitable jobs.

If this development of various organizations/institutions for allocating raw materials, capital and labour had not occurred, many exchanges favourable to all parties would not have taken place. Hand in hand with this material development of institutions for allocating production factors, the *professional knowledge* has increased for quality assurance of these *factors* and assessing their value and potential for success.

Nowadays, however, it is not the allocation of raw materials, capital and labour that chiefly limit development; instead the emphasis is increasingly on other limited resources of a more *immaterial character*, like leadership, creativity, knowledge creating, innovativeness, skills of intelligence and the willingness to change. Already in 1993, Drucker, in his book *Post-Capitalist Society*, argues convincingly that knowledge is not only another *production factor* along with the more traditional ones, but in reality is "the only meaningful resource today".

To claim that the skills of administrating as well as of adding/creating value to the knowledge and intelligence stock of companies and organizations presents perhaps the most intricate and most progressive field of work for business people (engaged in both theory and practice) now and in the future, should not be seen as an overstatement.

The role that graduates in Business Administration and Economics can play as *knowledge creators* (beyond their role as researchers/consultants/investigators) is definitely associated with their ability to do *knowledge work* in, at least, four areas:

1. To *improve* the process of creating knowledge of complementarity – to create a high degree of learning effectiveness in companies/organizations.
2. To *make sure* that learning effectiveness is also cost-effective – in other words, to uphold the *quality* of knowledge creating so that it has a *competitive potential* and belongs to the future based on its ultimate presumptions.
3. To *lower* transaction costs in the external, as well as the internal knowledge factor markets (virtually/concretely), for rapid and ongoing networks of various kinds of knowledge, *without* reducing long-term *variety*, into competitive and creative foci of solid business creation and development.
4. To *secure the ability* to "decode" the *inherent* presumptions of different knowledge of competitors and markets as a deeper kind of business and competitive intelligence.

The market is underdeveloped on each of these four counts. Our hope is that this third edition of *Methodology for Creating Business Knowledge* can also serve as a basis for the development of business in these areas – a kind of business "foundation" for *creating*, *auditing* and

Figure 15.1   Business Opportunity.

"decoding" knowledge/intelligence. It is truly no easy task for graduates in the fields of Business and Economics to be creators of knowledge in all these respects.

In this factor market it is natural for everything from sophisticated and serious ideas/recipes/ knowledge to various commercial tasks and "magical" truths to emerge; for everything, from what we are offered at specially arranged knowledge trade fairs around the world to be consumed as ready-made information in the hope of improving our knowledge-creating ability, to, somewhere else in the very same trade fairs, being warned that our existing knowledge is "rootless" and that "not even knowledge helps" to solve our problems. Knowledge audit and intelligence, therefore, is going to be a very subtle task to deal with.

Points 1–3 above we will treat under the concept of *knowledge audit* and point 4, which mainly concerns externally oriented activities, we describe under the concept of *knowledge intelligence*. Where the two *processes* of mainly internal and external character meet, a business developing/renewing *interface* is opened, which offers businesses and knowledge creators unexpected possibilities for quality assurance of, and excellence in, the production factor of creating knowledge (see Figure 15.1).

Creating knowledge as the most decisive *production factor* also means, really, that *this is the factor* that will continuously become *the critical resource* if there are disturbances in other production factors. It is by *creating knowledge* with high *crealiability* that we solve our problems, make our future businesses more effective and develop them.

KNOWLEDGE AUDIT

When we talk about knowledge creating as the totally superior factor for business development, it is also clear that *Methodology for Creating Business Knowledge* is more important than ever for this task in general, and for business ventures based on knowledge creation in particular. If *learning per invested day* is the foremost competitive factor – in everything from leadership to constructive customer relations, branding, creative financing, innovative market development, efficient manufacturing, business revival, image-promoting, internal education, entrepreneurship, and more – we can also see an important part of the tasks of graduates of Business and Economics is to be able to play an important role as a *knowledge creator*.

We can understand from this that owners of, as well as all employees in, a company should be seriously interested in upholding the *quality* of information about the basis that the business's learning and way of working rest on. Not only knowledge (the content), but also the *methods of creating* knowledge and *methods for learning* (the form) can become extinct and bankrupt. If the latter are not in tune with the times, a seeming paradox may take place: that a company becomes effective in creating and learning knowledge that is not cost-effective: in other words, an intensification of knowledge that results in a company with a diminished competitive potential and knowledge for the future. An upholdable *quality* of knowledge, of creating knowledge and of learning, must therefore have *content* as well as *form*.

The way of quality assurance (using our four areas of knowledge creation presented above as a starting point) must begin with the *ultimate presumptions* on which the different methods of knowledge creation are based. We have attempted in this book to give as rich a picture as possible of the language, the ideas, and the acts that compose the *three different worlds of knowledge creation* including the *methodology of complementarity*. In other words, knowledge-creating that has a very low cost-effectiveness can be pointed out and remedied by using *knowledge auditing*.

To be able to point out development trends and value shifts at an early stage, to invest in constructive future competitive advantages conceptually as well as actually, to develop "delivery routes" and "marketplaces" (what we call "creative foci" – area 3, see previous list) for the innovative creation of knowledge, will require that company boards and executive management in all firms have access to well-formulated action data that is based on a knowledge audit of what the knowledge that their learning, management and business is based on from a broad and deep perspective. This instrument – *the knowledge audit* – will be a *decisive point* on which business must be founded if we are to take to heart the message of knowledge-based business.

A knowledge audit contains a number of questions for the auditor and his/her assisting experts. And most of these business related methodological questions the reader will find in this book, especially in the chapters containing practical examples, if and when the reader has reached the necessary insight of the methodological grammar in question.

The information in this book is also offered as a foundation for knowledge audits, which we hereby introduce as a discipline in the subject of business to supplement traditional financial audits and other present and future audits.

This discipline has the objective of indicating whether the knowledge field – here described as the *knowledge*, the *methodology* of creating knowledge, and the *language* that is used to conduct business and, with the ultimate presumptions in mind, to develop new activities – can be expected to *create success* that is sustainable, powerful and in the right direction. Another task of the knowledge audit is to contribute to a creative rationalization of knowledge in order to increase cost-effectiveness in the company creating knowledge.

We introduced above a description of the *emergence* of new institutions/organizations for *allocating* production factors in society, because these *production factors* are important in development. The economic system works constantly on lowering the transaction costs for these exchanges and divisions. This increased efficiency has also been stimulated by tax policy and infrastructural investments. Inside the companies, these production factors have been further refined and continuously exposed to rationalization drives in relation to competition in the market.

Through various kinds of fiscal policy, society has been able to stimulate, and to some extent direct, the rationalization work of businesses; unfortunately it has also been able to prevent the changes that are necessary for achieving long-term sustainability. The tax shift from labour to energy and raw materials is also in line with the development of *knowledge-creating business*. This is because knowledge-creating businesses are intimately connected with human *creative and intellectual powers* – namely, people at work. And as we said above, *creating knowledge* as a production factor is also the most critical resource to solve those problems that may arise at disturbances of the other production factors.

A well-developed knowledge audit for knowledge rationalization, together with a tax shift, will make it possible for companies to pay more employees, at the same time that the rationalization interest is forced by market competition to raise the cost-effectiveness of the knowledge field per invested day. This will guarantee an ongoing productivity development toward long-term upholdability and a high competitive potential through business becoming smarter and more efficient in its use of capital, energy and raw materials.

We will probably also find, in the productivity development of the knowledge field, that *social inventions* have a great potential when combined with all the possibilities that information technology brings us. Our reason for advocating an audit for the rationalization of knowledge, therefore, is that it will be able to initiate a number of *social inventions* in the domain in combination with suitable technology. We are convinced that, if productivity development is to take place, *we have to bring into business more insight of ultimate presumptions of knowledge and of methodology of complementarity.*

Undoubtedly, the development of new social inventions that will allow us to rationalize the productive and innovative use of knowledge, to work at creating knowledge of complementarity, and to learn, is one of the major challenges in connection to the environmental challenge of our time.

A ground plan for knowledge audit

Methodology for Creating Business Knowledge as a ground plan for a knowledge audit emphasizes – regardless of what might be meant by success – that the *immaterial* production factor of knowledge, knowledge creation and learning must be upholdable, just like other production factors, if success is to be achieved. Inferior raw materials or poor capital conditions will hardly lead to what we associate with success. For these latter factors, which include labour, today's business has methods that are just as superior for upholding quality as it has methods that are inferior for upholding our *immaterial* production factor.

Upholding the quality of knowledge, knowledge creation and learning means that business can make sure that the methods that are used to handle knowledge, the creation of knowledge, and the development of learning, based on its ultimate presumptions, are in line with what the business hopes to realize in the long run. It is one thing to be able to express ourselves intelligently about what we might call a superficial or surface level, but something else entirely to have insight into the ultimate presumptions and premises for this level's manifold forms of expression.

With industry in a state of constant transformation in which different kinds of knowledge, learning and creative methods are offered in an unprecedented range, it is of the utmost importance that business economists develop a knowledge auditing profession: substantial and important economic, human and ecological values are at stake.

Conducting a knowledge audit is not one of the easiest activities, something that is probably evident from this book as a whole, nor can it be handled in the same way as an established financial audit. It must be developed as a kind of *thematic* judgement (see the Glossary), or as various methodological themes with reference to ultimate presumptions about what the knowledge within these themes is actually knowledge about in relation to the knowledge fields and the business language of the corporation. As a ground plan for these auditing activities, we have presented a *thematic language* of methodology, three methodological *views/approaches*, a methodology of *complementarity* and a quality assurance concept of *crealiability*.

We conclude the book by presenting some notions about knowledge intelligence related to knowledge creating and the methodology of complementarity as central tools in this subject of business creating.

KNOWLEDGE INTELLIGENCE

Knowledge intelligence is to us an overall concept to describe what we generally refer to as *intelligence* in relation to *business*. In this area we usually meet the concept in constellations like *business intelligence* and *competitive intelligence*. As knowledge creator it is possible to observe in those two contexts of intelligence a common low degree of awareness about what the point of departure from the theory of science and methodology can mean for what is collected and called "raw material" and "data/information" (see below).

This makes our methodological grammar highly relevant and interesting to introduce in these contexts of intelligence, as it is not only researchers/consultants/ investigators who come into contact with today's multifaceted science; *contradictory* scientific statements now commonly confront people involved in everyday business life. Sometimes these contradictions appear to be imaginary, sometimes invisible but tangible, and the like. How does *intelligence* relate, for example, to different methodological starting points and various data produced in the common name of science? How to handle, for instance, that data, according to some thinkers, are always theory laden? "observation is theory laden in that our theories influence what we see, and hence there is no actual separation between theory, interpretation and data" (Gill & Johnson, 2002: 179). Or as Hunt expresses it in the book *Controversy in Marketing Theory*. "Therefore, because all epistemically significant observation in research is theory-laden, objectivity is impossible" (2003: 278).

Some basic values are also so basic and are shared by so many that they are part of virtually invisible starting points for a given science. These values show themselves to some extent in what we earlier called *pre-scientific concepts*. This influence, conditioned by time and culture, is easily visible in a historical light, after necessary value shifts have taken place and the contrast sheds light on what has been. To be an *archaeologist of the present*, to put pressure on the present to get it to yield its basic *perspectives*, is no easy task for *knowledge intelligence*; particularly because it is full of conflicts. Nevertheless, this is often *precisely* how we trace new and brilliant businesses and how innovations come about. Therefore knowledge intelligence should also ask *impertinent* and *intricate* questions of a *theory of science/methodological* character to be able to come up with relevant material in the full extent of the word for decision making and business development.

Business and competitive intelligence

Let us pick up two relatively accepted definitions of the concepts of *business intelligence* (BI) and *competitive intelligence* (CI) from literature in the area.

Rustmann Jr defines BI as follows: "Generally, business intelligence can be broken down into three main categories: risk analysis, targeted collection, and counterintelligence" (2002: 6).

And Kahaner states: "Competitive intelligence is a systematic program for gathering and analyzing information about your competitors' activities and general business trends to further your own company's goals" (1997: 16).

These conceptualizations may seem unproblematic so far. What, however, quickly becomes clear when looking at the literature within the area of BI and CI, is, as mentioned above, a lack of elaborations based on theories of science and methodology. Discourses in texts around collecting and arranging information rarely if ever contain any treatments around what different methodological views for collection and arranging information mean for the results. This is something we have illustrated in a number of different ways throughout the book. We have also clearly shown the potential for deeper business insights that follows with such knowledge.

Unfortunately, within the BI and CI areas we find too often exactly what we were warning against in Box 1.2 (please read the box in full) when we wrote:

> ... methodological views make different assumptions about the reality they try to explain and/or understand. This, in turn, means that observations, collections of data, and results are determined to a large extent by the view chosen. Conscious development of knowledge in business – as in other subjects – is therefore far from "just" collecting data and making statements ...

What we, based on our conviction, are warning against is the somewhat naive belief that information is just there waiting to be collected, independent of methodological view, theories and methods. In the literature within BI and CI we also find concepts like "raw information" and "information is factual" and it is hardly any exaggeration to claim that the authors themselves often seem to be unaware of the ultimate presumptions of different methodological views. A few short examples will illustrate what we are referring to.

In the book *Competitor Intelligence – Turning Analysis into Success* (Hussey & Jenster, 1999: 95) it is expressed the following way: "What requires careful thought is how competitor information will be collected, organized, analysed, and disseminated." But the book does not in anyway touch upon any issue of theory of knowledge and science at the level of ultimate presumptions.

Kahaner writes:

> Companies with competitive intelligence programs engage in two kinds of collection procedures. First, they collect information ... for a specific reason or in response to a request from management. Second, they collect information that is saved and built into an ongoing data bank about one company, one industry, and so on. (1997: 56)

Similarly, as with Hussey & Jenster, there are no reflections of a theory of knowledge and methodology nature around the importance of the issues of methodological views for collecting information and stating knowledge results. The views they use themselves are consequently a blind spot to themselves – a pattern that is repeated in many books in this area. In books by authors like Gilad (2003) and Fuld (2006), for instance, it is also not possible to find any deeper aspects of what we are looking for and which we assert is of the utmost importance for potent and relevant BI and CI.

Rustmann Jr, with long experience of the CIA, follows in the same tracks as others referred to and writes in a committed way about collecting data/information without touching upon this very basic issue. The following illustrates what we mean: "Intelligence is not information. It is evaluated information" (2002: 27). But in the description of how the very evaluation of information is done, nothing of what we are searching for is in place here. Let us continue with some more quoted lines from his book *CIA, Inc. Espionage and the Craft of Business Intelligence*, where the *intelligence process* is described like this:

> Remember that intelligence is not just information; it is a circular process that involves several steps. ... In the first step, the decision maker ... makes a request for information that will assist him in making a particular decision. This request is then sent down to the collectors, who, in turn, use whatever sources are available to them to obtain information on that request. ... All of the information collected in this exercise is called "raw intelligence," or "raw reporting."
>
> Only after the raw information is reviewed, evaluated, collated, and written up in a coherent report for the decision maker is it called "finished intelligence." (Rustmann, 2002: 97)

What is expressed here is rather common for how intellection, reasoning, is operating within the area as far as *collecting* information is concerned – somebody wants information about something specific and sends *down* this request to somebody else, who in turn collects what is called raw data. What is then done with this raw information? Well, it has to be analysed and then we find descriptions like: "This is accomplished through some sort of reasoning process, usually through induction, deduction, abduction or a combination of these methods" (Rustmann, 2002: 98). And this is as close as one usually comes to the treatment of methodology in this type of literature. In other words, without in any way clarifying these three concepts and showing how they, by and large, belong to one methodological view, it is just stated that this is how it is done.

Nor do we find much of the type of discussion we are searching for in even such a well received book as Porter's (1998) *Competitive Strategy: Techniques for Analyzing Industries and Competitors*. His model "Five Forces" is lacking what should be of the utmost importance, the decoding of the *inherent* epistemical presumptions in different knowledge of competitors and markets with different "forces."

However, some "internal" criticism exists within BI and CI of what we could call overdone *"dataism"* (see Chapter 13). One person presenting such criticism is Walle (2000) in the book *Qualitative Research in Intelligence and Marketing*. His point of departure in terms of theory of science is in line with the actors view, but he is also working with some systems oriented conceptualizations, that is, what we call methodology of complementarity. When going through McDowell's ideas of development within intelligence, for instance, he writes:

> Stemming from McDowell's discussions, several disturbing developments in the field of intelligence serve as indicators of the decay or devolution of the field. They include: 1) An Overreliance upon Scientific/Quantitative Analysis. 2) An Overreliance upon Technology. 3) An Overreliance upon Computers and the Internet. (2000: 81)

This kind of "dataism" has, according to Walle and McDowell, in fact reduced the potential for intelligence and made it partly incapable of managing complex social circumstances (compare Figure 6.1).

In what we now denote as *knowledge intelligence* we are stressing the almost incomprehensible potential offered by analysing the *dominating concept of knowledge of a company, its way of knowledge-creating and learning* starting in our methodology of complementarity. Then we may also be able to decode the logic in the way of thinking and acting with the company. By understanding the internal logic in its very way of thinking and acting in relation to the market and society, we may also, in a simpler fashion come, to a conclusion about possible future acts by such a company. This, in turn, also provides us with increased possibilities to use *counter-intelligence* (to protect us from the intelligence from other companies).

In aspects mentioned here we look at our methodology, as a relatively complete basic tool to develop those skills that we claim must be in place in every activity seriously concerned with intelligence.

Business creating intelligence

To create new business ventures and conditions for improved business ventures always asks for a certain degree of creativity. Transferred to the area of *intelligence* as *creating business* we can see that there is no exception to this rule here either. Because, with creativity the ability to see something from several different angles is increased (see Chapter 2) which is also often a condition for *information* to start to "tell" its own story. Let us, in order to illustrate this, quote the following enlightening statement by Marti, an authority within BI/CI:

> Most people have lost the ability to fall in awe and wonder since they were kids. They have narrowed their attention span to a few things, and they rarely put into question their established mental models. Some of the best BI (Business Intelligence) professionals I know are like kids, enthusiastic about everything, open to all ideas and people, easy to reach by telephone (their secretary doesn't do much call filtering). They look for people that are stimulating and challenge their assumptions. In French we call this attitude "donner la chance à la chance" (give chance a chance). (1996: 128)

We have also asserted that effective intelligence requires insights into a theory of science as well as of a methodological nature. Our *principle of complementarity* (see Box 13.2) is directly applicable in every kind of intelligence as Walle can see: "that the complexity of people, organizations, and the world creates a situation that demands the use of diverse methods so phenomena can be viewed in all their depth" (Walle, 2000: 88).

In this combination of *creativity* and *complementarity* within *knowledge intelligence* we can also see how our concept of *crealiability* (see Figures 9.5 and 13.6) becomes useful. It is most likely that the core of *creativity* becomes one of the heaviest core elements when assessing necessary ingredients within the area of intelligence.

The model *ABC•IC* (see Figure 15.2) starts from the idea that the "collectors" already have the necessary methodological awareness of complementarity (i.e. to be knowledge creators) and the most important aspect in the model is; that the *knowledge audit* and the *knowledge intelligence* always work in concert with one another in this process of complementarity to gain the highest degree of crealiability in the above-mentioned sense.

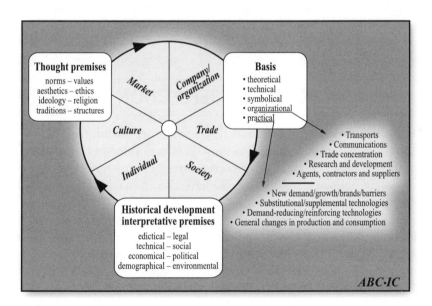

Figure 15.2   The Arbnor Business Creating • Intelligence Cycle

The model shows a circular process where information/data is arranged and "squeezed" of content and meaning in relation to the different sectors and boxes. Through this *multiperspectival* process and with an underlying awareness of our methodological *principle* of complementarity, a kind of business venture creating information material develops with high crealiability. In these cycles of *tightened information*, *contextualization* and *qualification*, a company can process its own situation as well as their competitors' and also match these "pictures" against each other.

For the *knowledge creator of intelligence* it is here about being able to combine different competencies, feelings and meanings and match them against facts, wisdom and creativity. If through *knowledge intelligence* one wants to confirm one's business development long-term potential, then one should also take the time to seriously search the individual business venture as well as the business activities as a whole in terms of an enlarged *dialogue of intelligence,* where the proponents of other and disparate opinions are also allowed to participate. This is rarely very time consuming and may provide exciting additions to the circular process.

At the same time as business creating intelligence to a large extent is about *creativity* we certainly want to stress that it is also about a very concrete and systematic way of *intellection* according to the *ABC•IC* model and in line with the methodological grammar presented in this book.

In this final chapter the methodological grammar from Chapters 1–14 has been the foundation for two processes that we have chosen to denote as knowledge audit and knowledge intelligence. We have contextualized these processes by relating them to an overall idea of creating knowledge as the most critical production factor for business in the twenty-first century. The chapter ends by presenting a model for business creating intelligence.

POINTS OF REFLECTION

1. In the chapter four different *production factors* are mentioned. What are they? What has continuously happened to these production factors over time?
2. One of these production factors has a certain *special position* as possibly more *critical* than others for business development. We have chosen to talk about this as the knowledge creating factor. What makes it so special?
3. In the chapter there is a description of *four different areas* in which a graduate in Business Administration and Economics as *knowledge creator* can expect to work in. Which way would you like to characterize area number four?
4. *Knowledge audit* and *knowledge intelligence* open up an exciting *interface* of business opportunities. What are these opportunities?
5. What is the very essence in *auditing knowledge* in a business operation?
6. In the chapter a *shortcoming/weakness* within the areas called business and competitive *intelligence* is mentioned. What is it and what might be the most tangible consequence of this shortcoming/weakness?
7. *Methodology of complementarity* is offered in the chapter as a prerequisite to create a basis with an almost incomprehensible *potential* for knowledge intelligence as well as counter-intelligence. What is meant by this potential?
8. Talking about intelligence with high *crealiability* one of the core elements is probably of higher importance than the others. Which, and why?
9. Give an account of the very *basic* idea behind processing information/data in the *ABC•IC* model?

RECOMMENDED FURTHER READING

See the end of the Appendix and visit the website below.

Become a worldwide partner as a *knowledge creator* in the development of *Methodology or Creating Business Knowledge* by visiting the website: **www.knowledge-creator.com**. Here you can contribute by asking your own questions and you will also find answers to the most frequently asked questions. The website has been developed alongside this third edition of the book and the questions posted there will be used to provide input for future editions.

INTRODUCTION

This Appendix introduces briefly into the discourse *some* philosophical/methodological orientations and their *relationships* to the *methodological grammar* and the three *methodological views* presented in this book. Methodology alone is indeed in itself an immense and complicated topic and we are in no way pretending that in this relatively short Appendix we can give more than a rough summary of its main points. We have selected, for the purpose of the book, some philosophical/methodological orientations and our selection is based on the following:

- They have had some, direct or indirect, influence on our own methodological thinking.
- They are frequently referred to and/or used in business research settings.

This Appendix will be divided into nine sections:

A1 Some ontological and epistemological perspectives   391
A2 Some philosophers on paradigm   392
   A2.1 Kuhn
   A2.2 Feyerabend
   A2.3 Törnebohm
   A2.4 Classifications of paradigms
A3 Explaining and understanding   394
A4 Explaining thinkers and theories   397
   A4.1 Positivism
   A4.2 Analytical philosophy
   A4.3 Holism
   A4.4 Structuralism
   A4.5 Marxism and critical theory
   A4.6 Systems thinking
   A4.7 Symbolic interactionism
   A4.8 Grounded theory
   A4.9 Sensemaking
A5 Understanding thinkers and theories   403
  A5.1 Hermeneutics
   A5.2 Phenomenology
   A5.3 Ethnomethodology
   A5.4 Social constructionism
   A5.5 Metaphorical thinking

A6 Can be seen as either explaining or understanding   408
    A6.1 Ethnography
    A6.2 Cultural studies
    A6.3 Narratives
A7 Two unique personalities   410
    A7.1 Michel Foucault
    A7.2 Ludwig Wittgenstein
A8 A summary   412
A9 Recommended further reading   413

The Appendix concludes with a list of proposals of texts for further reading for anyone who wants to deepen his/her knowledge.

A1 SOME ONTOLOGICAL AND EPISTEMOLOGICAL PERSPECTIVES

Empiricism (from Greek *empeiria*, experience) is an epistemological perspective, which claims that all knowledge of reality is derived from our *sensory* impressions (compare *induction* in Figure 4.3).

Rationalism (from Latin *ratio*, reason) claims, on the other hand, that it is possible to reach knowledge of reality or to justify it by our *reason* only. That is a kind of deductive methodological reasoning (compare relations to *deduction* in Figure 4.3).

It is, however, a great oversimplification to claim that these two concepts of epistemology are mutually exclusive. In a way, we could claim that they rather illustrate good points of departure in a methodology of complementarity where the *analytical view* is the transformative operator.

Pragmatism (from Greek *pragma*, act, deed) is a philosophical stream with great variety, primarily as a sociology toward the approach to find criteria of meaning and truth by practical consequences. A scientific result is thus judged by its usefulness and workability when applied in the *empirical* world. Hereby pragmatism rejects the opinions of *empiricism* and *rationalism* that knowledge can have a positive fundament. The concept of pragmatism is mainly rooted in our *systems view,* but can also be regarded as a weak undertone to our *actors view.*

Idealism (from Greek *idea*, appearance, state, art) is a collective term for a number of epistemological and metaphysical perspectives, which all stress that reality is shaped and constituted by knowledge and thinking such that no reality can exist which is independent of human consciousness or thinking. Our *actors view* has to a certain extent some of its roots in this kind of thought.

Traditional oppositions to idealism are *realism* (there is a world, independent of human consciousness) and *materialism*. Materialism (from Latin *materia*, stuff, material, matter) is a long tradition in European philosophy, which claims that all that exists in reality are things and processes and that they only have physical characteristics. It is, however, no exaggeration to claim that our two other views (*analytical* and *systems*) have to a certain degree some of their roots in this kind of thought.

Such branches as those mentioned above form a kind of historical undercurrent to our methodological views/approaches, and that's the reason why we have mentioned them here. They may possibly enter the methodological process when the meaning and content of various research results are discussed. It is true that the *start* of the analytical view, i.e. *positivism* (see below), stood on a firm *empirical* ground, but positivism as a clear-cut movement does not exist in business research today (even if it is true that its influences linger on with varying degrees of strength), and there exists elements of all the above branches in our three methodological views today.

A2 SOME PHILOSOPHERS ON PARADIGM

Philosophies as well as philosophers and other schools of thought and thinkers will appear in this Appendix in the order in which they would come in this book. This means that we start with some philosophers who are of interest to the concept of *paradigm* (see Box 1.6) after which come research and researchers whose goal is to *explain* and then research and researchers whose ambition is to *understand* (see Figure 3.1). The Appendix will finish with some further notions of the positions of our three methodological views in all this.

A2.1 Kuhn

The concept of *paradigm* (paradigm = model, pattern) was given a central place in the history of science by Kuhn (1922–1996). A paradigm can, as illustrated in Chapter 1, be seen as a set of assumptions, values and practices that forms a way of conceptualizing reality. According to Kuhn, major changes in scientific thinking (scientific revolutions) involve a change (a shift) in paradigm and such changes are rare. Kuhn's thesis is that when scientists work under a paradigm, they take part in what he calls *normal science*, trying to solve the problems thrown up by the theories they hold. This science then becomes a kind of puzzle solving.

Every so often, however, a scientific revolution occurs when the existing paradigm proves unable to cope with what appears to be *anomalous* situations (deviations from the normal or common order in the frame of a paradigm). Existing assumptions become so inadequate that they collapse and are replaced by a new set of assumptions. A new paradigm is then in a process of development. Such shifts of paradigms cannot occur within a normal – puzzle solving – science itself. That's why Kuhn talks about "scientific revolutions". One such example of how different assumptions pave the way for a new paradigm was illustrated in the beginning of Chapter 1, with the discovery of DNA.

In consequence, scientists working under different paradigms possess different concepts and make different observations. They cannot appeal to any theory-neutral observation and Kuhn considers the introduction of a neutral language of observation hopeless. In relation to this, we have in this book tried to realize a *thematic language* of methodology (see the

Glossary) to bridge some of the problems of language confusion between our three views/approaches.

A2.2 Feyerabend

Feyerabend (1924–1994) goes even further than does Kuhn in his anti-empiricism. In contrast to Kuhn, he is dealing much more with questions of epistemology and methodology. Kuhn primarily illustrates the development of science by historical narratives in an ambition to better understand the shifts.

According to Feyerabend, there should not be any generally valid norms or rules for science. Science should instead be an essentially anarchistic operation. As a research strategy, therefore, he recommends an extreme form of *methodological pluralism*, according to which the researcher must always be prepared to break with existing norms in order to be open to new types of research.

His central theme is that the *positivists* and the *rationalists* (see above) have misunderstood science as a process of rationality on its way to the idea of the "wholly true", where the right *method* should be the way. He also meant that science couldn't reasonably be the only way for developing knowledge with high credibility.

As a philosopher he was also concerned with the concept of *freedom* in relation to truth. For example: if science says that it has found some final truth, must we then give up our freedom to be sceptical?

In the development of our methodological grammar, certain clues from Feyerabend have had some impact on us. Our concept of *knowledge creator* (see Box 3.2) can be seen as an answer to his point of departure that not only science can be a part in creating reliable knowledge, especially in a business society based on knowledge, as can also our development of *crealiability*, as an extended concept of excellence in this domain. Our *actors view* has been influenced by Feyerabend too, especially by his creative research strategy, mentioned above, and his concept of freedom. Even our *methodology of complementarity* contains certain seeds from Feyerabend's thoughts. Apart from this we do not side with his, as we see it, pronounced relativism.

A2.3 Törnebohm

Törnebohm (b. 1919) was a professor of the theory of science. His works are mainly in the theory of physical science, influenced by, among others, Kuhn, but he has developed the theories of paradigms further, inspired by social science.

This book is in its entirety influenced by paradigmatic thinking. However, we prefer, in the main, Törnebohm's evolutionary theory over Kuhn's revolutionary one for three reasons:

1. Kuhn's discussions are exclusively devoted to physical science.
2. Scientific revolutions rarely, if ever, take place in social sciences. Paradigms there live together side-by-side and many social science methodologies do not deserve to be called developed and mature paradigms.
3. In our opinion, Törnebohm's theories fit better with the social sciences than do Kuhn's.

A2.4 Classifications of paradigms

We have *ontologically* and *epistemologically* classified various ultimate presumptions in relation to *methodology* and by that derived and developed three *methodological views*:

- the analytical view
- the systems view
- the actors view

We came up with this *classification* in the first edition of this book and we think it is still, together with our new developed principle of complementarity, quite complete and that every kind of methodological idea or action intended to deal with a problem of business can be related to it. We have also found it to be clear and useful worldwide. We continue therefore to use it in this third edition of our book.

There are other proposals for classifying paradigms, of course. Two quite recognized such classifications, also using the concepts of ontology, epistemology and methodology to classify, are by Burrell & Morgan (1985) and by Guba (1990). Burrell & Morgan talk about

- Functionalist paradigm
- Interpretive paradigm
- Radical humanist paradigm
- Radical structuralist paradigm

Guba talks about

- Post-positivism
- Critical science
- Constructivism

There are similarities between both these classifications and our own. One *important difference*, however, is that we do not find any of the two alternatives "complete". Burrell & Morgan assert that three of their paradigms (all but interpretive) are influenced by Marx. We do not find Marx that important and influential in business paradigms and methodological views. Furthermore, Guba is classifying paradigms for so-called qualitative research only. We also see much relevant quantitative research around in business.

A3 EXPLAINING AND UNDERSTANDING

To claim a clear difference between "explaining" and "understanding" may seem of little interest to some. However, it has become customary, *though by no means universal*, to distinguish between trying to describe *events* and trying to describe *actions*. It has also been suggested that the term *understanding*, in contrast to *explaining*, ought to be reserved for the latter. Let us look at this discussion in some historical light. We will see that there are variations on this theme today.

Since the inception of the discipline of social science, lines of controversy have been drawn between those who do and those who do not make a principal distinction between two presumed alternative modes of thought, that is, *natural* sciences and *social* sciences. Theorists rejecting any fundamental distinction between those modes have traditionally been called *positivists*. We may call them *knowledge creators solely interested in explaining*. They assume that the methods which historically have proved their value in the analysis of the physical world are applicable to the materials of social sciences, and that while these methods may have to be adapted to a special subject matter, *the logic of explanation* in physical and social sciences is the same.

Theorists who draw a distinction between "explaining" and "understanding" have been labelled *anti-positivists* or *hermeneuticians*. We may call them *knowledge creators solely interested in understanding*. The critical element in anti-positivism was that the methods of physical sciences, however modified, are intrinsically inadequate to the subject matter of social sciences; in the physical world man's knowledge, they insist, is *external* and empirical, while social sciences are concerned with knowledge which is *internal* to man and with various kind of experience.

The controversy between explaining and understanding is deeply rooted in Western thought. In its most elementary sense it is based on a presumed intrinsic difference between mind and all that is non-mind. The controversy cannot be eliminated by choosing between explaining and understanding, because, basically, they cannot be compared. Most researchers interested in *explaining*, for instance, claim that everything, in the natural world as well as in the human world, can be explained, at least in principle; while researchers interested in *understanding* claim that understanding is only for humans. Furthermore, there is no neutral position where you can choose between explaining and understanding in a businesslike or impartial way. One has to "choose" at the same time as, by necessity, being positioned in either the explaining or the understanding camp. Which is really no choice at all!

Furthermore: the purpose of explanations is to depict a *factive* (objective and/or subjective) reality in order to better predict its course from *outside*; the purpose of understanding is to develop *means* in order to better manage human existence from *within*. One explanation can replace another explanation; one understanding can replace another understanding. However, an explanation cannot (according to knowledge creators interested in understanding) replace an understanding (which it can according to knowledge creators interested in explaining).

According to von Wright (1971) and Apel (1984), the German philosopher of history Droysen (1808–1884) was the first, within science, to introduce the difference between "to explain" and "to understand" (in German, *erklären* and *verstehen* respectively), to ground historical sciences methodologically and to distinguish them from natural sciences. He did this in *Grundrisse der Historik*, which was published in 1858:

> According to the object and nature of human thought there are three possible scientific methods: the speculative (formulated in philosophy and theology), the mathematical or physical, and the historical. Their respective essences are to know, to explain, and to understand. (Droysen, 1858: 13)

Droysen's term "verstehen" can be traced back to the modern founders of hermeneutics, Schleiermacher (1768–1834) and Boeckh (1785–1867), among others, and was made more generally known through Weber (1852–1931). A historically significant form of the debate between understanding and explanation began with Dilthey (1833–1911).

Initially understanding gained a psychological character, which explanations lacked. This psychological element was emphasized by several of the nineteenth-century anti-positivist methodologists, perhaps above all by Simmel (1858–1918), who thought that understanding, as a method characteristic of the humanities, is a form of *empathy* (von Wright, 1971). But empathy is not a modern way of separating understanding from explanation. Understanding can today be associated with *intentionality*, for instance, in a way which explanation cannot. We will come back to this concept a little later.

Generally we can say that natural sciences, according to Fay (1996), require concepts that "permit the formation of testable laws and theories". Other issues, for instance, those deriving from ordinary language, are of less interest. "But in the human sciences another set of considerations exists as well: the concepts used to describe and explain human activity must be drawn at least in part *from the social life being studied*, not only from the scientists' theories." (Fay 1996: 114) (emphasis in original)

Scientific concepts then, according to Fay, "bear a fundamentally different relationship to social phenomena from that which they bear to natural phenomena. In the social sciences, concepts partially constitute the reality being studied while in the latter case they merely serve to describe and explain it" (1996: 114).

> It is possible to explain human behaviour. We do not try to understand an area of low pressure because it has no meaning. On the other hand we try to understand human beings because they are of the same kind as we are. (Liedman, 2002: 280; our translation)

The descriptions as far as explaining and understanding are concerned are, as we regard it, more mixed today than was historically the case. There is research aimed at explaining as well as at understanding in both scientific camps. Furthermore, as we will see later, explaining is no longer solely associated with positivism and understanding is no longer something done only by hermeneuticians.

Generally, we want to distinguish between two kinds of explanations:

⇨   explaining by causality ("because of" explanations)
⇨   explaining by finality ("in order to" explanations)

So, for instance, to explain why a company has a budget can be explained either by the fact that its senior management had previously introduced the procedure in that company ("because of") or explained by the fact that its senior management wants to control its economy better ("in order to").

We also want to distinguish between two kinds of understanding:

⇨   understanding by significance
⇨   understanding by intentionality

The first is based on the *understanding* by the knowledge creator of the study area, what he/she thinks is significant there. The second is based on the actors' understanding of themselves in everyday reality.

So, in general, the difference between explaining and understanding is that *explanation* provides a description, a *representation,* of a situation or a phenomenon. *Understanding* is a description that has a *meaning* to somebody, to the researcher or to the actors in the study area or to both. Another way to phrase it is to say that an explanation is *depicting* reality, while an understanding is *constituting* reality. We will see later that understanding by significance is associated with hermeneutics and understanding by intentionality is associated with phenomenology.

Some researchers talk about understanding also by knowing the reasons or motives behind somebody's behaviour. This, to us, is however, to explain something by bringing up subjective aspects of factive reality.

It is not unusual to say that researchers that are interested in explaining are building *models* and that researchers that are interested in understanding come up with *metaphorical interpretations*. However, one has to be careful with this terminology. Understanding can also mean to come up with models, but then as part of constituting reality (see Box 3.3 and Figure 3.14).

By studying Figure 3.1, the relevance of this illustration for our three methodological views/approaches can easily be seen.

A4 EXPLAINING THINKERS AND THEORIES

A4.1 Positivism

It was Comte (1789–1857) who gave the concept of *positivism* a prominent place in the history of philosophy. At the beginning of the nineteenth century, many academicians and philosophers had an unwavering faith in the possibilities of the natural sciences and claimed that they should be the foundation of what was then modern philosophy. This could also be seen, for instance, among the utilitarians Bentham (1748–1832) and Mill (1773–1836). By the mid-1900s, positivism had a revival in what became known as the *Vienna circle* with leading figures like Carnap (1891–1970) and Neurath (1882–1945). The preferred term was then *logical positivism* (later *logical empiricism*).

The following three statements, as far as the social sciences are concerned, can characterize the *positivist* movement:

- Explanations in social sciences should be of the same type as explanations in natural sciences, that is, statements expressed in the form "X causes Y."
- Social sciences should use the same methods as natural sciences when constructing and testing such explanations (*the unity of sciences*).
- Metaphysics does not belong to science.

Logical positivism (or logical empiricism) is today seen mainly as an abandoned direction in the Anglo-Saxon, so-called, *analytical philosophy,* and from around 1950 ceased to exist as an independent philosophical movement.

Even if logical positivism has ceased to exist as an independent movement, its influence still looms over many analytical creators of knowledge. We can therefore not neglect positivism in its different and later versions when we discuss the *analytical view*.

A4.2 Analytical philosophy

Analytical philosophy is a twentieth-century movement. *Conceptual analysis* was its central theme. Conceptual analysis was by analytical philosophy also made into a *logical analysis* (called a *conceptually* logical analysis unlike a *formally* logical analysis) and it was stated that it had to be so in order to be *objective*.

Moore (1873–1950) and Russell (1872–1970) turned logical analysis into a *definition process*. They wanted to come up with a definition of what is a "fact" and came to the conclusion that if the statement "knowledge is well established truth" is true, then it is an *analytical fact*.

Analytical philosophy is a name covering a number of directions in twentieth-century philosophy, mainly in the English-speaking world. In spite of large differences in theory as well as in practice, the various directions agree on some main points and basic ideas:

- They are based on a clearly averse attitude to metaphysical constructions.
- They build on the opinion that traditional philosophical problems only can be (dis)solved through a *clarification* of the content of those expressions that are central to the formulation of problems.
- A basic *empiristical* point of departure.

Analytical philosophy is the foundation of the *analytical view* in this our book. In spite of this very short illustration we can easily discover the roots for the analytical view's emphasis on definitions and focusing on problems and problem clarifications.

A4.3 Holism

According to the *Oxford English Dictionary*, the term *holism* was introduced by the South African statesman Smuts (1870–1950). He defined it as "The tendency in nature to form wholes that are greater than the sum of the parts through evolution". Holism comes from a Greek word *holos*, which means "all", "entire", "total".

Holism is, together with concepts such as determinism and individualism, one of different epistemological perspectives, and as such concerns central questions of *explanation* in the social sciences. Holism is, in this regard, the opposite of the idea of coming to the truth via a number of mere descriptive factors of something instead of a consideration of its totality (holism).

According to the *Encyclopedia Britannica*, Methodological holism

> maintains that at least some social phenomena must be studied at their own autonomous, macroscopic level of analysis, that at least some social "wholes" are not reducible to or completely explicable in terms of individuals' behaviour. … Semantic holism denies the claim that all meaningful statements about large-scale social phenomena (e.g., "The industrial revolution resulted in urbanization") can be translated without residue into statements about the actions, attitudes, relations, and circumstances of individuals.

Many thinkers have been classified as holists, for instance, the economist Schumpeter (1883–1950) in his evolutionary approach, the philosopher Morin (b. 1921) due to the transdisciplinary nature of his work, the sociologist Durkheim (1858–1917), when he opposed the notion that a society was nothing more than a simple collection of individuals and the psychologist Adler (1870–1937), claiming that the individual must be understood within the larger whole of society.

Our *systems view* is based on holistic thinking according to our first guiding principle of the view (see Figure 5.5).

A4.4 Structuralism

Structuralism generally means theories and methods within different scientific subjects which assert that individual elements cannot be analysed in isolation as they are determined by broader regularities and patterns; reality is *structured*. Only when the *determining* structures – the relationship between elements – have been uncovered, can individual elements be explained.

Structuralism can also mean, more specifically, that perspective which has been developed within *linguistics* starting from de Saussure (1857–1913). The term "structuralism" appeared in this perspective in the works of the anthropologist Lévi-Strauss (b. 1908). He aims at finding those universal structures which are behind all human conceptions. Along the same lines, the psychologist Piaget (1896–1980) studied those cognitive development stages that every human being, according to him, must pass in childhood.

Today, pure structuralism is less popular. It has often been criticized for being ahistorical and for favoring structural forces, as a kind of determinism, over the ability of individual people to act (we hear the same criticism from our *actors view* – see Chapter 13).

Structuralism has developed into perspectives like *post-structuralism* and *deconstructionism* (see "Recommended further reading: structuralism" at the end of this Appendix to explore further these two perspectives). However, the search is still for underlying structures in language. The claim is, that true and full knowledge of language cannot be reached at the individual level, only at a systems level. Therefore, we maintain that structuralism (with or without developments) is an important part of our *systems view*, as it supports our systems view in several fundamental aspects:

- A close connection between thought and language is pointed out, but the latter explains the former. So, for instance, if you talk about systems, you *think* systems and you *see* systems!
- We must look at the existence of language as a system rather than as the thoughts or activities of individuals. Not only are there systems, there is also a language *of* systems for us to take part in.
- Language exists independently of single individuals and cannot be completely described only at the level of single individuals. To think of language in terms of human systems is natural because it is something we share.

A4.5 Marxism and critical theory

Marxism is a political philosophy and practice derived from Marx (1818–1883) and Engels (1820–1895). Marx points out that philosophy is possible only as a critical analysis which has as its purpose to change praxis. In order to lay the foundation for this change of praxis, Marx introduces a new meaning of the term *materialism*, where materialism looks at man as an active creature, a creature who is able to put him/herself above nature and tries to rule it by realizing his/her human purposes and becoming free and able to determine him/herself. Man is creating *history*, but this possibility can be obscured and man may become a stranger to a him/herself, become *alienated*.

Engels supports Marx by adding among other things the term *dialectical* to *materialism*. *Historical materialism* is one part of this dialectical materialism. It has to do with the historical development of, for example, workers, social classes and societies. According to historical materialism, historical studies should have the *material* development of the societies as a starting point, and above all the different forms of production there.

The *Frankfurt School* (critical theory) attempts to develop a materialistic philosophy, which to some extent opposes dialectical materialism. The school generally claims that it is useless to speak of things or facts as independent of those *concepts* by which these things or facts are described.

The main proponents of the Frankfurt School are Horkheimer (1895–1973), Adorno (1903–1969), Fromm (1900–1980), Marcuse (1898–1979) and Habermas (b. 1929).

We claim that Marxism is closest to our *systems view* among our three methodological views/approaches due to its holistic orientation towards facts and reality and the risk of alienation (which in turn must be based on the belief of a factive self). The *critical theory* of the Frankfurt School has, to some extent, had an impact on us in our overarching notion of what it means to be a knowledge creator, whatever methodological view. Our actors view has also been influenced by *critical theory*, especially Fromm's humanistic approach to social science and to business as well.

A4.6 Systems thinking

There is really no philosophy that could be labelled *systems thinking*. However, there are some systems theories presented in the 1900s which have had an influence on the beginning of the development of our *systems view*:

- *Cybernetics* (from Greek *kybernetike*, the art of steermanship) is a scientific theory of control, established in 1948 by Wiener (1894–1964), which refers to studies of mathematical models for control systems. Cybernetics is researching communication technology problems related to control and internal information flow in complicated, preferably self-regulating, systems. Wiener's original definition of cybernetics pointed out similarities between biological, mechanical and electronic systems, but the cybernetic thought was later applied to economic, administrative and social systems as well.

- von Bertalanffy (1901–1972) was originally a biologist, and developed what he referred to a "holistic theory of life and nature". This was launched as a *general systems theory*. He saw in such a theory the possibility of developing principles and models applicable to all systems, regardless of their nature and organizational level. Von Bertalanffy claimed, therefore, that he was using more "organic" and "humanistic" opinions about human nature than the "mechanistic" and "robot-like" theories that were common at the time.
- Churchman (1913–2004) was a professor of Business Administration. He published in a number of different subjects, including ethics and value sciences. He is best known among business scholars for having launched, what he referred to as *the systems approach* in the 1960s as a framework for a further analysis of business problems. Churchman's interests can be seen as an extension of operations research and traditional decision theory.

A4.7 Symbolic interactionism

Mead (1863–1931) is a philosopher of the *pragmatic* school. He studied how our consciousness and the self are created in the social communication process. For pragmatists, meaning is primarily a property of *behaviour* and only secondarily a property of objects themselves. Meaning is seen as *stable* relations between a subject and a class of objects, defined in a way in which the latter is *typically* handled. Physical attributes are important, however, because they set limitations on what can be done. Meaning is also normally subject to social control in that the anticipated reactions of other people place additional restrictions on its usage.

Mead sets himself the task of formulating a scientific and empirical social psychology. Starting from situations of evolutionary biology he tries to *explain* how the human mind, the self, and self-consciousness come into existence.

Blumer (1900–1987) was a student of Mead and the sociologist who coined the term "symbolic interactionism". According to him this perspective rests on three "simple premises" (1986: p. 2):

1. Human beings act toward things on the basis of the meanings that the things have for them.
2. The meaning of such things is derived from, or arises out of, the social interaction that one has with one's fellows.
3. These meanings are handled in, and modified through, an interpretative process used by the person in dealing with the things he encounters.

Blumer looks upon the symbolic interactionism as an empirical social science. He asserts that: "its methodological principles have to meet the fundamental requirements of empirical science. ... an empirical science presupposes the existence of an empirical world. Such an empirical world exists as something available for observation, study, and analysis" (1986: 21).

Among Blumer's students we can find Strauss who is the co-founder of "Grounded theory" (see A4.8 below).

Social creators of knowledge who build on Mead's and Blumer's ideas are often called *symbolic interactionists*. They try to avoid the dilemma that behaviour is *caused* either by forces *internal* to the individual, such as instincts, or by social forces impinging from *outside*, by stressing the interaction of the two.

Our opinion is that symbolic interactionism may have an important part to play in the frame of our *systems view* due to its empirical and factive base. George Mead also claimed that he was a kind of social behaviourist.

A4.8 Grounded theory

Glaser (b. 1930) and Strauss (1916–1996) first developed grounded theory in their book *The Discovery of Grounded Theory* (1967). Glaser and Strauss emphasize *generation* of theory rather than its verification. They aim at formulating a number of more cogent and coherent collections of methodological rules to generate theory from empirical data. Glaser and Strauss originally presented their grounded theory as clearly influenced by positivism.

Grounded theory is based on the idea of systematically collecting and analysing data using an *iterative* process of considering and comparing earlier literature, its data and theories that emerge as the research process goes on (Glaser & Strauss, 1967; Strauss & Corbin, 1998).

The grounded theory research process starts with formulating the research question and defining some early concepts. References to existing earlier results of relevance can be made here. Thereafter, cases and groups are sampled in a theoretical manner, which means that the researcher does not look for representativity but for variations in key variables and other theoretically interesting characteristics of the units of analysis.

Researchers then move on to collection of data. When doing the data collection fieldwork or other forms of data collection, this is supposed to be done concurrently with analysis so as to be flexible to accommodate possible changes of plans in order to discover better theory.

Grounded theory researchers may, according to Mäkelä and Turcan (2007), benefit from triangulation of data collection methods, data types (for instance, along the quantitative-qualitative dimension) or investigators. If findings converge, this will enhance confidence in the quality of the study. If, on the other hand, findings are in conflict with each other, this will help prevent the premature closure of data collection or analysis.

We place grounded theory on the explaining side of our methodologies (see Figure 3.1). Even if Strauss himself considered grounded theory as qualitative research, this does not prevent it from being used in the name of explaining, as we know. A study based on this theory can develop into an *analytical approach* or a *systems approach* depending on the desirable outcome of the study. The result may become sets of cause–effect relations or systems structures.

A4.9 Sensemaking

Sensemaking is often associated with Weick (b. 1936). Weick's ideas can be summarized in the following points:

- Most of sensemaking is concerned with *recreating* and *confirming* those opinions we already hold about our reality.
- Sometimes, however, we stop and ask ourselves the question: "How can this make sense?" This takes place above all when we want to make *new* and *unknown* situations meaningful.
- This can be done by retrospectively selecting those aspects of these situations, which suit our opinion about what a reality is and should be. We may construct a *narrative*.
- In this way we *enact* another aspect of our perceived reality.
- This could *explain* why two persons may *experience* the same situation so differently.

Weick's sensemaking does not cover all aspects of life, but it fits, by and large, primarily those rare situations when we stop and think about the meaning of what we are doing and what is going on. It is generally understood that people handle their ordinary days with a fairly low degree of conscious thinking.

However, it sometimes seems like non-reflective scripts are controlling our behaviour. The basic idea of Weick's sensemaking is that cognition lies in the path of action. Action precedes cognition and focuses cognition. It has been pointed out that Weick's retrospective perspective is passive and lacks the proactive position of an organization, which includes creative chaos. Sensemaking, some claim, may also take place proactively.

Sensemaking is a process where people try to *make sensible explanations* of experienced situations. It is concerned with the future, but is retrospective in nature, and is based on earlier sensemaking in an *ongoing flow*.

Weick's version of it is definitely part of what we, in this book, refer to as the *systems view*. However, there are versions of sensemaking which are closer to our *actors view,* or rather to our *methodology of complementarity* with the actors view as a transformative operator.

A5 UNDERSTANDING THINKERS AND THEORIES

A5.1 Hermeneutics

Hermeneutics began as a discipline attempting to interpret biblical and legal texts. Now, however, it has been given a much wider application, so that the problem of *interpretation* is seen by many as being of central importance in the social sciences.

The main emphasis in hermeneutics is on *understanding* and *communication*. It aims to arrive through language at a common understanding or shared vision. Gadamer (1900–2002), who is regarded as one of the great authorities in social science hermeneutics, was of the opinion that "the world" is in language, rather than constituting its foundation. As a consequence he rejected all notions of a "world in itself" against which different conceptions of the world can be positioned.

According to Trigg (2000), philosophical presuppositions (compare our ultimate presumptions) are a necessary point of departure for social science. He writes in relation to Gadamer:

When language creates the categories with which we think, any attempt to understand those writing and acts at a different time and/or in a different language is fraught with difficulty. Their thoughts must be conditioned by their social situation, just as ours is by ours. Again and again, Gadamer emphasizes the primacy of language. Tradition is, he says, "linguistic in character", and he stresses, in a manner reminiscent of Wittgenstein, that "all forms of human community of life are forms of linguistic community". (2000: 220)

Several of Gadamer's influences can be traced in our methodological views. Gadamar's theories of hermeneutics – about language and interpretation – have been of great importance in the development of the *actors view*. However, in the respect that Gadamer stresses the importance of the interpretation made by the creator of knowledge, when he/she tries to come up with what is significant in the study area (even if only one interpretation among many) in the process of coming up with new knowledge, he has also influenced our *systems view* (in understanding mode).

A5.2 Phenomenology

The father of modern phenomenology is Husserl (1859–1938). Husserl's opinion about philosophy changed more than once, but he never wavered in his conviction concerning his indisputable demands of philosophers: they must look for complete clarity.

Husserl wanted in the beginning to understand the *essence* of things which consciousness has produced. This led to his *phenomenological method*, through which he hoped that the universal nature of things might be grasped. Husserl introduced, therefore, the concept of *transcendental-phenomenological reduction*. Roughly, this is a transition from an ordinary, natural, unconscious attitude toward the world and its objects to a position of oneself in a (transformatively creative) reflecting attitude (*free imaginative variation*). This process, which aims at discovering the essences in the world, starts by "bracketing" existence (Husserl called it *Epoché*), which does not mean the deny the world or question its existence, but methodologically to impose a limitation that permits one to make only judgements that do not depend on the world in time or space for validation.

Husserl claimed that when we perform this reduction we will discover what he called our "transcendental ego" or "pure consciousness". He was then interested in exploring and describing *the definite foundation of the experienced world*, a foundation that furthermore is not available to empirical observation but only to something Husserl called *eidetic intuition*.

Husserl held for a long time that the transcendental ego exists "absolutely" and that everything else exists "relative" to it. But toward the end of his life he changed his opinion about phenomenology one more time (including abandoning his belief in transcendental-phenomenological reduction as a progressive way to go in philosophizing):

- He now asserted that the transcendental ego was "correlated" to the world. It had lost its absolute status.
- He no longer claimed that the world had to be described starting from what it is to a transcendental individual but from an inter-subjective community of individuals.

• He made a sharp distinction between the world as known to science and the everyday reality in which we live, *der Lebenswelt*. Husserl was now of the opinion that scientific knowledge is only understandable if we understand this latter reality.

Husserl's phenomenology thereby acquired clear *dialectic* undercurrents.

A central concept to Husserl all along was *intentionality*, a concept which means that our consciousness is not fed by passive impressions but instead is always actively directed to *form* and *interpret* things around us, trying to make them meaningful; we are not referring here to objects as things in the outer world by themselves, but to things *intended*.

One can say that Husserl's final opinion is that phenomenology is not a description of a separate realm of experience but rather a reflection, and description, of *the ways in which our common experience comes to be and what the criteria are for different sorts of experiences and their adequacy*.

Husserl's later ideas were continued by one of his students, Schutz (1899–1959). He soon became one of the most recognized proponents in the field of *social phenomenology*. Standing with his feet in both the camps of philosophy and sociology, he developed a critical synthesis of Husserl's thinking and Weber's ideas about understanding. Schutz suggests that our experience of the world is directed by *the natural attitude*, where we take for granted that the world is built up by assumptions about groups of events in our language, so-called *typifications*, assumptions that we rarely question. For Schutz, it was always a matter of retracing and reconstructing the basis on which the construction of the life-world rests. In his *Collected Papers*, Vol. I, he developed such a base for a methodology of the social sciences.

Another person who ought to be named with respect to social phenomenology is Gurwitsch (1901–1973). His primary interest was the relation between phenomenology and Gestalt psychology.

Possibly the best-known social phenomenological publication known to business scholars is *The Social Construction of Reality*. This was published in 1966 by the sociologists Berger (b. 1929) and Luckmann (b. 1927). This book is based on Schutz's theories and even dedicated to him. This book is an attempt to answer the question: "What makes us produce the kinds of society that we do?"

Social phenomenology is the cornerstones for our *actors view*. The models of *typified cases* and the models of *constitutional ideals* (see Figure 6.11) and the construction of *ideal types* in the actors approach (see the end of Case III, Chapter 14) have, to a great extent, been inspired by the phenomenological idea of "free imaginative variation". These models are ideal states that can "imaginatively" reflect human freedom and the potential of life/business, and thereby engage various actors in procreating dialogues in which the potential will be transformed into the factual, that is, into a new social reality.

A5.3 Ethnomethodology

The ethnomethodological project focuses on the common-sense methods that we use to make sense of our experiences and constitute social reality. This project was started by Harold Garfinkel (b. 1917). The methods of special interest to ethnomethodologists are the various interpretive procedures that we routinely use to classify aspects of our experience and to establish connections between them. (Silverman, 1997: 28)

To put this social science movement in relation to other movements we can refer to Garfinkel himself and those persons he names that have influenced him most. Here we find name such as Husserl, Gurwitsch and Schutz (see A5.2 above).

Ethnomethodology can be seen as a branch of social phenomenology. As in phenomenology in general the development and the maintenance of our life-world is studied here. Criticism of traditional social science is strong.

Ethnomethodology is concerned with unconsidered and unquestioned background expectations and implicit rules that govern action in the quotidian world. Its method is to focus on micro processes that make it possible for the life-world to develop and to be maintained. Ethnomethodology has been criticized for studying the consequences of our everyday conventions, while ignoring the sources of these conventions.

In spite of being a branch of social phenomenology and in spite of the fact that Garfinkel denies the concept of social facts as having a reality of their own, it has only indirect bearing on the methodological treatments of our *actors view*.

A5.4 Social constructionism

There are a number of variations of social constructionism. They include elements of social phenomenology, ethnomethodology, discourse perspectives, semiotics and some varieties of post-structuralism, cultural concepts and gender perspectives.

There are, however, a number of similarities among all of the social constructionist movement:

- Person and reality are inseparable.
- Language produces and reproduces reality instead of being a result of reality.
- Knowledge is socially constructed, not objectively given.

Also, there are four basic working assumptions, emanating from Gergen, among social constructionist researchers to assure that the branch not merge into total relativism (Gergen, 1999):

1. Those terms by which we understand our world and ourselves are neither required nor demanded by "what there is". This has to do with the failure of language to map or picture an independent world. Another way of stating this assumption is to say that there are a potentially unlimited number of possible descriptions of "the situation in question" – and none of these descriptions can be ruled superior in terms of its capacity to map, picture or capture its features.
2. Our modes of description, understanding and/or representation are derived from relationship. Language and all other forms of representation are meaningful only in their relationships with people. Meaning and significance are born of coordination

between individuals – agreements, negotiations and affirmations. Nothing exists for us intelligible people before there are relationships.

3. As we describe or otherwise represent our reality, so do we fashion our future. Language is a major ingredient of our worlds of actions and therefore a part of building futures either as continuations of what already exists or as part of what will be new.

4. Reflection on our forms of understanding is vital to our future well-being. What shall we save, what shall we resist and destroy, what shall we create? There are no universal answers, only socially constructed ones.

We can say that our *actors view* is one variant of social constructionism. However, there are several differences, but one very important one is that the actors view illustrated in this book assumes that reality has an essence; most variations of social constructionism do not.

A5.5 Metaphorical thinking

A metaphor is in everyday life for most of us a figure of speech where things are compared in a symbolic way, as in "she is a dolphin" about a swimmer. Or, as the *Encyclopedia Britannica* describes it, a "figure of speech that implies comparison between two unlike entities, as distinguished from *simile,* an explicit comparison signalled by the words 'like' or 'as'". A metaphor may therefore in knowledge-creating pave the way for new perspectives. Some of the qualities of the intrinsic image of a metaphor are thus transferred to the idea or object in question. By using metaphors, the knowledge creator can also gain deeper insights into complex situations.

Metaphorical thinking provides us with effective means of dealing with complexity. It shows us how we can open our thought processes so that we can read one situation from multiple perspectives in a critical and informed way. But the opposite may also be the case.

In organizational theory, interpretations using metaphors are quite common (sometimes referred to as *poetic hermeneutics*). They often refer to Morgan (b. 1943). His argument is that researchers use metaphors, which are *taken for granted* and which are influencing their efforts. In order to get rid of their own implicit thoughts, it is important for them to become aware of the metaphors they use in their daily work. Those communities of theorists subscribe to relatively coherent perspectives (sometimes called *root metaphors or pre-scientific concepts* – see Chapter 2), which are based upon the acceptance and use of different kinds of metaphors as a foundation for inquiry.

Morgan does not, however, stop at pointing out the necessity for researchers to reflect on the metaphorical character of their knowledge. He also indicates a "method" of creating knowledge, which is based on the possibility of knowledge creators using different metaphors in their work, thus disclosing interesting aspects of the complex phenomenon of an organization. One interpretation of Morgan is that the researcher, if he/she is aware of the existence of different metaphors, can always consciously choose one or more metaphors to make his/her research a creative process. Examples of such metaphors could be: machine, organism, culture and psychic prison.

There are many ways to read what metaphors are and how they are used. In this book, we use it in the *systems view/approach* as a way to gain further insight into a factive reality, that is, when trying to come up with understanding in this approach, not only explanations. In the *actors view/approach*, however, it is especially common to make use of metaphors, from the very beginning of a knowledge-creating process to the procreative report. But the influence of Morgan is not very great, rather the actors view employs a real variety of influences from science to philosophy, from everyday language to poetry.

A6 CAN BE SEEN AS EITHER EXPLAINING OR UNDERSTANDING

A6.1 Ethnography

Ethnography is the study of people in their own naturally occurring settings or 'fields' by using methods of data collection which capture their social meanings and ordinary activities, involving the researcher participating him/herself directly in the setting, if not also in the activities, in order to come up with results in a systematic manner but without meaning being imposed on them externally. (Brewer, 2000: 6)

The following five features identify ethnographic research (Hammersley, 1990):

1 Behaviour is studied in everyday contexts. The researcher is not to impose any unnatural or experimental circumstances.
2 Observation is the primary means of data collection. However, other techniques can be used as well.
3 Data collection is flexible and unstructured in order to avoid imposing categories on what people say and do.
4 Focus is normally on a single setting or group.
5 The data are analysed by attributing meanings to the human actions described.

The word ethnography often refers to research methods used in cultural anthropology or to written text produced by such efforts. In this respect ethnography has also influenced, and been influenced by, literary theory.

Similarly to how we later in this Appendix will talk about narratives, there are, in a broad sense, two kinds of ethnography. One could be called ethnographical *realism* and the other could be called ethnographical *constructionism* (or constitutive ethnography; partly related to ethnomethodology, see A5.3). In the first case, the knowledge creators try, in an *explaining* mode, to depict people in their natural settings "*as they are*". This can be associated with our *analytical* or our *systems view*. The other takes a more *understanding* position in the sense of our *actors view*.

A6.2 Cultural studies

Culture can be seen in many different ways. In its widest sense one can say that culture is everything not given to man by nature, but produced by man himself. However, one can see culture either as something that exists as a *fact* (as a factive reality) or something which is *constituted* only *between* human beings (as a factified reality), something which is triggered only when people meet, people who have some cultural aspects in common, and is not something which is stored as objects in people's minds. In such a case, we can compare it with the modern concept of memory. Memory exists only as dispositions in people's brains. Every time we remember something, we are reconstructing what we believe we remember. It is not like the computer, where all retrieved documents are exactly the same as when they were last stored, or like a book, which when once again is picked off the bookshelf contains the same text and the same pictures as before. The brain must create anew every time we "remember".

Further aspects of culture can be picked up from Geertz (1926–2006), a cultural anthropologist and a researcher more interested in understanding than in explaining. (We discussed Geertz in Chapter 5.) Our interpretation of him is that he is looking for systems *results*. However, he often uses concepts that seem to be very *actors view* oriented, but when doing so, he always uses, in our methodological language, the *systems view* as a *transformative operator*.

- There is a difference between "thin" and "thick" descriptions. In the former case we can read what an actor is doing; in the latter case we can read what meaning underlies the action. The latter is the object of *ethnography*, according to Geertz.
- Culture is public because meaning is. The cognitivist fallacy – that culture consists of mental phenomena, which can be analysed by formal methods similar to those of mathematics and logic – is as destructive for an effective use of the concept, according to Geertz, as are the behaviourist and idealist fallacies to which it is a "misdrawn correction".
- A human being not influenced by his//her environment does not exist, has never existed, and most important, could not in the very nature of the case exist.
- To draw a line between what is natural, universal and constant is extraordinarily difficult. To draw such a line may even be seen as falsifying the human situation.
- Language and culture are intimately related. One can say that they mirror each other.

Explaining and *understanding* provide different perspectives of what culture is (the same way as we earlier saw alternative perspectives behind doing ethnographic research). *Explaining* looks at culture as an aspect of a firm alongside other aspects such as strategy and structure (compare Figure 5.2, where "shared values" can be seen as culture), while *understanding* can envisage the whole situation *as* culture being socially constructed. Research in the first case could be associated with our *systems view*; research in the second case with our *actors view*.

A6.3 Narratives

To construct a narrative is to reconstruct experience in a story. An issue discussed among social scientists (similar to the discussion we have had in the case of ethnographic research and cultural studies) is whether narratives are useful as a tool for researchers to get a new kind of order into what they are studying, or whether reality, as we approach it and try to understand it as human beings, means constructing our own narratives in our life-world. According to Fay (1996), the first we may call *narrative realism*, the second *narrative constructionism*. He asserts that narrative realism presumes that narratives *exist* in our human world and the mission for a creator of knowledge is to *depict* them, that is, to have people in the study area to tell them. Narrative constructionism presumes that we *impose* stories on our lives to make them more meaningful. In other words, in the latter case, narratives are *constructed*, not discovered.

So, as in the case of ethnography and cultural studies, (see above), we have *explaining* as well as *understanding* modes of researching narratives. In this sense we may say that *narrative realism* can be seen as related to our *systems view* and *narrative constructionism* as related to our *actors view*.

A7 TWO UNIQUE PERSONALITIES

There are two philosophers/thinkers that are particularly difficult to position in our *methodological views*, i.e. Foucault and Wittgenstein. In spite of that, they have influenced our work, alongside the others, with respect to the three views/approaches presented in the book.

A7.1 Michel Foucault

The strength of the work of Foucault (1926–1984) lies not so much in the problems he treats, but in the particular kind of analyses he performs. They all concern the modern organization of theoretical and practical knowledge and their relation to certain practices and forms of social organization. As a philosopher, sociologist and historian he has been named as a "structuralist" as well as a "post-structuralist", and also described as "postmodernist", labels he himself has rejected.

Foucault's radical/critical intellection has powerful implications for theoretical work within the social sciences. This should be taken in two senses. First, his particular analyses of the relation between forms of knowledge and social practices implicated in psychiatry or criminology throw into question a number of widespread epistemological and sociological assumptions, which govern conventional analyses. Second, he provides an analysis of the human sciences themselves, together with the ancillary fields of criminology and psychiatry. If Foucault's analyses are accepted it is clear that many a conventional position in the social sciences could be questioned.

The analyses of Foucault are in the most obvious sense historical. He believed that the large question he posed regarding the meaning of human existence today could be answered only within the context of humanity's understanding of the past. The changing order of knowledge and power is historically conditioned and our ignorance of these conditions leads us to believe that our present state of existence is the epitome of humanity. The theoretical disciplines that Foucault's reflection incorporates, according to Kendall and Wickham, 1999, are *genealogy* – the theory of power practice – and *archaeology* – the theory of discourse and knowledge.

Foucault is probably best known for his analyses of power. It is his conviction that power is the principle of development and integration within our society. If this assertion is accepted as a general rule, then power, as a practical principle must also apply as a principle for a theoretical system of knowledge. In fact, power and knowledge are the main themes of Foucault's work. What Foucault calls the *episteme* are the conditions of knowledge within which organized knowledge is structured. He has developed this in *Power/Knowledge* (Foucault, 1980).

Foucault uses the term *discourse* here to analyse diverse configurations of assumptions, categories, logics, claims and modes of orientation. The configurations provide persons with coherent interpretive frameworks and discursive practice for bringing up different realities, within which particular kinds of people reside, relationships prevail and opportunities are likely to emerge. According to Foucault, the production of discourses in any society is controlled, selected, organized and redistributed by certain procedures.

Foucault is also working with the history of ideas and he is using unconventional methods while doing so. But, basically, his working hypothesis is that underlying structures control different products within a given epoch. There is a system of concepts or a code which determines what can be thought within the epoch.

Foucault refused, as mentioned above, to accept any kind of scientific label on his thoughts. It is our opinion that, among our three views, we are closest to his intellection with our *systems view*. For most of his life he talks about necessary and "hidden" structures influencing our possibility to know and learn and to exert power. It is not until late in life that he is discusses how men can get around these structures and release their free will. This later train of thought turns him partly, as we regard it, towards what we refer to as the *actors view*.

A7.2 Ludwig Wittgenstein

Wittgenstein (1889–1951) is one of the most influential and most widely discussed philosopher of the twentieth century. One of those rare human beings who radically differs from the mainstream, but still remains relevant and of his time, he is also rare in another sense. He really knows the meaning of a paradigmatic shift (see A2.1 above). He made one himself.

Wittgenstein is mainly a language philosopher and he was a professor at the University of Cambridge. It is common to speak of his two periods. The first preceded his doctoral theses *Tractactus Logico-Philosophicus*. The second began around 1930 and continued to his death. In this period he rejected practically every aspect of his conceptions of language as presented in his thesis. It is these later radical thoughts on how to learn a language, on meaning in language and on language itself, which are of interest here. According to Pears (1971), this is also normally the case in most other contexts.

As Wittgenstein looks at it in his second period, language is something we do. To understand a language is not, according to him, a matter of grasping some inner essence of meaning, but rather of knowing how to perform. The emphasis falls on the "functions" of words rather than their "content". Wittgenstein refers to this as *language games*.

If language is seen as human *activity* rather than a collection of labels for categories of phenomena, then we will not be surprised to find systematic inconsistencies in it – not as a fault or as problems, but as essential to its function. Further, if language is seen as human activity, that activity may be carried out in quite different ways, depending on what the talking human beings are up to. Furthermore, if words need not be used for referring and their meaning is not their reference, and if concepts may be internally inconsistent, then many of our traditional and common-sense assumptions about the relationship between language and reality are called into question. The way Ziff (1960) looks at it, one could, according to Wittgenstein, say that the essential language function is *not to comment on factual circumstances but to be together*. We can say that Wittgenstein's opinion of the meaning of "understanding" is related to action:

> Try not to think of understanding as a 'mental process' at all. For *that* is the expression which confuses you. But ask yourself: in what sort of case, in what kind of circumstances, do we say: "Now I know how to go on". (Wittgenstein, 1953: 61)

Wittgenstein calls the regularities of our life in language "forms of life". In other words, human life as we live and observe it is not just a random, continuous flow, but displays recurrent patterns, regularities, characteristic ways of doing and being, of feeling and acting, of speaking and interacting. Because they are patterns, regularities, configuration, Wittgenstein calls them "forms", and because they are patterns in the fabric of human existence and activity on earth, he describes them as "of life". The idea is clearly related to the idea of language games, and more generally to Wittgenstein's action-oriented perspective of language as Pitkin (1972) has pointed out. "The speaking of language", Wittgenstein says, "is a part of an activity, or a form of life" (Wittgenstein, 1953: 23).

Wittgenstein talks much about rules and patterns, but he never leaves the level of humans as actors. He also stresses the *constituting* rather than the *depicting* purpose of language. In the language of this book, we could, with the greatest humility, say that Wittgenstein is using systems concepts in an *actors view*.

A8 A SUMMARY

It isn't an easy task to relate philosophical thoughts and concepts to each other and to different philosophical branches. It's a slightly hazardous business, where you continuously risk treading on somebody's toes. In this Appendix we have made our descriptions only in respect to how various branches, movements, perspectives, thinkers, etc. have influenced the development of our three methodological views. To summarize this briefly:

- The *analytical* view is still today influenced by positivism, but its modern foundation is analytical philosophy. We have adapted the analytical view to business by giving subjective facts the same methodological status as objective facts, in the frame of the ultimate presumption of a factive reality. We have illustrated the ontological and epistemological roots of the view, from empiricism to rationalism, and related it to such branches as grounded theory and ethnography in the senses of explanation.
- The *systems* view is our name for all sorts of research/consulting/investigating based on systemic, holistic and structuralistic thinking either as explaining or as understanding. In the latter case, hermeneutics, symbolic interactionism, sense-making, metaphorical thinking, etc. enter the picture.
- The *actors* view is based on social phenomenology and has a social constructionist aspect. However, as a methodological view/approach, as presented in this book, it is a genuine development by us, especially by Arbnor. Phenomenological thinkers rarely concern themselves with concrete research methodology, even less with creating business knowledge. Furthermore, the actors view is, besides the above-mentioned philosophers/thinkers, also influenced by figures like Bergson (1859–1941), Heidegger (1889–1976), Habermas (b. 1929), Sartre (1905–1980) and Ricoeur (1913–2005) and has therefore an orientation to the philosophy of human life itself, which the other two methodological views have not.

What makes this book unique, on top of its combining of philosophy of science, methodology and business, is that we have developed a *methodology of complementarity*, which means that the book is a complete package of methodology for creating business knowledge.

A9 RECOMMENDED FURTHER READING

(Visit: www.knowledge-creator.com)

Theory of science

Fay, B. (1996), *Contemporary Philosophy of Social Science*. Oxford: Blackwell Publishers.
Potter, E. (2006), *Feminism and Philosophy of Science*. London: Taylor & Francis Ltd.
Rosenberg, A. (2007), *Philosophy of Social Science*. Boulder: The Perseus Books Group.

Paradigms

Burrell, G. & Morgan, G. (1985), *Sociological Paradigms and Organizational Analysis – Elements of the Sociology of Corporate Life*. Aldershot: Ashgate Publishing Group.
Guba, E.G. (ed.) (1990), *The Paradigm Dialog*. Newbury Park: Sage.
Kuhn, T. (1996), *The Structure of Scientific Revolution*. Chicago: The University of Chicago Press.

Explaining and understanding

Apel, K.O. (1984), *Understanding and Explanation*. Cambridge, MA: The MIT Press.
Manicas, P.T. (2006) *A Realist Philosophy of Social Science: Explanation and Understanding*. Cambridge: Cambridge University Press.
von Wright, G.H. (1971), *Explanation and Understanding*. London: Routledge.

Positivism

Friedman, M. (1999), *Reconsidering Logical Positivism*. Cambridge: Cambridge University Press.
Richardson, A. & Uebel, T. (2007), *The Cambridge Companion to Logical Empiricism*. Cambridge: Cambridge University Press.

Analytical philosophy

Austin, J.L. (1979), *Philosophical Papers*. Oxford: Clarendon Press.
Martinick, A. & Soza, E.D. (2001), *Analytical Philosophy: An Anthology*. Oxford: Blackwell Publishers.
Stroll. A. (2007), *Twentieth-Century Analytical Philosophy*. Dehli: Motilal Banarsidass.

Systems thinking

Bertalanffy, L. (1973), *General Systems Theory* (rev. edn.). New York: Brazilier.
Buckley, W. (ed.) (1968), *Modern Systems Research for the Behavioural Scientist*. Hawthorne, NY: Aldine.
Jackson, M.C. (2003), *Systems Thinking: Creative Holism for Managers*. Chichester: John Wiley and Sons Ltd.
Skyttner, L. (2001), *General Systems Theory*. Singapore: World Scientific Publishing Co. Pte Ltd.

Holism

James, S. (1984), *The Content of Social Explanation*. Cambridge: Cambridge University Press.
Laszlo, E. (1996), *Systems View of the World: A Holistic Vision for Our Time*. Cress Kill, NJ: Hampton Press.
Phillips, D.C. (1976), *Holistic Thought in Social Science*. Stanford: Stanford University Press.

Structuralism

Dosse, F. (1998), *History of Structuralism* (two volumes). Minneapolis, MI. University of Minnesota Press.
Hawkes, T. (2003), *Structuralism and Semiotics*. London: Taylor & Francis Ltd.
Norris, C. (2002), *Deconstruction: Theory and Practice*. London: Taylor & Francis Ltd.
Sturroch, J. & Rabaté, J.M. (2003), *Structuralism*. Malden: Blackwell Publishing Ltd.
Williams, J. (2005), *Understanding Poststructuralism*. London: Acumen Publishing.

Marxism

D'Amato, P. (2006), *The Meaning of Marxism*. Chicago, IL: Haymarket Books.
Therborn, G. (2008), *From Marxism to Post-Marxism*. New York: Verso.

Grounded theory

Charmaz, K. (2006), *Constructing Grounded Theory. A Practical Guide Through Qualitative Analysis*. London: Sage.
Glaser, B.G. (1992), *Basics of Grounded Theory Research*. Mill Valley, CA: Sociology Press.
Glaser, B.G. & Strauss, A.L. (1967/1999), *The Discovery of Grounded Theory*. Edison: Transaction Publishers.

Sensemaking

Weick, K.E. (1995), *Sensemaking in Organizations*. Thousand Oaks, CA: Sage.
Weick, K.E. (2000), *Making Sense of the Organization*. Malden, MA: Blackwell Publishing Ltd.

Symbolic interactionism

Blumer, H. (1986), *Symbolic Interactionism: Perspective and Method*. Berkeley: University of California Press.
Charon, J.M. (2006), *Symbolic Interactionism: An Introduction, An Interpretation*. Englewood Cliffs, NJ: Prentice-Hall.

Metaphorical thinking

Morgan, G. (ed.) (1983), *Beyond Method*. Newbury Park: Sage.
Pugh, S.L., Hicks, J.W., Davis, M. & Ventra, T. (1992), *Briding: A Teacher's Guide to Metaphorical Thinking*. Urbana, IL: National Council of Teachers.

Hermeneutics

Bauman, Z. (1978), *Hermeneutics and Social Science. Approaches to Understanding*. London: Hutchinson and Sons.
Gadamer, H.G. (2004), *Truth and Method*. London: Continuum International Publishing Group Ltd.
Jasper, D. (2004), *A Short Introduction to Hermeneutics*. Louisville: Westminster John Knox Press.

Phenomenology

Husserl, E. (1931/2002), *Ideas: General Introduction to Pure Phenomenology*. London: Allen & Unwin.
Moran, D. (2000), *Introduction to Phenomenology*. London: Routledge.
Sokolowski, R. (1999), *Introduction to Phenomenology*. Cambridge, Cambridge University Press.

Social Phenomenology

Schutz, A. (1962–1970), *Collected Papers Vol. I: The Problem of Social Reality, Vol. II: Studies in Social Theory, Vol. III: Studies in Phenomenological Philosophy*. Leiden: Martinus Nijhoff Publishers.
Schutz, A. (1967), *The Phenomenology of the Social World*. Evanston: Northwestern University Press.

Ethnomethodology

Garfinkel, H. (1984), *Studies in Ethnomethodology*. Oxford: Blackwell Publishers.

Social constructionism

Burr, V. (2003), *Social Constructionism,* London: Routledge.
Gergen, K.J. (1999), *An Invitation to Social Construction*. London: Sage.

Ethnography

Atkinson, P. & Hammersley, M. (2007) *Ethnography: Principles in Practice*. London: Taylor & Francis Ltd.
Madison, D.S. (2005), *Critical Ethnography*. London: Sage.
Rose, D. (1990), *Living the Ethnographic Life*. Newbury Park: Sage.

Cultural studies

Alvesson, M. (1993), *Cultural Perspectives on Organizations*. Cambridge: Cambridge University Press.
Bjerke, B. (1999), *Business Leadership and Culture*. Cheltenham: Edward Elgar.
Geertz, C. (1983), *Local Knowledge*. New York: Basic Books.

Narratives

Czarniawska, B. (1998), *A Narrative Approach to Organization Studies*. Thousand Oaks, CA: Sage.
Mitchell, W.J.T. (ed.) (1981), *On Narrative*. Chicago: University of Chicago Press.

Michel Foucault

Foucault, M. (2002), *The Archeology of Knowledge*. London: Taylor & Francis Ltd.
Foucault, M. (1988), *Power/Knowledge*. New York: Random House.
Hoy, D. (ed.) (1986), *Foucault. A Critical Reader*. Oxford: Blackwell Publishers.

Ludwig Wittgenstein

Pears, D. (1997), *Wittgenstein*. London: Fontana Press.
Pitkin, H.F. (1976), *Wittgenstein and Justice*. Los Angeles: University of California Press.
Wittgenstein, L. (1967/2001), *Philosophical Investigations*. Oxford: Blackwell Publishers.

GLOSSARY

Each word in italics in the Glossary is possible to find as a cross-reference. We strongly recommend going further with such references if they are not already familiar to the reader.

ABC • IC The Arbnor Business Creating • Intelligence Cycle (see Figure 15.2).

abduction To place a single case (the result) from the *study area* in a *hypothetical* pattern to be confirmed by *theoretical* "rules" and/or new observations; a kind of combination of *induction* and *deduction*; associated with the *analytical view*.

actors approach *Actors view* in application.

actors view A *methodology* for creating knowledge devoted to *understanding*, creating and *vivifying meaning* in reality, where this reality is presumed to be *socially constructed*.

analysis An analysis can be made within all three of the *methodological views*. An analysis, according to the *analytical view*, consists of dissecting an object into its parts. An analysis in the *systems view* consists of *explaining* and/or *understanding* the relations of an object's parts to each other, to the *totality*. The analysis concept is also used in the *actors view* (however, more common is *diagnosis*) in order to emphasize an interest in looking at different parts and their *dialectic* relations to each other.

analytical approach *Analytical view* in application.

analytical philosophy A generic term for a philosophical movement, which has made the *methodological* use of conceptual *analysis* and formal logic its central theme; associated with the *analytical view*.

analytical view A *methodology* for creating knowledge devoted to *explain causality* in reality, where this reality is presumed to be *factive* and built up *summatively*.

anomaly A deviation from the normal or common order in the frame of a *paradigm*.

antithesis A *dialectical* element of a process, where this second (*antithesis*) is the contrasting part of the first (*thesis*), with the first inherent in itself; associated with the *actors view*.

approach See *methodological approach*.

Arbnor/Bjerke Methodological Principle of Complementarity The potential interdependency in opposite methodological opinions of similar problems is to be used for excellent explanations and/or understanding of them. The principle implies that there are many such problems with this kind of inherent interdependency, which cannot fully be treated by only one of the approaches, in question. Therefore, it is possible and desirable to use complementarity in studies faced with multifaced problems.

Arbnor Uncertainty Principle "The more precisely you determine isolated characteristics of a human being and her activities, quantitatively and statistically, the less you understand of her as a whole. And the better you understand her as a whole, the more uncertain the quantitative/statistic aspects become."

artistics The way in which the actors *creator of knowledge* expresses his/her knowledge-creating as a *procreative* language of description. Also, the final expression format of this interpretive pictorial language creating meaning and new prespectives (opposite: statistics).

atomism A philosophical/scientific perspective, presuming that aspects of a given situation can be determined or *explained summatively* by its parts (opposite: *holism*).

base view/approach A denotation of a *methodological view/approach* when used as a *transformative operator* in a *methodology of complementarity*.

causality A presumed relationship between an explaining factor (*cause*) and a factor being explained (*effect*); associated with the *analytical view*.

cause See *causality*.

ceteris paribus "Everything else being equal"; circumstances presumed to be *valid* for *explanations* in the *analytical view*.

complementarity A concept describing how a potential interdependency in opposite *methodological* opinions of similar problems can be used in a *reconciliation* for excellent *explanations* and/or *understanding* of them.

complementary procedure A *transformative operation*, where a *technique/method/theory* from one *methodological view* is being brought into another *methodological view* and inevitably transformed by being so (opposite: *primary procedure*). Compare *methodical procedure*.

consistency A concept of quality assurance, according to knowledge creating. Degree of methodological syntactical match in relation to *ultimate presumptions* of a *methodological view*. The concept is an essential core element of the overall scientific concept, *crealiability*, for excellence in knowledge creating work.

consistency of complementarity A concept of quality assurance, according to knowledge creating of complementarity. Degree of methodological syntactical match of complementarity in relation to the ultimate presumptions of the *transformative operator*. The concept is an essential core element of the overall scientific concept, *crealiability of complementarity*, for excellence in knowledge creating work.

constitutional factors Factors, which are *socially constructed*, by which reality is built up socially; associated with the *actors view*.

constitutional ideal A more "general" principle for how reality is *socially constructed* and how it could be if the potential in what is *factual* was delivered; associated with the *actors view*.

constitutive interpretive procedures "Rules" by which creators of knowledge *interpret/ understand* the reality which the actors and the *creators of knowledge* are part of *socially con- structing* themselves; associated with the *actors view*.

constitutive understanding *Understanding* which is seen as an inevitable part of reality, where this reality is presumed to be *socially constructed*; associated with the *actors view* (opposite: *representative understanding*).

constructionism See the Appendix.

constructivism See *constructionism*.

crealiability The concept is a compound of creativity and liability and the prefix "crea" denotes, in scientific contexts, to be creative, to have imagination and ingenuity, this con- nected to the suffix "liability" in the sense of responsibility, obligation and duty. Crealiability is our concept for excellence in knowledge-creating work and consists of the four core ele- ments: creativity, *objectivity (validity/reliability)*, *stringency* and *consistency*.

creator of knowledge (also *knowledge creator*) A conscious researcher, consultant and/or investigator who has the will to apply curiosity and imagination, has the insight that knowl- edge also contains manifestations of *ultimate presumptions*, and uses his/her training in the concrete handicraft to develop knowledge, and to present new knowledge to others and be accountable for it.

culture Fundamental values, assumptions and beliefs associated with members of a social group (can also be seen as, or including, how a social group manifests itself in various arti- facts, including language).

cybernetics A generic term, taken from Wiener around 1950, to describe *teleological* struc- tures, interactions, responses, feedbacks, etc. in complex systems. The "art of steering and control" of multifaceted systems structures, especially communication processes.

deduction Inference of specific forecasts/conclusions from general *theories/premises*; associ- ated with the *analytical view* (compare: *induction* and *abduction*).

denotation of conceptual meaning A fundamental ambition of *the actors view*, that is, to come up with pictures/descriptions/*metaphors* of how actors attach *meaning* to their lan- guage and actions.

depiction A "map" of reality, where this reality is presumed to be *factive*; associated with the *analytical view* and the *systems view* in the *explanatory* mode.

determinism A philosophical concept, presuming that every phenomenon or event, includ- ing human acts and behaviour, has a cause – is *causally* determined by a link of previous occurrences; partly associated with the *analytical view* and the *systems view*.

diagnosis A way to interactively *interpret* and *understand* actors in situations of *everyday* life through deeper insight and broadened perspectives; associated with the *actors view*.

dialectics The process of *thesis, antithesis* and *synthesis*, that is, relationships and situations where people constantly reinterpret and give different meaning value. This is also the process where the knowledge-creator gives scientific meaning to his/her interactive *diagnosis*; associated with the *actors view*.

dialogue The interplay between "talking" and "listening" that takes place on equal terms for the participants. A dialogue is to clarify differences in order to transgress them toward something new, in a deepened *understanding* and *meaning* of life, that is, the parties of the dialogues are looking for an agreement through what is different; associated with the *actors view*.

discourse A praxis in communication, governed by (often implicit) rules. In social science applications it involves concepts, methods and skills with specific purposes. This means, in general, that the chosen discourse delivers a way of thinking and a style of communicating. The concept is mostly connected with the work of Foucault (see the Appendix).

eclectic maze A jumbled mixture of what appear to be best *techniques*, *theories*, and so on, without any reflection in relation to *ultimate presumptions* on the various *methodological views*.

effect See *causality*.

egological sphere The internal logic of an actor that constitutes his/her *finite province of meaning*, and by which he/she orients him/herself; associated with the *actors view*.

emancipative understanding Come to an *understanding* that one's reality is seen through the "lenses" of a language and that those lenses can be shifted, thereby providing another *understanding*; associated with the *actors view*.

emancipatory interactive action Action taken by the *creator of knowledge* together with other actors in the *study area*, aiming at providing *emancipative understanding* by delivering the potential in what is factual; associated with the *actors view*.

empirical Pertaining to human experience.

empiricism A philosophical movement, presuming that all knowledge of reality, seen as *factive*, is derived from our sensory impressions (opposite: *rationalism*).

epistemology A set of philosophical presumptions concerning human knowledge and learning. The philosophical *"theory"* of the nature and grounds of knowledge.

ethnography See the Appendix.

ethnomethodology See the Appendix.

everyday reality See *life-world*.

explaining Providing objective and/or subjective reasons for phenomena or events, presumed to be independent of us as *creators of knowledge*; associated with the *analytical view* and the *systems view* in the explanatory mode.

externalization The process by which we make our subjectivity available to others ("society is a human result"); associated with the *actors view*.

factified reality See *factual reality*.

factive reality A reality presumed to be built of by objective and/or subjective facts and independent of us as *creators of knowledge*; associated with the *analytical view* and the *systems view*.

factual reality A reality presumed to be *socially constructed* but treated as a fact without being one in the sense of the *analytical view* and the *systems view* (can also be called *factified reality*); associated with the *actors view*.

falsification If a theory is to be regarded as scientific, according to the concept of falsification, it has also to specify results that, if found, would disprove the theory. Falsification means therefore to direct the researcher's attention to look for refuting or counter instances as well. Conclusions in the theoretical reality for prediction are open for falsification, that is denial in empirical reality that some conclusion derived in the theoretical reality is valid; associated with the *analytical view* (opposite: *verification*). The concept is connected with the work of Popper.

finality A presumed relationship between an *explaining* factor (*producer*) and a factor being explained (*product*), that is, to *explain* by the purpose they serve rather than by postulated previous *causes* (see *causality*); associated with the *systems view*.

finite province of meaning An actor's picture/concept of reality – the actor's subjective reality in its entirety – more or less socially shared by a larger or a smaller number of other actors (includes also parts of which are not shared with anybody else); associated with the *actors view*.

functionalism A philosophical/scientific thought, having made the relationship between patterns and their *factive* consequences a central theme; associated with the *systems view*.

General Systems Theory A scientific attempt to come up with a *holistic theory* of life and nature, based on systems principles; a forerunner to the *systems view*.

grounded theory A scientific branch, based on the idea of systematically collecting and *analyzing* data from the study area instead of starting from "grand theories", mainly associated with the *analytical view* or the *systems view*.

hermeneutics See the Appendix.

holism A philosophical/scientific perspective, presuming that all aspects of a given situation cannot be determined or *explained* by its parts only; associated with the *systems view* (opposite: *atomism* or *reductionism*).

hypothesis In a strict sense: a *cause–effect* (see *causality*) relationship proposal, not yet verified or falsified; associated with the *analytical view*. In a loose sense: supposition, idea, point of departure, etc.; mainly associated with the *systems view* and the *actors view*.

idealism See the Appendix.

ideal-typified language A more "general" language constituted by *typified cases* and the *constitutional ideal*; associated with the *actors view*.

induction Generation of general *theories* from individual facts in the *empirical* (*factive*) reality; associated with the *analytical view* (compare: *deduction* and *abduction*).

institutions An institution emerges according to the *actors view* when common *typifications* of habitual acts are established. By "institution" can be meant everything from established concepts of description – lingoes/clichés – to different public authorities; associated with the *actors view*.

institutionalization The process of establishing values, norms, routines, etc. as *institutions* in the *socially constructed reality*; associated with the *actors view*.

internalization The process by which we take over the world in which others already live ("humans are a societal result"); associated with the *actors view*.

interpretation To decode something contextually and through that coming up with an *understanding*, either by a *metaphor* provided by the *creator of knowledge* in the *understanding* mode of the *systems view*, or by a denotation of conceptual *meaning* in the *actors view*.

intentionality The dimension, process and structure behind intention that gives a *meaning* to experience; associated with the *actors view*.

intersubjectivity Agreement between results from *creators of knowledge*, working independently of each other; mainly associated with the *analytical view*.

knowledge creator See *creator of knowledge*.

legitimization The process of the justification of *institutions* in *socially constructed reality*; associated with the *actors view*.

life-world (also called *everyday reality*) The world regarded as the one immediately given to us in everyday life and not imposed by any scientific models or one's own interpretations. In a society where scientific results continuously influence us, this is a crucial concept (compare: *self-reference*); associated with the *actors view*.

magnifying level Degree of details contained in systems models or systems *interpretations*; associated with the *systems view*.

materialism See the Appendix.

meaning Significant sense-quality (value and importance) that actors attached to their situation; associated with the *actors view*.

meaning structure A more "complete" built-up of *meaning* relations in a group of actors; associated with the *actors view*.

metaphor In everyday life for most of us, a figure of speech where things are compared in a symbolic way, as in "she is a dolphin" about a swimmer. In science, a concept, an abstraction or image placed by the creator of knowledge on one situation in the study area, taken from another and different situation, where the qualities of the intrinsic sense of the metaphor thus are transferred to the object in question in the first situation. A metaphor may therefore in knowledge-creating pave the way for new perspectives; associated with the *systems view* and the *actors view*.

metaphysics Branch of philosophy that deals with "being" (*ontology*) and "knowing" (*epistemology*), that is, the ultimate nature of reality. These kinds of studies have been subjected to many criticisms regarded as too subtle and theoretical. Since the middle of the nineteenth century the predominant social science course has been *positivism*, which denies the value of any metaphysical assertion.

metatheories The background theories in the conception of science that are held by *creators of knowledge* and that, in general terms, guide their practical knowledge-creating. More fundamental "theories of theories", which inevitably include the people using them; associated with the *actors view*.

method Guiding principle for creation of knowledge and choosing among *techniques*.

methodical procedure The way the *creator of knowledge* incorporates, develops and/or modifies a technique or a previous result and/or theory in a *methodological view*; can be of a *primary* or a *complementary* type.

methodics Applying *methodical procedures* in a plan and/or in an implementation of a study.

methodological approach A *methodological view* in application.

methodological view A consistent set-up of *ultimate presumptions*, concepts and principles guiding creation of knowledge. Three such *views* are: the *analytical view*, the *systems view* and the *actors view*.

methodology A *theory* and a grammar of the modes of thinking and acting for knowledge creating.

methodology of complementarity A complete grammar for creating knowledge containing *primary* as well as *complementary procedures* open for all kinds of *transformative operations* within the three *base views/approaches*.

model A deliberately simplified picture of the *factive reality*; mainly associated with the *analytical view* and the *systems view* in *explanatory* mode. The concept may also be used by the *actors view* in "painting" the *socially constructed reality*, both in the sense of visualizing aspects of it and *vivifying* the potential in what is *factual*, but, of course, then with a totally different meaning of the concept than with the two other views.

narrative A story guided by specific rules, either seen as a part of the *factive reality* in the *systems view* (narrative *realism*) or as told by actors as part of the *factified reality* (narrative *constructionism*).

objectification The process by which an *externalized* human thought and/or act might attain the characteristics of a *socially constructed objectivity* ("society is an objective reality"); associated with the *actors view*.

objectified Something seen as *objective* in the *actors view* without being so in the sense of the other two *views*; this means that this *objectivity* of reality can be questioned and changed in the logic of delivering what is potential in what is *factual*.

objective Characteristic of the non-subjective part of the *factive reality*, presumed to be general and independent of any single individual; mainly associated with the *analytical view*.

objectivity See *objectified* and *objective*. As a concept of quality assurance in *knowledge creating* and as a core element of *crealiability* it will signify different substances in relation to the various *methodological views*. (See "The problem of objectivity" in Chapter 7.)

ontology A set of philosophical thoughts and presumptions concerning the set-up and constitution of all reality and the problems/opportunities of existence. (See *metaphysics*.)

operative paradigm A consistent arrangement of *methodical procedures* and *methodics* as a bridge between a *methodological view/approach* and a *study area*.

paradigm A philosophical and *theoretical* framework of presumptive and guiding principles which are governing knowledge and the creation of knowledge, but which cannot be *empirically* or logically tested.

phenomenology A philosophical branch, which has made the study of human consciousness or subjective experience, neglecting questions of truth in the sense of traditional *analytical philosophy*, a central theme. The *intentional diagnosis* of *everyday* life from the point of departure of the actors who are living it, is a central theme; associated with the *actors view*.

positivism A philosophical/scientific branch presuming that classic natural sciences are the path to true knowledge. By using the *methods* of these sciences, suggesting that human behaviour is an *effect* of social, economic, biological, etc. *causes,* the truth of the *factive reality* will be mapped; mainly associated with the *analytical view*.

pragmatism A school of philosophy, based on the principle that a scientific result is judged by its usefulness, workability, etc. when applied in the *empirical* world; mainly associated with the *systems view*.

pre-scientific concept A concept that will be taken for granted when conducting a study, because of its belonging to the special subject, the lingo of the profession, the study area, etc. in question.

primary procedure The term for a *methodical procedure* when applied in a *methodology of complementarity* (opposite, in this frame of methodology: *complementary procedure*).

problematization To make what is common uncommon – to question what is taken for granted. To pave the way for new points of departure for orientation and by this discover new aspects. Problematization is therefore intimately connected to both the act of knowing and the concrete situations in the *study area*, as well as the act of creativity.

producer–product relationship Same as *finality* relationship; associated with the *systems view*.

procreative report A written report with ambitions to communicate *procreative understanding*; associated with the *actors view*.

procreative understanding A kind of higher form of consciousness that fertilizes the mental power to create, to transform, to *vivify* and to change in uniquely and desirable directions; associated with the *actors view*.

procreative word Concept in language development that is "loaded" by the right kind of fertilizing energy for the *study area* and for the *knowledge creator's* own development *of procreative understanding:* associated with the *actors view.*

rationalism See the Appendix.

realism A philosophical perspective, regarding reality as independent of human consciousness (opposite: *idealism*).

reconciliation A process of getting two opposite thoughts/things to correspond in a knowledge-creating mode. Compare: *complementarity* and *methodology of complementarity.*

reductionism A philosophical/scientific thought presuming that events and circumstances at a given level of nature or society can be *explained* at a lower level of nature or society, for instance, providing psychological *explanations* to sociological phenomena (opposite: *holism*).

reification Looking at immaterial concepts such as being, having soul, etc. as concrete objects, that is, humans giving them characteristics as "mechanical" components and as such neglecting the fact that meanings and actions are made by people, mainly associated with the *actors view.*

relativism A philosophical branch presuming that there are different, possibly self-contained, traditions, ethics, knowledge and ways of life, each to be judged only in accordance with its own arbitrary standard, dependent upon circumstances.

reliability As a concept of quality assurance in *knowledge creating* and as a subcore element of *crealiability* it will signify different substances in relation to the various *methodological views.* (See "Measurement techniques and techniques for controlling reliability" in Chapter 7.)

representative understanding Understanding, which is seen as a *depiction* (map) of reality, where this reality is presumed to be *factive*; associated with the *systems view* (opposite: *constitutive understanding*).

self-reference A phenomenon, according to the *actors view,* that exists between scientific results and the development of society. The social scientist will therefore always, when doing research, also research the influence of his/her own earlier results, without any possibility of clear-cut results. The existing social science knowledge representation of generality, normality, clichés, uniformity, etc. in individual human beings will always be there as an *everyday reality.*

sensemaking See the Appendix.

social construction (of reality) A reality, which is built and rebuilt by its members in a *dialectical* process and does not exist independently of, or beyond, these members, including its *knowledge creators*; associated with the *actors view.*

social phenomenology A critical *synthesis*, created by Schutz, of Husserl's *phenomenology* and Weber's thoughts about *understanding*; associated with the *actors view.*

stringency A concept of quality assurance, according to knowledge-creating, including a degree of rigorous performance and standard of attainments. The quality of being stringent in the frame of a *methodological view*. The concept is an essential core element of the over-all scientific concept, *crealiability*, for excellence in knowledge-creating work.

stringency of complementarity A concept of quality assurance, according to knowledge cre-ating of complementarity, including a degree of rigorous performance and standard of attainments. The quality of being stringent in the frame of the *complementarity* in question. The concept is an essential core element of the overall scientific concept, *crealiability* of *com-plementarity,* for excellence in knowledge-creating work.

structuralism A philosophical branch, generally looking at the study area as patterned or, more specifically, derived from linguistics and applied to other fields, presuming that phe-nomena should be *explained* or *understood* in terms of invariant underlying structures of organization; associated with the *systems view*.

study area The field of focus and interest in an effort to create knowledge.

subjectification The process of consciousness by which we create and constitute ourselves as *intentional* subjects ("humans are a subjective reality"); associated with the *actors view*.

summative Built up *ceteris paribus*, that is, the belief that any new finding when creating knowledge can be added to a previous finding without any complications or additions for the latter one; associated with the *analytical view*.

synergy A principle that *totality* is presumed to be more or less than the sum of its parts; mainly associated with the *systems view*.

synthesis The *dialectical* "end" of a process, where the first (*thesis*) has been contrasted by the second (*antithesis*), with the first inherent in itself, and at the "end" both the *thesis* and the *antithesis* have been moved up into a higher form, the synthesis; associated with the *actors view*.

systems approach *Systems view* in application.

systems view A *methodology* for creating knowledge, devoted to *explaining* and/or *under-standing* reality, presumed to be built up *holistically*.

technique Rules given a priori for using various tools to create knowledge in practice.

teleology See *finality*.

theory A word with an unambiguous sense as well as an ambiguous one, depending on in which *methodological view* it appears and under which circumstances. In the former sense, for example: empirical (experiential) laws *explaining* regularities existing in objects and events of a *study area;* associated with the *analytical view*. In the latter sense: A set of asser-tions or main beliefs devised to *explain* and/or *understand* a set of facts or phenomena; associated with the *systems view* and the *actors view*.

thesis The first *dialectical* element of a process, where this first (*thesis*) is going to be con-trasted by the second (*antithesis*); associated with the *actors view*.

thematic language of methodology A "neutral" language, developed in this book to bridge the problems of knowledge creation and knowledge quality between various contexts of research, consultation and/or investigation, containing: *paradigm, ultimate presumption, factive reality, factified reality, methodological view/approach, operative paradigm, methodical procedure, methodics, method, technique, reconciliation, methodology of complementarity, base view, transformative operator, primary procedure, complementary procedure, study area, crealiability, and crealiability of complementarity.*

totality A world, presumed to be an entity, where the parts are more or less dependent on each other; mainly associated with the first guiding principle of the *systems view*.

transformative operation The total amount of *methodical procedures, primary* as well as *complementary*, in connection with the *methodics* will form the *operative paradigm*, and the overall concept for all these operations in a *methodology of complementary* is thus transformative operations.

transformative operator The concept for a *methodological approach* when acting as a base of *complementarity* for *transformative operations*.

typification Describing our way of attaching various labels and typical designations to – and having different understandings of – the people and things around us. We expect, and then take for granted, that what is typified behaves according to the understanding mediated by the typification; associated with the *actors view*.

typified cases Knowledge-illustrations with an ideal character describing various ideal states that "imaginatively" can reflect the potential, and thereby engage various actors in *procreating dialogues* in which the potential will be transformed into the *factual*, that is, into a new *social reality*. Typified cases, in spite of being ideal, have a strong connection to the "living" social reality.

ultimate presumption Fundamental belief of reality and life (same as normative thesis), which cannot be empirically or logically tested, but which influences and steers each and every one of us when acting as *knowledge creators*.

understanding Providing knowledge based on the creator of knowledge, attempting to gain a "deeper" knowledge of his/her *study area*, associated with the *systems view* in an understanding mode, or knowledge based on the actors *denotation of conceptual meaning*, associated with the *actors view*.

validity As a concept of quality assurance in *knowledge-creating* and as a subcore element of *crealiability*, it will signify different substances in relation to the various *methodological views*. (See "Validation techniques" in Chapter 7).

verification Confirmation in *empirical* reality of some conclusion derived in the *theoretical* reality; associated with the *analytical view* (opposite: falsification).

verstehen See the Appendix.

view See *methodological view*.

vivify To give new energy to life, ennoble the values of life, provide reinforcement to what is unique; associated with the *actors view*.

REFERENCES

Ahl, H. (2007), "A Foucauldian framework for discourse analysis" in H. Neergaard & J.P. Ulhøi (eds), *Handbook of Qualitative Research Methods in Entrepreneurship*. Cheltenham, UK and Northampton, MA, USA: Edward Elgar, pp. 216–50.

Apel, K.-O. (1984), *Understanding and Explanation*. Cambridge, MA: The MIT Press.

Arbnor, I. (1976), *Vetenskapsteoretiska bilder* [Images from the theory of science]. Malmö: Liber Läromedel.

Arbnor, I. (2004), *Vägen från klockrike* [On the road from the Industrial Clockdom]. Stockholm: SNS Förlag.

Arbnor, I. (2006), *Entreprenörskap i världsklass – Koenigsegg* [World class Entrepreneurship – Koenigsegg]. Malmö: Liber.

Ashworth, A. (2005), *Contractual Procedures in the Construction Industry*. New Jersey: Pearson Education.

Berger, P.L. & Luckmann, T. (1966), *The Social Construction of Reality*. Garden City, NY: Doubleday.

Blumer, H. (1979), *Critiques of Research in the Social Sciences*. London: Transaction Publishers.

Blumer, H. (1986), *Social Interactionism: Perspective and Method*. Berkeley: California University Press.

Bohr, N. (1928), "The Quantum Postulate and Recent Developments in Atomic Theory", *Nature* 121 (Suppl.): 580–90.

Bosma, N. & Harding, R. (2007) *Global Entrepreneurship*. GEM 2006 Summary Results, Babson College, Babson Park, MA, USA and London Business School, London, UK.

Brewer, J.D. (2000), *Ethnography*. Milton Keynes: Open University Press.

Buckley, W. (ed.) (1968), *Modern Systems Research for the Behaviorial Scientist*. Hawthorne, NY: Aldine.

Burns, T. & Stalker, G. (1961), *The Management of Innovation*. London: Tavistock.

Burrell, G. & Morgan, G. (1985), *Sociological Paradigms and Organizational Analysis – Elements of the Sociology of Corporate Life*. London: Heinemann.

Byars, L.L. (1987), *Strategic Management* (2nd edn). New York: Harper & Row.

Churchman, W. (1968), *The Systems Approach*, New York: Dell.

Czinkota, M.R., Rivoli, P. & Ronkainen, J.A. (1994), *International Business* (3rd edn). Orlando, FL: Harcourt Brace.

Deal, T. & Kennedy, A. (1988), *Corporate Cultures*. London: Penguin Books.

DePree, M. (1992), *Leadership Jazz*, New York: Dell.

Dredge, C.P. (1985), "Corporate culture: the challenge to expatriate managers and multinational corporations" in H.V. Wortzel & L.H. Wortzel (eds), *Strategic Management and Multinational Corporations: The Essentials*. New York: John Wiley & Sons, pp. 410–24.

Droysen, J.G. (1858), *Grundrisse der Historik*, published (1897) as *Outline of the Principles of History* (trans. E.B. Andrews). Boston, MA: Ginn & Co.

Drucker, P.F. (1993), *Post-Capitalist Society*. New York: HarperCollins.

Emery, J. (1969), *Organizational Planning and Control Systems*. New York: Reinhold.

Etzioni, A. (1966), *Moderna organisationer* [Modern organizations]. Stockholm: Aldus/Bonniers.

Fay, B. (1996), *Contemporary Philosophy of Social Science*. Oxford: Blackwell Publishing.

Feyerabend, P. (1993), *Against Method*. London: Verso Books.

Foucault, M. (1980), *Power/Knowledge*. New York: Pantheon.

Fuld, L.M. (2006), *The Secret Language of Competitive Intelligence: How to See Through and Stay Ahead of Business Disruptions, Distortions, Rumors, and Smoke Screens*. New York: Crown Business.

Geertz, C. (1973), *The Interpretation of Culture*. New York: Basic Books.

Gergen, K.J. (1999), *An Invitation to Social Construction*. London: Sage.

Gilad, B. (2003), *Early Warning – Using Competitive Intelligence to Anticipate Market Shifts, Control Risk and Create Powerful Strategies*. New York: AMACOM.

Gill, J. & Johnson, P. (2002), *Research Methods for Managers*. London: Sage.

Glaser, B.G. & Strauss, A.L. (1967/1999), *The Discovery of Grounded Theory*. Edison: Transaction Publishers.

Guba, E.G. (1990), "The alternative paradigm dialog" in E.G. Guba (ed.), *The Paradigm Dialog*. Newbury Park: Sage, pp. 17–27.

Hunt, S.D. (2003), *Controversy in Marketing Theory*. London: M.E. Sharp.

Hammer, M. & Champy, J. (1993), *Reengineering the Corporation*. New York: Harper Collins.

Hammersley, M. (1990), *Reading Ethnographic Research*. Harlow: Longman.

Husserl, E. (1931), *Ideas*. London: Allen & Unwin.

Hussey, D. & Jenster, P. (1999), *Competitor Intelligence, Turning Analysis into Success*. New York: John Wiley & Sons.

Jeffcutt, P., Small, R.G. & Linstead, S. (1996), "Organization as a theatre of performance", *Culture and Organization*, 2(1): 3–8.

Johnson, G. & Scholes, K. (1999) *Exploring Corporate Strategy* (5th edn). Englewood Cliffs, NJ: Prentice-Hall.

Jones, A.H. (1916), "The problem of objectivity", *The Philosophical Review*, 25(6). Cornell University, USA.

Kahaner, L. (1997), *Competitive Intelligence – How to Gather, Analyze, and Use Information to Move Your Business to the Top*. New York: Simon & Schuster.

Kamprad, I. (1993), *Snålands allehanda* [Internal IKEA journal]. Älmhult, Sweden: IKEA.

Kao, J. (1997), *Jamming: The Art and Discipline of Business Creativity*. New York: HarperBusiness.

Katz, D. & Kahn, R. (1966), *The Social Psychology of Organizations*. New York: John Wiley.

Kelly, G. (1991), *The Psychology of Personal Constructs*. New York: Routledge.

Kendall, G. & Wickham, G. (1999), *Using Foucault's Methods*. London: Sage.

Kilmann, R.H. (1984), *Beyond the Quick Fix: Managing Five Tracks to Organizational Success*. San Francisco: Jossey-Bass.

Kuhn, T. (1970/1962), *The Structure of Scientific Revolutions*. Chicago: University of Chicago Press.

Kunde, J. (2002), *Unique Now – Or Never*. London: Financial Times Prentice Hall.

Lasserre, P. & Schütte, H. (1995), *Strategies for Asia Pacific*. London: Macmillan Press Ltd.

Lawrence, P. & Lorch, J. (1969), *Developing Organizations: Diagnosis and Action*. Reading, MA: Addison-Wesley.

Liedman, S-E. (2002), *Ett oändligt äventyr* [An infinite adventure]. Stockholm: Albert Bonniers Förlag.

Lindqvist, S. (1978), *Gräv där du står* [Dig where you stand]. Stockholm: Bonniers.

March, J. & Simon, H. (1958), *Organizations*. New York: John Wiley.

Marti Y-M. (1996), "A Typology of Information Needs" in B. Gilad & J.P. Herring (eds), *The Art and Science of Business Intelligence Analysis*. Greenwich: JAI Press, pp. 121–31.

Matheson, D. & Matheson, J.E. (1998) *The Smart Organization: Creating Value Through Strategic R&D*. Harvard Business School Press.

May, R. (1969), *Love and Will*, New York: W W Norton & Company.

Mertins, K., Heisig, P. & Vorbeck, J. (2003), *Knowledge Management: Concepts and Best Practices*. Berlin: Springer.

Miller, J.G. (1977), *Living Systems*. New York: McGraw-Hill.

Morgan, G. (1998), *Images of the Organization*. Thousand Oaks, CA: Sage.

Myrdal, G, (1969), *Objectivity in Social Research*. London: Gerald Duckworth.

Normann, R. (2001), *Reframing Business. When the Map Changes the Landscape*. New York: John Wiley & Sons.

Mäkelä, M.M. & Turcan, R.V. (2007), "Building grounded theory in entrepreneurship research" in H. Neergaard & J.P. Ulhøi (eds), *Handbook of Qualitative Research Methods in Entrepreneurship*. Cheltenham: Edward Elgar Publishing Ltd. pp. 122–43.

Pears, D. (1971), *Wittgenstein*. London: Fontana Press.

Peirce, C.S., Houser, N. & Eller, J.R. (1998), *The Essential Peirce: Selected Philosophical Writings, 1893–1913*. Bloomington, IN: Indiana University Press.

Pfeffer, J. (1992), *Managing with Power: Politics and Influence in Organizations*. Boston: Harvard Business School Press.

Pitkin, H.F. (1972), *Wittgenstein and Justice*. Los Angeles: University of California Press.

Porter, M.E. (1990), *The Competitive Advantage of Nations*. New York: The Free Press.

Porter, M.E. (1998), *Competitive Strategy: Techniques for Analyzing Industries and Competitors*. London: Simon & Schuster Ltd.

Reynolds, P., Bosma, N., Autio, E., Hunt, S., de Bono, N., Servais, I., Lopez-Garcia, P. & Chin, N. (2005), "Global Entrepreneurship Monitor: Data collection design and implementation 1998–2003", *Small Business Economics*, 24: 205–31.

Rustmann Jr, F.W. (2002), *CIA, Inc. Espionage and the Craft of Business Intelligence*. Washington, DC: Brassey's Inc.

Salzer-Mörling, M. (1998), *Företag som kulturella uttryck* [Companies as cultural expressions]. Lund: Academia Adacta.

Saxenian, A. (1996), *Regional Advantage*. Cambridge, MA and London: Harvard University Press.

Schon, D. (1972), *Blindgångare mot framtiden* [Beyond the stable state]. Stockholm: Pan/Norstedt.

Schutz, A. (1962), *Collected Papers Vol. I: The Problem of Social Reality*. Leiden: Martinus Nijhoff Publishers.

Schwartz, H. & Davis, S.M. (1981), "Matching corporate culture and business strategy", *Organizational Dynamics*, Summer: 30–48.

Shapira, P. (1995), *The R&D Workers: Managing Innovation in Britain, Germany, Japan, and the United States*. Westport: Greenwood Publishing.

Shattuck, R. & Watson Taylor, S. (1965), *Alfred Jarry. Selected Works of Alfred Jarry*. New York: Grove Press.

Shaw, E. & Conway, S. (2000), "Networking and the small firm" in S. Carter & D. Jones-Evans (eds), *Enterprise and Small Business. Principles, Practice and Policy*. Upper Saddle River, NJ: Prentice-Hall, pp. 367–83.

Silverman, D. (1997), *Qualitative Research: Theory, Method and Practice*. Thousand Oaks, CA: Sage.

Stent, G.S. (2002), *Paradoxes of Free Will*. Darby: Diane Publishing Co.

Strauss, A. & Corbin, J. (1998), *Basics of Qualitative Research: Techniques and Procedures for Developing Grounded Theory*. Thousand Oaks, CA: Sage.

Thompson, J.D. (1967), *Organization in Action*. New York: McGraw-Hill.

Thorsrud, E. & Emery, F. (1964), *Mot en ny bedriftsorganisation* [Democracy at work]. Oslo: Tanum.

Trigg, R. (2000), *Understanding Social Science*. Oxford: Blackwell Publishing.

Törnebohm, H. (1974), *Paradigm i vetenskapernas värld och vetenskapsteorin* [Paradigms in the world and theory of sciences]. Gothenburg: University of Gothenburg Press.

von Bertalanffy, L. (1968), *General Systems Theory*. New York: George Braziller.

von Wright, G.H. (1971), *Explanation and Understanding*. London: Routledge & Kegan Paul.

von Wright, G.H. (1986), *Vetenskapen of förnuftet* [Science and Reason]. Stockholm: Albert Bonniers Förlag.

Walle, A.H. (2000), *Qualitative Research in Intelligence and Marketing: The New Strategic Convergence*. Westport, CT: Greenwood Publishing Group.

Watson, G.D. (1969), *The Double Helix*. New York: Atheneum.

Whitman, M.E. & Woszczynski, A.B. (2003) *The Handbook of Information Systems Research*. Harrisburg: Idea Group Inc.

Winch, P. (1958), *The Idea of a Social Science*. London: Routledge & Kegan Paul.

Wittgenstein, L. (1953/2001), *Philosophical Investigations*. Oxford: Basil Blackwell.

Zairi, M. (1998), *Benchmarking for Best Practice: Continuous Learning through Sustainable Innovation*. Oxford: Butterworth-Heinemann.

Zairi, M. (1999), *Best Practice: Process Innovation Management*. Oxford: Butterworth-Heinemann.

Ziff, P. (1960), *Semantic Analysis*. Ithaca: Cornell University Press.

INDEX

Words in **bold** are concepts which can also be found in the Glossary

abduction 91–2
action 142–3, 156, 242
actor 66, 138
actors view
  and entrepreneurship 41–5
  and prerequisites, explanations,
    understanding and results
    58–60, 67–75
  and reality assumptions 54–5
analogies 57, 61, 75, 156, 338
analysis 66, 93–4
analytical philosophy 398
analytical view
  and entrepreneurship 36–8
  and prerequisites, explanations,
    understanding and results 56–7, 60–3
  and reality assumptions 54–5
antithesis 68, 158, 372
Arbnor Business Creating•Intelligence Cycle
  (*ABC•IC*) 387
Arbnor/Bjerke Methodological Principle of
  Complementarity 330, 387
Arbnor Uncertainty Principle 132
artistics 201
average 60

base view/approach (*see* methodological base
  approach)
business creating intelligence 386–8
business intelligence 383–8

case studies 194–5
causality 85–8, 396
causal relations 56–7, 61–2
ceteris paribus 56, 94

competitive intelligence 383–8
complementarity 325, 330, 342, 355
complementarity procedure (*see* procedures)
complex 103, 134, 335
complexity 134, 239, 335, 356, 368
consistency 272, 347
constitutional factors 58–9, 72–3
constitutive understanding 52, 58
crealiability 247–8
crealiability of complementarity 346–7, 378
creator of knowledge 6, 50, 77
critical theory 400
cultural studies 409
cybernetics 400

dataism 332, 386
decision model 234
deduction 91, 191, 391
denotation of conceptual meaning 133,
  161–5, 242
descriptive language 71–2, 163–5
determinism 132, 332, 398
diagnosis 139–141, 159–161
dialectic relations 68, 70, 137, 145
dialectics 58–9, 136–8
dialogue 135–6, 195–7
direct observation 181, 183–4
discourse 126–7, 406, 411
dissociation 139, 159, 243–6

egological sphere 69, 146, 161
emancipate 59
emancipatory interactive action 59, 74,
  132, 198
empathy 305, 396

empiricism 48, 391
engagement 159, 243–6
episteme 411
epistemology 15, 201
equifinality 65
ethnography 408
ethnomethodology 405–6
everyday reality (*see* life-world)
    149–151, 167
experiments 182–5
explaining 50–2, 394–7
explorative studies 89
externalization 144–7

factive reality 51, 81–2, 115
factual reality (*see* factified reality) 51, 409
falsification 56
finality relations 57, 396
finite province of meaning 55, 67–9, 140
first hand expressions 44, 152, 158, 189

General Systems Theory 66, 102–3, 401
grounded theory 91, 402, 413

hermeneutics 395, 403–4
holism 103, 398–9
hypothesis 62–3, 83–4

idealism 391
ideal type 60, 72, 369–74
ideal-typified language 59, 70, 71–2, 163–5
induction 90, 239
information
    primary 180–5
    secondary 180–5
institutionalization 144, 147, 245
intentionality 133–4, 204, 396, 405
internalization 144, 148–9, 197
interpretation 104, 157–65, 397
intersubjectivity 204
interviews 181–4
invariance 81–3

knowledge audit 380–3
knowledge creator (*see* creator of knowledge)
knowledge-creating 5–6, 29, 247
knowledge intelligence 380, 383–4, 386

language development 141–2, 197–200
language game 154, 364, 412
Lebenswelt (*see* life-world)
legitimization 144, 147–8
life-world (*see* everyday reality)
    70, 299, 405

magnifying level 112, 117
materialism 391, 400
meaning structures 54, 69, 200
measurement scales 185
metaphor 52, 104, 142, 216, 367
metaphorical thinking 407–8
metatheories 58, 151–4
methodical procedure 17–8, 175–6, 267,
    278, 300
methodics 17–8, 175–6, 256, 279, 304
methodological approach 19
methodological base approach (*see* base
    view/approach) 330
methodological view 3, 11, 15
methodology 17
methods 7–8, 11, 176–7
model 51, 82, 129, 163
multifinality 65
mutuality 119, 360

narratives 410
normative theses 7, 202

ontology 102, 394
objectification 66, 144–5, 147–8
objectified reality 67–8
objectivity 201–6
observactor 139
operational definitions 92–3
operative paradigm 12, 17, 175–6

paradigm 10, 14–6, 392–4
perspective 29–30, 36
phenomenology 166, 404–5
positivism 95, 395–7
potential in what is factual 143, 200
pragmatism 121, 186, 391
precision 185–6, 205
pre-scientific concepts 16, 24, 48, 383, 407
primary procedure (*see* procedures)

principle of 239, 360
  complexity 112
  mutuality 119
  relativity 113
  totality 112
  unpredictability 119
problematization 29, 34
procedures
  complementary 342–4, 346, 356,
    362, 369
  primary 342–4
procreative 134, 243
  report 168, 200–1, 307
  words 198, 302
production factors 378–82

rationalism 391
realism 391, 410
reconciliation 340
reductionism 103
relativity 113, 239, 356
reliability 24, 185–6
representativity 179

sampling 94, 189–91
scientific 47–9
self-reference 41, 135, 340
sensemaking 402–3
sensitivity 185–6
significance 166, 396
social constructionism 406–7
socially constructed reality 52, 58, 67,
  144–9, 179
social phenomenology 166–7, 405
stringency 349
structuralism 103, 399
study plan
  for actors studies 243–7
  for analytical studies 229
  for descriptive studies 229–32
  for determining finality relations 237–40
  for determining problems 228–9
  for explanatory studies 232
  for forecasting studies 233, 240
  for guiding studies 233–5, 240–1

subjectification 144–6, 200, 370
summative 36, 39, 255
symbolic interactionism 401–2
synergy 53, 63–4, 122, 336
synthesis 68, 72, 74, 136, 372
systems theory 102–3, 122
systems thinking 53, 103, 400–1
systems view
  and entrepreneurship 39–41
  and prerequisites, explanations,
    understanding and results 57, 63–7
  and reality assumptions 54–5

techniques 8–9, 176
  common: - for collecting data 180–5
    for measurement and controlling
      reliability 185–6
    for selecting units to study 178–80
    for validation 186–9
  specific: - the actors approach
    195–201
    the analytical approach 189–92
    the systems approach 192–5
thematic language of methodology
  331, 347, 392–3
theory 82
thesis 68, 74, 136, 372
tools 176
totality 112, 239, 372
transformative operation 329, 344
transformative operator 320, 342–3
typical 60
typification 144, 147,
  161, 405
typified 60, 72–3, 164, 405
typified cases 59, 72, 164

ultimate presumptions 4, 6–9, 11, 25
understanding 50–2, 394–7
unpredictability 119, 214, 360

validity 186–9, 191–2
verification 91
Vienna circle 397
vivify 59, 141, 197, 299

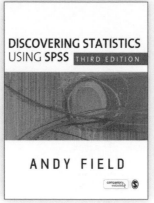
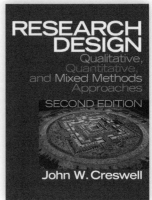

The Qualitative Research Kit

Edited by Uwe Flick

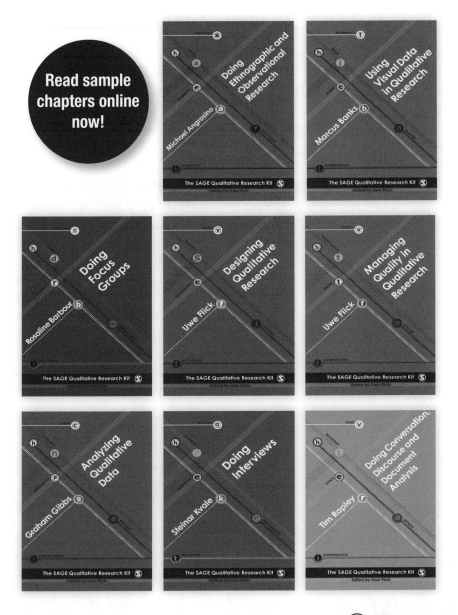

Read sample chapters online now!

Doing Ethnographic and Observational Research — Michael Angrosino

Using Visual Data in Qualitative Research — Marcus Banks

Doing Focus Groups — Rosaline Barbour

Designing Qualitative Research — Uwe Flick

Managing Quality in Qualitative Research — Uwe Flick

Analyzing Qualitative Data — Graham Gibbs

Doing Interviews — Steinar Kvale

Doing Conversation, Discourse and Document Analysis — Tim Rapley

The SAGE Qualitative Research Kit
Edited by Uwe Flick

www.sagepub.co.uk